THE URBAN RETAILING SYSTEM

To
Virginia
and
Glad and Bob

The Urban Retailing System

Location, Cognition and Behaviour

ROBERT B. POTTER
Bedford College,
University of London

Gower
and
Retailing and Planning Associates

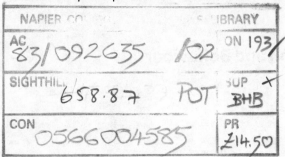

Published by
Gower Publishing Company Limited
Gower House, Croft Road, Aldershot, Hants GU11 3HR, England

British Library Cataloguing in Publication Data

Potter, Robert B.
Urban retailing system.
1. Retail trade - Great Britain
I. Title
658.8'7'00941 HF5429.6.G7

ISBN 0-566-00458-5

Printed and bound in Great Britain by
Robert Hartnoll Limited,
Bodmin, Cornwall.

Contents

Figures

Tables

Preface

This book reflects the author's interest in spatial and structural patterns of urban retailing, a concern that commenced with the preparation of a short undergraduate dissertation on retailing structure in 1971, and burgeoned out into a doctoral thesis completed in 1975, which witnessed a broadening of interest to include aspects of consumer spatial behaviour and perception. Throughout this period, as well as long before, interest has been shown in various aspects of retailing and marketing by specialists from all manner of disciplines, employing a number of paradigms. This volume seeks to order and review the literature in this important applied field, and to present a number of previously unpublished research case studies undertaken by the present author. As with any volume of this length, however, the selection of topics for discussion and the emphasis placed on them is very much a reflection of the author's views, experience and inevitably, although hopefully unwittingly, his prejudices too. As such it is tempting to quote the prefatory words of Haggett (1965, p. vi) and say that 'This volume is clearly then a report from an active battlefront rather than a well-rounded and reflective essay', although hopefully, readers will not find it entirely devoid of merit in the latter respect.

Given the vast volume of academic and applied research that is published today, it has become almost customary for authors to acknowledge the fact that it is increasingly difficult to separate their own ideas from those of others. This is certainly true in the present case and to all those from whose work I have drawn concepts, facts or inspiration, I owe a great debt. I hope that this has been adequately documented both in the text and in the bibliography. More specifically, a number of authors and publishers have been kind enough to allow me to reproduce in revised or redrawn form, copyright diagrams and figures. This has been acknowledged in the captions to the figures concerned in the normal way.

I should also like to thank the Social Science Research Council for a three year Research Studentship Award from 1971 to 1974, which allowed me to work on my PhD thesis. Further, I was fortunate enough to be granted a Younger Research Workers Interchange Scheme Award from the British Council and the Dutch Department of Education and Science. This enabled me to visit Dr Harry Timmermans of the Department of Architecture, Building and Planning at the Technical University of Eindhoven, The Netherlands, in December 1980, in order to discuss our mutual research interests in retailing structure, central place theory and consumer behaviour. These discussions were of great value in that they gave me the chance to air many of the evolving ideas that are presented in this book, before writing itself began.

I also owe a great debt to three reviewers who read and provided invaluable, detailed and most constructive comments on various draft chapters. Dr John Marshall and Dr John Parr both read several of the chapters on retail structure, and their informative responses, especially in relation to Chapter 2, were much appreciated. A special word of thanks must, however, go to Dr Harry Timmermans who gave unstintingly of his time and energy, and willingly read the entire draft manuscript as it evolved chapter by chapter. I count myself extremely fortunate to have had such enthusiastic, well-informed, positive and efficient criticism. I can only add the all important proviso that any remaining errors of fact, interpretation or presentation in the final product are mine and mine alone. Further, I hope my reviewers will forgive me if in some places I have not been able to fully follow their sound recommendations due either to constraints of time or space. I should also like to thank Dr Ross Davies who encouraged me to first consider writing this volume. Finally, the raw data on the structure of the urban retailing system of Swansea, which is used as the backdrop for the analysis of consumer behaviour in Chapter 7, was collected by two former undergraduate students of the Department of Geography, Bedford College, Ian Cowling and John Munro, as a part of independent field work completed under my supervision.

A particular vote of thanks must go to Miss Claire Wastie, Cartographer in the Department of Geography, Bedford College, who drew the majority of the figures new to this volume most expertly and efficiently from my roughs. At one time it looked as though as a consequence she might need hexagonal shaped spectacles! Mr Ron Halfhide and Gillian Collins drew a number of other figures. None of these is to be held responsible, however, for the remaining figures which were drawn by the author. Mrs Rosemary Dawe typed both the draft and final manuscripts. By now she is familiar with many of my idiosyncracies, both calligraphic and stylistic, and managed to combine speed with efficiency in producing an exemplary manuscript.

I should also like to thank Virginia, who read through the manuscript for linguistic lunacies and helped with proof reading, and in many other ways besides. It goes without saying that her interest in shops, particularly those selling apparel, is frequently far more earnest and practical than mine. Finally, I thank my parents for all their help and encouragement over the past years. This volume is dedicated to these three individuals as a small token of my appreciation.

London,
November 1981

ROBERT B. POTTER

1 The Urban Retailing System: An Introduction

> 'Patterns of day to day travel by consumers result from the spatial layout of society. Conversely, these intricate patterns of movement are important agents in affecting the spatial structure of society' (Huff, 1960, p. 159).

Shops, shopping centres and shopping as a spatial activity all constitute vital ingredients of our day-to-day existence. This crucial role played by retailing applies both in the context of technologically advanced economies and developing countries alike, although it is obvious that the ensuing spatial form of the retailing system and the behaviour of consumers are likely to vary considerably between such contrasting area types. The common denominator, however, as Huff's quotation serves to imply is that wherever they occur, shops and markets constitute a very significant component of the physical fabric of man-made environments. However, it is equally salient that such retailing fabric is itself in great part a reflection of consumers' effective demand and associated travel and purchasing patterns. As a consequence, retailing facilities often bestow centrality on specific locations or, viewed alternatively, reflect the existence of such centrality (Bird, 1977). Logically, therefore, retailing facilities may be regarded as constituting focal reference points in our awareness and organization of space, both in rural and urban environments. Thus, there is a complex interrelation and interdependence between retail structural organization on the one hand, and the spatial cognitions and overt behaviour of consumers on the other. This relationship and its spatial implications constitute the subject matter of the present book.

RETAILING RESEARCH

It is not difficult to appreciate, therefore, that the study of retailing systems is of great potential relevance to a broad range of social science disciplines, amongst which may certainly be listed economics, history, sociology, marketing, geography and planning. Scholars from each of these subjects have made significant contributions to our knowledge regarding retailing systems. As will be discussed subsequently, increasingly, other social sciences such as psychology, architecture, building, operational research, regional science and politics are also making distinctive inroads on retailing research.

Despite this catholic appeal and the longstanding practical relevance of retailing research, historically, the field has not been without its problems. Frequently, those objects which comprise part of what may be described as our 'taken-for-granted world' (Ley, 1977) and which play an important, albeit a common or garden role in our daily lives tend to be neglected by researchers and scholars. Thus, in a recent major review of investigations into urban travel and transport, the authors note with dismay the fact that '... the everyday, humdrum web of local shopping activity excites few students' (Daniels and Warnes, 1980, p. 158). This is a surprising situation when viewed in the light of another quotation, this time taken from the very first sentence of the preface to a recent major work dealing with the marketing environment:

> 'Almost everyone who looks at this book is in direct daily contact with the marketing system whether in buying a ballpoint refill at the student co-operative store, purchasing their daily bread, fighting the vans and trucks on their urban delivery rounds or gazing at the advertisements on the way to work' (Dawson, 1979a, p, 13).

In this connection, it is scarcely an exaggeration to suggest that it has virtually become a tradition to commence books on the general topic of retailing by offering excuses, apologies and disclaimers. In a frequently cited passage, Smith (1948, p.l) has highlighted this problem in venturing that:

> 'Among those prejudices, inhibitions, and predilections which compose the English tradition a prominent place is occupied by the conviction that there is an essential element of unworthiness about retail trade, a blend of the sinister and the ridiculous'

so that:

> 'the result has been that while most people, economists included, have been agreed that there are important problems arising out of retail trade, until very recently economists have preferred to concern themselves with subjects of which the titles carried a more dignified and scholarly connotation.'

Such predilections would be of marginal interest if they reflected a transitory neglect of retailing on the part of academics merely during the period when Smith was writing, but this has clearly not been the case. Thus, much nearer to the present, but in a remarkably similar vein, Scott (1970, p.11) after quoting Smith, has observed that 'despite its economic importance retail distribution has remained until recently a comparatively neglected field of academic enquiry'. In this sense at least, the study of retailing might almost be regarded as the 'cinderella' of the social sciences: somehow and in a quite paradoxical manner, the very familiarity of the subject matter seems to conspire to make prospective scholars feel that its study is trivial, obvious perhaps, or even less than honourable. A final quotation, this time taken from the opening account of a text focussing on the economics of retailing serves to exemplify the arguments presented thus far:

> 'Everybody knows about retailing. By its nature, retailing is ubiquitous, in rich and poor countries alike. Children, students and housewives who do not participate in the economic system as producers of goods or services for monetary reward nevertheless have frequent and numerous contacts with retailing firms and their activities. Retailing is also visible.' (Tucker and Yamey, 1973, p. 9).

In direct contrast, however, the same authors were forced to conclude that the

> 'fact is that in much of the ostensibly relevant branches of economic theory and analysis the favoured treatment abstracts from the presence of intermediaries, such as retailers, between the production and consumption of goods and services: the treatment is as if the producer sold to the consumer' (Tucker and Yamey, 1973, p. 9).

It may be argued that such caveats and associated reticence on the part of potential researchers are far from necessary: retailing is manifestly an important and worthy topic for study. In fact, enough has probably already been said to convey the general impression that retailing is a relatively complex topic which has considerable theoretical underpinnings and a great deal of applied relevance, both in connection with commercial decision-making and the formulation of planning policy. Stated simply, this relevance and significance stems from the fact that the process of distribution directly touches each of our daily lives, as noted by Tucker and Yamey (1973) and Dawson (1979a). This is particularly the case at the present given the rate of retail change occurring in Western European countries and North America, and the role that the growth of tertiary activities is playing in what is commonly referred to as the 'informal sector' of the economies of cities in the Third World.

This book is concerned with the study of both urban retailing structural organization and the spatial cognitions and overt shopping behaviour of consumers in urban environments, principally, although by no means exclusively, within western-industrialized societies. Further, it focuses on the interrelations existing between such spatial patterns of location and organization on the one hand, and spatial processes of consumer behaviour on the other. As this implies, the primary emphasis is a *spatial-geographic* one, for the distance dimension is fundamental to the structural organization and operation of urban retailing systems wherever they occur. This chapter describes the overall aims, content and approach of the present volume. However, before these are considered in detail, it is necessary to outline the general field of interest and to define the nomenclature basic to its study.

THE NATURE OF RETAILING

As retailing is such a commonplace and familiar activity, there is almost a temptation not to offer a concrete definition of its nature and precise functions at the outset of such a work, regarding such an exercise as little more than pedantry. In fact, a number of texts written on retailing and marketing succumb to this temptation. Thus, books by Berry (1967), Scott (1970) and more recently by Guy (1980), whilst all incorporating the words 'retail' or 'retailing' in their titles, do not endeavour to provide explicit definitions of these terms.

If the *Concise Oxford Dictionary* is consulted, it is found that the noun 'retail' is defined as 'the sale of goods in small quantities'. This definition certainly points to the principal function of the retailer, that is to act as the middleman or intermediary between the consumer on the one hand, and the producer and/or wholesaler on the other, in the process of the physical distribution of goods. However, such a definition is deceptively simple, for retailers do not, in fact, perform a single function, but rather fulfil a variety of roles in the process of offering goods for sale to members of the public. The retailer essentially provides a service, but this consists of many different component parts. The main functions of the retailer in the chain of distribution include buying, selling, the storage of goods, bulk breaking, risk sharing, the display of goods and the provision of choice and assistance with choice, the provision of information and the offering of credit, personal service and sometimes the delivery of goods as well (Lipsey, 1971; Dawson, 1979a). However, as Dawson (1979a, p. 149) has concluded, the 'central function is the aggregation of assortments of goods to make them available, in small lots, for the consumer'. In fact, the attribute of smallness seems to be the hallmark of retailing as an activity within the economic system, so that Dawson (1979a) observes that one apparent reason for the large number of shops is that retail businesses are characteristically small. With the evident trend towards larger retailing units, affording greater economies of scale, the term 'relatively small' seems to be increasingly appropriate.

The definition of retailing provided above,like all definitions to some degree or another requires further qualification. This is especially the case since it is obvious that the once clearly distinct roles of retailer and wholesaler are changing greatly and becoming less easy to disentangle. A quote from Davies (1976, p. 47) serves to exemplify the extent of this transformation, for he notes that some:

> 'wholesalers are now owners of retail outlets and may also use their warehouse depots as discount shops; likewise, many retailers have increasingly developed their own system of wholesaling by dealing more directly with the producers. In addition, it is often found that the producers themselves distribute goods immediately to consumers without the aid of intermediaries, through the use of postal deliveries or direct shipments'.

All of this means that the simplest, traditional three-stage marketing channel, consisting of the passage of goods from the producer to a wholesaler and then via the retailer to the consumer is becoming less common in practice. However, the basic activity of retailing as the linking mechanism between the production of goods by firms and their final consumption by households and other units of consumption within the economy remains largely unchanged.

Notwithstanding these developments, a clear distinction must be drawn between *retail selling techniques* as opposed to forms of *retailing organization*. The latter refers to the characteristics of ownership or business structure and three basic organizational types are usually recognized - the independent retailer, multiple retailers (sometimes referred to as corporate chains) and consumer co-operatives (Scott, 1970; Davies, 1976; Dawson, 1979a). The distinguishing feature of the co-operative is that its ownership and management are vested with members of the consumer society, whilst the distinction between independents and multiple retailers is generally made on the basis of the number of branches. In the British context, for example, a threshold of ten establishments was employed in the 1971 Census of Distribution to differentiate between these organisational forms Dawson, 1979a). Independents, usually small in size, have customarily comprised an important component of the retailing system, although in recent years their competitive position has become increasingly precarious. A salient development has been the formation of voluntary trading groups, whereby a number of retailers get together and co-operate, often under the aegis of a common trading symbol. In 1971, independent stores accounted for 52.9 per cent of the total retail turnover of Britain, being followed by multiple groups which took 25.8 per cent and co-operatives with 7.2 per cent. The residual turnover was accounted for by Department stores and mail order sales, these taking 10.2 and 3.8 per cent respectively (Davies, 1976). However, one of the most significant changes in the retailing system during the twentieth century has been the expansion of the proportion of total retail turnover taken by multiples at the expense of both independent operators and co-operatives. Closely associated with this has been the development of new large scale forms of retailing such as the hypermarket and the superstore (Jefferys, 1954; Alexander, 1970; Davies, 1976; Dawson, 1979a, 1980a; Pacione, 1980).

This latter fact brings us to the second concept, namely, the form of selling technique employed by retailers. This represents the precise mode of contact occurring between the retailer and the consumer at the point of transaction. There are many different forms of selling and each one may be employed by any one of the organisational forms of retailing. When considering them it is necessary to think in terms of the periodicity and permanency of retailing establishments. Thus, although we are inclined to think of retailing in terms of shops, not all forms of retailing involve fixed premises at fixed locations. More accurately, a continuum exists which extends through fixed shops, daily markets to periodic markets and peripatetic sellers (Hodder, 1968; Bird, 1977). Thus, itinerant trading (pedling), hawking and street vending are all forms of retail selling that do not involve fixed retail premises, permanent locations or even necessarily fixed operating times. Street markets and stalls represent another selling type in which although the location is normally fixed, the premises need not necessarily be, and trading may be periodic in a temporal sense. The character of such retailing types is concisely described by Scott (1970, p. 127) when he defines a market as 'a public gathering of buyers and sellers at an appointed place and at regular intervals for the purpose of doing business under specific conditions'. Periodic marketing systems are frequently associated with the rural areas of less developed countries (Stine, 1962; Skinner, 1964) where it is argued that low density of effective demand, poor storage and transport infrastructure are met by markets moving in circuits, so that time is substituted for space (Ullman, 1974). The attributes and aetiology of such systems have been studied in some detail (Hay, 1971; Tinkler, 1973; Webber and Symanski, 1973; Bromley, Symanski and Good, 1975; Hay and Smith, 1980) and they exist in both the rural and urban environs of Third World countries, as is shown by Mabogunje (1964) in the intra-urban case of Lagos, Nigeria. Frequently, in fact, traditional markets exist alongside a modern retailing sector of department stores and supermarkets in Third World countries, comprising what Santos (1979) has described as the *lower* and *upper circuits* of the urban economy respectively (see also Mabogunje, 1964 and Gwynne, 1978). However, the fact should not be overlooked that periodic marketing systems formed the predominant mode of selling in Britain during the Medieval period (Fox, 1970) and relict features still exist today in the form of fairs and street markets. In the United Kingdom in 1971, for instance, although accounting for less than 1.0 per cent of the total volume of retail trade, there were as many as

32,000 mobile shops and market stalls so that they still represented an important ingredient of the urban retailing system (Davies, 1976; Beaujeu-Garnier and Delobez, 1979). In fact, a century ago markets constituted the main retail outlets for foods and it is argued that it was only in the latter half of the nineteenth century that fixed shop retailing became so general in Britain that it started to take over from itinerant traders and market stalls (Jefferys, 1954; Davis, 1966; Scola, 1975; Alexander,1970; Wild and Shaw, 1975, 1979).

Subsequently, however, counter retailing increased progressively in importance and today is probably the most frequently occurring method employed in fixed location retailing, as noted by Dawson (1979a). More recently, supermarketing based on self-service selling techniques, superstores and hypermarkets can all be seen as modern variants of retail selling, their significance deriving from the fact that they have enabled shop size and associated economies of scale to be progressively increased. At the smaller scale, automatic vending from machines and mail order are further selling types which do not involve personal face-to-face contact between the consumer and the retailer. Finally, mobile shops may be seen as a latter-day variety of periodic marketing.

However, even when fixed shop retailing occurs, definitional problems remain, for the precise definition of a retail shop is itself a more difficult task than at first might appear to be the case. NEDO (1970, p. 121) have defined retail shops as 'shops whose main business is selling goods to the public'. This itself leads to a further basic distinction between *convenience goods shops*, whose principal trade is in foods, grocery, confectionary, newsagency, tobacco and other frequently required items, and *comparison goods shops* which provide other more durable retail commodities.

Generally speaking, therefore, retailing is associated with the sale of tangible commodities to consumers, but as Davies (1976, p. 55) observes 'certain service activities are incorporated into the retail classification of the Census of Distribution because they obviously function in the same way as shops, and exhibit similar locational characteristics'. Here it is essential to recognize that pure retailing comprises but a part of what is referred to as the 'tertiary sector' of the economy. Tertiary activities are generally united in that they are concerned with the exchange and consumption of goods and services and their product is normally intangible and non-transferable. However, there is a diverse range of such functions, including service activities (vacational, recreational, medical, educational, religious, business, and administrative), financial activities (banking, insurance, real estate) and trade activities (wholesaling and retailing).

The distinction between such functions, particularly in a locational sense is a very complex matter and presents a possible bone of contention in a volume such as this. Thus, Beaujeu-Garnier and Delobez (1979) follow the definition of retailing proposed by Jefferys and Knee (1962, p. 250) as including 'all establishments, fixed or not, and all persons - owners, family workers, employees, full-time or not - engaged wholly or mainly in the sale of goods, in a state ready for final consumption or use, to private consumers'. Excluded from this definition in customary manner are 'units that sell primarily services, e.g. cafés, restaurants, dry cleaners, laundries and repairers ...' (p. 250). A similar schism occurs in British town planning practice as noted by Guy (1980) and Fernie and Carrick (1981). The Town and Country Planning (Use Classes) Order, 1972 includes under the category "Class 1 - Shops", retail shops along with services such as hairdresser, undertaker, travel agent, ticket agents, post office and premises for the reception of goods to be washed, cleaned and repaired. In contrast, other service activities such as banks, estate agents, building societies, car hire, driving schools and employment agencies are aggregated under "Class II - Offices". To complicate matters still further, restaurants, betting offices and launderettes, public houses and premises for the sale of hot food all represent unspecified uses. Such a classification would appear to have a strong arbitrary element and it is tempting to suggest that some of the Class II and unspecified uses are really complementary to the retail shops and service establishments enumerated in Class I.

The argument presented by Davies (1976) is thus a strong one, and in the present work a relatively broad definition of urban retailing is adopted which includes both the selling of goods and the provision of certain pure services which tend to occur in a complementary functional manner and in close spatial proximity to strictly defined retail units. An impression of this sort of definition is given by the classification of retail functions and major groups presented in Table 1.1. This was developed and employed by the present author in an empirical study of retailing in a medium-sized British town. Although by no means intended as a comprehensive or definitive checklist, the typology does provide a framework for discussion and analysis. It is worth recording that during the field survey associated with this study, the main commodities and services offered by establishments in shopping centres were noted, but no prior categorisation of functional types was adopted due to the frequent occurrence of dual and multiple functional shops. On the basis of the functional types enumerated in the field case study and with some recourse to the typologies used by other workers (Berry, 1963; Price, 1967; Tarrant, 1967; Davies, 1974), the classification of major retail shop functions shown in Table 1.1 was produced (Potter, 1976a, 1981b). This consists of some sixty-nine separate functional types forming ten major functional divisions (food, clothing, household, personal, motor, sports, professional, miscellaneous, plus a separate category for large retail units such as supermarkets and department stores and also for vacant premises). In most of the categories, closely allied service activities have been incorporated along with the pure retail functions identified. Reference will be made to this classification when empirical studies of urban retailing are examined in detail in Chapters 3 and 4.

In conclusion, therefore, a definition of a retailing shop is advanced which closely reflects the detailed considerations outlined above, and which also draws on the definition proposed by Price (1967). Thereby it is suggested that *a shop may be regarded as a permanent or semi-permanent structure which is either wholly or partly devoted to the conduct of retail trade or complementary service and catering activities, and which is accessible to the general public or prescribed segments of that public.* By simple extension, therefore, a retail or shopping centre may be defined as any readily discernible spatial grouping of such retail outlets.

Table 1.1
A classification of urban retailing functions

I. FOOD : 1 Butcher, 2 Baker, 3 Greengrocer, 4 Baker/Confectioner, 5 Fishmonger/Poulterer, 6 Off Licence, 7 Tobacconist/Sweets, 8 Public House, 9 Restaurant/Café, 10 Fried/Take-away Food.

II. CLOTHING : 11 Women's clothing, 12 Men's clothing, 13 Children's clothing, 14 Footwear, 15 Shoe repair, 16 Millinery, 17 Wool/Needlework.

III. HOUSEHOLD : 18 Decorating Supplies, 19 Hardware/Gardening, 20 China/Glass, 21 Furniture, 22 Gas Showroom, 23 Electricity Showroom, 24 T.V./Radio/Electrical, 25 Antiques, 26 Carpets, 27 Lighting, 28 D.I.Y./Timber/Glass, 29 Drapery/Fabrics, 30 Office Equipment, 31 Plumbing/Heating.

IV. PERSONAL : 32 Women's Hairdressing, 33 Men's Barber, 34 Chemist, 35 Medical/Surgical, 36 Jewellery.

V. MOTOR : 37 Car Sales, 38 Motorcycle Sales/Repair, 39 Motor Spares/Accessories, 40 Garage/Filling Station.

VI. SPORTS and RECREATIONAL : 41 Sports Equipment, 42 Pet Stores, 43 Fishing Tackle, 44 Photographic Equipment, 45 Toys and Games, 46 Bookshop, 47 Musical Equipment, 48 Records, 49 Travel Agents, 50 Photographic Studio.

VII. MISCELLANEOUS : 51 Florist, 52 Greetings cards, 53 Betting Office, 54 Optician, 55 Dry cleaners, 56 Launderette, 57 Luggage/Leather Goods, 58 Stationery/Art Supplies, 59 Newsagent, 60 Prams/Baby care, 61 Cycles, 62 Other specialist.

VIII. PROFESSIONAL and FINANCIAL : 63 Banks, 64 Post office, 65 Estate Agent, 66 Professional service.

IX. LARGE RETAIL OUTLETS : 67 Supermarket, 68 Department Store.

X. VACANT : 69 Vacant Units.

(Source: Potter, 1976a, 1981b)

THE URBAN RETAILING SYSTEM

Having defined the terms and concepts basic to this work a suitable juncture has now been reached at which to assess in some detail the nature and importance of retailing in the urban setting. The aggregate significance of retailing as a sector of the economy has been implied, but a precise impression of its physical and behavioural importance within the urban economy has not yet been provided.

In terms of the dynamics of retail change and planning, it is the spatial connotations of urban retailing that serve to make it a topic worthy of detailed examination. The process of distribution involves the movement of both commodities and consumers within urban areas. The producers of particular commodities dispatch their goods to retail outlets which serve different localities and their dispersed populations. On the other hand, certain retail outlets offering different goods and services tend to cluster together in what may be termed 'shopping centres', so as to be readily accessible to consumers who will frequently want to undertake multiple purpose shopping trips. Such a spatial arrangement necessitates either the movement of consumers between their places of residence and retail centres in order to obtain the goods they desire, or the shipment of the goods to the consumer at his home. The distribution of goods and services is therefore of great importance, not only in relation to the structure and land use characteristics of urban areas, but also in relation to the daily lives and activity patterns of the denizens of such settlements. The structural organization of the urban retailing system and the behaviour of consumers are thereby inextricably bound together within the urban economic system. In the British setting, such a conclusion is of especial relevance as virtually 80 per cent of the total population is to be found living within urban areas, so that the preponderance of shopping trips are executed at the intra-urban scale. However, as the process of 'tertiarisation' of economies appears to be a fundamental concomitant of economic development (Clark, 1940; Kay, 1975), the relation between consumer behaviour and urban structure is in fact of universal significance.

Although it is true that only a relatively small proportion of the total land area of any urban region is devoted to retailing purposes, as argued by Dawson and Kirby (1980) this is disproportionate to the significance of such land use in terms of its functional importance and the employment and traffic that is generated. In a study of commercial structure in Chicago, for instance, Berry (1963) has shown that nine out of a total of 224 square miles, or approximately 4 per cent of the city was devoted to retail and service use. One square mile of this total was located within the Central Business District (C.B.D.), the other eight square miles being taken up by some 55,000 suburban retail and service establishments (although it is notable that this ratio conflicts with the observation of Lowenstein (1963) that the amount of land in the C.B.D. devoted to retail activities is generally equal to that in the rest of the urban area). Berry observed that to 'devote less than 4 per cent of the city's area to outlying business uses is hardly impressive, but the layout of the eight square miles brings business into every neighbourhood of the city' (Berry, 1963, p. 15). The author continues giving a general impression of the scope of urban retailing in Chicago - of the total ground floor area of buildings in the entire city, 13.3 per cent was in retail and service use. This proportion was as high as 26.8 per cent in the C.B.D. and fell to 9.94 per cent in the peripheral areas of the city. Such statistics show in striking manner the spatial and functional importance of retailing in urban zones. The distribution of shops is at once both highly dispersed at the macro spatial scale and highly concentrated at the micro urban scale.

The composite structural significance of urban retailing is also attested by shop numbers. The ubiquity of shops has been noted above and it is true to say that after people and houses they represent the most frequently occurring unit in urban areas. In Britain, there is on average one shop per 100 people or one shop to roughly every forty residences (Thorpe, 1978). In a survey conducted by the present author (Potter, 1976a) it was found that in 1972, some 2,345 shops served a total urban population in Stockport of 139,633, so that there was one shop for every 59.54 inhabitants. Comparable statistics for major urban areas in Britain were cited from the 1951 Census of Distribution by Parker (1962): Croydon 100, Liverpool 97, Leeds 82, Sheffield 77, Manchester 70. Although in total the number of individual shops is showing a marked tendency to decline, data from the Census of Distribution 1971 reveal the following average population levels per shop at the regional level in England and Wales: South East 124, North 122, Scotland 121, East Midlands 113, Greater London 109, Wales 97, North West 93 (Davies, 1976). Comparative European data is to be gained from Jefferys and Knee (1962), where it is stated that the number of people per shop is 105 in Spain, 89 in Portugal, 84 in Greece, 59 for Italy and as low as 34 in Belgium. In the case of the United States, the relation between shops and inhabitants has changed from one shop per 148 persons in 1948 to one shop per 175 persons in 1967, whilst in France at the latter date there was on average one shop per 88 people (Beaujeu-Garnier and Delobez, 1979). Naturally enough such ratios have become a part of town planning practice so that in 1946, the New Towns Committee in Britain proposed a standard of one shop for every 100-150 people (Low, 1975).

Finally, the importance of urban retailing is also reflected in its role as a major employer. Alexander and Dawson (1979, p. 408) have recently directed attention to this neglected aspect of the urban economy and have noted that 'not only is retailing a major quantitative component in the metropolitan workforce; it is currently a very dynamic component with a strong spatial element', due to the increasing suburbanization of shopping facilities offering part-time and female employment. Generally, commerce accounts for 15 per cent of total employment in developed countries and around 8 per cent in less developed economies (Alexander and Dawson, 1979). In a functional classification of American cities, Nelson (1955) found that on average, 19.25 per cent of the total urban work force was employed in retailing with a standard deviation of 3.63 per cent. In the British context, 12 per cent of the entire labour force is currently employed in shops (Thorpe, 1978), and Scott (1970, p. 11) has observed that

> 'retail distribution is an important sector of the national economy. In Britain, for example, retail sales account for more than one-half of total consumer expenditure, and the retail trade employs as many as one in every ten insured workers, or more than twice the work force engaged in the primary industries of agriculture, fisheries, and forestry. Although total employment in retailing is less than one-third that in manufacturing, retailing as measured by establishments is the largest single industry in many British towns.'

In like manner, Davies (1976) notes that retailing in Britain in 1971 generated sales of more than £15,000 million and thereby provided some 2.5 million jobs making it the third greatest contributor to national output after manufacturing and office services. In Britain, distribution now accounts for as much as 17 per cent of private sector gross domestic product (Thorpe, 1978). This vital role performed by retailing is true of most economies. For example, in Barbados, a small Third World nation, in 1979 wholesale and retail trade represented the single most important sector of the economy, constituting 19.8 per cent of gross domestic product.

However, the significance of retailing is probably most evident to us as individuals by virtue of its influence on our daily life styles and activity patterns. This importance springs from the fact that shopping trips generally occur relatively frequently and characteristically involve short distance moves. Thus, 'if all shopping journeys are considered, including those made on foot, their number in any urban area is probably roughly equivalent to the number of journeys to work' (Daniels and Warnes, 1980, p. 157). The basic characteristics of intra-urban shopping journeys are exemplified by the data shown in Table 1.2. This summarises selected aspects of the normal shopping behaviour of a sample of 192 consumers within the Stockport urban region. The study from which these figures emanate was carried out by the present author (Potter, 1976a, 1980b), and the questionnaire survey employed is reproduced in Appendix 1 of this book. The marked frequency of trips to purchase items such as bread, cigarettes, and regular purchases such as meat and groceries is clearly discernible, along with the short distance of such trips and their dependence on walking.

Table 1.2
Selected aspects of intra-urban shopping behaviour amongst sample consumers in Stockport

Commodity type	Mean distance travelled km.	Mean no. of days between trips	Percentage of respondents travelling by:				
			Foot	Bus	Cycle	Train	Car
Casual purchases	0.55	2.02	83.96	6.42	0.53	0.00	9.09
Regular purchases	1.11	5.49	58.94	14.74	0.53	0.00	25.79
Minor household	1.17	37.67	47.04	24.32	0.53	0.00	28.11
Minor clothing	2.08	66.81	23.78	45.41	0.00	0.00	30.81
Major purchase	3.13	164.71	10.40	44.51	0.00	4.05	41.04
Expensive goods	3.86	286.98	5.43	37.98	0.00	6.98	49.61

(Source: Potter, 1980b)

The importance of shopping as a major trip generator within urban settlements is similarly indicated by other recent studies of consumer shopping behaviour. Daws and Bruce (1971) studied the Watford urban area, interviewing 1,350 housewives. An average of four shopping trips were made during the course of a week by the sample housewives, although the modal category was as high as six trips per week, with 33 per cent of all housewives falling into this category. In fact, as high a proportion as 76 per cent of the housewives made three or more separate shopping trips per week. Perhaps just as significantly, the weekly frequency of shopping trips varied according to the characteristics of the shoppers; thus, housewives from the upper social groups, those with two cars and those from the outer part of the Watford area tended on average to shop less frequently. Interestingly, the ideal number of shopping trips per week according to the sampled housewives averaged 3.1. Clearly, therefore, the respondents wanted to shop less frequently than they did at the time of the survey and the authors concluded that equilibrium between behaviour and preference had therefore not yet been reached. Davies (1973a) completed a diary survey of shopping behaviour in Coventry amongst 487 households. In this case, an average of 6.4 shopping trips per week were undertaken by the survey respondents; five trips on average were initial shopping trips, one a link trip to another centre after the initial trip, and 0.4 represented entirely separate second shopping outings on the same day.

These data illustrate in clear fashion the fact that households undertake frequent shopping trips within urban areas. Another way of looking at this is to examine the proportion of total personal trips that are devoted to shopping purposes and the amount of time spent on such journeys. In this regard, an impressive array of relevant statistics has recently been presented by Daniels and Warnes (1980). They refer, for example, to the London Transport Travel Survey undertaken in 1954, which showed that shopping trips accounted for 8.11 per cent of all movements amongst the 4,000 households surveyed, thereby contributing the third most important reason for travel after work trips and a miscellaneous trip category. The same general level of importance of shopping trips was shown by a survey of bus travel in Newcastle carried out in 1964 by Burns (1967). Here, 17.6 per cent of all the journeys were for the purpose of shopping, making it the third most important trip generator after work and recreational based trips. It should be stressed, however, that by design these two studies did not include walking based trips, but other studies have shown that generally, shopping trips represent 10-17per cent of all intra-urban movements. Daniels and Warnes (1980) also quote statistics derived from Bullock *et al.* (1974), who completed a time budget study of adults in Reading. It was found that the average time spent on shopping and personal business activity per day was 0.3 hour for men, 0.5 hour for working women and 0.6 hour for non-working women. Further, it was estimated by Daniels and Warnes that these figures amounted to 5 per cent of all travel time for men, 10.9 per cent of the total for working women and 54.5 per cent for non-working women. The particular importance of shopping based trips to certain groups of the population has been further exemplified by Kutter (1973) who looked at the activities of a random sample of 2,536 people in three West German towns. Of the entire sample population, 30.4 per cent comprised a group of housewives and retired people for whom shopping and business trips were by far the most important generator of movements.

APPROACHES TO THE STUDY OF URBAN RETAILING

It is evident, therefore, that both the supply based facets of the structural distribution of shops within urban areas and the demand associated patterns of intra-urban consumer movement are highly complex, and that their spatial ramifications are of great potential significance. In fact, the foregoing account serves to return us to a point made earlier, namely that a variety of academic disciplines have a vested interest in the study of retailing.

Similarly, it has already been emphasized that the overall perspective adopted in the present work is primarily a *spatial-geographical* one. Naturally, this focus reflects in part the interests and experience of the author, but perhaps more significantly, the view that the adoption of such an approach is imperative in contemporary retail studies. In order to set this viewpoint in its wider context, an interdisciplinary framework for spatial-geographical studies of retailing has been derived in Figure 1.1. If it is accepted that geography as an academic subject

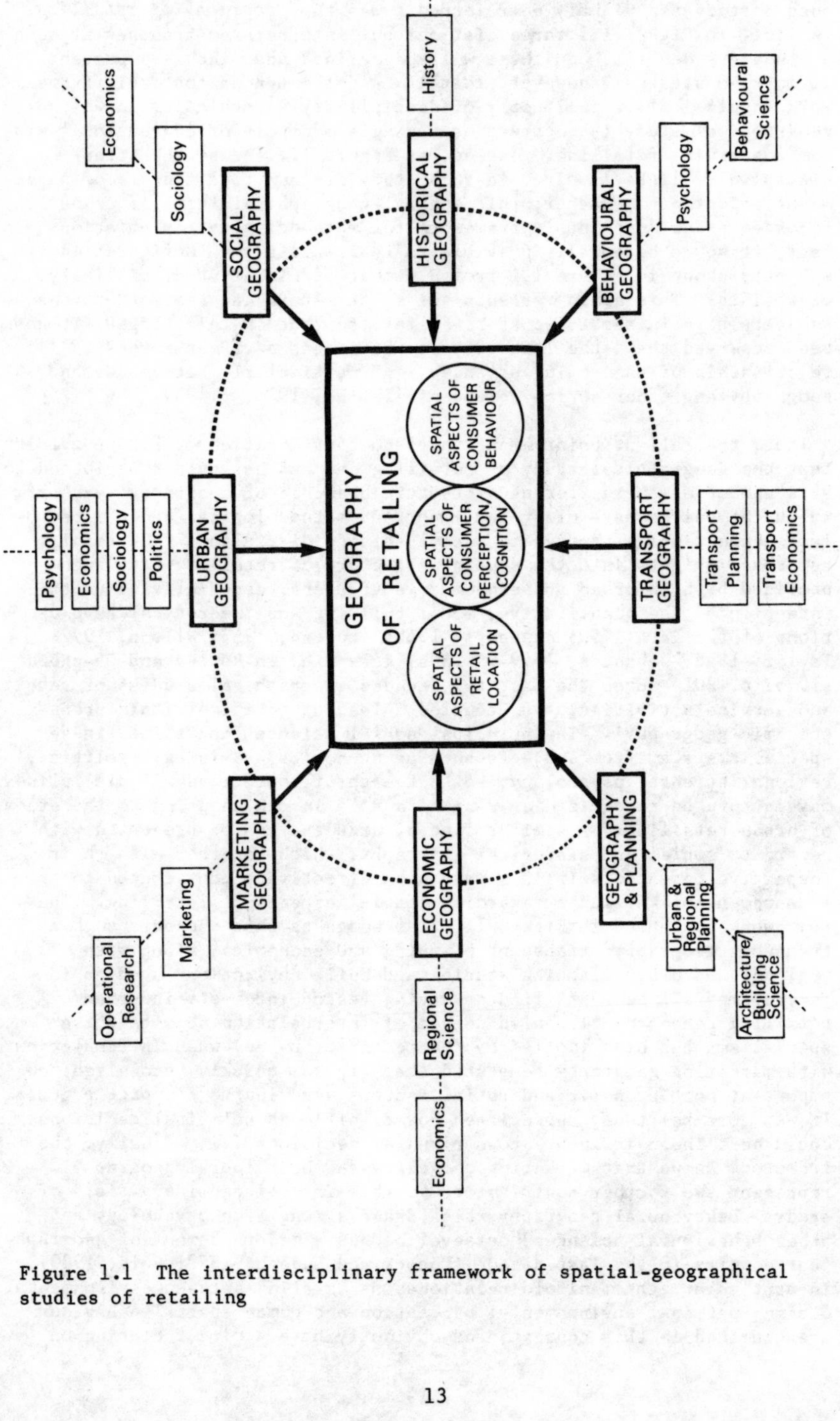

Figure 1.1 The interdisciplinary framework of spatial-geographical studies of retailing

seeks to study spatial patterns and their associated processes, then such a study can rightly be referred to as the *geography of retailing*. In fact, in Figure 1.1 three distinct but interrelated branches of such a study are denoted, and these will be defined and discussed presently. It must be stressed, however, that it is not intended that this framework should imply a philosophy of disciplinary parochialism in which geographical study is regarded as having a monopoly of conventional wisdom concerning retailing. Indeed, as Figure 1.1 shows, the interdisciplinary links involved in such study are numerous and are of paramount importance. Rather, this spatial-geographical theme is to be regarded as no more than a framework for methodological orientation. In fact, it would be equally possible to reorientate the configuration of subjects shown in Figure 1.1 from a number of different disciplinary viewpoints. This again reflects the close mutual interests that these subjects have in the topic of retailing, so that in this respect it has been observed that 'the last 13 years have seen a closer interrelationship of the social sciences, and particularly between human geography and other social sciences' (Thorpe, 1978, p. 96).

Thus, the salient point emanating from consideration of Figure 1.1 is that the geographical study of retailing can and has been contributed to by a number of the different systematic branches of geography, each of which themselves have clear and important methodological and philosophical connections with cognate social science disciplines. Certainly, numerous insights into the spatial structure of retailing have been provided by both urban and economic geographers, especially since the inception of the quantitative, model building and theoretical revolutions of the late 1950s and early 1960s (Burton, 1963; Wilson, 1972; Taylor, 1976; Johnston, 1979). Thus, according to Rowley and Shepherd (1976, p. 201) 'over the past two decades geographical studies of retail and service activities have occupied a leading position within urban-economic geography'. The principal social science inputs into these specialisms stem from subjects such as economics, sociology, politics, regional science, psychology, so that each of these academic disciplines may in turn be recognized as playing a role in contributing to the study of urban retailing. A similar line of argument can be presented with regard to social and historical geography, which together with their respective parent disciplines have also effectively contributed to the advancement of knowledge regarding spatial aspects of retailing. The framework presented in Figure 1.1 also suggests that subjects such as transport geography, transport planning and economics, along with regional and urban planning studies and built environment studies in general may all be identified as having vested interests in urban retailing research. The high degree of interrelation between these specialisms has been implied by Thorpe (1978, p. 96) when in connection with marketing geography he stated that 'it was quickly recognized how important both economic and social factors were in the shopping process. It was more belatedly appreciated how significant political decisions could be. These influence town planning decisions...' Finally, the framework shows that marketing geography and behavioural geography represent two further contributors to this interdisciplinary field of study. Behavioural geography which draws strongly on psychology and other behavioural sciences has developed as a major element of geographical enquiry in the last decade (Pocock and Hudson, 1978; Gold, 1980). In particular, the manifold relationships existing between environmental design, personal environmental perception and human spatial behaviour are examined in this context, and obviously have a direct bearing on studies of the urban retailing environment.

The field of marketing geography depicted in Figure 1.1 perhaps deserves special and separate mention. Marketing geography is a well established and quite distinguished field of geographical endeavour, which if strictly defined seeks to examine the spatial connotations of the entire process of distribution within the economy (Dawson, 1973, 1979a; Davies, 1976; Beaujeu-Garnier and Delobez, 1979). In fact, the development of such a field owes much to American geographers, in particular William Applebaum (see, for example, Applebaum, 1954, 1961; Murphy, 1961). Despite the intended scope of marketing geography, a review of the literature suggests that its practitioners have tended to concentrate heavily on the study of retailing activities rather than the full gamut of marketing functions. Thus, topics such as store locational analysis, the determination of trade areas and the movement of goods have received much attention within the field. The emphasis placed on these topics probably reflects the view of Applebaum (1954) that marketing geography should not be a purely academic subject, but should essentially be an applied field of study directly related to the interests and needs of retail businesses. This applied orientation has also been subscribed to by British researchers, notable among them being Davies (1976, 1977a) and Thorpe (1978). Whilst the practical relevance of marketing geography is undoubtedly great, it may be argued that there is an inherent danger involved in adopting exclusively such an approach, for it can lead to a situation where the needs of retail businesses are promoted above the research requirements of comprehensive academic retailing and distributional studies. Thus, in the words of Warnes and Daniels (1980, p. 133)

> 'those primarily concerned with short-term contract research commissioned by retail firms or planning agencies are prone to neglect the distributional characteristics of retailing; this could have a long-term regressive effect for retail geography'.

In conclusion, the important point to note is that both the disciplines of marketing and marketing geography have made substantial contributions to the study of retailing. This was particularly the case in the 1950s and 1960s when few sociologists or economists turned their attentions to retail research (Dawson, 1980b). Further, in terms of overall scope and practice, it has also to be stressed that recent developments in the field have meant that 'retail geography, particularly since Scott's important survey (1970), has become a sub-branch of geography almost as important as marketing geography which encompasses it' (Dawson, 1979a, p. 25).

LOCATION, COGNITION AND BEHAVIOUR

A clear and important theme has emerged from the foregoing discussions, namely that retail locational patterns and consumer behavioural traits are closely interrelated. Stated in the simplest terms this implies that retail location affects possible courses of behaviour in the short run period, although in the medium to long run periods, changes in consumer demand and behaviour may well be reflected in changing retail locational patterns through the birth and death of firms.

The heart of Figure 1.1 suggests that three substantive topics dominate geographical studies of the retailing system. Firstly, such studies have traditionally focused on *spatial aspects of retail location.* This theme has come to be associated with a deductive theory concerning the location of tertiary activities known as central place theory and its propagation owes much to the quantitative revolution in geography. Secondly, as shown on the right hand side of the central box in Figure 1.1, retailing geography has also had a longstanding interest in *spatial aspects of overt consumer behaviour*; considering, for example, the distance, direction and frequency of the trips made by consumers. Thirdly, serving to link these examinations of the nature of the retail environment on the one hand and the characteristics of consumer movements on the other, there have been studies of the *spatial attributes of consumers' perception and cognition* of the retail system. Such studies have essentially been interested in two main things. First, the amount of knowledge that consumers have regarding retailing facilities. For example, is it the case that some consumers possess more information about retailing facilities than others; are there distinctive spatial patterns in consumers' awareness of facilities? Secondly, work has also focused on how individuals feel about the shops and centres comprising what may be termed their 'information zones' and 'mental maps'. This approach within retail geography, along with the overt behavioural perspective owes much to the rise of behavioural geography as a whole during the 1970s (Dawson, 1980b).

One of the central arguments advanced in the present work, therefore, is that the locational and cognitive-behavioural aspects of the urban retailing system should be considered in conjunction. The need for such a unified approach is clearly illustrated by the fact that singular examination of one of these topics requires the adoption of assumptions regarding the other. Thus, it is hard, if not impossible to study consumer spatial behaviour or perceptions without paying due heed to the circumstances of retail location and structure whilst equally, it is difficult to derive a model of retail location unless assumptions are made as to how consumers behave within the system.

This important methodological consideration is ably demonstrated by the approaches that have been employed by researchers to study urban retailing phenomena in the past. The earliest generally concentrated on facets of retail location, both empirically (Proudfoot, 1937a, 1937b), and via theoretical formulations (Garrison *et al.*,1959; Berry and Garrison, 1958a, 1958b; Berry *et al.*, 1963). It was in this latter connection that increasing recourse was made to central place theory. At this early stage of research, consumer behaviour was rarely considered in explicit terms (Shepherd and Thomas, 1980). The early deductive models that were employed to explain the spatial configuration of retail and service activities assumed first, a uniform or 'isotropic' environmental context and secondly, the existence of entirely rational businessmen and consumers. In this manner, the vagaries of differential consumer behaviour and perception were assumed away in such studies. In fact, a model of human behaviour subsequently referred to as *Economic Man* was effectively being adopted. In the words of Wolpert (1964, p. 537) such location theory assumed that the decision-maker 'has a single profit goal (or cost or space utility), omniscient powers of perception, reasoning and computation, and is blessed with perfect predictive abilities'.

The central place models developed by Christaller (1933) and Lösch

(1938, 1940) may thereby be regarded as reflecting a form of economic determinism. The retail locational and trade area patterns envisaged by these two theorists are shown in Figure 1.2. In both of these resultant

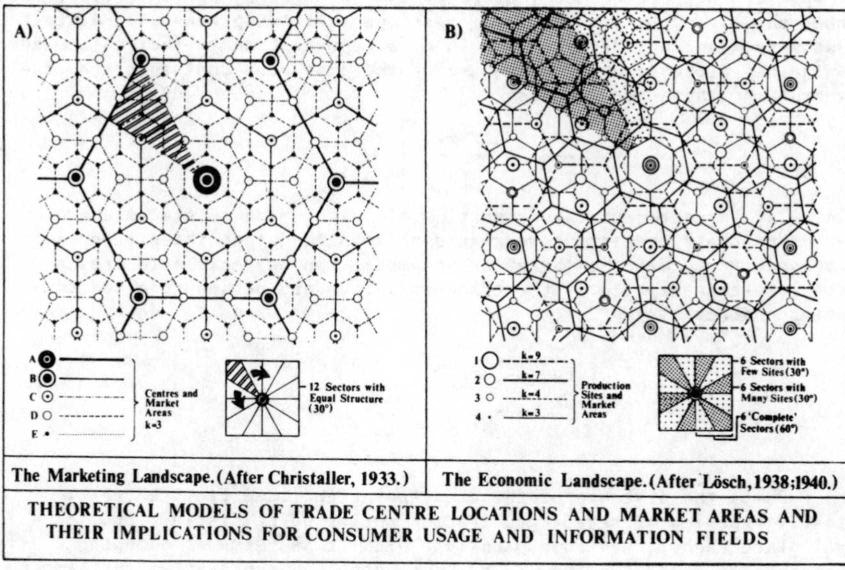

Figure 1.2 Retailing models and their implications for consumer behaviour and perception (Reproduced by permission from Potter, 1977c)

systems, since consumers are assumed to have perfect knowledge and to behave in a perfectly rational economic manner at the outset, they will visit the nearest centre that provides the goods or services they require. Purely economic reasoning then gives rise to the distinctive geometrical-hierarchical patterns of retailing centres shown in Figures 1.2A and B.

Interestingly, both of these models yield retailing landscapes that consist of structurally symmetrical sectors radiating from the urban core. The marketing system derived by Christaller, for example, renders twelve radial sectors of equal structure extending outward from the highest-order central place. Thus, a consumer located anywhere within the system would be able to purchase all goods and services by visiting the shopping centres that lie in a 30° zone incorporating his home (Figure 1.2A). The Löschian landscape consists of six 60° sectors of identical retail structure and a similar behavioural argument can be applied with respect to it (Figure 1.2B).

These models are clearly dominated by retail structural considerations so that they negate the influence of diversity in consumer behaviour and perception at the outset. This fact coupled with the symmetrical structure of the retail system will lead to consumers shopping in wedge-shaped or sectoral zones, the apex of which is focused on the town centre (Potter, 1977c). In essence this gives rise to the empirical notion of a size dominated urban retailing system, so that consumer choice may be viewed as basically involving a trade-off between centre size and the distance of location of the centre from the consumer's home (Hudson, 1975). In fact, this size-distance principle is commonly employed to view consumer behaviour and is embodied in the basic gravity or spatial interaction model of retailing advanced by Reilly (1931). Thus, the *law of retail gravitation* states that two places will attract custom from an intermediate area in direct proportion to their size and in inverse proportion to the square of the distances that separate consumers from these two centres:

$$\frac{Ta}{Tb} = \frac{Pa}{Pb} \left[\frac{db}{da}\right]^2$$

where Ta, Tb represent the proportion of trade drawn to places a and b, Pa and Pb their respective population sizes and da, db the distances involved. From this the 'break-point' model can be derived in order to calculate the position of the trade area boundary between the two competing centres:

$$Db = \frac{dab}{1 + \sqrt{\frac{Pa}{Pb}}}$$

where Db is the distance of the break-point in trade from centre b. Clearly, the law of retail gravitation whilst being distinct from central place theory, has some parallels with it in terms of shopping centre trade areas (Davies, 1976), and adopts an aggregative and almost mechanical view of consumer behaviour (Timmermans, 1980a). The size of centres is thereby regarded as the basic determinant of their attractiveness and this is only compensated for by the closeness of other smaller centres to the consumer. No other factors are taken into account in this basic gravity formulation.

The notion that the world is inhabited by economic optimizers is clearly untenable, and was first critically appraised by Simon (1957, 1959), who argued that the concept of economic man has little or no relevance in a situation of imperfect or spatial competition. Simon argued that decision-makers generally search for a satisfactory outcome rather than an optimal one, and thereby he introduced the principle of *satisficing*. It was suggested that the concept of economic man should be replaced by that of *bounded rationality*. Essentially this reflects the fact that decision-makers are regarded as constructing a simplified model or representation of the situation they are dealing with, because of the extreme complexity of reality. It is argued that individuals then behave rationally with respect to this model rather than with respect to reality itself, thereby allowing for the occurrence of wide variations in decision-making and behaviour.

Such perspectives opened up the possibility of a behavioural-perceptual approach to the study of consumer behaviour, and this was taken up by workers such as Huff (1960) and Thompson (1963, 1966). Thus, in identifying future directions for retail research, Thompson (1966, p. 17) commented that

> 'the fundamental factor affecting the geographic distribution of retail trade is the manner in which consumers organize their

perceptions of the external environment with which they are faced. Adoption of this hypothesis forces the empiricist to abandon his preoccupation with objective phenomena and necessarily to focus on the more subjective aspects of human behaviour'.

In fact, in the 1960s and subsequently, a series of empirical investigations showed that consumers do not invariably patronize the nearest centres that offer the commodities they require (Golledge, Rushton and Clark, 1966; Rushton, Golledge and Clark, 1967; Clark, 1968; Clark and Rushton, 1970; Eyles, 1971; Fingleton, 1975). One explanation that may be advanced for this is that retail centres of the same overall size may well be markedly different from one another in terms of their qualitative tone, degree of compactness, protection from the weather or precise functional mix. This might itself induce different perceptions and decisions regarding ultimate behaviour on the part of consumers.

Inherent differences between consumers themselves may represent another factor which promotes variant consumer behavioural patterns. This idea of diversity in decision-making has been developed by Pred (1967) using what he terms the *behavioural matrix*, the basic characteristics of which are depicted in Figure 1.3A. It may be argued that all spatial-economic decisions can be regarded from two points of view; first, the quantity and quality of the apposite information available to the decision-maker and secondly, his ability to employ this information in a sound manner. These two variables prescribe the axes of the behavioural matrix which may be regarded as a series of pigeon holes that can be employed in order to classify the efficacy of locational decisions. A decision placed at B_{11}, for instance, would be characterised by little available information and a poor ability to use it. At B_{nn}, however, the decision-maker has all of the relevant information at his disposal and a marked ability to employ this in coming to a rational decision. Pred also followed the classification of economic activities into *adaptive* and *adoptive* first provided by Alchian (1950). Some enterprises may be seen as rationally adapting their operations to the prevailing conditions, as a result of the accurate information they have and their ability to use it. In contrast, others act in relative ignorance and almost by chance some are adapted by the environment and succeed. This allows the matrix to be divided into four quarters on the basis of an adaptive-adoptive dichotomy on the one hand and a successful-unsuccessful division on the other (Figure 1.3). The traditional economic man of normative economic location theory would be found located in the successful adaption category at the bottom right of the matrix.

Such a framework recognises the realities of satisficing behaviour and acknowledges that decisions are frequently taken on the basis of imperfect levels of information and in the absence of the desire or ability to achieve an optimal solution. This idea is illustrated with regard to the location of urban retailing facilities in Figure 1.3B. Here, the majority of retail establishments are located in what is deemed to be a rational pattern, but those at A and B represent unsuccessful adopters who are likely to make a loss and go out of business soon. Similarly, the approach is also applicable to the spatial shopping behaviour of consumers. Thus, in Figure 1.3C, although the majority of shoppers visit their nearest centres, those at A and B travel to far distant places. This may represent behaviour which is thought irrational on purely economic grounds but which is entirely consistent when viewed in terms of the wider aims and aspirations of the consumers

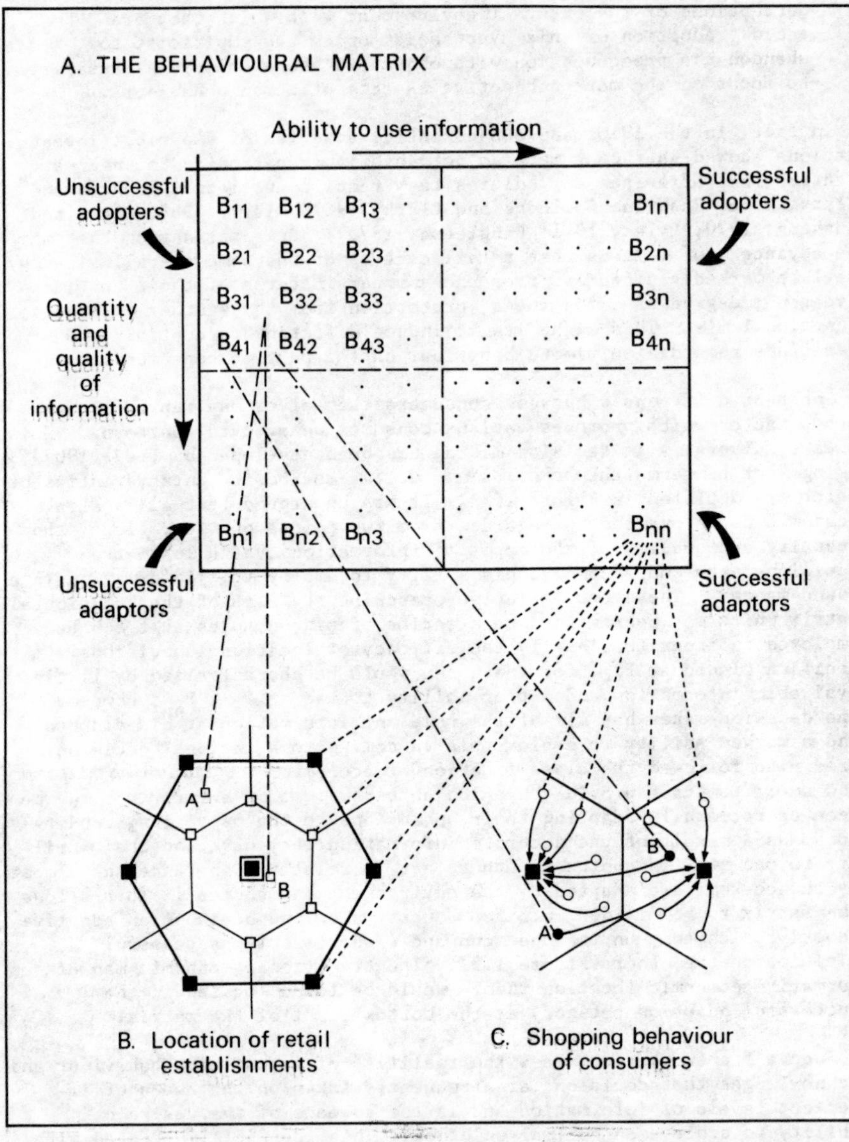

Figure 1.3 The behavioural matrix applied to retail location and shopping behavioural patterns (Adapted by permission from Pred, 1967)

concerned. Although some have argued that Pred's behavioural matrix is little more than a statement of the obvious and that it is incapable of further refinement (Adams, 1968; Webber, 1972), its influence on location theory and empirical research has undoubtedly been considerable.

It is hoped that this section and the previous one have given some impression of the nature, scope and importance of urban retailing studies, so that the aims and organization of the present work may now be elaborated in full.

AIMS AND STRUCTURE OF THE PRESENT WORK

This book seeks to examine in detail the knowledge that has been accrued concerning the structural characteristics of intra-urban retailing centres and the overt behaviour, spatial cognitions and perceptions of consumers in urban environments. Further, the reciprocal links existing between these topics is also considered. This objective is pursued by means of detailed reviews of the existing literature in these fields and the volume thereby focuses on the theories, techniques and empirical findings of studies by geographers, planners, sociologists, psychologists, marketing specialists and others in a variety of urban contexts. Particular emphasis is also placed on the author's own research carried out in Stockport and Swansea, and previously unpublished case studies of both urban retailing structural organization and consumer spatial behaviour-cognition are provided.

It has already been stressed that the study of retailing constitutes a relatively complex topic which has considerable applied relevance in relation to both commercial decision-making and the formation of planning policies. Although a substantial amount of research has been completed in the general field of retailing, relatively little attempt has been made to consider in detail 'the interdependent adjustment process between retail structure and shopping behaviour' (Thorpe, 1978, p. 93), that is between spatial aspects of supply and spatial aspects of demand.

In the first part of the book theories, models and empirical studies of urban retailing locational and structural patterns are presented and critically evaluated. Chapter 2, for instance, provides a detailed review of the mainly deductive theories and models that have been developed in order to explain the patterning of retail and service activities within urban areas. In the light of such work, in Chapter 3, an empirical case study of urban retailing structure based on the present author's research is presented. This subsequently leads on to a more rounded consideration of empirically based studies of urban retailing structural patterns in Chapter 4. Through this work, the importance of the size, quality, morphological and functional variables is stressed, along with the nature of the interrelations existing between these key retail area attributes. The theme here is that in studies of urban retailing structure, whilst the relationship between the size and location of urban retail centres has received much attention, equally important structural traits such as retail area quality levels and their morphology have received relatively scant attention. These variables are likely to be of as much importance as retail centre size. Thus, the recent development of techniques to measure and analyse these retail area characteristics is of considerable interest. Finally, in Chapter 4, an effort is made to summarize these points and a simple model of the spatial evolution and structure of urban retailing is advanced and tested against the findings of empirical research.

Turning to the cognitive-behavioural domain, although the size and location of urban retailing facilities are two factors that are obviously employed by consumers to assess retail areas, factors such as their morphology, qualitative tone and degree of functional specialisation are equally likely to influence consumer decision-making via the mechanism of differential cognition and perception. Thus, in the second part of the book, the focus is very much on the consumer, with respect to the spatial characteristics of his overt shopping behaviour and the nature of both his designative (informational) and appraisive (emotional) perceptions of the constituent elements of the urban retailing system. In Chapter 5, an effort is first made to review extant models of consumer spatial behaviour and cognition, and the motivations of consumers are also examined. A simple graphical model of consumer behaviour is presented which develops the idea of analysing the usage and information fields of urban consumers. The findings of a wide variety of studies designed to ascertain the spatial nature of intra-urban retailing trips are also reviewed in detail. In Chapter 6, the focus is on empirical investigations of designative and appraisive aspects of consumer perception and cognition and their implications. Subsequently, the findings of a study of consumer behaviour and perception which was carried out by the author in the Swansea urban area in 1978 are reported (Chapter 7). Finally, an effort is made to conclude in Chapter 8 by summarizing the practical planning implications of the material reviewed previously in the volume.

Much research has recently been completed in the broad field of urban retailing studies and the time seems ripe for a volume which attempts to synthesize this material. It must be stressed, however, that in terms of overall coverage, the present volume is perforce selective and illustrative rather than exhaustive. Hence, certain important topics such as the mathematical modelling of consumer behaviour, receive comparatively little attention. Unfortunately, such an approach is necessary in a volume of this length. Although there are a number of textbooks dealing with various aspects of marketing and retailing geography (Berry, 1967; Scott, 1970; Davies, 1976; Beaujeu-Garnier and Delobez, 1979; Dawson, 1979a, 1980a), this is the first to deal exclusively with the *urban retailing system*. As such it is hoped that it will be of interest and use to geographers, planners, sociologists, psychologists, marketing specialists and other social scientists who are concerned with topics such as the spatial connotations of marketing systems, urban retail planning and aspects of environmental design and perception.

2 Theories and Models of Urban Retail Location

The debate or what may perhaps be described more accurately as the controversy concerning the efficacy and appropriateness of existing models and theories of the location of retailing activities within urban areas continues at the research frontiers of both retailing geography and spatial marketing studies. This preoccupation with locational matters remains despite the fact that such questions have now commanded the attention of workers in the field for some considerable time. The currency of this interest is amply illustrated by the observation of White and Case (1974) that during the period 1960 to 1974, as many as five hundred papers were published in mainstream journals on the general topic of the theory of location of tertiary economic activities.

The basic aims of this chapter are twofold. First, it presents reviews of the leading theories and models that have been developed which purport to explain the salient features of urban retailing structural organisation. It is hoped that this material will serve as a basic introduction to the field for those who have little prior knowledge of such works. Subsequently, efforts are made to elucidate the salient characteristics of such models along with their implications. This leads on to the second aim, which is to evaluate the contemporary relevance of these formulations. In this context, the emphasis is placed primarily on work published since 1970. In particular, an effort is made to assess the validity of the models when viewed with respect to the most important changes that are occurring in the urban retailing system.

BACKGROUND CONSIDERATIONS

Recently, there has been a considerable growth of literature and associated theories, models and generalisations concerning not only the overall pattern of location of tertiary economic activities in urban areas (Teitz, 1968; Davies, 1973b), but also the distributional characteristics of the various sub-components of the urban tertiary domain (see, for example, the reviews by Thomas, 1976; Warnes and Daniels, 1979; Dawson and Kirby, 1980; Kivell and Shaw, 1980). In broad terms, such research has sought to establish whether or not the basic tenets of *classical central place theory*, as expounded by Christaller (1933) and Lösch (1938, 1940) apply with respect to the intra-urban location of tertiary activities, either collectively or singularly. Thus, for example, the locational configuration of wholesaling establishments within urban areas has been examined and a great deal of discussion has ensued concerning the relevance of central place theory in accounting for it (Vance, 1970, 1973; Teitz, 1971; Rabiega and Lamoureux, 1973). Similar attention has been addressed to the spatial incidence of recreational and vacational establishments (Campbell, 1966; Mercer, 1970) and also with reference to the placement of various health care and medical facilities in towns and cities (Morrill and Earickson, 1968; Morrill, Earickson and Rees, 1970; Schultz, 1970; Parr, 1980a). The importance of promoting and/or achieving a sound and efficient system of location for such public facilities hardly requires stressing, for this will obviously be an important agent affecting the distribution of social welfare and equity in any society.

As retail goods and services are also essential to the conduct of our daily lives, writers such as Harvey (1973) and Guy (1980) have argued that retailing may properly be regarded as a semi-public good. This is attested by the fact that consumers generally expect an adequate level of shop provision in their localities regardless of considerations of pure commercial viability. This serves to emphasise the need for careful commercial planning imperatives, based on apposite theories and generalisations concerning retailing structural organisation.

The highly controversial nature of the congruence perceived to exist between urban retail structural patterns in theoretical formulations and in reality is probably most clearly illustrated if the views expressed in a number of recently published works on spatial aspects of marketing are examined. These are extremely divergent. Thus, on the one hand, Dawson and Kirby (1980) are quite unequivocal in their condemnation of the lack of relevance of traditional theory to the contemporary urban setting, for it is ventured that

> 'Whilst central place theory may have been an adequate model of the intra-urban retail system in the 1950s the retail industry has changed in the last quarter century to such an extent that the tenets of that theory no longer have relevance to modern marketing practice and present day cities' (Dawson and Kirby, 1980, p.87-8).

Similar views have recently been proferred by the same author elsewhere (Dawson, 1979a, 1980a). Despite this, however, Dawson (1979a) has observed that central place theory has frequently been employed as a framework for retail planning policy at both the inter- and intra-urban scales. At the national scale, for example, central place based ideas have been employed in planning service centre hierarchies in Israel, the Dutch Polders (Davies, 1976) and Barbados (Potter and Hunte, 1979). With respect to the urban situation, whilst Dawson has noted that the retail infrastructure of places such as London and Sydney, along with the British new towns and certain other smaller settlements have been planned on a hierarchical basis, it is still concluded that the retail 'industry has passed into another phase of development at least in urban Britain and central place theory is now of little relevance' (Dawson, 1979a, p. 337). However, in almost total contrast, Beaujeu-Garnier and Delobez (1979) at the conclusion of a lengthy review of the theory and practice of commercial location imply the universal applicability of a hierarchical principle of spatial organisation for retailing and other tertiary activities.

> 'The conclusion clearly indicated by the study of all these examples is this: that the "equipment" of commerce is distributed in certain functional gradations that correspond to an equally hierarchical spatial distribution based on distances apart and

areas served. This is the case in the most highly developed countries, while in the others there is a tendency to copy the model closely, either by strict planning as in the socialist countries or through normal economic evolution' (Beaujeu-Garnier and Delobez, 1979, p. 148).

Thus, when the basic question of the utility of existing theory is asked in the context of the urban environment, a clear and resounding answer is given by the authors; 'can we apply the elements of the hierarchical theory of commercial centres, within the towns themselves? Most authors would agree that we can' (Beaujeu-Garnier and Delobez, 1979, p. 170).

The ambivalence displayed by marketing geographers in their reactions to central place theory is further illustrated by Davies (1976, p. 29) who maintains that 'The hierarchy concept has been especially important in urban planning in Britain, where it represents the main organisational principle not only for retail provisions but also for educational, medical and other welfare services'. Somewhat later in the same book, however, this positive view is qualified when it is stated that 'central place theory contains much that is relevant to the domestic shopping system in Britain but it does not illuminate the locational requirements of service activities or even certain specialised retailing activities' (Davies, 1976, p. 289).

Collectively these quotations and the views they express serve to exemplify the complexity of debate concerning the contemporary relevance and applicability of general theories of urban retail location, and this topic forms the theme of the present chapter. However, before such works are reviewed in any detail, it is necessary to look briefly at the general issue of the nature of theories and models and their relation to empirical research work.

THE NATURE OF THEORIES AND MODELS OF URBAN RETAILING

Although this chapter is entitled 'theories and models of urban retail location', it would be inappropriate to place undue emphasis on the single feature of *location*. In fact, the spatial placement of retail centres is not the only variable considered in such theories and models, although it is obviously the dominant one. Other vital attributes, such as the numerical frequency of retail centres by size orders, their functional characteristics and degrees of specialisation are considered *inter alia* in such formulations. This is an important point and will be returned to subsequently.

Further, it must be stressed that this chapter deals almost exclusively with theories and models of urban retailing rather than the findings of purely empirically based research. An *empirical* study is one that is based on observation of reality or on experimentation. As such the approach basically follows an *inductive* mode of explanation, working from the particular to the general. Thus, the end product of empirical research may well be a generalised statement or 'theory'. The model of urban commercial structure derived by Berry (1963), which will be examined later falls into this category. On the other hand, a pure *theory* may be regarded as a set of statements which seek to explain how the phenomenon under study works or how it is structured. Frequently, theory formulation derives from the application of a *deductive* approach, the set of statements having been developed by a process of logical reasoning in advance of intensive observation of the phenomena under study in the field. In this respect, Einstein's view of theories as free creations of the human mind becomes clear and thus defined, any speculative fantasy concerning the structure of the real world may quite legitimately be regarded as a theory. From an academic viewpoint, however, a more fruitful definition of a theory as 'a set of propositions which purports to explain the structure of some system and/or how the system develops' (Wilson, 1972, p. 32) may be adopted. It is of note, however, that a special class of what may be regarded as idealistic theories may be identified. These are generally referred to as *normative theories* and seek to explain how a system should be structured for efficiency or some other goal, rather than how it is actually believed to be structured. Thus, *a theory of urban retail location may be defined as a set of propositions that seeks to explain the spatial structuring of the urban retailing system and which hopefully also casts some light on the development of the system and/or its ideal state.*

The differences existing between the deductive and inductive orders and to a lesser degree between normative and other theories give credence to the distinction that is commonly drawn between *theory* and *practice*. It is important to emphasise that in the retailing context, this distinction should be seen as a matter of degree only and not as the generator of a dichotomy as is so often implied. Quite simply, theories about retailing, in common with those concerning many other phenomena are rarely derived without recourse to the 'real world'. Thus, even normative theories are developed by individuals who observe the external world on a daily basis. Certainly, the very ubiquity of shops should serve to discourage the derivation of abstruse theories. Thus, a focus should be placed firmly on the search for general statements about retailing which are of wide applicability (*nomothetic* studies), as opposed to studies that stress unique facets of the retail structure of particular towns (the *idiographic* approach). However, it is to be appreciated that such generalisations can be derived via both empirical and theoretically oriented studies of retailing phenomena.

This leads on to the second term used, that of *model*. The attributes of models and the precise nature of their relation to theories are both thorny problems. The word 'model' can be employed to denote a degree of perfection, a representation of something or a demonstration. As commonly used in an academic setting, a model may essentially be regarded as a selective and highly simplified representation of reality. Thereby, the hallmark of a sound model is that it presents in a generalised manner, only those attributes of the study object that are deemed to be important. Thus, models are selective, structured and hopefully also suggestive. As defined, therefore, models and theories are closely interrelated, so that Harvey (1969) has commented that a model is to be regarded as the formalised expression of a theory. Thus, simplified models are frequently derived in order to represent a theory. As a consequence, it is sometimes suggested that whilst all theories and laws are models, not all models may be regarded as constituting theories or laws.

As previously explained, this chapter examines theories and models of urban retail location - that is sets of ideas, often of a highly selective nature which endeavour to explain the spatial structure and development of urban retailing systems. Stated in this manner, the derivation of sound models and theories of retailing appears as a formidable and important task. This mirrors the fact that such formulations should embody and clearly express the general principles which influence retail locational patterns, and in this way they play a significant role in providing a framework for empirical analyses and planning.

THE CLASSICAL CENTRAL PLACE THEORY OF CHRISTALLER

The basic principles affecting the location of tertiary economic activities were first deduced in a comprehensive manner by a German geographer, Walter Christaller. He laid down the bases of his theory in a book entitled *Central Places in Southern Germany* which appeared in 1933, and in 1966 as an English translation. It is important to stress that Christaller was concerned with identifying the pure principles of location for all tertiary activities, including administrative, cultural, religious, health and sanitation, social, economic, commercial and financial, labour, professional, transport and communications functions and associated institutions (see Christaller, 1966, p. 140-1 for a full listing of such activities). Thus, the work was conceived at the level of the urban system and focused on urban settlements at the national or regional scales. However, the wide ranging appeal and utility of central place theory cannot be overstressed. One recent writer has been moved to comment that 'central place theory may be called the most important contribution of geography to theoretical social science' (Saey, 1973, p. 181), whilst Bunge (1962, p. 129) has contended that 'the initial and growing beauty of central place theory is geography's finest intellectual product and puts Christaller in a place of great honour'. Certainly one is bound to agree with Parr (1978a, p. 31) that there 'can be little question that central place theory continues to occupy an important position in urban and regional analysis', and it is frequently employed as a basis for planning and prediction (Turner and Cole, 1980).

Such is the theoretical and applied importance of Christaller's work that is receives detailed coverage in most books on spatial economic structure and a number of more detailed expositions also exist (Berry and Pred, 1961; Berry, 1967; Marshall, 1969; Beavon, 1975, 1977; Haggett, Cliff and Frey, 1977; Lloyd and Dicken, 1977; Yeates and Garner, 1980; King and Golledge, 1978; Carter, 1981). Thus, only a basic outline of Christaller's work is provided here as a foundation for the studies which follow.

Christaller's work was motivated by the apparently simple question 'are there laws which determine the number, sizes and distribution of towns?' (Christaller, 1966, p. 1). In reply, he argued that such features cannot be explained by recourse to essentially environmental-geographical factors, but rather by the purely economic factor of demand in space. It was suggested therefore, that special 'economic-geographical' laws or tendencies of tertiary location could be identified.

Significantly, in terms of methodology, Christaller's thesis began 'not with a descriptive statement of reality, but with a general and purely deductive theory' (Christaller, 1966, p. 4). The theory of central places is a normative spatial economic formulation and it therefore makes use of a partial equilibrium approach wherein the influence of some variables is negated by the adoption of limiting assumptions. Further, it is important to note that places performing functions for a wider nodal or functional region were defined by Christaller as *central places* and were seen as standing in direct contrast to *dispersed places* such as those based on transport functions or the existence of special resources. This is an important distinction which as we shall see is parallelled in the urban setting. Further, it served to limit Christaller's attention to the *tertiary component* of the economic system *alone*, a fact frequently ignored in introductory accounts of the theory.

As noted above, Christaller adopted a number of assumptions at the outset of his theory. These have been summarised by Parr and Denike (1970, p. 568):

> 'a) a homogeneous plain with a uniform rural population; b) a system of f.o.b. pricing, i.e., the consumer pays the price at the point of production (the f.o.b. price) plus the cost of transportation to the consumer's location; c) an identical demand by all consumers at any real price (i.e., the f.o.b. price plus the appropriate transportation cost); d) no institutional or legal restrictions on the entry of producers into the market.'

Recently, some debate has ensued regarding the first assumption, Saey (1973) and Beavon (1975, 1979) having argued that the Christallerian system does not require a homogeneous isotropic plain, and that it is sufficient to have a homogeneous transport system with a regular but not necessarily even distribution of population. However, for general purposes it is adequate to assume a high degree of physical and socio-economic uniformity and the behavioural existence of economic men.

Notwithstanding these deliberations, the basic concept of central place theory is neatly embodied in a single quotation from Christaller (1966, p. 19): 'Central goods and services are produced and offered at a few necessarily central points in order to be consumed at many scattered points', so that the derivation of the theory can briefly be explained as follows. Christaller noted for any good offered at a central point, the f.o.b. cost incurred by the consumer increases with his distance of location from the centre, due to the transport charge. At a certain distance from the market, therefore, a point will be reached at which the demand for the good will be zero. This maximum distance over which the consumers are prepared to travel or over which they are willing to ship the good is known as its *range*. Under competitive conditions there will also be a *lower limit to the range*. This has subsequently come to be known as the '*threshold*', that is the minimum sales volume or market area needed to ensure the viability of firms offering the good. Christaller by and large developed his theory, however, in terms of the upper limit of the range and not on the basis of thresholds (Beavon, 1975, 1977; Beavon and Hay, 1978). As Saey (1973) notes, a number of authors are in error in the sense that they have developed the system in terms of the threshold requirement (Berry, 1967; Marshall, 1969; Lloyd and Dicken, 1972).

Firms will enter the plain so as to command a market area equal to the range. Accordingly, the plain will come to be covered by central place establishments which have circular market areas. Under these conditions the firms will be earning *excess profits*, that is a return higher than the threshold for viability. The amount of land unserved will be minimised and the packing maximised when the firms are evenly spaced in a triangular arrangement, each trade area being tangential to six others. This leaves unserved areas in the interstices between market areas however, and these can only be eradicated if the areas overlap at their margins. As consumers are assumed to act in a rational economic manner, they will minimise their costs by visiting the nearest place offering the good. Hence, the segments of overlaps between trade areas will be bisected, rendering a contiguous set of hexagonal market areas and a triangular lattice of firms.

A wide variety of goods and services must be supplied to the dispersed population of the area. Each good will be characterised by a different range. If a triangular system of higher order A-centres and their attendant hexagonal trade areas is developed to supply the good with the largest range (good *n*) in the manner outlined above, then the conditions of supply of the good with the next largest range (*n-1*) may be considered. This can also be supplied from the A centres, but the range will prescribe a smaller circular trade zone and an area will remain unserved between any three of the existing A centres. As goods with successively lower ranges are introduced, a good is finally reached, say good *n-p*, for which the interstitial population and purchasing power between any three existing A centres is equal to the range of the good in question. Good *n-p* is referred to as a *hierarchical marginal good* (Berry and Garrison, 1958a), and with it second-order or B centres will develop at the exact mid-points between any three existing A centres. The B centres obviously will not supply goods with range requirements greater than that of good *n-p*, but will supply all goods with a lower range than this.

In fact this process of location can be continued to give third, fourth and fifth levels of central places, each of these being associated with further lower-order hierarchical marginal goods and thereby with distinctive sets of tertiary functions. The spatial pattern of retail location which results is shown in Figure 2.1A. This is referred to as the *k=3* or *marketing principle*, where *k* is the ratio of the equivalent number of market areas existing at a particular functional level to the number of market areas existing at the next higher level. This can be illustrated by recourse to the market area of the first order central place located at the middle of Figure 2.1A. Thus, we take one such first order central place. There are six second order centres located on the boundary of the first order market area. However, each of these is split between three adjacent first order centres, so that there is the equivalent of (6 x ⅓), or two second order centres for every one of the first order. Turning to the third order centres, there are six whole centres nested within the first order market area. Further, there are 12 entire fourth order centres plus 12 that lie on the first order market area boundary, and which are split in half; hence, there are 12 + (12 x ½) or the equivalent of 18 fourth level centres. Thus, the numerical frequency of centres by size group is 1, 2, 6, 18 ... *etc*.. As each centre of a particular level also carries out the functions of centres of the next lowest and successively lower orders, the progression of market areas and the total number of centres performing functions at a given level runs in a sequence of 1, 3, 9, 27 ... *etc*.. This gives the geometric bifurcation ratio of 3. Alternatively, k can be regarded as the ratio of market area sizes between hierarchic levels (Marshall, 1977a). As Timmermans (1979a) has pointed out, k does not refer to the numerical sequence of centres by size orders at each discrete level, an error made in several works (e.g. Johnson, 1967; Garner, 1967; Haggett, Cliff and Frey, 1977).

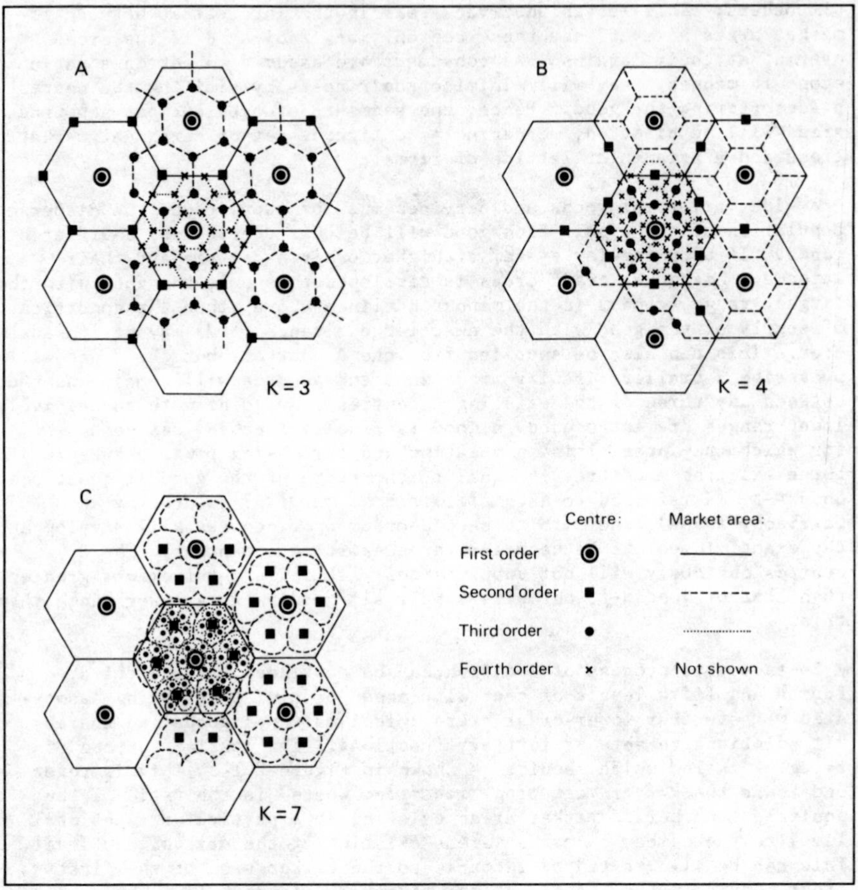

Figure 2.1 The k=3, 4 and 7 central place systems developed by Christaller

The marketing landscape basically represents an areal solution in which a region is supplied with all goods and services in the most efficient economic manner. The system thereby minimises the number of centres and consumer travel. But the location of successively lower order centres at the mid-points between three higher order places results in two shortcomings. First, a difficulty in constructing an efficient transport network and second, that of providing for administrative efficiency.

The problems involved in establishing a satisfactory traffic system within the marketing landscape are illustrated in Figure 2.2. The need is to construct priority routes between the highest order A places (Figure 2.2A). The logical solution is to develop a net of six major radial-routes extending from each A centre to each of the six A centres surrounding it. Such high priority connections will bisect the line joining any adjacent pair of B centres at its mid-point. In other

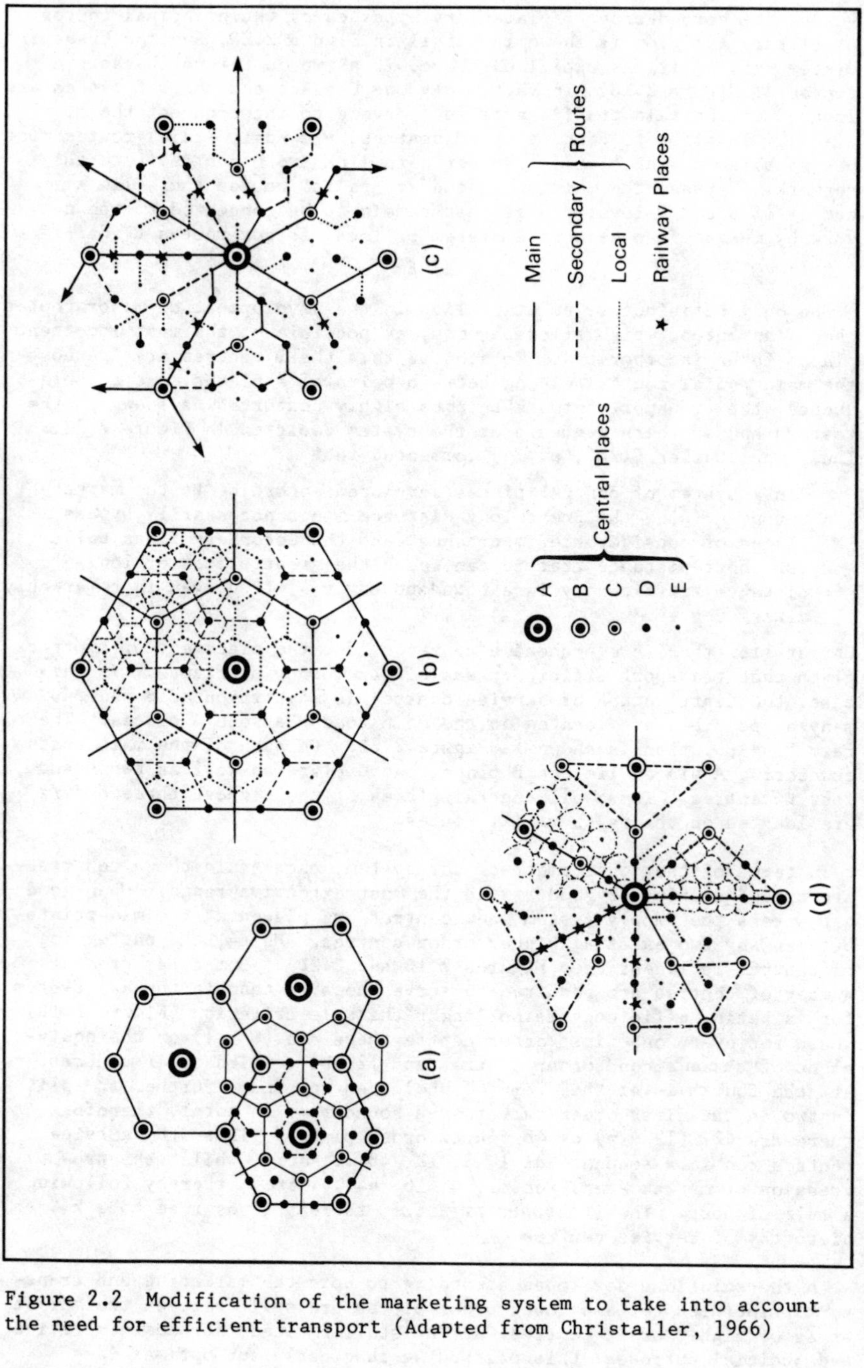

Figure 2.2 Modification of the marketing system to take into account the need for efficient transport (Adapted from Christaller, 1966)

words, the second-order B places are bypassed by the principal routes. A solitary A region is shown in detail in Figure 2.2B, and the transport system serving it, as explained above, is shown in the north-eastern sector of Figure 2.2C. In fact, only one C place and three E places are located on the main traffic arteries serving to interconnect the A places. In order to connect the B centres, secondary radial routes must be established, which will also serve to link two D centres into the network. Between the main and secondary radial routes there lie a number of E and D level places that remain to be connected to the network by means of an elaborate system of local feeder routes (Figure 2.2C).

The only satisfactory solution lies in the development of major routes the alignment of which allows as many as possible of the most important places to be incorporated. To achieve this the B centres are linked by the main radial routes running between pairs of A places. As a consequence, the transport network becomes highly contorted as shown in the western and southern segments of the system depicted in Figure 2.2C. Thus, Christaller (1966, p. 74) commented that

> 'In a system of central places developed according to the marketing principle, the great long-distance lines necessarily bypass places of considerable importance, and the secondary lines built for short-distance traffic can reach the great places of long-distance traffic only in a roundabout way - often even in remarkably zigzag routes.'

Christaller therefore proceeded to reconsider the placement of centres given that transport efficiency was of paramount importance. In this case, the distribution of service centres is most favourable when as many as possible are located on the main roads between A places. The resulting solution is shown in Figure 2.2D. On each of the main roads connecting A places lie one B place, one C place as well as two D and four E centres. Thus, all central places of the highest three orders are located on the major radial routes.

In terms of the development of the system, once again the A centres are spaced evenly for good n with the most extensive range. When good $n-p$ enters the supply system, new centres are placed at the mid-points between any two existing higher order centres. Hence, the patterning of centres is linear (see Figures 2.1B and 2.2D). But a far greater number of centres are required to serve the area than in the k=3 system, for marketing efficiency is no longer the sole criterion (Figure 2.1B). Thus, for every one first order centre there are (6 x ½) or the equivalent of three second order centres and 12 whole third order centres. At the fourth level there are 42 whole centres and a further 12 split in two on the first order market area boundary. In total, therefore, there are 42+ (12 x ½) or 48 fourth order places. Thus, the service centres run in a sequence of 1, 3, 12, 48 ... etc., whilst the progression of market areas runs 1, 4, 16, 64 ... etc., thereby following a rule of four. The *transport principle* thereby gives rise to a k=4 hierarchy of service centres.

In the solutions developed according to both the marketing and transport principles certain lower order places are split between the market areas of higher order centres. As Christaller noted, for administrative and judicial purposes, this patterning is clearly sub-optimal (see Figures 2.1A and B). Hence, the *administrative principle* was developed.

The allegiance of lower order centres is never split between higher order places. Thus, given a uniform distribution of first order places, when the hierarchical marginal good *n-p* enters the system, six whole second order centres are placed around each first order place. Hence, the number of centres at each level runs 1, 6, 42, 294 ... etc., whilst the number of market areas is 1, 7, 49, 343 ... etc. (Figure 2.1C). This is the k=7 *administrative principle* of tertiary location.

The elegance and beauty of Christaller's three hierarchical principles of tertiary location is hard to refute, but their true significance lies beyond such characteristics. Their full structural implications have been usefully listed by Marshall (1969, p. 23 *et seq.*).

1. *Spatial interdependence of centres* - for example, the second order centres depend on those of the first order for higher order goods.

2. *Functional wholeness of the system* - taken together, therefore, the centres of different orders comprise a functional entity.

3. *Discrete stratification of centrality* - the centres of a given functional order are identical. Thus, 'differences in functional complexity between the various levels are greater than the differences within each level; the latter, in fact, are zero' (Marshall, 1969, p. 25).

4. *Interstitial placement of orders* - centres are located in a uniform geometrical pattern; lower order places are sited between higher order places.

5. *Incremental baskets of goods* - as developed, Christaller's systems mean that higher order centres provide the goods supplied by lower order centres, plus a further distinctive set. Parr (1978a), following Schultz (1970), refers to this as a 'successively inclusive type hierarchy' and it is a very important characteristic. Incremental sets are related to the appearance of hierarchical marginal goods.

6. *A minimum of three orders* - this is required according to Marshall to give a true hierarchy.

7. *A numerical pyramid in order membership* - each order of centres contains more places than the next higher order so that a true numerical hierarchy exists

These seven diagnostic criteria may be used as an empirical test of perfect hierarchical structuring. A basic feature is that Christaller produced *fixed k* central place systems. Thus, if the k value between the first and the second order centres is 3 (i.e. k_{12}=3), then it will also apply to all other levels of the hierarchy (e.g. k_{23}=3, k_{34}=3, etc.). As a result, some regard the Christaller systems as inflexible, unduly rigid and frequently incapable of describing the observed frequency of central places by size (Parr, 1978a, 1978b, 1980b, 1981). This is certainly a valid criticism of the models as developed, although Christaller did suggest that the patterns prevailing in any area would likely take the form of a compromise arrangement between different principles. This fact is often disregarded in reviews of Christaller's work, although it is clearly noted by Parr (1978a, 1978b) and Warnes and

Daniels (1979). This gives rise to a fascinating possibility for developing more flexible and realistic central place models, as is shown subsequently.

Another notable characteristic of the Christallerian systems is a stepped hierarchy of centres. The models are dominated by the size variable and functions are located in a complementary fashion in the largest centres, so that the only form of functional variation is that which occurs by size (Potter, 1981b). Thus, centres of the same size are identical. This of course reflects the adoption of uniform behavioural assumptions at the outset. As Rushton (1971a) has noted, if these postulates are changed, so will the location of centres, a point stressed in Chapter 1, and which will receive empirical verification in subsequent chapters.

On the positive side, Marshall (1977a) has argued that Christaller's models have the advantage of being realistic, plausible and not overly complex. Further, Christaller gives a certain degree of priority to the operation of the *economies of spatial agglomeration*, and thereby also takes into account, to some extent at least, the importance of multipurpose trips by consumers (Parr and Denike, 1970). These characteristics are both useful in the urban setting. However, there are a number of problems to be faced if Christaller's systems are used normatively in the urban context. First, as Warnes and Daniels (1979) have implied, the k=3 and k=4 systems fail to take account of the finite nature of urban areas. In the k=3 and 4 models at the intra-urban scale, the second order places would be the major district centres. As we have already seen, these second ranking places are located on the boundary of the market areas of the first order centres. Thus, the district centres would be located at the very periphery of the urban zone - a highly unlikely spatial configuration (see Figure 2.2B, for example). Only in the case of the k=7 system are the district centres and their trade areas located wholly within the town (Figure 2.1C), but this is not a very efficient pattern for retailing purposes. Finally, within an urban setting, central places do not always take the form of discrete nodes in space; they often string out along major routes. Although this is taken into account to some degree in the k=4 system, it remains a problem for strictly defined central place models.

THE CLASSICAL ECONOMIC LANDSCAPE OF LÖSCH

When bringing the work of Lösch (1938, 1940) into juxtaposition with that of Christaller there is a tendency to stress their differences. But as Parr and Denike (1970) have noted, the salient fact is that using essentially different lines of reasoning, Christaller and Lösch arrived at remarkably similar conclusions. Lösch, another German scholar but this time an economist produced his major book, *The Economics of Location* in 1940, the English translation appearing in 1954. His work was far ranging and has received many accolades. Valavanis (1955, p. 637) has remarked that the book 'belongs to that class of works, of which each generation produces very few, that both introduce a new subject and exhaust it' and that 'the main ideas are few and appear utterly simple once popularized'. However, a great deal of research continues on the Löschian system of economic regions and the subject is by no means as exhausted or simple as Valavanis implies (see, for example, Leven, 1969; Parr, 1970, 1973; Tarrant, 1973; Beavon, 1973, 1978b,

1978c; Beavon and Mabin, 1975, 1976; Haites, 1976; Marshall, 1975, 1977a, 1977b; Funck and Parr, 1978).

Lösch adopted similar assumptions to those of Christaller, commenting that the work started from 'radical assumptions in order that no spatial differences may be concealed in what we assume' (Lösch, 1954, p. 105). Thus, economic raw materials were assumed to be ubiquitous and the area homogeneous in all other respects, save for self-sufficient farms being regularly distributed in a triangular fashion. Lösch sought to produce a spatial equilibrium pattern of location from this uniform starting position.

Let it be assumed that a single farmer produces a good over and above the subsistence level and wishes to market this excess. Lösch showed that the cost of the good will increase with distance from the farm due to the transport charge (Figure 2.3A). As the quantity of a good demanded tends to fall with its increasing price (Figure 2.3B), demand will increase with distance from the point of supply, giving a circular market area and a demand cone (Figure 2.3C). Lösch indicated how a system of such market areas may be packed together to form hexagons (Figures 2.3Di to 2.3Diii). Finally, the hexagonal market area may be reduced in size until it ultimately covers the threshold purchasing volume, so that the farmer is earning *normal profits* (Figure 2.3Div).

The proposition enumerated above holds for every good, the size of the market area being determined by the sales required to make production viable. Lösch then established the size of the successively larger trade areas that can be constructed around a single supply point in the basic lattice. The k=3, 4 and 7 hexagons were shown to be the three smallest such areas that can be drawn, subject to the constraints that each hexagon forms part of a wider network, and that the centres coincide with places in the basic settlement lattice. Other market area sizes such as k=3.5 or 5 can be constructed, but in such cases the supply points will not coincide with the basic farms (Beavon and Mabin, 1976).

The three smallest market areas are shown in Figure 2.3E. In the k=3 case, the central point of supply serves a third of the entire requirements of six of the basic settlements, plus itself. Hence, the equivalent number of farms served is $(6 \times \frac{1}{3}) + 1$, or 3. Thus, in the Löschian case, k represents the number of basic settlements served by a central place. The k=4 market area serves $(6 \times \frac{1}{2}) + 1$, or 4 of the farms. In the k=7 pattern, the equivalent of seven whole farms are supplied. In fact, there is a whole series of market areas that can be drawn around a supply point serving 9, 12, 13, 16, 19, 21, 25 of the basic units of demand. Lösch identified 150 such nets up to k=511 times the basic unit of demand. This is in fact an arbitrary number, and there is an infinity of Löschian numbers. However, as Marshall (1977b, 1978a) notes, the real world does not contain an infinity of different goods.

The nine smallest Löschian market areas are depicted in Figure 2.4. The diagram indicates that these are obtained by increasing the size of each hexagonal unit and changing its orientation vis-à-vis the basic lattice of places. In Figure 2.4D, for instance, the higher order centre serves six entire lower order places, along with one-third of the requirements of a further six places, plus itself. Hence, $k = 6 + (6 \times \frac{1}{3}) + 1 = 9$. Similarly, in Figure 2.4E, the higher order centre

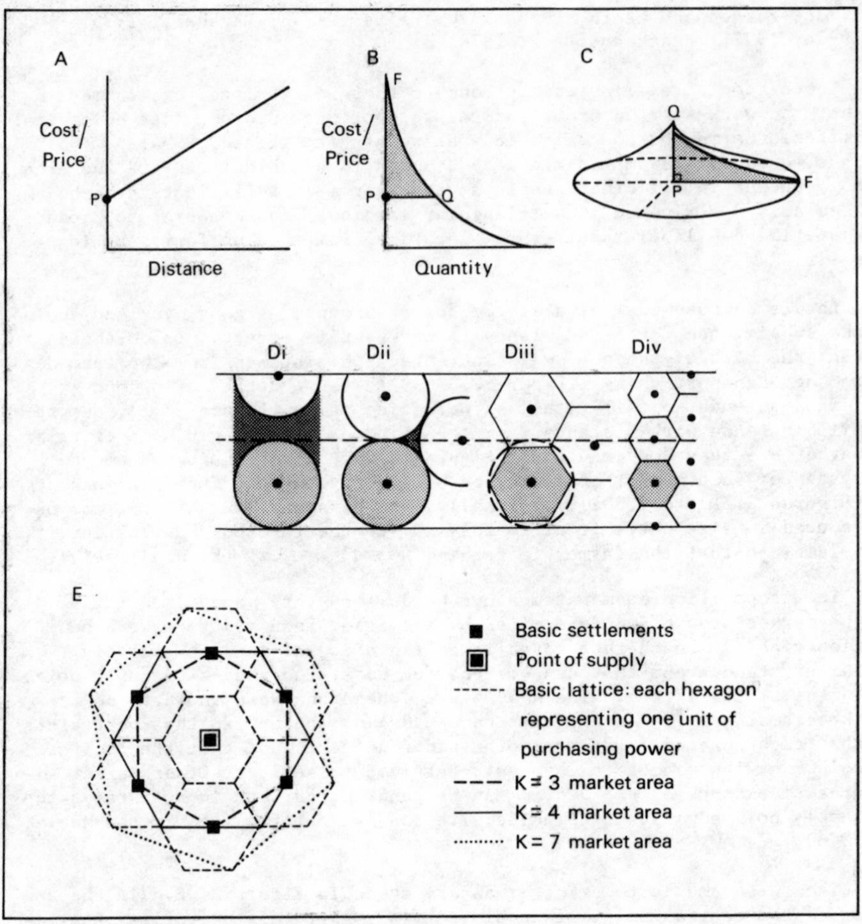

Figure 2.3 Basic aspects of the Löschian system of market areas (Adapted from Lösch, 1954)

serves six entire places, one-third the requirements of a further six, one half those of another six, plus itself, so that $k = 6 + (6 \times \frac{1}{3}) + (6 \times \frac{1}{2}) + 1 = 12$.

Thus, Lösch initially derived entirely separate networks of market areas and centres for goods with different thresholds, no attention having been paid to the spatial coincidence or agglomeration of such functions. However, Lösch (1954, p. 124) observed: 'despite the resulting confusion, every place would lie in the market area of every good. Yet it is worth while to bring order out of this chaos by means of a few reflections'. First, Lösch laid the nets down in such a manner that they all coincided at one point, giving a metropolitan centre (Figure 2.5A). Next, Lösch argued that the nets should be rotated about this common centre in such a way as to produce six sectors in which many market centres coincide and six where few coin-

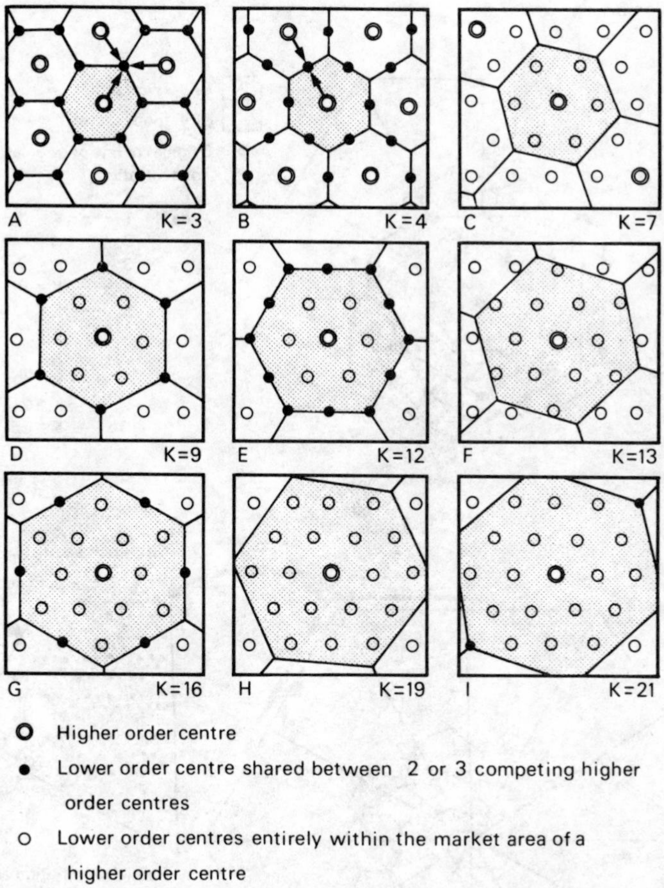

Figure 2.4 Löschian market areas from k=3 to k=21 (Redrawn by permission from Haggett, Cliff and Frey, 1977)

cide. This process of superimposition and rotation has been examined in detail recently by Beavon (1973), Beavon and Mabin (1975, 1976), Tarrant (1973) and Marshall (1977b). The product of this is the 'cog-wheel' or 'city rich - city poor' economic landscape commonly associated with Lösch's work (Figure 2.5B). It is clear that the productio of such sectors is a constraint on the rotation procedure and not the outcome of it (Tarrant, 1973). The entire system is composed of six identical 60° sectors, each one being made up of one 30° city rich zo and one 30° city poor zone (Figure 2.5; see also Figure 1.2B). Althou the existence of such sectors in the theoretical landscape has recent been fiercely debated by Marshall (1977b, 1978b, 1979) and Beavon (1978a, 1979), it seems likely that if they occur in reality they are related to the spatial disposition of intrametropolitan traffic arteries as argued by Parr (1973) and Marshall (1977b) in the intra-metropolitan context.

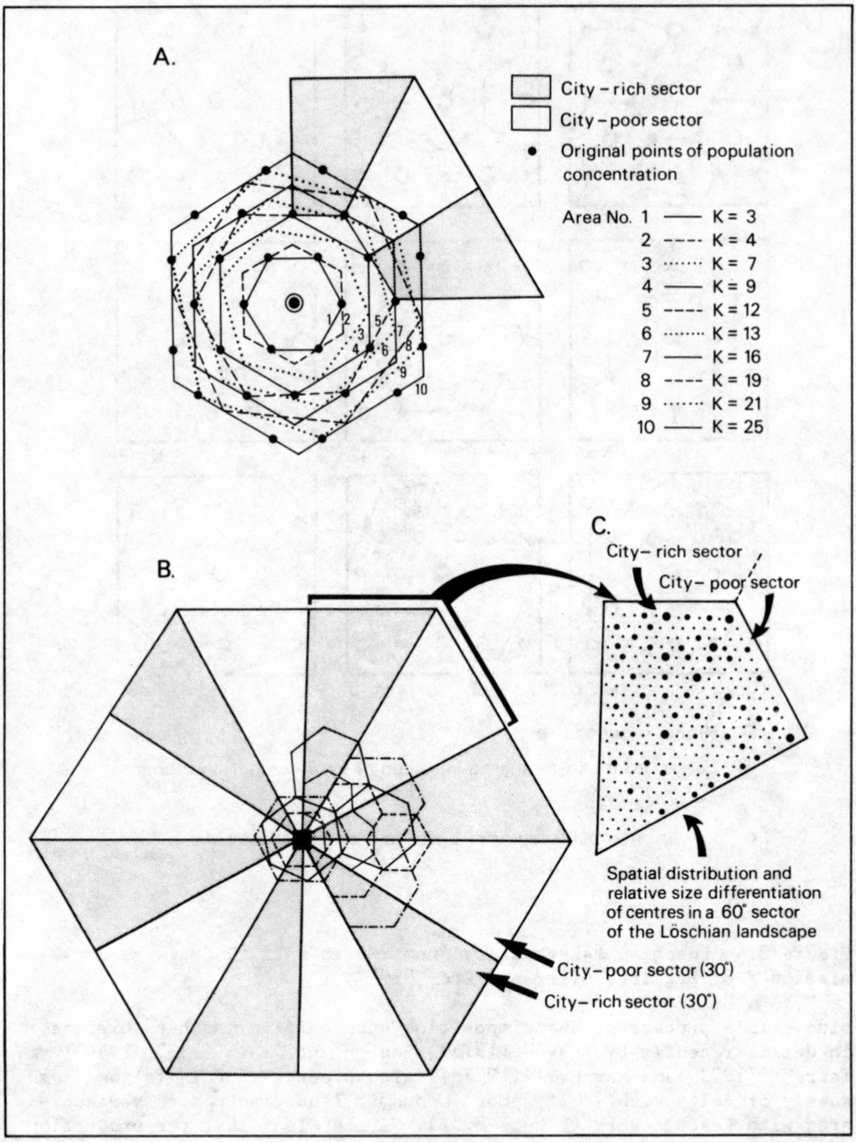

Figure 2.5 The derivation of the Löschian economic landscape (Adapted from Lösch, 1954)

Lösch's model is essentially a *nonhierarchical system*. Further, as the centres of the various market area networks occur at different distances apart, the centres which offer high threshold functions do not necessarily perform lower threshold functions as well. Thus, a form of non-size related functional specialisation occurs within the system and incremental baskets of goods as envisaged in the Christaller model do not occur. As a consequence, if the centres are classified by size, they tend to show a continuum rather than the discrete stratification of centrality. Although Parr (1973) has shown that a step-like hierarchy may be developed in a Löschian system, the size differentiation question is generally seen as a major contrast between the models of Christaller and Lösch, and has come to assume considerable importance regarding the applicability of the systems. The spatial distribution and relative size characteristics of the centres in one of the identical 60° sectors of the Löschian landscape is shown in Figure 2.5C. Despite the model being core dominated, a distinct overall pattern emerges in which market centres tend to increase in size as one travels out from the metropolitan centre.

The construction of the Löschian system is relatively complex and it has been argued that Lösch did not fully describe the procedures involved (Tarrant, 1973; Beavon, 1973, 1977; Beavon and Mabin, 1975, 1976), and that this has led to the popularity of Christaller's model over that of Lösch. However, the fact that the system is finally based on the superimposition of a series of independently derived sub-systems leads to a major inconsistency (Parr and Denike, 1970). It is that Lösch gave little priority to the agglomeration of marketing activity save for the minimal amount that results from the rotation of the separate market area networks. As a further consequence, therefore, the system also fails to account for multi-purpose shopping behaviour by consumers. Marshall (1978a, p. 125) has been moved to comment that 'we are thus faced with a crisis of plausibility', a comment that certainly does not bode well for the model's application in the urban setting. Of note here is the fact that it is no more than an operational assumption on the part of Lösch to regard each market area type as being appropriate for only one commodity. Some market areas could be suited to the supply of several goods (Marshall, 1977b), thereby allowing for a somewhat greater degree of agglomeration.

Despite such problems, however, it has been posited that the Löschian model is most relevant to the location of tertiary activities within cities. This view has recently been stressed by Beavon (see Beavon and Mabin, 1975; Beavon, 1977) who cites other researchers presenting a similar argument (Stolper, 1955; Dacey, 1965; Haggett, Cliff and Frey, 1977; Parr, 1973; Yeates and Garner, 1971). It is true that initially Lösch was presenting a model of market oriented manufacturing, but as the influence of raw materials is negated at the outset, the end product certainly amounts to a theory of tertiary location (Marshall, 1977b). The veracity of Beavon's argument, however, remains to be fully investigated subsequently.

It may be concluded that Lösch's model is more flexible than Christaller's formulation, but as a result it is also much more difficult to empirically recognise, test and verify (Parr, 1973, 1978a; von Böventer, 1962). However, the principal cause for concern is the poor performance of the model with respect to the occurrence of functional complementarity, agglomeration and multi-purpose travel, so that Marshall (1978a, p. 125) has stated that 'It is difficult to avoid the conclusion that the Löschian approach is too implausible to serve as a basis for empirical work'.

THE THEORY OF TERTIARY ACTIVITY

The foregoing account has intimated that certain problems are to be faced if classical central place theory is applied in an unmodified form to the intra-urban distribution of retailing activities. As well as the considerations previously enumerated, it is clear that population densities, the socio-economic composition of the population, purchasing power and propensities to consume are anything but uniform within large urban areas. A major step, however, came with the work of Berry and Garrison (1958a), when they produced a reformulation of central place theory under heterogeneous environmental conditions.

Berry and Garrison maintained that given the operation of the economic mechanisms of the threshold and range, a hierarchy of tertiary centres will occur even if an isotropic surface is not assumed beforehand. Consider, for example, the simple case of population density declining away from an urban centre. The highest order A centres will not be located uniformly, but with increasing distance from one another with increasing remove from the urban core, so that the area around each centre contains approximately the same level of population and purchasing power. Thus, market areas will no longer take the form of perfect hexagons but will be spatially transformed (Rushton, 1972; Beavon, 1974a), so that the range is not a fixed areal measure but reflects relative demand and purchasing power. When the hierarchical marginal good *n-p* enters the system, the second order centres can still be located at the mid-points between three higher order centres, and so on. The resulting pattern in the case of a k=3 system in an urban area is shown in Figure 2.6B for three levels of the hierarchy and is compared with the uniform Christaller distribution in Figure 2.6A.

A complete hierarchy is thereby developed free of the original Christaller assumption that population density and effective demand are uniformly distributed. This reformulation led to the argument that '*whatever* the distribution of purchasing power (and whether in open countryside or within a large metropolis) a hierarchical spatial structure of central places supplying central goods will emerge' (Berry and Garrison, 1958a, p. 111). This was the first clear statement that Christallerian central place theory, albeit in modified form, applies within cities, and the ideas have come to be referred to as the *theory of tertiary activity*. It is of note that this reformulated theory is characterised by the same general features as the classical Christaller models, so that Marshall's diagnostic criteria for hierarchical structuring are applicable. Further, the Berry-Garrison argument can easily be extended to the k=4 and 7 systems (Marshall, 1969, pp. 33-7).

The adoption of a variable pattern of market centre location and distorted market areas is a simple but important expedient. The same principle can also be applied with regard to the Löschian economic landscape (Figure 2.7). An inconsistency arises in the basic Löschian model in that a situation of regularly distributed population leads to one of unequal industrial productivity and marketing activity. This was recognised by Isard (1956) who modified the standard Löschian system of nets of market areas (Figure 2.7A) to take into account the fact that population density will decrease away from the metropolitan core (Figure 2.7B). Isard's graphical solution to this problem may therefore be regarded as a direct precursor to the Berry-Garrison reformulation.

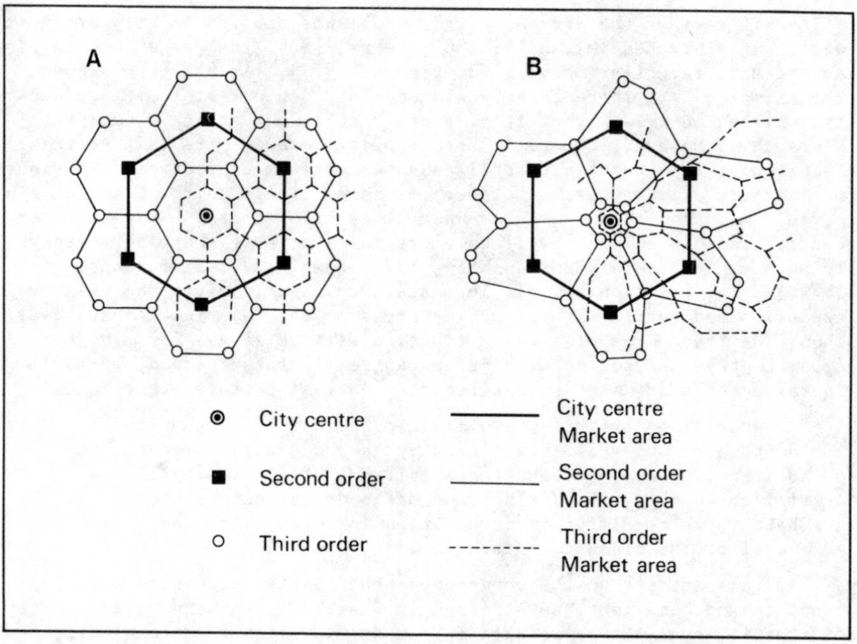

Figure 2.6 Spatial aspects of the theory of tertiary activity

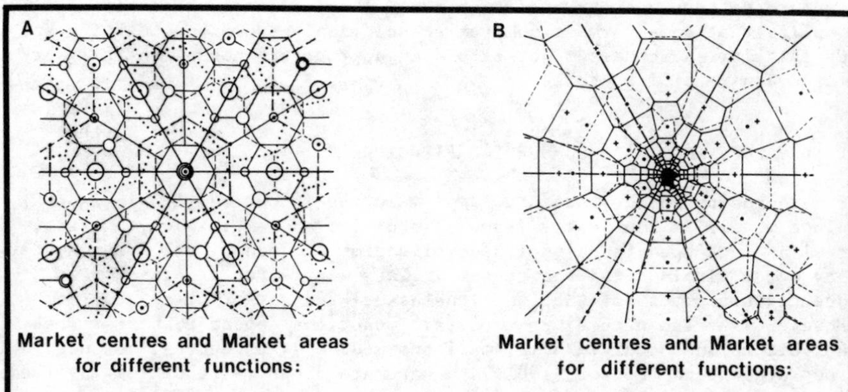

Figure 2.7 A heterogeneous modification of a Löschian landscape
(Adapted by permission from Isard, 1956)

The efficacy of the Berry-Garrison model was debated shortly after it was first published (Marshall, 1964; Berry, 1964) and has also been discussed more recently (Saey, 1973; Beavon, 1977). It has been argued, for example, that there is no real need for such a restatement of central place theory and that it does not result in a strictly defined hierarchy. However, a more important point to note here is that the theory of tertiary activity still assumes uniform-stereotyped behaviour on the part of consumers. However, it seems likely that the range of a given commodity will be greater when it is offered from a higher order centre, because shoppers will complete multi-purpose shopping journeys to such centres (Clark and Rushton, 1970; Saey, 1973; Timmermans, 1979a). The solution to this inconsistency also involves the relative expansion and contraction of market areas of the same functional level. Thus, the trade area of a given function will be larger for a higher order centre than for a lower order centre. Rushton (1971a, p. 140), in taking this argument to its logical conclusion states that

> 'a spatial behavioral postulate closer to reality than that adopted by Christaller yields a system of central places that differs in one important respect from that derived by Christaller; namely, the arrangement of goods in centers occurs in batches which differ in composition for centers at the same level of the classical hierarchy.'

This fact attests to the congruence that exists between retail location and behaviour, as stressed in Chapter 1. A more realistic set of starting assumptions results in a model in which functional differences occur between centres of the same overall size. Further, the spatial geometry of the original system no longer pertains. It is interesting to observe, therefore, that the dictates of multi-purpose travel suggest that whilst Lösch underestimated the degree of agglomeration of retail functions occurring within the real world, Christaller appears to have overstressed such spatial coincidence. This in itself implies that some form of compromise solution between the Löschian and Christallerian schemes might afford an appropriate normative framework for urban retailing studies.

LAND VALUES AND URBAN COMMERCIAL STRUCTURE

The degree to which *functional agglomeration* is catered for in central place models is thus a key issue. Intuition and experience, in fact, tell us that both functional specialisation and functional complementarity occur within retailing systems. Thus, large retail areas frequently house most of the functions associated with smaller centres. However, it also happens that certain functions appear to be far less ubiquitous and occur in some small and medium size centres, but not in the larger ones (Potter, 1981b). There are other difficulties involved in the application of pure central place notions to urban retailing. At this micro-spatial scale, the models developed at the inter-urban level take no account of the fact that retail areas exhibit very diverse morphological forms. Some, for instance are highly compact, whilst others string out in a linear fashion making it extremely difficult to think of shopping centres as discrete entities. It would appear that these variations reflect the differential accessibility of sites to urban consumers. In the simplest case of the monocentric city, accessibility will probably decline regularly with distance from the centre.

The rent that a user can pay for a plot will be proportional to the profit that can be derived at that site (Alonso, 1960). Hence, a process of competitive bidding will mean that land values will fall progressively with distance from the urban core (Figure 2.8A). However, accessibility and therefore land values are likely to be higher along the main radial routes that extend from the city centre (Figures 2.8B and C). In fact, most western cities have a transport network consisting of radial and ring routes. In such a situation, the generalised outward decline, and the ridges of higher land values along arterials will be complemented by land value peaks where ring and radial routes intersect (Figure 2.8D). This results in the complex three dimensional patterning of urban land values observed by Berry (1963) which is depicted in Figure 2.8E. Empirical research has confirmed that these hypothesised accessibility and land value patterns are typical of metropolitan areas (Hayes, 1957; Knos, 1962; Yeates, 1965).

Thus, it is logical to posit that shopping centre location and function will also be closely related to accessibility and land rent variations. Spatially compact or *nucleated centres* may be located at the major transport intersections, coinciding with land value peaks. Linear or *ribbon shopping developments* may string out in a less compact manner along the main arterial routes in response to land value ridges. The resultant pattern is expressed in Figure 2.8F, yielding a more complex morphological portrait than that envisaged in classical and modified central place formulations. The first attempt to clearly link these ideas in order to produce a model of urban retailing and commercial activities was made by Brian Berry in 1963. Berry's threefold typology was based on literature reviews (Berry, 1962) and on empirical investigations in American cities (Berry, 1959, 1960). The inductive foundations of this scheme will receive detailed attention in Chapter 4. The typology, shown in Figure 2.9, comprises three basic elements, those of *nucleated centres*, *ribbon developments* and *specialised functional areas*. Berry suggested that the first of these represents a hierarchy of business centres, these being either planned or unplanned. Four clear grades of centre were identified below the C.B.D. (Figure 2.9) and these were assumed to be located centrally with respect to their potential consumers, so that they conform with the dictates of the theory of tertiary activity. Also, it was noted that there is a pressure for different stores to group together so that consumers can complete multi-purpose functional shopping trips.

The second component of the typology, the system of ribbons is particularly conspicuous in the North American situation (Yeates and Garner, 1980; Hartshorn, 1980), but is of considerable relevance in most urban settings. Such ribbon types are mainly distinguished in terms of the accessibility and space requirements of certain tertiary functions, although they are highly varied. The *traditional shopping street* may be seen as little more than a linear extension of a nucleated centre (Figure 2.9). *Urban arterial* developments house a range of functions which require access to the urban market, but function efficiently outside of the nucleations, due to their need for space and the behaviour of their clientele. Amongst such uses Berry recognised specialised automobile repair establishments, furniture and appliance stores and discount houses. *New suburban ribbons* are simply a chronological variant of this type. *Highway oriented ribbons* develop to meet the needs originating along major trunk routes between places and are essentially

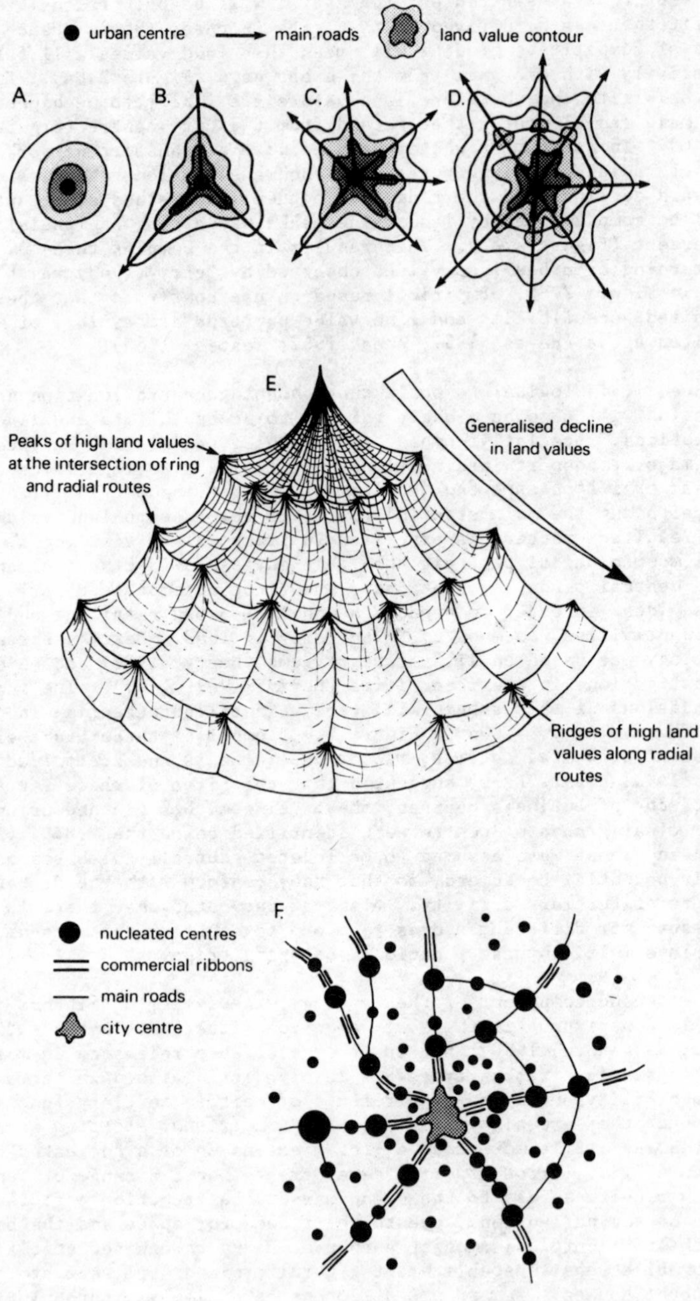

Figure 2.8 Urban land values and retail structure (Diagram E redrawn by permission from Berry, 1963)

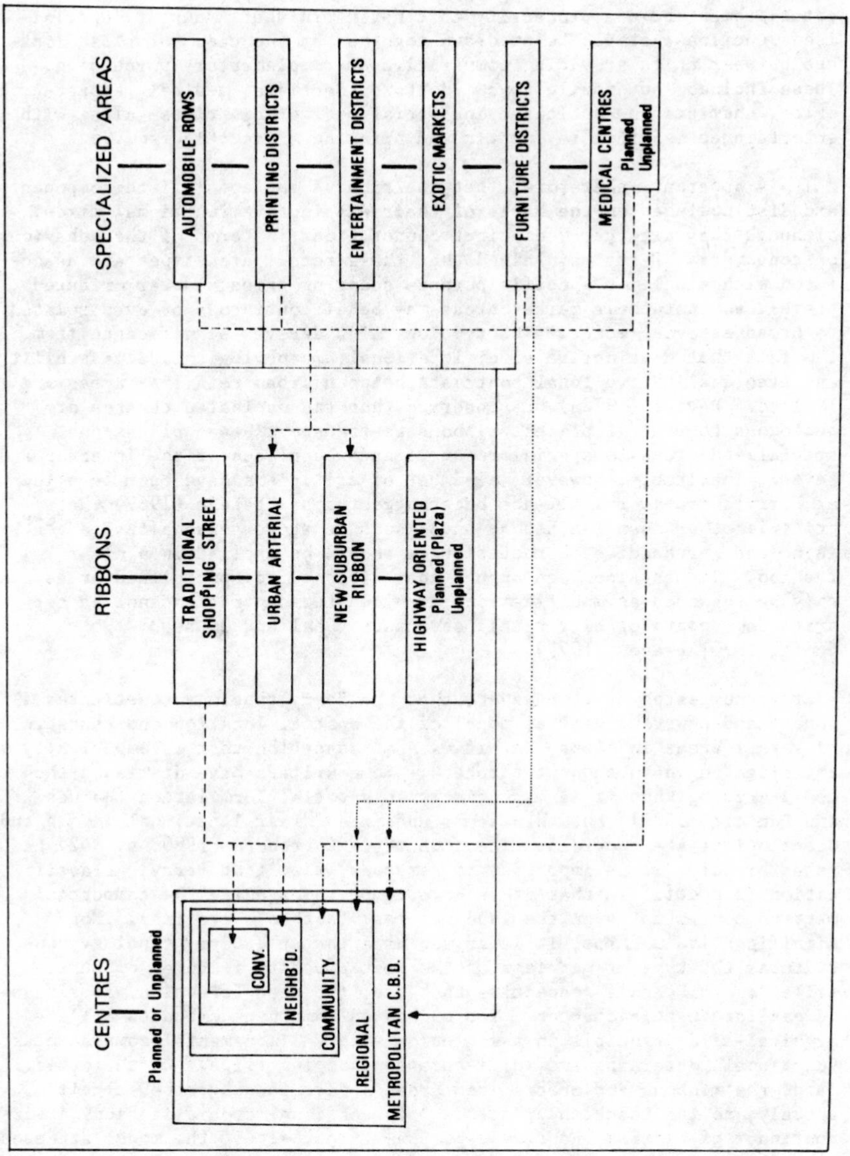

Figure 2.9 B. J. L. Berry's typology of urban commercial structure (Redrawn by permission from Berry, 1963)

'strip' developments. Typical associated functions are service and petrol stations, motels, restaurants, produce and vegetable stands. As a third major element, Berry argued that several types of commercial establishment have a propensity to cluster in what amount to specialised functional areas, being drawn together by the need for close linkage between units providing comparative or complementary purchasing. These include 'automobile rows', doctors, dentists, medical laboratories, chemists and opticians in special medical districts, along with entertainment, furniture, exotic and printing areas (Figure 2.9).

It is apparent, therefore, that the ribbons and specialised components are distinguished on the basis of their distinctive functional mixes, although they also carry distinct connotations in terms of the behaviour of consumers. Berry maintained that these retail area types are associated with single or specific purpose shopping trips and car oriented travel, so that their market areas may be discontinuous or even related to broad arterial zones. The typology also derives significance from the fact that distinctive size, locational, morphological, accessibility and even qualitative/tonal contrasts between urban retailing areas are implied. Davies (1972a) has observed that the nucleated centres are analogous to central places, ribbons to transport based places and specialised areas to special resource endowed places at the inter-urban level. Inevitably, however, a number of criticisms have been levelled at Berry's framework. It has been suggested by Epstein (1969) that criteria other than functional ones, such as store personality, advertising and merchandise characteristics should be applied in a clear fashion. It has also been argued that ribbons and specialised areas can only be regarded as modifications of nucleated centres and not as separate components of city retail structure (Boal and Johnson, 1965; Scott, 1970; Beavon, 1977).

It is suggested here, however, that the Berry typology constitutes a robust and powerful general model of the spatial location and character of retail areas in towns and cities - an assertion that is empirically investigated in subsequent chapters. Some writers have dismissed the model arguing that it is essentially an aspatial formulation (Warnes and Daniels, 1980), but this seems unfair as clear locational labels and descriptions are provided. Thus, Dent (in Hartshorn, 1980, p. 342) has recently said 'It is important to remember, too, that Berry's classification is *spatial* in that it is an attempt to organise the commercial pattern conceptually on the land use map' (author's italics). More significantly, perhaps, it is argued here that the Berry typology constitutes the type of marriage of the most apposite features of Christaller's and Lösch's respective theories, the need for which was stressed earlier in this chapter. The nucleated component embodies a hierarchical-size principle in association with an incremental-complementary functional patterning and multi-purpose shopping trips. On the other hand, the ribbons and specialised areas appear to subscribe, albeit loosely, to the Löschian principles of functional specialisation, a size continuum of centres and single-purpose trips. Thus, the model stresses that the perfect principles of size differentiation and a numerical hierarchy are gross oversimplifications. Thereby the model is salient not only in terms of its structural implications but equally with respect to its allusion to more realistic and flexible modes of behaviour on the part of consumers in urban areas.

MODELS OF HIERARCHICAL SUB-SYSTEMS

Berry's threefold framework was also instrumental in the metropolitan context in that it stressed that rather than being composed of monotonic elements located according to a single set of locational principles, the urban retailing system is made-up of a number of constituent sub-components. This stricture was verified in a series of American empirical studies carried out after the appearance of Berry's model. These demonstrated that nucleated shopping centres themselves tend to form into separate sub-components serving different ethnic and socio-economic groups. In so doing, such studies also perhaps indicated the efficacy of the theory of tertiary activity for the urban nucleations in the Berry typology.

In one of the first of these studies, Pred (1963) showed that in Chicago the shopping centres in Black areas contained a higher proportion of bars, cafes, general stores and pool-parlours than those of White areas. This finding was affirmed for Chicago in a more comprehensive study published by Berry, also in 1963. It was shown that retail centres in the high income areas of the city generally contained more stores and a greater floorspace than the same types of retail areas located in the low income districts. Thus, for example, what were described as 'smaller shopping goods centres' had an average of 150 establishments when located in high income areas, but only 100 in low income tracts. A similar contrast was found for neighbourhood level centres. Such variants in the hierarchy of outlying business centres in Chicago according to socio-economic status were confirmed in a subsequent study conducted by Garner (1966).

These findings were significant and acted as the catalyst for a similar enquiry based on Leeds in Britain by Davies (1968). This looked at the retail provisions of two contrasting estates in Leeds. Although there were more establishments in the shopping centres serving the high income residential area, these tended to be of a more specialised functional nature. The retail areas of the low income districts were slightly smaller but tended to provide a much wider range of functions and thereby presumably played a more dominant role in the residents' shopping activities, due to their lower income and mobility levels. It was also observed that clear qualitative differences were discernible between retail establishments in the two socio-economic areas.

The lesson is a relatively simple but very important one - once income and mobility levels and the behaviour of consumer groups display divergencies, so the urban retail system will become increasingly complex and differentiated as a consequence. Such empirically derived generalisations do not invalidate the tenets of central place models but rather serve to stress their strong normative basis.

These types of structural and behavioural contrasts were developed into a developmental model of the emergence of hierarchical sub-systems of urban retailing centres by Davies (1972a). In this, Davies (1972a, 1976) stresses that in many cities the majority of lower income residents tend to be located in the inner city in close proximity to the retail facilities of the central area. The developmental model is reproduced in Figure 2.10. A perfect central place type hierarchy is shown schematically for three distinct income areas in Stage 1. Separ-

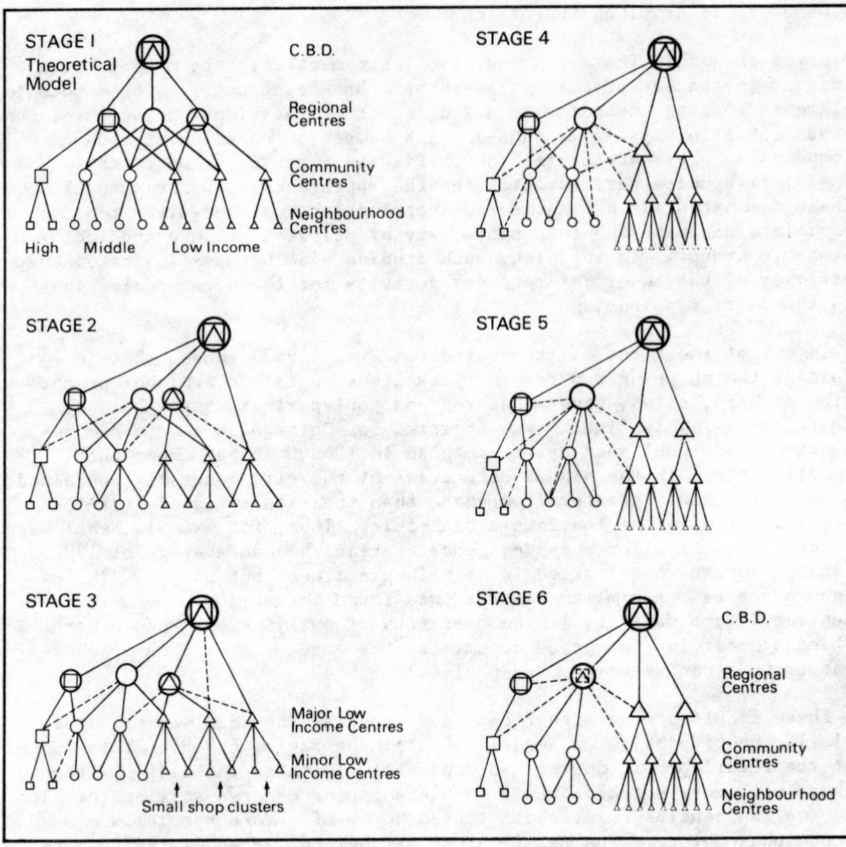

Figure 2.10 A model of the development of hierarchical sub-systems (Redrawn by permission from Davies, 1972a)

ate sets of neighbourhood and community level centres develop to serve the demands originating in the different social areas of the city. The higher order centres are shared by these different consumer segments. In Stage 2, the notion that low income residents live at higher densities near to the urban centre is introduced, so that retail facilities are more densely concentrated in the low income inner parts of the city. Also, the regional centres serving the low income consumers become overshadowed by the central area, often being by-passed on shopping trips. Thus, the regional centres in the middle income districts tend to gain in trade. This leads to the emergence of a variant shopping centre hierarchy in Stage 3. The importance of smaller centres is enhanced in the low income areas and they become functionally more diverse. Major and minor low income centres may develop which perform regional through to neighbourhood level functions respectively. With time, an almost entirely separate hierarchical sub-system may emerge for the low income areas (Stage 4). Considerable shopping movements are assumed to occur between the middle and high income sub-components, thereby furthering the growth of the middle income regional centres. A stage of competition between the central area and the middle income regional centres is then envisaged, so that some of the middle income consumers may also by-pass smaller centres and begin to erode the lower levels of their own sub-system. The final outcome is represented in Stage 6. Three distinct sub-systems of nucleations have developed. The middle income areas of the city are now characterised by the largest regional centres, whilst the low income areas show the greatest concentration of small centres.

The model thereby embodies many of the types of regularity identified in the empirical studies carried out in the 1960s and the size dominated, perfect incremental hierarchy of urban retail areas becomes distorted. Qualitative differences will become apparent between retail districts of approximately the same size and functional range. Presumably the size differentiation of nucleations is no longer stepped, but forms more of a continuum, particularly at the lower levels of the retail system. Superimposed on this complex pattern will be a further set of specialised areas and ribbon developments based on single-purpose trips. In essence, therefore, the assumption of diverse behavioural patterns on the part of consumers leads to a more realistic and complex structural pattern of urban retailing facilities.

VARIABLE K CENTRAL PLACE MODELS

The point that regularities in the size differentiation of urban retailing areas are not likely to be either simple or constant is coming to the fore. In this respect at least, theory formation has kept pace with empirical findings, for a notable development in the 1970s has been that of the *variable k* or *general hierarchical model* of central places. This family of models, just like those of Christaller and Lösch has been derived at the inter-urban scale, but is equally applicable to the intra-urban retailing system.

The precursors to the general hierarchical model are to be found in Christaller's original work, when he acknowledged that real world size-location patterns will be the outcome of all three central place principles acting in unison rather than singly. As noted by Parr (1978b) and Warnes and Daniels (1979), in a later publication Christaller (1950) endeavoured to modify this shortcoming in a theoretical hierarchy produced by the simultaneous operation of the k=3, 4 and 7 principles. Later, it was suggested that an average k value of 3.3 would result (Christaller, 1962). The idea of a mixed-hierarchy was extended by Woldenberg (1968) who argued that market area size can be derived by the geometric means of the numbers produced by the three principles operating independently at each level of the hierarchy.

However, another response to the challenge of flexibility and applicability in central place systems is possible. This has recently been developed in an imaginative and original manner by Parr (1978a, 1978b), although the idea had been noted in other earlier papers (Parr, 1970; Beckmann and McPherson, 1970; Parr, Denike and Mulligan, 1975; Marshall, 1977a). This involves the operation of different locating principles at the various levels of the hierarchy. Parr (1978b) tried to produce a model that is similar to that of Christaller, but which is far less rigid. This *GH* or general hierarchical model starts with similar assumptions to those of Lösch and Christaller regarding population density and purchasing power. However, there are two principal features of the GH model that differentiate it from these earlier systems. First, market area sizes increase from the smallest to the largest at a rate that is not necessarily constant, making it different from Christaller's model. Second, the centre of a market area of a given functional level is also the centre of market areas of each smaller size. This means that the GH model is akin to Christaller's model in that it caters for incremental baskets of goods and multiple purpose travel, but serves to distinguish it from the Löschian system. Thus, in the GH model k, the ratio of the number of market areas at different levels of the hierarchy is not necessarily constant, but may *vary between the levels*. If there are N levels in the system, there will be n-1 nesting factors or k values.

An example of such a variable k system is shown in Figure 2.11A. For the one first order centre there are ($6 \times \frac{1}{2}$) or the equivalent of three second order places. Adding the first order centre there are effectively four market areas at this level. Thus, $k_{12}=4$ and the transport principle of spatial location is operative (Figure 2.11A). Turning to the third order, within the first order market there are ($6 \times \frac{1}{3}$) + 6 or the equivalent of eight centres. This makes a total of 8 + 4 = 12 market regions at this level. Thus, $k_{23}=3$ and the marketing principle is discernible. Finally, although not fully shown in the diagram, there are 24 entire fourth order centres within the first order market. Adding these to the 12 existing market areas at this level gives a total of 36, so that $k_{34}=3$ and the marketing principle of spatial placement has again been followed. Another example of a variable k hierarchy is given in Figure 2.11B and a similar analysis can be performed. This reveals that $k_{12}=3$, $k_{23}=4$ and $k_{34}=3$, illustrating the inherent flexibility of the GH central place model.

The principal merit of the GH model is the potential ease with which it fits the numerical complexities of observed retail and service hierarchies. This has already been illustrated in a series of articles by Parr (1978a, 1978b, 1980b). Christaller's fixed k models may in fact be regarded as a special limited case of the GH model, which in turn, is a set of special cases of the Löschian landscape. In a sense, therefore, Parr's model is intermediate between those of Christaller which are narrow and relatively simple and the general Löschian model which is broad but very complex (Parr, 1978b).

In Parr's (1978b) paper, it is ventured that a 'further area of application of the alternative model concerns public policy decisions within an intra-urban setting. One possible application might relate to the regulation of shopping centres and other commercial nodes' (p. 43). Certainly as an intermediary between the systems of Christaller and Lösch it might be concluded that the GH model has much to recommend its application to urban retail patterns. Further, in this connection it is of note that the system is not incompatible with the rank-size distribution or a continuum of centres by size (Parr, 1978a). This possible intra-urban extension of the GH model has been taken up by Warnes and Daniels (1978, 1979). The type of variable k urban landscape that they initially propose is shown in Figure 2.11C. Thus, with regard to a given town centre, the second order or district centres are located according to the administrative principle ($k_{12}=7$) in order to ensure the functional autonomy of the C.B.D. However, it can be posited that the sep-

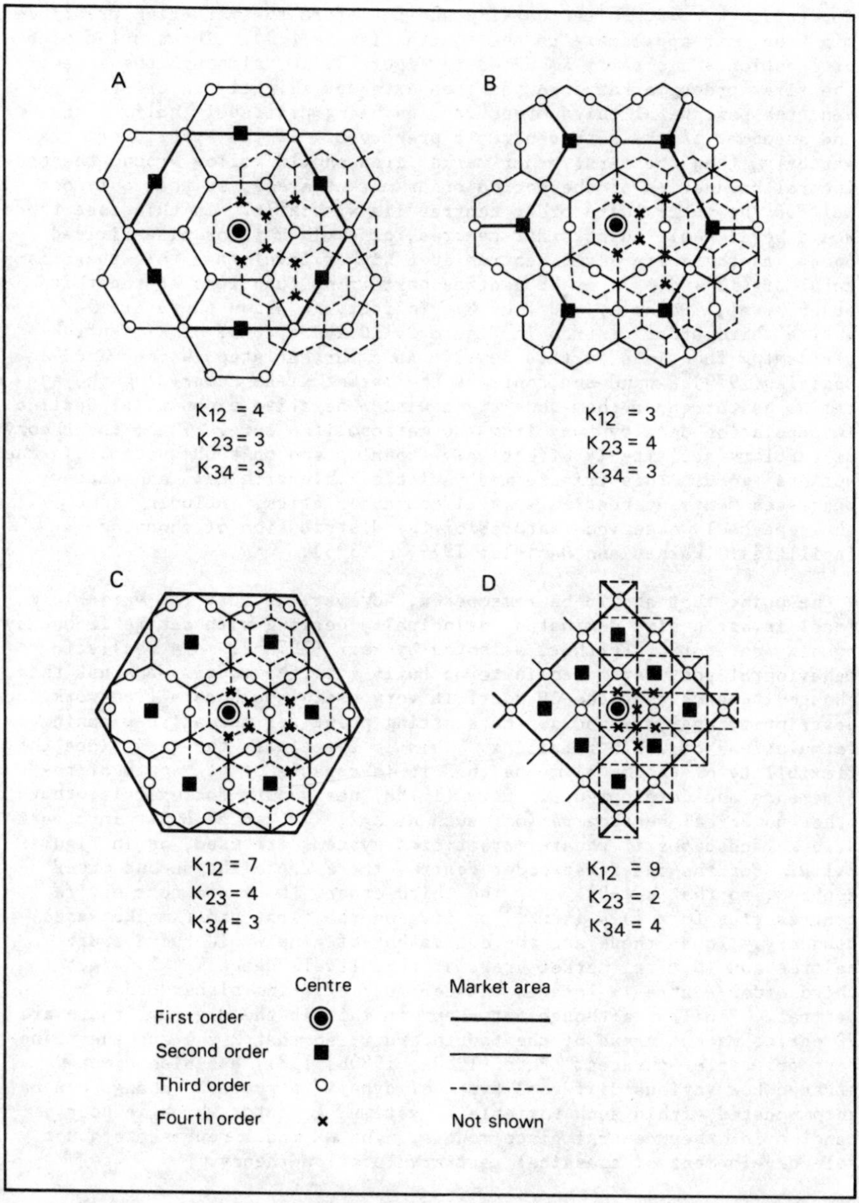

Figure 2.11 Examples of variable k hierarchical central place models (Diagrams A, B and D redrawn by permission from Parr, 1978a, 1978b, Parr et al., 1975. Diagram C adapted by permission from Warnes and Daniels, 1979)

aration principle is of little relevance to the placement of the third order centres. Perhaps the transport principle would be most realistic for these ($k_{23}=4$), whilst walking and therefore the marketing principle might be most applicable to the fourth tier ($k_{34}=3$). These principles of location are clearly embodied in Figure 2.11C, although the size of the first order market area has been extended slightly in order to prevent the peripheral third order centres being divided in half. Thus, the autonomy of the city centre is preserved. If the system were drawn strictly, then the first order market area should follow around the peripheral boundaries of the second order market areas, so that only one half of the outer third order centres lie within it. In this case there would be 12 whole third order centres, plus ($18 \times \frac{1}{2}$) or nine divided ones. As there are seven centres at a higher level than this there is a total of (12 + 9 + 7) or 28 centres performing functions at the third order level. Hence $k_{23}=28/7$ or 4. In fact, as drawn there are 30 entire third order centres in Figure 2.11C and a total of 37 centres performing functions at this level. As a further step, Warnes and Daniels (1979) expand and contract the market areas comprising the system so as to render them consistent with a negative exponential decline in population density away from the metropolitan core. Thus, the theory of tertiary activity is effectively superimposed on a GH system. In the authors' words 'this transformed variable k hierarchical landscape possesses many interesting spatial characteristics, including some of the repeatedly observed features of the distribution of shopping facilities' (Warnes and Daniels, 1979, p. 396).

One point that should be remembered, however, is that the variable k model is again size dominated, principally dealing with centre frequency by size category. Further, as noted by Parr (1978b), more realistic behavioural postulates remain to be built into the model. Against this though it seems that the GH model is very useful both as a framework for descriptive analysis and as the starting point for normative-planning formulations of urban retailing. This is especially the case since the flexibility of the model means that it is capable of all sorts of refinements and developments. Parr (1978a) has shown, for example, that other numerical nesting ratios, such as k=2, k=9 can be built into variable k landscapes if square market area systems are used, as in Figure 2.11D. For the one first order centre, there are eight second order centres, so that $k_{12}=9$). For the third order, there are four entire centres plus ($8 \times \frac{1}{2}$) + ($4 \times \frac{1}{4}$) or five on the first order market area boundary. Thus, there are the equivalent of nine whole third order centres and 18 total market areas at this level, hence $k_{23}=2$. Each third order centre is located between four existing higher order centres. Finally, although not shown in full in the diagram, there are 72 entire market areas of the fourth order, so that $k_{34}=4$ and the transport principle operates. Parr (1980a, 1980b, 1981) has also demonstrated how various different types of dynamic structural change can be accommodated within such variable k systems, a factor which is poorly handled in other central place models. The GH model represents a notable development of classical tertiary location theory.

AN INTRA-URBAN FORMULATION OF THE LÖSCHIAN SYSTEM

The overall debate continues, however, for in a major review and reevaluation of classical central place theories, Beavon (1977) has argued that the Löschian system holds the key to the meaningful understanding of the empirical structure of retailing facilities in urban areas. Primarily, it is suggested that the Löschian formulation was disregarded by geographers at the time when central place theory was being extended into the urban setting by Berry and Garrison, mainly as a result of the difficulty of comprehending the theory (Beavon, 1973, 1977; Beavon and Mabin, 1975, 1976). Further, Beavon (1972, 1974b) argues that a continuum of centres by size invariably characterises urban retailing systems and that this is inconsistent with classical Christallerian theory and the theory of tertiary activity, both of which give rise to stepped hierarchies of retailing centres.

The development of the intra-urban Löschian model has been described in detail by Beavon (1974a, 1974b, 1977) and follows closely the original approach of Lösch at the inter-urban scale. An isotropic plane with an economic base sufficient to maintain a growing population is the starting point. In the urban context, each market area in the system may be regarded as reflecting different threshold volumes. The model retains the merit of building up from the lowest to highest threshold good, as population and demand grow. The overall system is core dominated, with the smallest threshold area business type spreading out from the city centre as population increases, thereby determining the location of future urban retail sites. Thus, in a similar fashion to the inter-urban model, the development of metropolitan business-rich, business-poor sectors is envisaged. The urban area thereby comes to be dominated by a continuum of centres and it is concluded that 'the work of Lösch provides a sounder and more realistic theoretical framework for the study of the intra-urban location of tertiary activities' (Beavon and Mabin, 1976, p. 37). This argument has been stressed in a series of closely linked articles (Beavon, 1974a, 1974b, 1975, 1976; Beavon and Mabin, 1975, 1976).

Naturally, the criticisms that were made of Lösch's general theory as a model of retailing location can also be levelled at Beavon's work, although its full appraisal must await detailed empirical investigation. However, the question must be asked whether the Löschian model is just too flexible and complex to be fully verified in an urban region. Perhaps more fundamental is the point that the model is once again largely based on the single attribute of centre size, and factors such as retail area morphology, accessibility, quality and age are entirely ignored. Further, the model suggests that the size of centres will increase outward from the city centre, and this prediction contravenes reality where many large centres are concentrated relatively close to the urban core (Warnes and Daniels, 1979). Although this factor can be taken into account to a certain degree by allowing for the duplication of functions in centres with increases in population density and by the spatial transformation of market areas (Beavon, 1974b, 1977), it remains a shortcoming of the basic model. Further, it is debatable whether it is realistic to assume that generally speaking entirely separate market area networks will develop to supply different goods in urban areas. In this respect the intra-urban Löschian model appears to overstress the occurrence of functional specialisation and, therefore, does not cater sufficiently for multi-purpose consumer trips. Thus, in a review of Beavon's book, Rushton (1980, p. 283) has observed that

> 'the main weakness of the proposed model is the lack of attention to the behavioral foundations of both firms and consumers and the processes of mutual adjustment that explain, at least to the

> comfort of those from the economic-behavioral school, the intrametropolitan spatial distribution of business activity.'

Such criticisms have also been acknowledged in other reviews of Beavon's work, either explicitly (Thomas, 1978) or implicitly by failing to mention its intra-urban connotations (Lewis, 1980). Another major weakness is that in arguing that a continuum of centres by size is not accounted for in existing theory, Beavon is effectively ignoring Berry's typology of commercial structure, Davies' hierarchical sub-systems model and variable k central place formulations, all of which provide the rationale for such a characteristic. Finally, Beavon's model is heavily based on the argument that Lösch's work has been ignored by researchers, especially by Berry. However, examination of Berry's work indicates that this assertion is not fully justified. Thus, Berry (1967) argued that a degree of locational specialisation is an essential characteristic of retailing within urban areas, so that the 'classical hierarchy of central places is replaced by a pattern of business centres, ribbons, and specialized areas, with additional variations resulting from income differences or ethnicity' (p. 123). Developing this theme, Berry (1967, p. 124) commented that increasing mobility and rising real incomes in western metropolitan areas will mean that

> 'Centres must compete, and to achieve some margin of safety seek all means to differentiate themselves from their competitors ... The only real safety is in the economies introduced by further specialization, and the result of widening of living spaces is to increase the locational specialization of individual functional areas and ribbons, and introduces specialization among shopping centers of the same level of the hierarchy.
>
> The Christaller type of hierarchy thus breaks down. The new form of specialization said to be emerging has never been specified in the discussions. However, Lösch's model of non-hierarchical retail specialization may be applicable.'

This is an important line of argument and certainly seems to challenge the structural and behavioural bases of Beavon's intra-urban reformulation of the Löschian model. The concept of retail change and increasing functional specialisation seems once more to favour the development of a composite model of urban retailing in which salient properties of both the Christallerian and Löschian models are juxtaposed. It is reiterated here that Berry's threefold commercial typology appears to afford such a framework, a point that is picked up in the conclusion of this chapter.

MODELS OF CITY CENTRE RETAILING STRUCTURE

No account of theories and models of urban retail location would be complete without some attention being paid to the structure of the retail core. Despite the trend towards the suburbanisation of retailing in the countries of Western Europe and North America, the central area or C.B.D. generally remains as the major retail focus in urban areas (Murphy, 1972; Davies, 1976). This is particularly the case in Britain where a considerable amount of central area redevelopment has occurred in the post war period. Given this importance it is surprising that as Davies (1976, p. 141) has noted 'there have been few attempts to construct theories or concepts about the particular locational attributes of business activities inside the central area'.

Perhaps the earliest attempt to provide a framework for analysis was that of Horwood and Boyce (1959), when they proposed the core-frame model of C.B.D. functional differentiation. This did little more than recognise that there is a zone of intensive land use known as the C.B.D. core, which is encircled by a less intensive frame. The core is the district of highest buildings and the greatest land use intensity within the urban area. It is the centre of specialised functions and a focus for offices, professional and business services. The frame is basically a zone of land use transition in which there is a peripheral dispersion of less intensive land use clusters, such as wholesaling, warehousing, medical, motor, service and manufacturing activities.

The core-frame model of functional distribution clearly reflects the occurrence of accessibility and land value variations within the central retailing area. As such the framework is analogous to the model of the internal functional organisation of retail nucleations devised by Garner (1966, 1967). In this it is proposed that retail functions are generally arranged in a consistent pattern within such centres. Thus, establishments performing low order threshold functions tend to occur towards the edge of shopping centres whilst higher order functions tend to be located near to their cores. This distribution at the intra-shopping centre level appears to represent the type of meeting of central place and rent theory notions that is witnessed at the intra-urban level by Berry's three-fold typology. In a further scale modification, therefore, Davies (1972a, 1972b) has used these ideas to develop a comprehensive model of central area retailing structure, as outlined in Figure 2.12. In the words of Davies (1972b, p. 6): 'It is argued that if the central area forms the apex to a central place hierarchy of nucleations, it will also reflect on other retailing characteristics found in the rest of the city, such as are described by Berry (1963)'. Thus, the retail structure of the central area is regarded as reflecting a composite set of nucleated, ribbon and special area characteristics. The nucleated functional component is envisaged as being laid out in broad concentric divisions which reflect diminishing threshold values and general levels of accessibility, as in Garner's intra-centre model. Hence, the most central facilities command the greatest volume of consumers (Figure 2.12A). Ribbon developments are seen as occurring mainly toward the periphery of the central area and are related to particular roads leading from the centre. These may vary from traditional shopping street functional groupings to auto related functions (Figure 2.12B). Special area characteristics on the other hand represent clusters of shops that are similar either in terms of their functional status and/or their quality levels. For example, it may be argued that high quality retail outlets will group in a special prestige area reflecting their high threshold values, whilst middle quality groups will be associated with the peak land value intersection and a mass market clientele. Low quality outlets would then inhabit the peripheral zones of the central retailing core (Figure 2.12C). Inevitably, a composite model can be derived if all three structural components are superimposed. According to Davies, the derived model should not be regarded as a stereotype but merely as an outline (Figure 2.12D). A complex of concentric, sectoral and linear spatial variations are recognised within the C.B.D. The dashed lines indicate that the retail core merges almost imperceptibly with the frame area, wherein the major specialised functional zones are to be found. The outer parts of the core are the most complicated and confused areas of retail structuring.

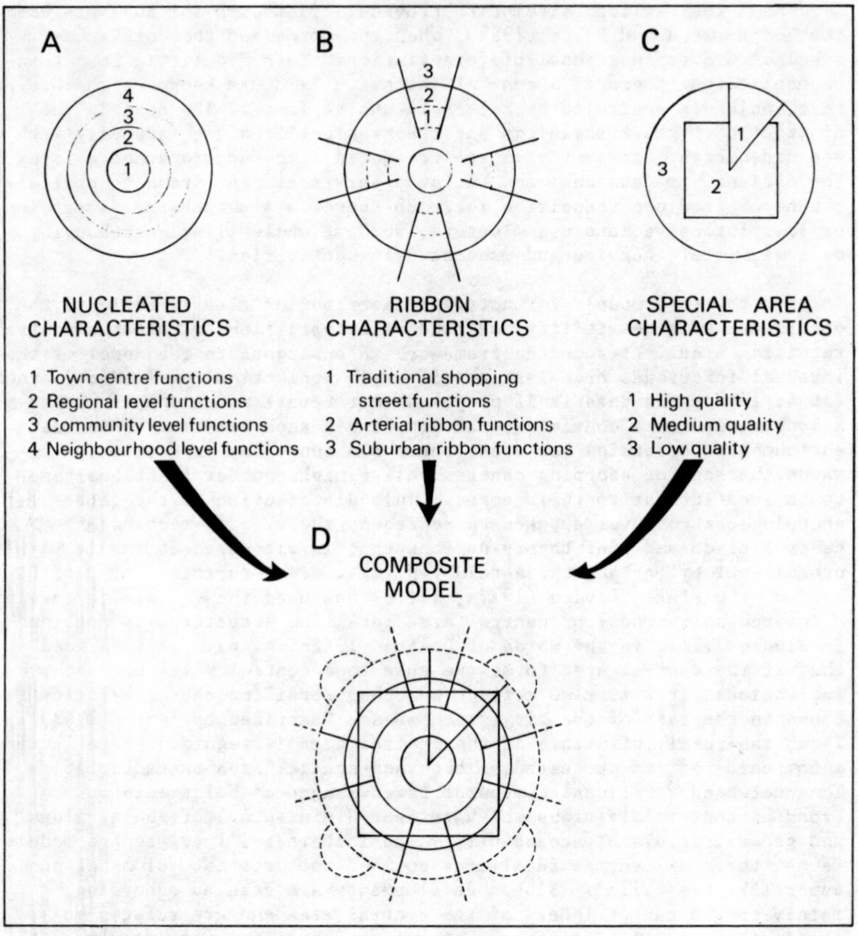

Figure 2.12 A composite model of city centre retail structure (Adapted by permission from Davies, 1972a)

The significance of this simple model is that it acknowledges the occurrence and interrelation of hierarchical, functional and qualitative, tonal variations within the core retailing areas of cities. Further, it demonstrates the undoubted versatility of joint land rent-central place formulations, particularly Berry's threefold typology of nucleations, ribbons and special functional areas. This type of structuring would seem to apply to the retail system from the inter-urban to the intra-retail area scales.

CONCLUSIONS: RETAIL MODELS AND RETAIL CHANGE

This chapter has attempted to provide a broad overview of the various theories and models that have been used to explain urban retailing locational and structural patterns. The account has basically been chronological, tracing ideas from the development of Christaller and Lösch's general theories of tertiary location, to the extension and modification of central place theory in the 1950s, through to the latest theories and models. At the conclusion of such a review it is tempting to argue that the efficacy of these formulations can only be judged by means of detailed empirical testing. However, this assertion ignores the fact that such models are essentially simplified normative formulations based on particular limiting assumptions. Thus, as shown, the types of assumption that are adopted about the spatial behaviour of consumers will influence the structural predictions of any such model. To quote Parr (1981, p. 97) 'To criticise central-place theory for its lack of generality does not therefore seem to be reasonable: it is a case of a theory being criticised for failing to do what it was never intended to do'. It is suggested here that theories should provide a sound and plausible framework for understanding retail structure, and act as a background for analysing real world patterns and for promoting new planned systems. Central place theory is neither true or false, although its relevance and realism may be debated at any given time or place. It is in this sense that it may be argued that central place theory and its derivatives remain of great significance in spatial studies of the urban retailing system. To argue that central place theory is no longer of any relevance to retailing studies is to misrepresent the original and continuing aims of the theory.

This is not to deny, however, that the urban retailing system is at present experiencing very rapid and fundamental changes in most Western countries. Some commentators have gone so far as to argue that in the late twentieth century we are in the throes of a 'marketing revolution', the effects of which are likely to be as significant as those of the industrial revolution in the nineteenth century (Dawson, 1979b; Dawson and Kirby, 1980). A number of important changes in retail distribution, consumer behaviour and the wider economic environment have occurred in Britain, for example, since 1945 (NEDO, 1971; Davies, 1976; Guy, 1980; Dawson and Kirby, 1980). The major changes in retail distribution have been a sharp decline in the overall number of shops and the enhanced importance of multiple firms. As a consequence, the average size and the real turnover of shops have increased markedly. During the same period, consumer behaviour and the general retailing environment have also changed. There has, for instance, been an overall growth in real disposable incomes and this together with the higher levels of female participation in the labour force has led to a greater emphasis on weekly bulk-buying and one stop shopping. This trend has also been encouraged by growing car ownership and personal mobility, and the increasing ownership of domestic refrigerators and freezers. Other aspects of change have been the growth of durable goods and clothing shops and the dramatic rise of self-service as a method of retailing.

In terms of retail location, these changes have become associated with two major trends. First, a net outward movement of shopping facilities in urban areas, mirroring the suburbanisation of both employment opportunities and population. Secondly, economies of scale in retail management and store operation are leading to the development of large free standing stores. Collectively, these two factors have culminated in pressures for the construction of edge-of-town and out-of-town superstores, hypermarkets and regional shopping centres. Further, new multi-functional centres combining retail and an array of other tertiary functions are gaining in importance, along with theme or specialist centres, particularly in North America.

Whilst it is tempting to suggest that these developments constitute a complete break with established urban retailing traditions, it nevertheless seems premature to reject central place type frameworks outright. Thus, it may be argued that concepts such as range, threshold, hierarchical marginal goods, incremental functional sets are all still valid, at least in so far as they aid analysis. Hypermarkets with their emphasis on car-borne one stop shopping might be seen as a new variant to be added to Berry's specialised and arterial sub-components of the urban commercial system. In this respect, it is also interesting to note that Beaujeu-Garnier and Delobez (1979) have recently presented a schematic map of shopping facilities in an 'average French town' which depicts peripheral hypermarkets within a basically hierarchical framework. In terms of the market areas of such developments we can think of city-wide but discontinuous spatial zones, perhaps an ultimate middle income culmination of Davies' hierarchical sub-systems model. The increasing size of market areas associated with economies of scale can be related to the dynamic merging of the existing market areas of industrial enterprises within a Löschian framework proposed by Watts (1977). Multi-functional and specialised centres can also be accommodated at the respective poles of the Berry threefold typology. Further, it is worthy of note that planning intervention has also increasingly entered the retailing scene. Interestingly, two of the major goals of planners have been to bolster nucleated centres in suburban locations and to encourage the disappearance of arterial ribbons, both policies potentially leading to the preservation of a hierarchical structure.

It is concluded that models and theories still have an important role to play in studies of urban retailing, although it is becoming increasingly unrealistic to expect any one formulation to match every facet of reality. All models have both merits and limitations. For example, it has been argued that existing theory has had the adverse effect of focusing undue attention on the single attribute of the *size differentiation* of retail centres, whilst other equally salient properties have been relatively neglected. A sound model should be robust enough to enable changing economic, social, and technological circumstances and their spatial expressions to be mapped into it. In this connection, Berry's typology is regarded with considerable approbation, as indicated in this and the previous sections. In essence, however, all of the models and theories reviewed have something to contribute, whether it be to analysis, description or design. This reflects the argument of Lösch (1940) that we should perhaps expect reality to be more like theory, rather than expecting theory to mirror reality in all its complexity.

3 A Case Study of Urban Retailing Structure

This chapter presents the findings of a study undertaken by the present author in an effort to examine the principal features of the location and structural organisation of retail facilities in a medium-sized British town. The undertaking of such a project might at first seem superfluous given the ubiquity and familiar nature of shopping facilities in urban areas. However, there have been relatively few comprehensive field based studies of urban retailing structure in the recent past. Thus, Warnes and Daniels (1980, p. 135) have observed that 'it is surprising how few British studies have addressed themselves to the basic spatial question of describing the distribution of urban shopping facilities'. Instead, they maintain, unusual and idiographic developments, such as the impact of a particular hypermarket tend to have received ample attention but studies of the 'omnipresent and mundane features of shops' (p. 135) have not been updated. Further, the suggestion is made that central place theory has been rejected prematurely for the purpose of intra-urban research because of this lack of corroborative empirical evidence. A similar conclusion has been forwarded by Giggs (1977), who identified four lacunae in our knowledge of British urban retailing patterns. First, it is suggested that our understanding of the commercial structure of British cities is less developed than that of the North American urban area. Second, that British studies have rarely proceeded beyond attempts to identify a stepped size distribution of centres. Thirdly, that the research that has been done has related to medium and large cities rather than small ones. Finally, that dynamic aspects of retail change through time have been neglected. In fact, since the early pioneering works of the late 1950s and early 1960s, it is probably fair to say that these comments apply equally well in the North American context. It is as if retail distribution studies went into eclipse with the transformation from the quantitative to the behavioural paradigms in geography.

The present simple descriptive case study is offered in the light of the argument put forward by Davies, W.K.D. (1968a) and Warnes and Daniels (1980) that there is a vital need to update and to replicate studies of retail spatial distribution. Whilst not intended as an explicit testing of theories and models of urban retailing, for the reasons outlined in the last chapter, it is perhaps inevitable that comparisons will be drawn between reality and theory. In particular, the debate raised in Chapter 2, concerning the identification of a 'realistic' model of urban retailing structure will be reconsidered. However, the identification of the main features of the urban retailing system remains the principal aim of this work. Subsidiary aims involve the recommendation of variables which warrant further detailed empirical study, and the presentation of a set of simple methods that may be used to gain an overview of the retail structure of any given urban area.

THE STUDY DESIGN

A detailed field survey covering all of the urban retailing facilities of the then County Borough of Stockport was completed in the summer of 1972. Although the administrative area of Stockport forms part of the wider Manchester conurbation, nevertheless it was considered to represent a suitable study area in terms of its overall areal extent, population size and degree of functional independence. In 1971, the town had a total resident population of 139,644 persons. It can be argued that Stockport has in fact maintained its significance as a distinct functional entity within the wider urban region (Freeman, 1959; Potter, 1976a, 1981b).

The initial orientation of the field survey was based on the distribution of commercial land depicted on the land use maps compiled by the Stockport Borough Town Planning Office. The definition of a retail outlet followed closely that presented in Chapter 1 and a complete and detailed inventory of all shops in the town was carried out. The 69 main functional types identified followed the classification previously shown in Table 1.1. It thereby included a range of allied service activities along with strictly defined retail shops. Separate categories for large retail units and vacant premises were included.

For each retail establishment, its precise location was recorded along with a listing of the main commodity types and services offered. Further, a detailed qualitative grading was made of each shop, the aggregate results of which will be mentioned in this chapter, although a detailed consideration of this variable awaits presentation in Chapter 4. This data allowed the following aspects of retail structuring to be viewed: (i) the overall distribution of commercial land, (ii) the delimitation and location of shopping centres, (iii) the size characteristics of retail areas, (iv) the spatial configuration of retail size differences and (v) the functional structure of the retailing system. Each of these topics is considered in turn in the following account.

THE DISTRIBUTION OF COMMERCIAL ACTIVITIES

The precise distribution of commercial land uses observed in Stockport is shown in relation to the road network in Figure 3.1. Isolated stores have been omitted from the map, so that only the main retail outlets and blocks are shown. Four major types of retail concentration are apparent. The most striking feature is the intensive concentration of commercial activities within the inner urban area. A second noticeable feature is the clustering of retail and service activities along the main arterial routes that radiate from the town centre. In this regard, the main A6 trunk route which passes through the urban centre on its south-east to north-west path through the town is particularly important. A third feature is the high density of commercial premises in the inner urban zone just to the south of the town centre. Finally, the sporadic

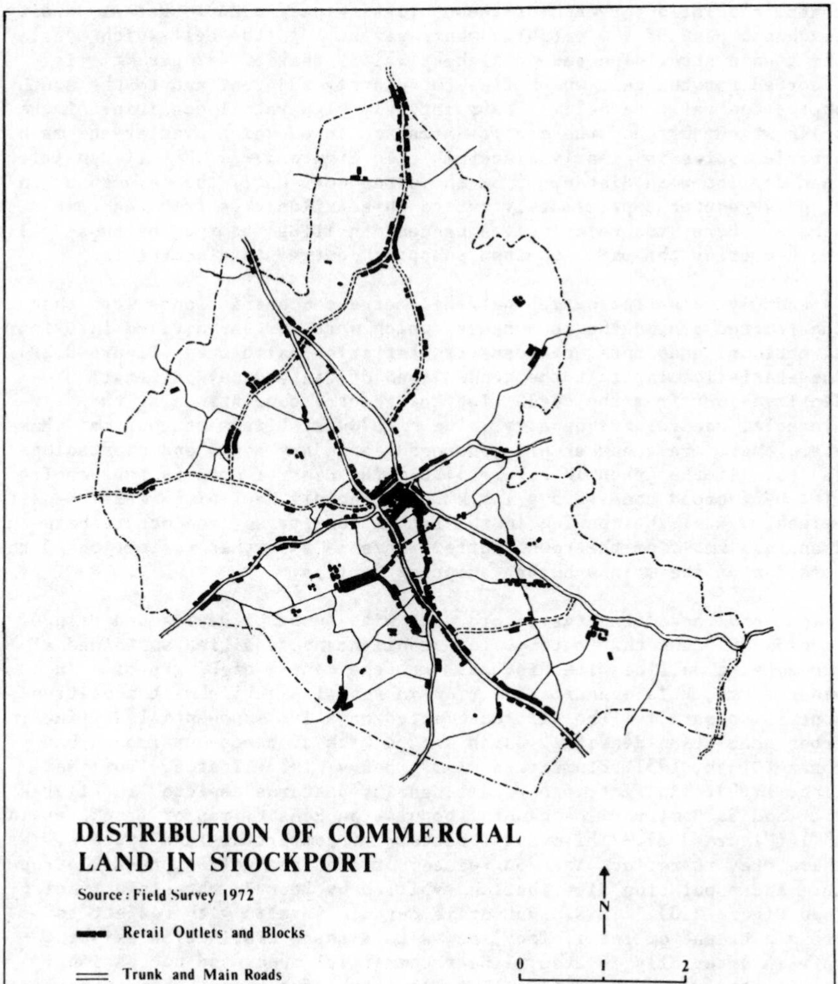

Figure 3.1 The spatial configuration of commercial land in Stockport

concentration of activities in the main suburban residential areas of the town is apparent. Overall, this patterning exemplifies the distinction between nucleated and linear components of the urban business pattern and illustrates the importance of centre morphology.

To look at the situation in greater detail, the town was divided into a mosaic of kilometre grid squares and the density of retail establishments calculated for each of these areas (Figure 3.2A). Retail density reaches a peak of 550 establishments per km^2. in the cell which overlays the town centre. The second highest value, that of 282 per km^2. is recorded for the cell which lies immediately adjacent and to the south of the central area cell. The relatively high retail densities of the cells which surround the central area and those which overlay the main arterial spine is clearly discernible in Figure 3.2A. Retail densities then decline with distance from the urban core until the main suburban ring is reached approximately two to three kilometres from the town centre. Here, the relatively enhanced densities recorded by those cells which overlay the main suburban shopping centres is discernible.

Secondly, a series of ten half-kilometre concentric zones were then constructed around the town centre which were further divided into four directional quadrants, and density statistics calculated (Figure 3.2B). The statistics indicate the generalised distance decay in retail densities out from the core. The town centre zone stands as the pinnacle, recording a density value of 670 establishments per km^2. However, there are a number of pronounced secondary peaks and depressions as shown in the graph in Figure 3.2C. The central area is thus encircled by a broad zone (0.5 - 1.5 km.) of rapidly declining retail density values. A slight upswing in the retail density surface occurs between 2 and 3.5 km. from the town centre. This is a further reflection of the location of the main suburban shopping centres.

In fact, these findings accord well with those of Davies and Briggs (1967) who found that automobile establishment densities sustained a progressive decline with distance from the centre of Liverpool. In wider terms, this overall reduction in retail establishment densities appears to parallel the well documented negative exponential decline in urban population densities which occurs with distance out from urban cores (Clark, 1951; Blumenfeld, 1959; Berry, 1963; Yeates, 1965; Newling, 1969). In fact, the retail density patterns depicted in Figures 3.2B and 3.2C mirror the general population density map of Stockport in 1971 (Figure 3.3). The overall pattern of commercial land appears, therefore, to reflect the congruence between land values, retail structure and population distribution typified by Berry's threefold typology (see Figure 2.8). This argument is certainly valid with respect to broad patterns of retail location, with a sharp distinction existing between arterially located, linear commercial areas and nucleations. Whether the contrast applies in terms of the functional characteristics of centres is another matter. Finally, it was found that retail densities were closely related to the socio-economic characteristics of areas, again probably reflecting net residential densities. The overall density level for the town was 61.7 shops per km^2.. This varied from a high value of 174.5 per km^2. in the low status residential areas to 50.0 per km^2. in the medium status areas and a low of 27.2 shops per km^2. in the case of the high status tracts.

THE DELIMITATION AND SPACING OF CENTRES

The overall distribution of individual retail units thereby indicated a tendency toward their location in spatially discrete clusters. These assemblages of retail outlets are customarily referred to as 'shopping centres' although even a cursory examination of Figure 3.1 shows that

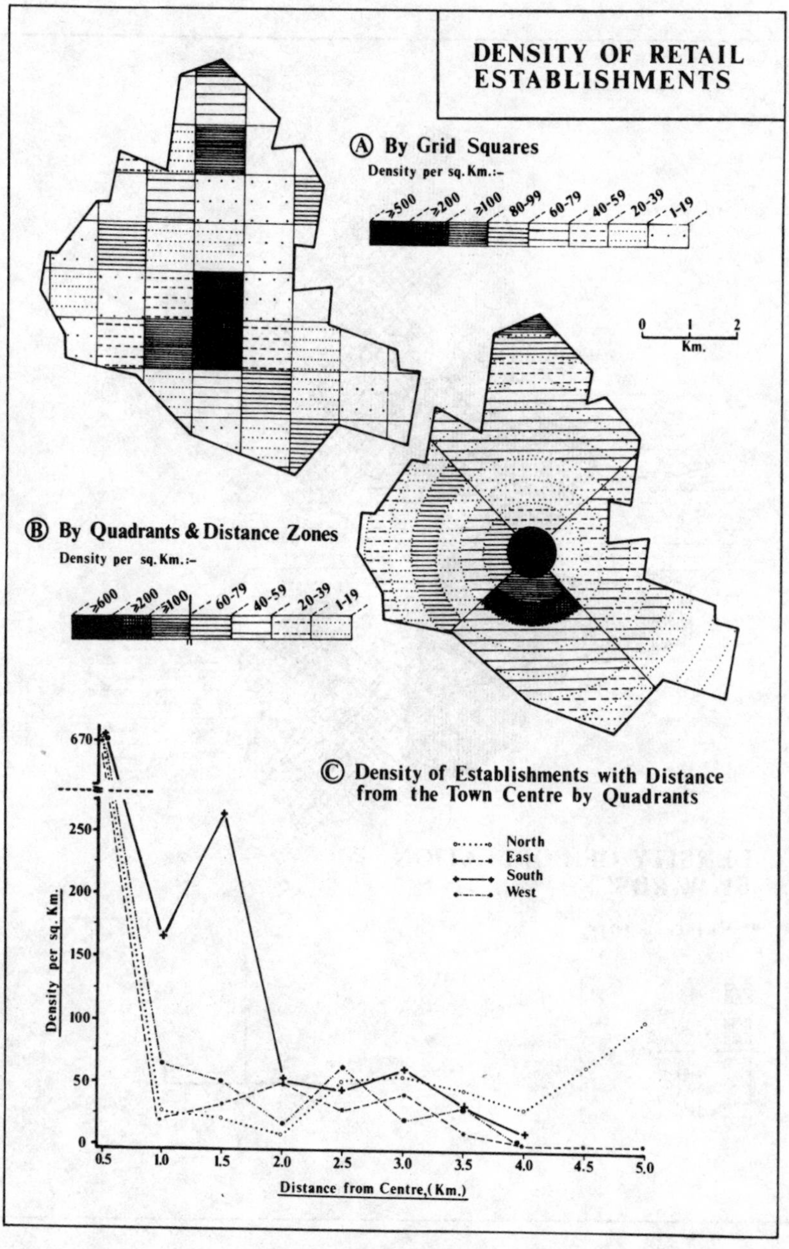

Figure 3.2 Retail establishment density variations in Stockport

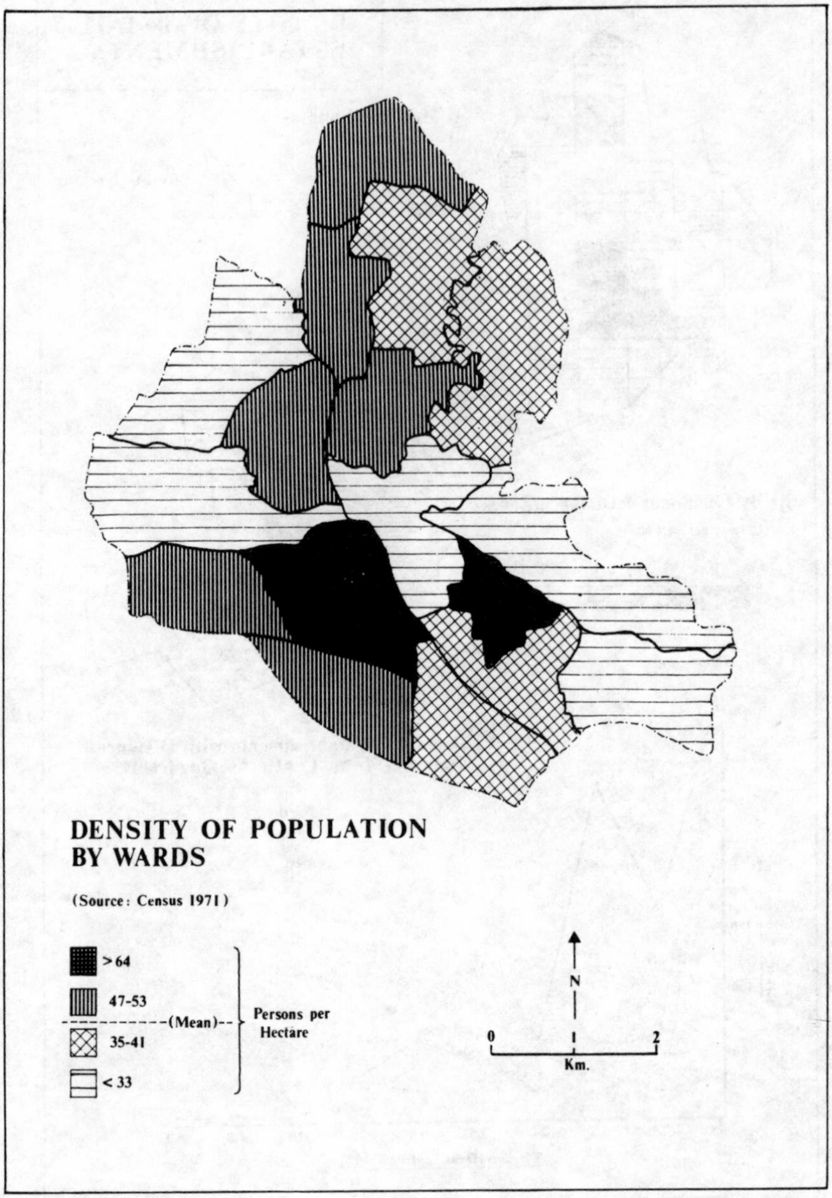

Figure 3.3 Density of population by wards in Stockport

they are by no means all strictly nuclear in form. This patterning of dispersal within the townscape and concentration at certain localities may be viewed in terms of the general principle of centrifugal and centripetal forces outlined by Colby (1933).

In the present study a centre was defined at the lowest level as an association of three or more shops, at least two of which occupied neighbouring premises. Some 247 outlets were thereby classified as isolated stores. The difficulties involved in the delimitation of shopping centres are formidable, and have been usefully reviewed by Scott (1970) who notes that the majority of early studies tended to gloss over this problem. The 1961 Census of Distribution, however, defined the edge of a centre as that point where the ratio of shops to all properties fell below one in three. Lomas (1964) argued that this was too liberal a criterion, but researchers have continued to broaden it. Thus, Davies (1967) included a shop in a centre if it lay within the equivalent distance of four terraced houses of another shop. Garrison et al. (1959) and Clark (1967) included an establishment if it was within 200 feet of another, whilst Logan (1968) relaxed this distance constraint to 300 feet. In the present study, a separation criterion of the equivalent distance of five residential units was adopted. The employment of any such standard is likely to be extremely arbitrary in certain situations. This is particularly likely to be so where loosely knit rows of shops are spread out in an almost continuous chain along a main road. This is a difficult and very complex issue and illustrates the importance of the enhanced accessibility of arterial sites in urban areas and the inappropriateness of strictly defined central place notions in dealing with them. In operational terms, where contentious cases occurred in the field, note was taken of the local recognition of shopping centres (for example, amongst store owners). This problem is also encountered in the behavioural context in that some workers have posited that consumers do not think in terms of entire shopping centres, but rather in terms of particular shops (Downs, 1970).

Notwithstanding these difficulties, a total of 71 suburban retail centres over and above the town centre were delimited. Their location is shown in Figure 3.4 and they are identified by a numerical notation that represents a rank ordering according to the total number of retail establishments comprising each centre. It is necessary to emphasise that the town centre is omitted from the analyses which follow in this chapter. That the centres so defined exhibit a multiplicity of relative sizes, locations and spacings within the town is clearly attested by Figure 3.4 (see, in particular, the linear fabric extensions that are to be recognised). The spacing of retail centres has received much attention in the literature, mainly using the nearest neighbour statistic as a measure (Dacey, 1962; Getis, 1964; Clark, 1969; Rogers, 1969a, 1969b; Sherwood, 1970; Sibley, 1972). Centres were defined by their geometric mid-points, as shown by the solid squares in Figure 3.4. Nearest neighbour statistics (*Rn*) were then calculated for centres in various divisions of the town. The Rn value of 1.16 for the entire distribution of retail centres in the town indicates that the general pattern is one of apparently 'random' spatial placement. However, retail centres are more evenly spaced in the northern half of the town (Rn=1.37), and show a near random patterning in the southern half (Rn=0.98). If equivalent statistics are computed for centres in the four quadrants employed in Figure 3.2B, then the western sector emerges as the area with the most even spacing of centres (Rn=1.35). However, in

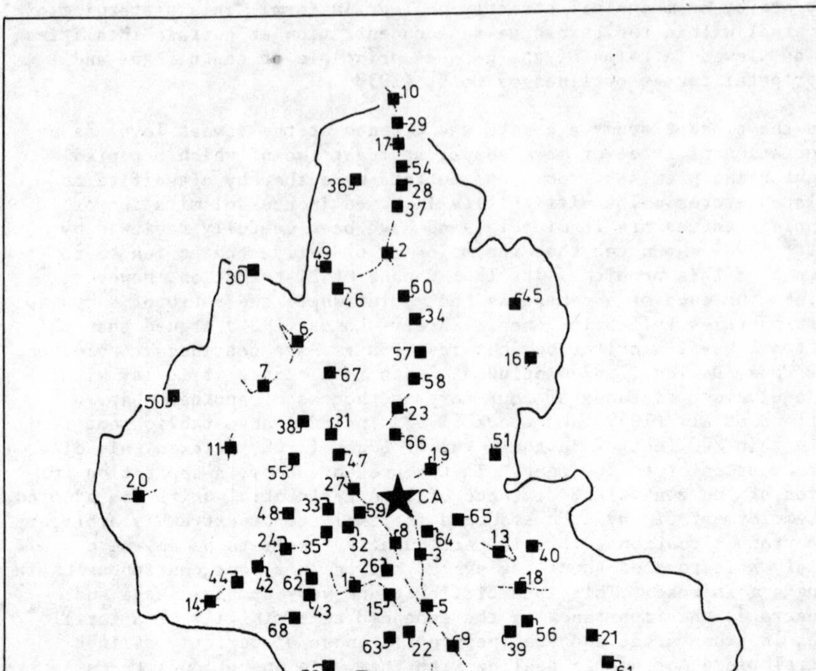

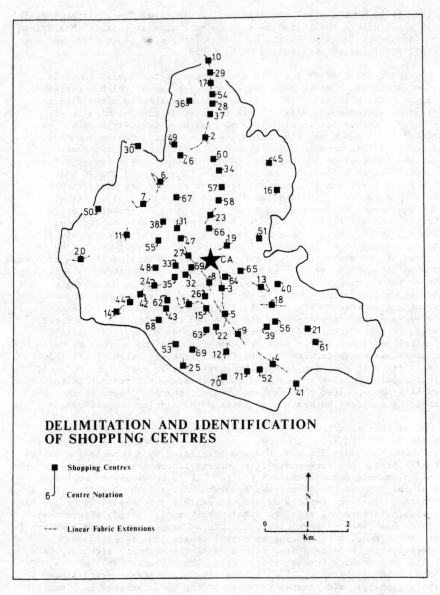

Figure 3.4 The spatial distribution of retail centres in Stockport

general the analysis indicates that the system of centres tends towards an ostensibly random spatial patterning. This undoubtedly suggests that the non-isotropic character of the townscape is aetiological, so that the spacing of centres appears to reflect population density, socio-economic and accessibility levels within the town.

One feature of importance is that there appears to be a close correspondence between the location of centres by size and the hierarchical structure of the transport network (Figure 3.5). In Figure 3.5A, the centres are shown disaggregated into rank-size groups according to a rule of tens. The ten largest shopping centres are located in an axial belt which closely follows the path of the main A6 traffic artery through the town (Figure 3.5B). The location of the next ten largest centres tends to prescribe lines along the remaining primary and secondary routes, whilst the next rank group locations extend along the secondary routes. It is not until the centres of the twenty-first to thirtieth rank are reached that these connecting lines push out along the local feeder routes (Figure 3.5B). These facts suggest once more that the theory of tertiary activity and Berry's system of centres and ribbons may be of some descriptive relevance.

THE SIZE DIFFERENTIATION OF CENTRES

It is clear, therefore, that the set of retail centres also exhibit considerable variations with regard to their relative sizes. At the intra-urban scale of investigation, a range of variables, such as counts of total retail establishments, total functions performed, retail sales, floorspace, front footage and total employment may be used to assess the size and importance of centres. The relative merits and degree of comparability of these various measures have been assessed in a number of studies (Davies, W.K.D., 1965, 1966; McEvoy, 1968; Davies, R.L., 1970). On the basis of the field collated data, it was possible to construct a detailed inventory of the functions present and their numerical frequency at each of the centres (Figure 3.6). The functions are numbered along the 69 columns and the ten-fold major functional groups are named below (see Table 1.1 for a detailed listing of these). The centres are shown in rank order by establishment totals in the rows from 1 to 71. The data entries are the frequency of occurrence of the 69 functions in the 71 centres.

From this data set it is possible to derive a number of simple measures of the size of the retail centres. Firstly, the *total number of establishments* may be counted along the rows and secondly, the *total number of functions* performed by centres may be enumerated. The *total number of functional outlets* may be calculated if the total number of establishments is adjusted by the number of multi-functional shops. As a quality score ranging from 1 to 5 was given to each shop, the *total quality score* achieved by each centre may be employed as a weighting of total establishments by assessed quality level. A further measure which takes into account both establishment and functional counts, the *total functional index* technique, may also be employed. This very useful method was developed by Davies, W.K.D. (1967) and has subsequently been employed by other workers in the field (McEvoy, 1968; Marshall, 1969). The basic advantage of the method is that it considers the relative frequency of occurrence of functions within the system. Location coefficients (C) are calculated for every function in the retail system, thus:

$$C = \frac{100\,t}{T}$$

where t represents a given retail function and T the total number of

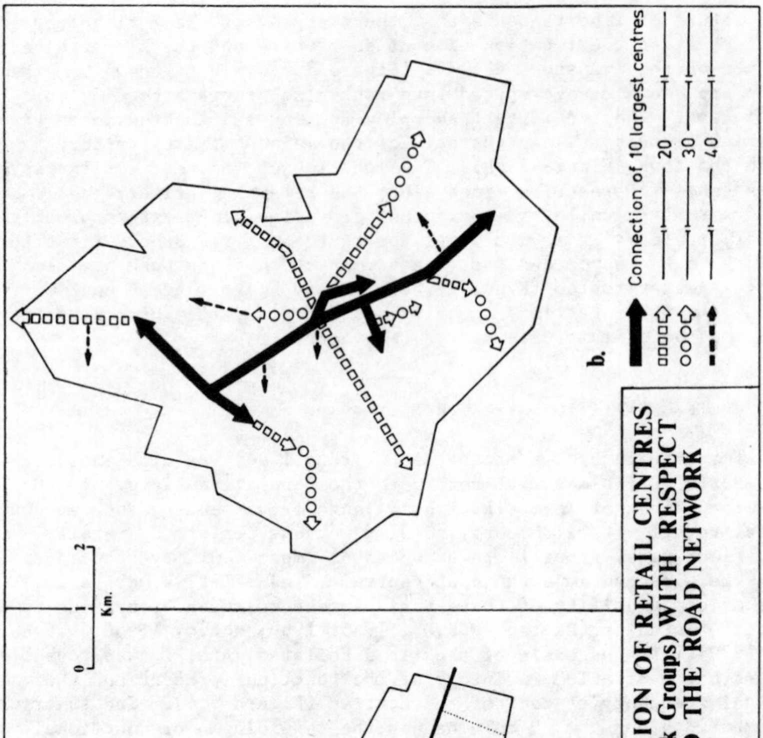

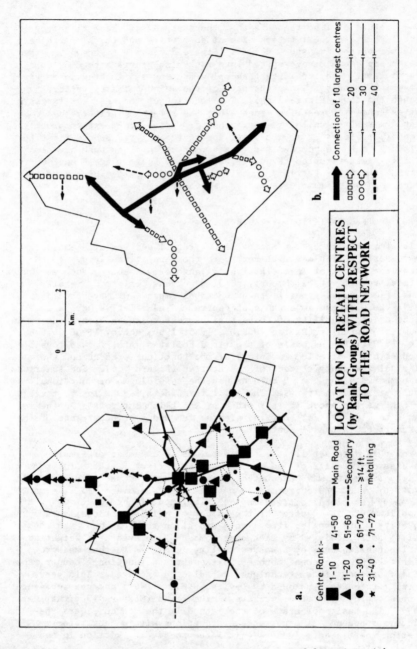

Figure 3.5 The relationship between centre size and location with respect to the transport network

FUNCTIONAL SURVEY
Data Matrix

FUNCTIONS →

CENTRES ↓ (Ranked according to Number of Establishments)

Function groups: Food. | Clothing. | Household. | Personal. | Motor. | Sport & Recreational. | Miscellaneous. | Prof'l Service. | Lg Units. | Vacant.

CENTRES	FUNCTIONS 1–69 (123456789012345678901234567890123456789012345678901234567890123456789)
1	*456118724*423014462310722111005220101200101720011222221014124220021*
2	8655158243*3423032402113110200282201211213103001102211222161113111406
3	9714103*245201200230500330013203220116520100102000001111107014110100*
4	273402931452313012620002011000041301302511011002101110111131111133200
5	03100142437221101111500043222003001010121100300000110222102003111*004
6	373411510331201001410001001100151201202411213000100111110041122110005
7	353311422161211001311002100010030100000100002000001201212030012111201
8	01000034312000101010100001100100011020010000110111010100012003104*001
9	321111421240210021311020100010130200121301002000000110010030130101003
10	343221310141102012200004010020010100001201001000101011111010101000102
11	212101511141210011220001000100021101000000000100120111012002000112220 3
12	422301500140010001201001010100111201000000000100000111011002000210110 0
13	333201111110101001100000000000022200000010100300000011021002110010010 2
14	232101412211200001100000100000002010000010020020001012100100100011101 01
15	111101111110011000211000000310011000000000101000000000000010010101003
16	123111101222111000010000000000102111000000000100010101011000000110020 0
17	211201202100011100211100200010000110100010000100000000100111100101100 00
18	360100110210101022100000000100110200000000000200000000111003000011000 0
19	010200231400000000001001000100101000010200000000000000101100100300000 09
20	211101110120000001111000100100041100000000000000000011000012001110000 4
21	222101210120110011100000000010010100000010000100000000100200200000001 01
22	221100010000100001200001101000111000000100100000000000010001000010000 0
23	222100300120100000100001000000010000000101100000000001010001000010000 3
24	231000012111110000020000000010000100000000000012000000100100000000100 005
25	232101210201100010100000000000001000000000000100000000100000100001000 00
26	010000001000100000000000200000011000000000211000000000000000000000000 8000
27	000000014100000000010100010000010100110320100100000000000000000100000 0000
28	111100110020100010200000000000001010000000010010000000001000100000000 00
29	231001100010000000001001010000020000010000001000001000000001001000000 1
30	011000201010000000100000000000000100001022001010000000000000001002000 0000
31	001100100100000000000000000000011000021020000000000000100000100000000 00
32	000000001010000000000010010003000100000000000000000000000000000000100 001
33	100101110100000000000000000000010000001000000000000000000000001000000 000
34	120111010010000000010000000000000000000000000000000000000000100001000 00
35	011000201011011001000001000000000000000000000000000000000010000000000
36	120101110100000000000000000000000000000000000000000000110000010000100 000
37	011001100000000010000000000000000000011000000000000000001001000000 01
38	131110000000000000000000000000000000000000000000000010010000100000
39	111101100110100000000000000000000000000000100000000000010010000000 000
40	121100100000000010200000000000000000000000100000001000000010000000 0000
41	010000200000000000000000011000001000000000100000000000000002000000000 00
42	000011100100000000000000110000001000000000000000000000000001000000000 0
43	110100110010000000010000000100000000000000000000100000000000000000000 00
44	120001000000000000100000000000000000000000010000000000000001100000010 00
45	120100110100000000000000000000000000000000010000000000000010000000000 0
46	011110100100000000000000000000010000000000000100000000000000100000001 00
47	000000010010000000000020000000001000000000000000000000000000000000100 000
48	111100100110100000000000000000000000000000000000000000001000010000 1
49	221100100100000000000000000000000000000010000000000000001000000000 00
50	111000100000000000100000000000010000000000000100000000000000000000100 000
51	100001110000000000000000000000000001000000100000000000000001000010000 0
52	131000100010100000100000000000000000000000001000000000000000000000000 0
53	111100010011000000000000000000000000000000100000000000000010000100000
54	011001100010100000000000000000000000000000000000000100001000000000000
55	110000110100000000000000000000000000000000001000000000000001000000010 0
56	011100200010100000100000000000000000000000000000010000001000000000 0
57	010000110000000000000000000000001000000000000000000001000001000000000 0
58	010001100010100000000000000000000100000000000000000000000000000000000
59	010000110000000000000000000000000100000010000000000000000010000000000 0
60	011001100010100000100000000000000000000000000001000000000000000000000 0
61	101000100100000000000000000000000000000000000000000000001000000010 0
62	000000100000100010000000000000001000000000000000001000001000000000000
63	011000010100000000000000000000000000000000000000010000000000000000000
64	000000010000000000000001000000000000000010000000000000000000000000 3
65	010000100000000000100000000000000000000000000000000000000100001000 00
66	010100100000000000000000000000000000000000000000000000100100000000 1
67	010100100000000000000000000000000000000000000000000000001000010000 0
68	010000000101000000000000000000000000000000000010000000001000100001000 00
69	010000100000000000000000000000000001000000000000000000000000001000000 000
70	010000110000000000000000000000000000000000000000010000000000001000010 0001
71	010100000000000000000000000000000000000000000010000000000000100001000 00

* Denotes score ≥10

Figure 3.6 Functional matrix for the urban retailing system of Stockport establishments performing that function within the study area. For each centre, the number of shops performing each function (n) may be multiplied by the appropriate 'location coefficients' (C) and these scores summed to give the total functional index value (Fj):

$$Fj = \sum_{t=1}^{n} Ct$$

These five measures were used to examine the overall size characteristics of intra-urban retail centres in Stockport. For each of the measures, the range of values pertaining to the array of centres is shown in relation to the means and standard deviations in Table 3.1.

Table 3.1
Range, mean and standard deviation
for the six measures of retail centre size

Measure	Range	Mean	S.D.
Total establishments	3 - 140	22.53	29.74
Total functions	3 - 57	16.66	13.48
Total functional outlets	3 - 158	26.99	33.69
Functional index scores	4 - 873	97.83	160.88
Total quality score	1 - 234	31.68	46.04

In general terms, the data show that the size frequency distribution for each of the five variables is noticeably skewed toward small centre size levels. Thus, however size is defined, there are a large number of small centres and only a relatively small number of large ones. The former satisfy the needs of consumers to be close to basic facilities and to minimise travel, whilst the latter allow for the operation of economies of agglomeration and scale, and multi-purpose shopping trips.

With respect to establishment totals, the centres ranged from three to 140 shops and the mean of 22.53 clearly reflects the preponderance of small centres; in fact, only 20 having more establishments than this average level. Total functional index scores show a far greater range, from four to 873 with a mean of 97.83 and a standard deviation of 160.88. This measure, however, tends to highlight those centres which perform relatively sporadic functions. The functional index scores of the 71 centres are shown mapped in Figure 3.7. The relative importance of the cluster of inner urban retail areas in this respect is clearly revealed. The map also renders an overall impression of the relative size differentiation of centres within the town.

The general accordance existing between these five measures of centre size and functional importance is shown if they are inter-related (Table 3.2). Each of the correlation coefficients (*r*) is significant beyond the 0.1% probability level. As in overall terms these measures are so closely related, the size classification of centres may be further considered with respect to a single variable, for example, retail establishment totals. Such a univariate analysis is shown in the rank size graph of Figure 3.8. The grouping criterion advanced by Clark and Evans (1954), that each member of a group must be closer to some other member of that group than to any member of another group may

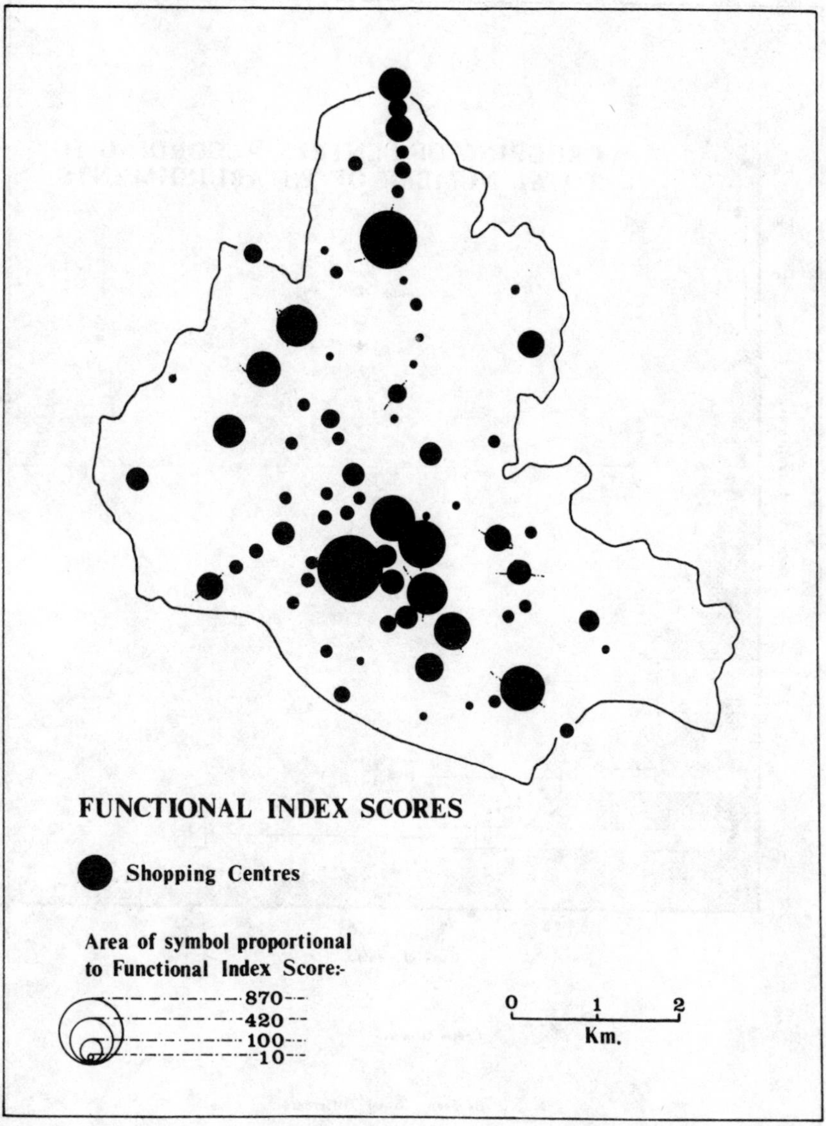

Figure 3.7 Functional index scores for retail centres in Stockport

be employed. In this way, six distinct size groups of centres were identified (Figure 3.8 and Table 3.3), such that the between group differences in establishment totals was in each case greater than the maximum within group difference. Significantly, this grouping of centres on the basis of a single variable produced a numerical pyramid of order membership. This runs in a 2, 3, 6, 9, 9, 42 sequence down through the identified size divisions.

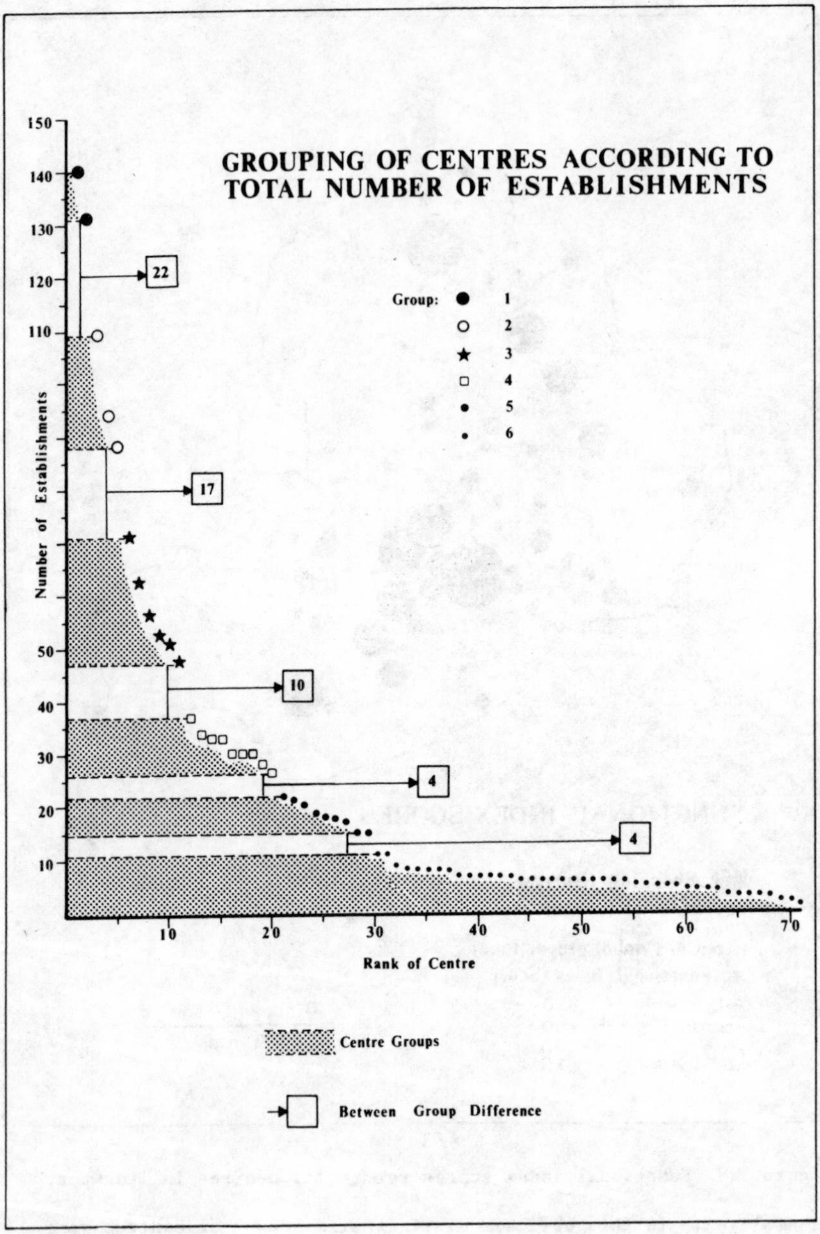

Figure 3.8 The size differentiation of retail centres in Stockport according to establishment totals

Table 3.2
Correlations between measures of centre size

Measure	1 T.E.	2 T.F.	3 T.Q.S.	4 T.F.O.	5 F.I.S.
1. Total establishments	1.00	0.94	0.98	1.00	0.97
2. Total functions		1.00	0.94	0.95	0.88
3. Total quality score			1.00	0.98	0.99
4. Total functional outlets				1.00	0.97
5. Functional index scores					1.00

Table 3.3
Grouping of retail centres
according to establishment totals

Group	Total no. of centres	Maximum within-group difference	Between-group difference
1	2	9	→ 22
2	3	15	→ 17
3	6	9	→ 10
4	9	3	→ 4
5	9	2	→ 4
6	42	2	

The size differentiation of centres may also be examined with respect to a combination of variables. Such a bivariate analysis appears in Figure 3.9 where the number of functions performed by each centre is graphed against establishment totals. The close positive correlation (r=0.94) between these two variables is such that 88.36% of the variation in functional diversity is explained by establishment totals. It also indicates, however, that there is a residual form of functional variability that is not accounted for by centre size. The regression line of total functions (F) on total establishments (E) is described by the equation:

$$F = 0.43E + 7.10$$

The Clark-Evans criterion was employed to group centres on the basis of their joint functional and establishment totals. By this means, six main size groups were recognised (1, 2A, 2B, 3A, 3B, 4 in Figure 3.9). For each of these, the between group difference in bivariate space is in excess of the maximum within group difference. Considering the relative between group differences in greater detail, four main size divisions were recognised (1-4). Thus, the middle four size divisions were regarded as forming two main groups, each composed of two subgroups. The validity of this grouping scheme may be partially assessed by calculating the mean values of the groups on each of the five size

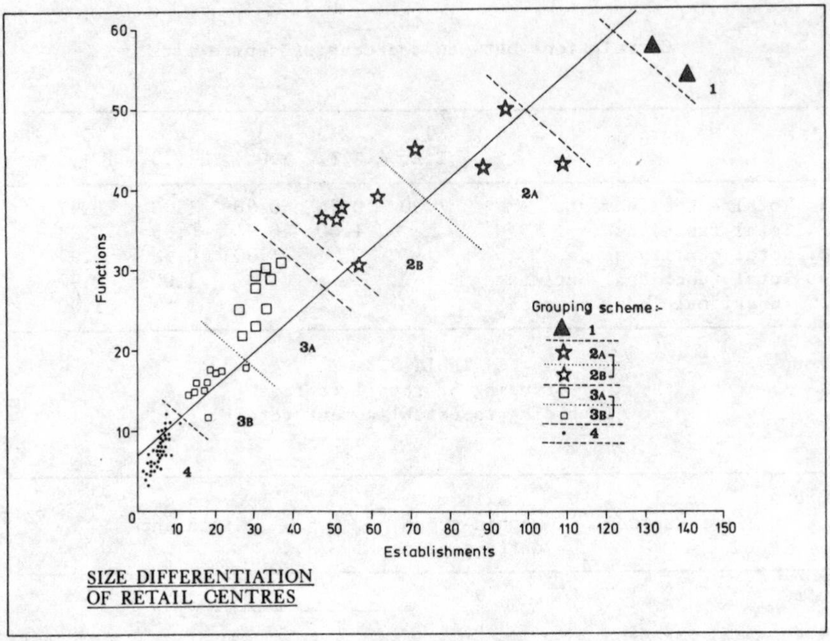

Figure 3.9 The size differentiation of retail centres in Stockport according to total functions and establishments

variables. The results, listed in Table 3.4, give the impression that the centre groups show the discrete stratification of centrality. This, together with the numerical pyramid of centres gives rise to the suspicion of the existence of an overall hierarchy of centres that broadly conforms with Marshall's criteria for a Christallerian or Berry-Garrison type system.

Table 3.4
Mean size measures for centre groups identified

Centre group	Mean : Establishments	Functions	Functional outlets	Functional Index score	Total Quality score
1	135.50	55.50	155.50	749.50	214.50
2A	90.50	45.00	104.00	435.00	130.75
2B	53.60	36.20	62.60	262.80	79.40
3A	30.55	27.00	36.89	112.44	45.11
3B	18.20	15.80	21.40	63.70	20.10
4	5.58	7.56	8.05	17.22	7.15

Furthermore, the size grouping of centres renders a 2, 4, 5, 9, 10, 41 numerical sequence of order membership which becomes a 2, 9, 19, 41 numerical sequence when the four-fold size classification is employed. This numerical sequence may be compared with that associated with a perfect Christallerian k=3 marketing system (Table 3.5). In the case

Table 3.5
Numerical frequency of retail centres by hierarchical group

Stockport study area				Christaller's k=3 system	
Size group	Number of centres	Number of market areas	k	Number of centres	Number of market areas
Central area	1	1	-	1	1
1	2	3	3	2	3
2	9	12	4	6	9
3	19	31	2.58	18	27
4	41	72	2.32	54	81
Isolated scores	247	319	4.43	162	243

of the Stockport study area, the town centre has been included above the suburban centre groups, whilst below them the total number of isolated stores has been inserted. The actual k values for the six levels of the system vary from k=4.43 to 2.32, with an average of 3.27. In fact, the reasonably close correspondence between the observed frequency of centres by size orders and the sequence envisaged by Christaller's marketing system is apparent. This was tested for the sequence of complementary market regions and the X^2 value of 5.75 indicates that the null hypothesis must be accepted at the 5% probability level. The k values in Table 3.5 also serve to indicate the possible relevance of variable k central place models in the intra-urban retailing context.

THE SPATIAL CONFIGURATION OF THE HIERARCHY

The size differentiation and associated grouping of retail centres within Stockport thereby produced a system of discrete size-order groups. The spatial manifestations of this structuring remain to be examined. It has already been shown that the retail centres are not evenly spaced throughout the town. The hierarchical classification of centres is spatially expressed in relation to the configuration of built-up areas and the network of major transport routes in Figure 3.10. On the basis of the relative spatial location of centres by size-orders within the town and the commonly employed urban retail area nomenclature (Hoyt, 1958; Berry, 1967), the centre size groups were labelled thus: *regional centres*(group 1), *major district* (2A), *minor district* (2B), *major community* (3A), *minor community* (3B) and *neigh-*

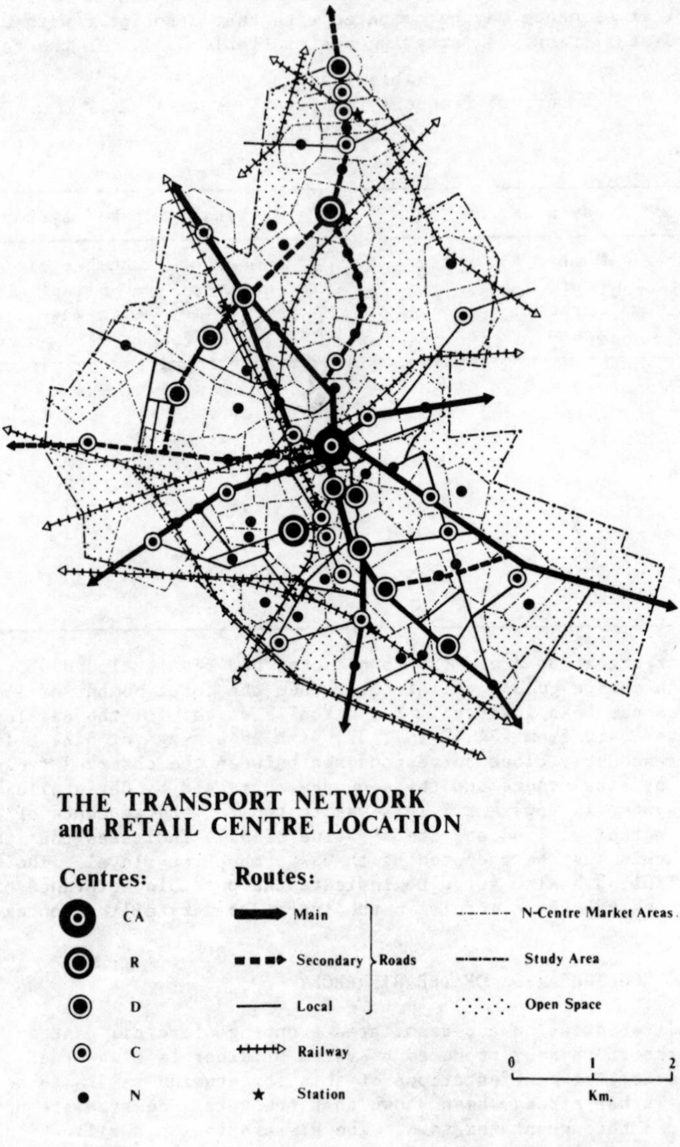

Figure 3.10 Hierarchical classification of retail centres in Stockport

bourhood centres (group 4).

In Figure 3.10, the components of the retailing system are subdivided into their major hierarchical classes of regional (R), district (D), community (C) and neighbourhood (N) centres. The transport network is represented by the main, secondary and local routes, plus the railway lines. The spatial configuration of the N-level market regions is shown as inferred from the construction of thiessen polygons, which give proximal regions for each centre (Dixon, 1972; Haggett, 1965). The distribution of open spaces is clearly depicted in relation to the pattern of market areas.

This spatial arrangement brings several points into focus. First, there appears to be a general tendency toward the interstitial placement of hierarchical orders. Thus, a ring of high order centres exists some 2.5-3.0 km. from the town centre. These higher order centres are particularly apparent in the more continuously built-up north-western, western and south-western suburbs. On the other hand, the neighbourhood level centres tend to be located in the interstitial areas between the scatter of district and community level centres. However, this nesting pattern is far from perfect and may be viewed as the outcome of the adjustment of the hierarchy to a series of non-isotropic townscape features. Thus, the distribution of centres is closely associated with the configuration of built-up areas and roads in the town and this possibly explains the overall tendency toward the near 'random' spacing exhibited by the entire set of retail areas. Further, the distribution of centres by size orders mirrors the pattern of population density variations in the town. This is particularly noticeable in connection with the concentration of higher order centres in the southern inner-town area where it may be remembered, population densities reach their peak.

From this viewpoint, at least, the pattern within the study area may be seen to resemble the more flexible central place systems of Berry and Garrison (1958a) and Isard (1956). The relative expansion in the size of the N level market areas outward from the urban core is noticeable. Further, the pattern of centres is clearly related to the geometry of the transport network. Thus, in several sectors of the town, as previously noted, the retail areas tend to be located almost exclusively on the main arterial routes. In such cases, the alternation of centre size groups along the roads visually suggests the operation of Christaller's traffic principle. In the suburban interstices an areal solution more akin to the k=3 patterning is observable. This composite pattern bears a passing resemblance to the more flexible economic landscape suggested by Lösch. Indeed, if this broad suggestion is adopted, it becomes a temptation to identify six main radial transport corridors, each surrounded by a built-up wedge containing many centres. These 'business-rich' sectors are separated by a series of 'green-field' or partly built 'business-poor' sectors. In some senses, however, this almost represents a case of forcing real world patterns to fit a theory, and further exemplifies the difficulties involved in the testing of the Löschian system.

The spatial character of the hierarchy within Stockport can also be given some quantitative expression if mean separating distances are calculated for centres at its different levels. The general tendency towards the interstitial placement of orders within the hierarchy is signified by the increasing mean separation distance recorded for successively higher order centre groups. Thus, the two regional centres are located 4.10 km. apart, the district centres 1.10 km., the community centres 0.63 km. and the neighbourhood level centres 0.38 km. apart. In a Christallerian perfect marketing landscape, if Da is the separating distance between the lowest order centres, then the mean spacing between centres of the next hierarchical group (Db) would be:

$$Db = Da \cdot \sqrt{3}$$

For the study area, the separation distance of 0.38 km. pertaining to the neighbourhood centres may be taken and the formula applied to estimate the theoretical separating distances for the three higher orders. This gives a theoretical sequence of 0.38, 0.66, 1.09 and 1.90 km. for the four groups. The agreement between the predicted and actual separating distances for the community and district level centres in relation to the neighbourhood spacing distance is striking.

THE FUNCTIONAL STRUCTURE OF THE HIERARCHY

The analysis has shown that a broadly defined hierarchy of retailing areas was found within Stockport. It will be recalled that Marshall (1969) stated that a service centre hierarchy should constitute a functional whole and that centres therefore exhibit a high degree of spatial correspondence. It was also stated that a hierarchy should exhibit the discrete stratification of centrality, a numerical pyramid of order membership, the interstitial placement of orders, a minimum of three levels and incremental baskets of goods. In the foregoing analysis it has been indicated that the study system accords tolerably well with the first six criteria, and attention is now focused on the final one.

The question of the functional structuring of the size groups identified within a system is a vitally important one for it is a distinctive feature of a Christallerian hierarchy that incremental baskets of goods occur, whereas, centres specialise far more within a Löschian type system. This aspect of retail structuring therefore has a bearing on the overall efficacy of models and theories.

In order to examine functional structuring within the Stockport study area, the columns of the original functional survey data matrix (Figure 3.6) were rearranged so that the functions ran from 1 to 68 according to their overall frequency of occurrence within the system. The most frequently occurring activity, grocery, appears on the left of the matrix, the least frequent, department stores, on the extreme right. Vacancy levels have been omitted from this analysis. The centres are ranked from the largest to the smallest in the 71 rows of the data matrix, and the broad divisions of the hierarchy indicated.

The functional matrix (Figure 3.11) shows that the larger centres generally tend to offer the goods and services that are supplied by the smaller ones, whilst also offering a further range of functions not performed by the lower order centres. Thus, there is a clear general tendency toward functional incrementality within the urban retailing system. These features of functional composition are further illus-

RETAIL FUNCTION MATRIX
(Numerical)

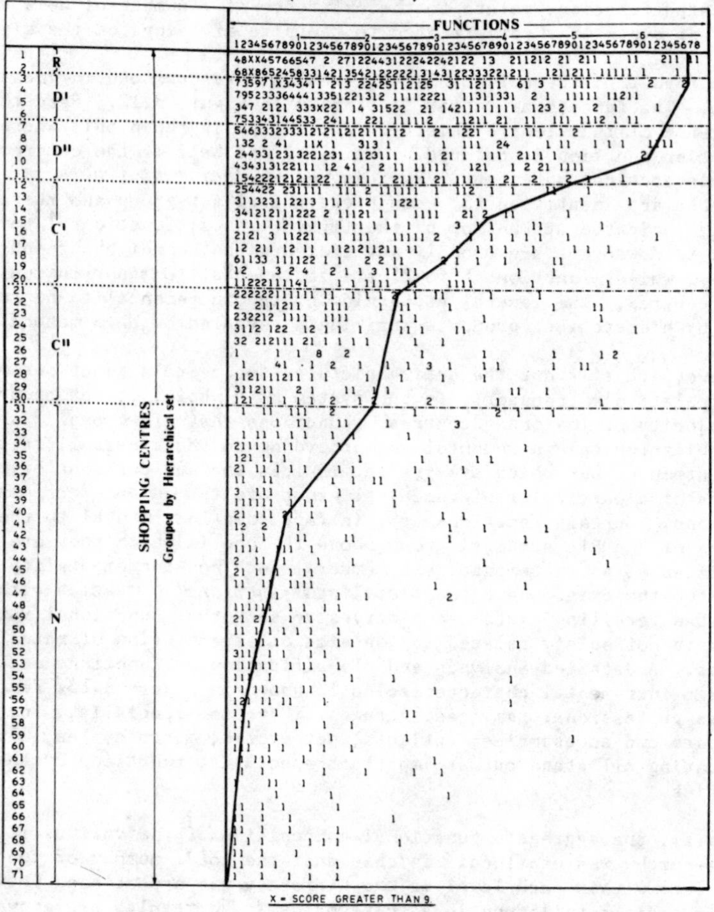

KEY TO RETAIL FUNCTIONS

1 GROCER
2 SWEETS/TOBACCO
3 WOMEN'S CLOTHING
4 BUTCHER
5 NEWSAGENT
6 GREENGROCER
7 PUBLIC HOUSE
8 HOUSEHOLD
9 BAKER
10 WOMEN'S HAIRDRESSING
11 FRIED FISH
12 TOYS
13 OTHER PROFESSIONAL
14 INFANTSCLOTHING
15 GARAGE/FILLING STATION
16 POST OFFICE
17 TV/RADIO
18 OFF LICENCE
19 CAFE
20 CHEMIST
21 OTHER SPECIALIST
22 WALLPAPER/PAINT
23 FURNITURE
24 LAUNDERETTE
25 DRY CLEANERS
26 MENS BARBER
27 BETTING OFFICE
28 MENS CLOTHING
29 SPARES/ACCESSORIES
30 SUPERMARKET
31 WOOL
32 ANTIQUES
33 D.I.Y/TIMBER
34 CARDS
35 BANKS
36 SHOE REPAIR
37 PET STORES
38 FOOTWEAR
39 CAR SALES
40 ESTATE AGENT
41 FLORIST
42 MOTOR CYCLES
43 FISH/POULTRY
44 CHINA/GLASS
45 FABRICS/DRAPERY
46 CARPETS
47 PLUMBING/HEATING
48 OPTICIAN
49 TRAVEL AGENT
50 LUGGAGE
51 CYCLES
52 JEWELLERY/WATCHMAKER
53 LIGHTING
54 FISHING EQUIPMENT
55 STATIONERY
56 SPORTS EQUIPMENT
57 RECORDS
58 PRAMS
59 PHOTOGRAPHIC
60 ELECTRICITY
61 OFFICE EQUIPMENT
62 MEDICAL GOODS
63 BOOKSHOP
64 PHOTO STUDIO
65 GAS
66 MUSICAL EQUIPMENT
67 MILLINERY
68 DEPARTMENTAL STORES

Figure 3.11 Hierarchical functional matrix for the urban retail system of Stockport trated if functions are considered only where they are replicated in centres. The generalised curve shown in Figure 3.11 joining commonly replicated functions points to the existence of a number of well defined breaks of slope which are related to the size divisions of the hierarchy.

As a result of these findings, the analysis was pursued in greater detail. The functional matrix is redrawn in Figure 3.12. Here the occurrence of functions by hierarchical groups is shown only where a particular function is offered by at least one half of the centres in each hierarchical sub-group. By this means, *incremental sets of functions* are identified for each hierarchical sub-group and these are clearly indicated at the top of the figure. Thus, functions 1 to 5, grocer to newsagent are broadly associated with the neighbourhood level centres, whilst functions 6 to 25 are incremental to minor community (Cii) centres. The general patterning of the incrementality of functions by hierarchical group is strikingly revealed by this method.

However, this is not the entire picture, for certain functions which occur relatively frequently in the system as a whole, do not occur in the majority of low order centres. Functions that are grouped in a given hierarchical-incremental set according to their overall frequency of occurrence, but which are present in less than 50 per cent of the centres of a particular hierarchical group are termed *non-incremental* functions. Certain functions are, in fact, non-incremental to the centres of the hierarchical group above the one in which they are first classified as an incremental set member. Such non-incrementality indicates the existence of a *specialised functional dimension* within the urban retailing system, and serves to show that functional variability is not solely related to the size differentiation of retail centres. A detailed analysis and classification of functions according to their incremental characteristics is shown in Figure 3.13. Functions such as professional services, garages, TV/radio, specialist, furniture, car spare and accessories, antiques, pet stores, motor cycles, plumbing and heating all stand out as important specialist functions by this yardstick.

Finally, the aggregate functional composition of the various levels of the hierarchy was examined. To this end, the total number of functional outlets within each level of the hierarchy was apportioned between the nine main retail functional categories. The results are shown in the first four columns of Figure 3.14 and a number of decipherable size related functional trends are apparent. For successively lower orders of the hierarchy, the proportion of functional outlets offering food commodities tends to increase progressively. In contrast, the proportion performing clothing and household functions shows a progressive decline. Further, the proportion of large retail units and those performing recreational and sports functions show a consistent reduction with movement down the hierarchy. Miscellaneous functions represent an almost constant proportion of total functional outlets at the various levels. In contrast, however, the functions of personal services, motor goods and professional services show a less decipherable hierarchic related variation. In fact, they seem to witness once more the existence of a specialised functional component. A close scrutiny of the functional matrix revealed that these functions are concentrated in a relatively small number of arterially located centres. For this reason, the main linear and arterially located centres were subject-

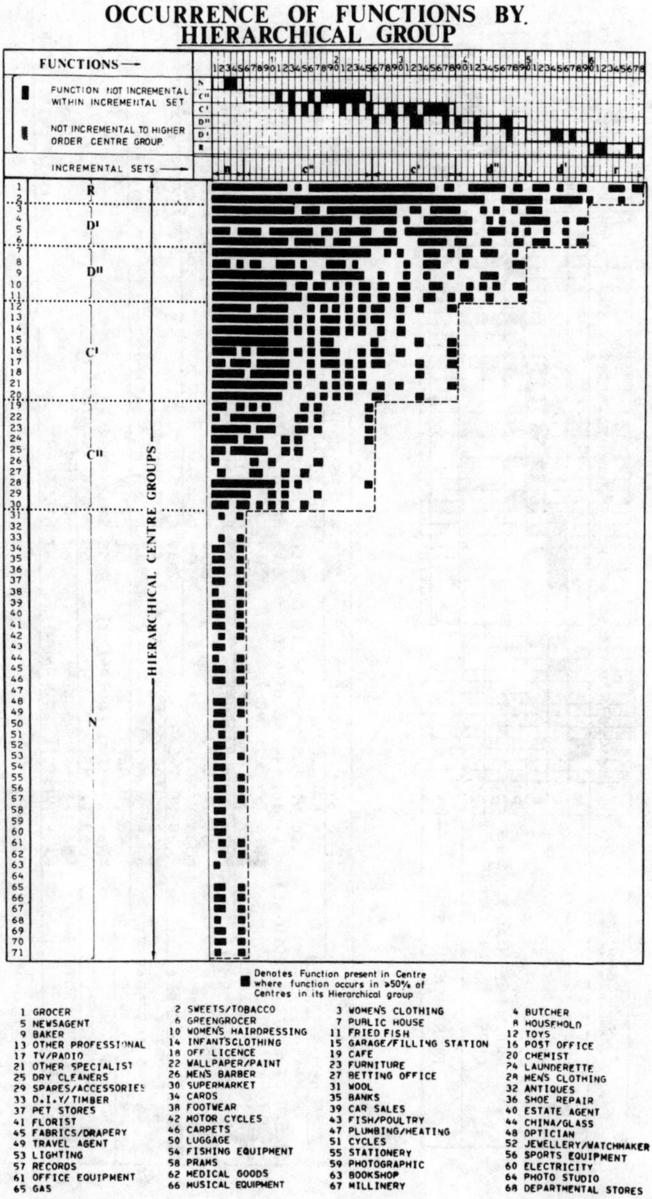
OCCURRENCE OF FUNCTIONS BY HIERARCHICAL GROUP
FUNCTIONS
FUNCTION NOT INCREMENTAL WITHIN INCREMENTAL SET
NOT INCREMENTAL TO HIGHER ORDER CENTRE GROUP
INCREMENTAL SETS
R
D'
D''
C'
C''
N
HIERARCHICAL CENTRE GROUPS
Denotes Function present in Centre where function occurs in ≥50% of Centres in its Hierarchical group
1 GROCER
2 SWEETS/TOBACCO
3 WOMEN'S CLOTHING
4 BUTCHER
5 NEWSAGENT
6 GREENGROCER
7 PUBLIC HOUSE
8 HOUSEHOLD
9 BAKER
10 WOMEN'S HAIRDRESSING
11 FRIED FISH
12 TOYS
13 OTHER PROFESSIONAL
14 INFANTSCLOTHING
15 GARAGE/FILLING STATION
16 POST OFFICE
17 TV/RADIO
18 OFF LICENCE
19 CAFE
20 CHEMIST
21 OTHER SPECIALIST
22 WALLPAPER/PAINT
23 FURNITURE
24 LAUNDERETTE
25 DRY CLEANERS
26 MEN'S BARBER
27 BETTING OFFICE
28 MEN'S CLOTHING
29 SPARES/ACCESSORIES
30 SUPERMARKET
31 WOOL
32 ANTIQUES
33 D.I.Y/TIMBER
34 CARDS
35 BANKS
36 SHOE REPAIR
37 PET STORES
38 FOOTWEAR
39 CAR SALES
40 ESTATE AGENT
41 FLORIST
42 MOTOR CYCLES
43 FISH/POULTRY
44 CHINA/GLASS
45 FABRICS/DRAPERY
46 CARPETS
47 PLUMBING/HEATING
48 OPTICIAN
49 TRAVEL AGENT
50 LUGGAGE
51 CYCLES
52 JEWELLERY/WATCHMAKER
53 LIGHTING
54 FISHING EQUIPMENT
55 STATIONERY
56 SPORTS EQUIPMENT
57 RECORDS
58 PRAMS
59 PHOTOGRAPHIC
60 ELECTRICITY
61 OFFICE EQUIPMENT
62 MEDICAL GOODS
63 BOOKSHOP
64 PHOTO STUDIO
65 GAS
66 MUSICAL EQUIPMENT
67 MILLINERY
68 DEPARTMENTAL STORES

Figure 3.12 Occurrence of retail functions by hierarchical group

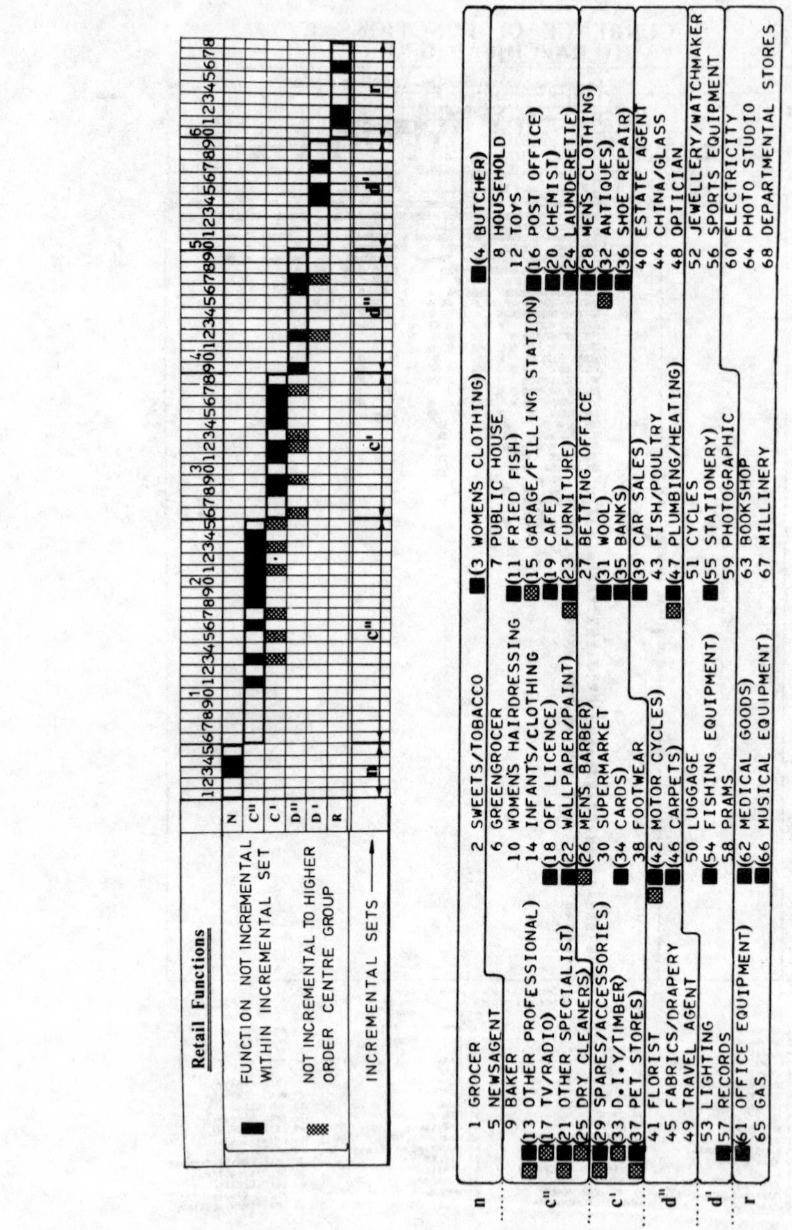

Figure 3.13 Incrementality of urban retail functions by hierarchical group

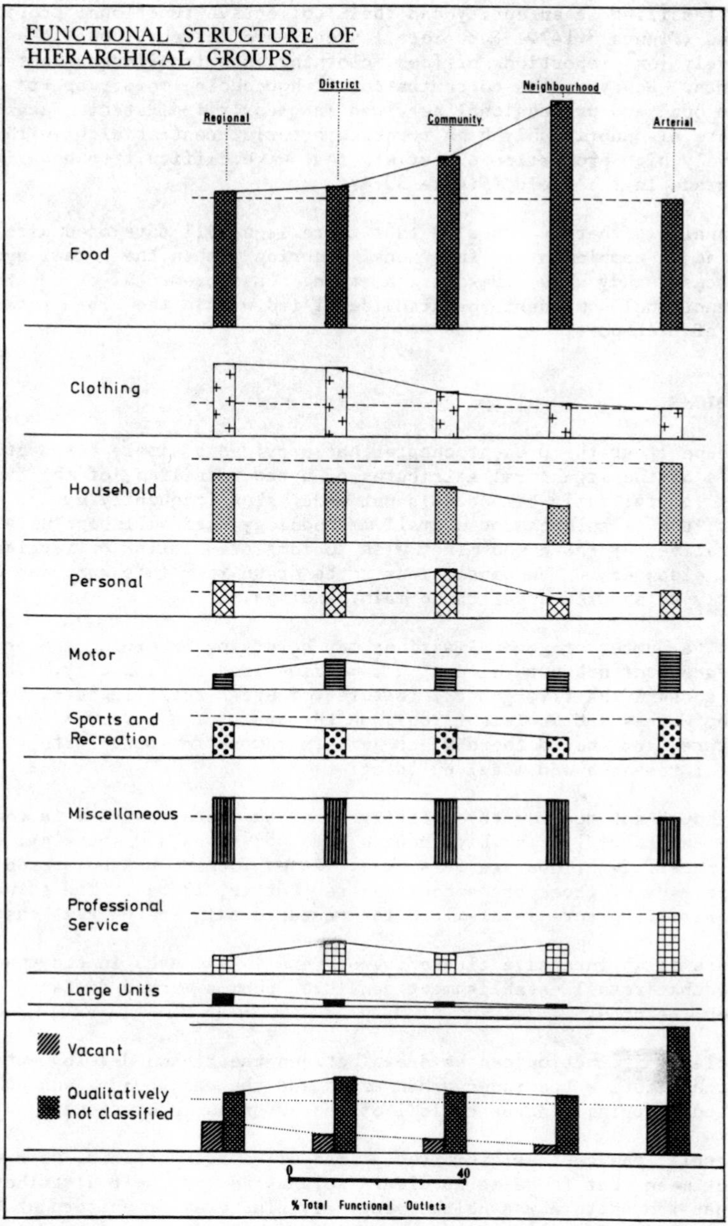

Figure 3.14 The functional structure of the retail system of Stockport

ively classified as an entity and their collective functional profile examined (Figure 3.14). Such retail areas were thereby shown to have relatively low proportions of food, clothing and miscellaneous establlishments. However, the concentration of household, motor, sports and recreational and professional services is clearly indicated. Vacancy rates are also noticeably high for such arterial centres along with the relatively high proportion of outlets that were difficult to quantitatively grade in the field (Figure 3.14).

The analysis thereby revealed that there is a well developed size dominated or complementary functional ordering within the retail system of the case study area. However, a strong non-incremental or specialised functional component was also identified within the urban retailing system of Stockport.

CONCLUSIONS

It is hoped that the present chapter has provided a simple but useful analysis of the structural attributes of urban retailing, of the type that it was initially bemoaned is not undertaken frequently enough. Further, the techniques and overall methodology used will hopefully be illustrative for those who might wish to complete similar or replicative studies elsewhere. The conclusions to be drawn from this work can conveniently be handled under three main headings.

First, a number of generalisations may be drawn concerning the principal facets of urban retailing in a middle-sized British city. These points subsume the five general features of urban retailing structure cited by Warnes and Daniels (1980), on the basis of a review of the literature, and should thereby act as a framework for both further empirical research and model building:

1. Although not dealt with explicity here, the retail system is dominated by the central area which houses some 484 shops and where all 69 listed retail functions are performed. Redevelopment has bolstered the clear primacy of Stockport's town centre (Potter, 1976a). The structure of the retailing core is examined in greater detail in the next chapter.

2. There is an intensive clustering of retail land uses in the inner city so that retail establishment densities show a marked distance decay out from the core.

3. A clear distinction can be drawn between the ribbon developments which characterise the inner urban areas and the main roads, and the nucleated shopping centres typical of the suburban interstices.

4. Overall, the centres exhibited a 'random' spacing. This, however, does not mean that there is no clear explanation for their distribution, only that the pattern was neither entirely clustered or uniform at the level of the entire town.

5. A relative concentration of large retail centres occurs close to the urban core reflecting population density, accessibility and possibly socio-economic conditions.

6. A decipherable size differentiation of retail centres was found to

exist such that discrete size clusters were identified. However, this size distribution was neither perfectly stepped nor perfectly continuous.

7. Additionally, the system of retail centres was characterised by a true numerical hierarchy, the discrete stratification of centrality and the interstitial placement of centres by size orders.

8. Both functional incremental baskets of goods and a separate specialised functional component were shown to exist.

The second major set of conclusions involve the implications of these findings for the debate on the development and adoption of relevant models of urban retailing structural organisation. The analysis implies that several aspects of the Christallerian central place system are apposite. In particular, the incremental patterning of the majority of the functions is interesting. These appear to be hierarchic in nature and are presumably related to multi-purpose shopping trips on the part of consumers. Further, elements of the k=3 and k=4 locational patterns appeared to be clearly identifiable. Other broad Christallerian characteristics, such as those listed under 7. above were also noted. The average observed k value for the system was 3.27 and the variable k general hierarchical formulation is at least conceptually relevant for the different levels of the hierarchy. However, the structure of the entire system cannot be explained in these terms alone, although equally, it is true that the Löschian system is not readily identifiable or applicable due to its extreme complexity. It is only in respect of the occurrence of some non-incremental functional patterns that the economic landscape of Lösch is of any real descriptive relevance. This fact, along with the generalisations listed above points to the empirical inappropriateness of Beavon's recent reworking of Löschian theory at the intra-urban scale. Clearly, however, some elements of the theory of tertiary activity and Davies' model of hierarchical sub-systems are discernible in the empirical ordering of the system, especially in terms of population density induced variations. However, the overall correspondence shown by accessibility levels, commercial structure and inferred land values within Stockport tends to be spatially reminiscent of Berry's typology of centres, ribbons and specialised components. This also clearly mirrors the existence of separate specialised and incremental functional components within the system.

Whilst it is true that in a number of facets the features of the study area seem to match certain aspects of these theories and models, it is of course not realistic to expect these formulations to fit all aspects and cases of reality. As argued in Chapter 2, this is not their prime function and they are basically to be regarded as normative guides for description and planning. The third major conclusion, therefore, is that the generalised models that do exist cannot possibly take into account all of the manifold aspects of urban retail centre variability and their complex interrelations. In particular, these formulations tend to concentrate perhaps too much attention on the size differentiation of retail centres. This approach tends to neglect other salient aspects of retail variation such as centre morphology, contiguity of fabric, qualitative tone, age, accessibility and functional mix. Thus, the present study has furnished strong evidence that although the size ordering of retail centres is an important ingredient of the structural organisation of the urban retailing system, it is by no means an omnipotent factor. This conclusion acts as the overall theme for the detailed review of empirical urban retail research that is presented in the following chapter.

4 Empirical Perspectives on Urban Retail Structure

Attention is focused on the methods, techniques and substantive findings of empirical studies of urban retailing structure in this chapter. As defined in Chapter 2, empirical studies are normally associated with the inductive mode of reasoning, that is they look at particular circumstances or examples and on the basis of these, endeavour to derive generalisations which have wider relevance and applicability. Thus, the hallmark of such work is its reliance on experimentation and direct observation of real world structural patterns. The utility of such an approach was hopefully exemplified in the last chapter, where a single empirical case study was presented. However, many such enquiries have been carried out and together they constitute a corpus of knowledge concerning urban retailing structural patterns.

In the first part of this account, an effort is made to look at the findings of early classifications and typologies of urban retailing centres, these having principally been carried out in North America and Western Europe. This concludes with an examination of the methods which may be used to classify retail centres into discrete groups. These two sections serve to indicate some of the variables which hitherto have received relatively little explicit attention in retail studies. Here the argument concurs with that presented in Chapter 3, that research on the size-related characteristics of retail centres has been overemphasised at the expense of examination of other attributes that are possibly of equal importance, particularly to consumers in their decision-making and spatial behaviour. In the following parts of the chapter, these variables are considered in detail, for example, centre morphology, the question of their qualitative tone and their functional disposition. The difficulties involved in measuring such properties are reviewed along with the range of techniques that may be employed. In each of these sections, empirical evidence is drawn from as wide a range of sources as possible, but considerable emphasis is placed on the author's research in the Stockport urban area. A synthesis is then attempted when the possible interrelations between the various retail area attributes are examined and the implications of these associations assessed. A short section follows on these types of variation within the city centre, again illustrated by the example of Stockport. In conclusion, empirical research on historical aspects of retail development and dynamic change is examined. Finally, a graphical model of urban retail structural organisation is presented which it is suggested is both locationally and behaviourally sensitive. This formulation keeps the link between behaviour and structure to the fore and in this sense represents the culmination of this first half of the book.

EARLY EMPIRICAL STUDIES OF URBAN RETAILING

Much descriptive and analytical research on urban retailing patterns was undertaken during the 1950s and 1960s, but there is a body of empirical work which predates this, and such research is initially considered here. Most of these early descriptions, which also advanced retail centre typologies were based on American cities and have been fully summarised by Berry in Garrison *et al.* (1959, Chapter 3). The initial account which follows draws heavily on the extended reviews that are to be found in that source, along with the original works.

Perhaps the earliest comprehensive empirical investigation of urban retailing was completed by Rolph (1929) in the city of Baltimore. Here it was concluded that five main types of centre could be recognised, these being (1) *the central business district*, (2) *retail subcentres*, (3) *string streets*, (4) *neighbourhood facility groups* and (5) *nonconcentrated businesses*. The significance of this typology as pointed out by Garrison *et al.* (1959, p. 40) is that 'it was one of the first to show that various types of business centers exist, and that their functional make-up differs'. In particular, food and clothing functions were seen to be associated with the retail subcentres, whilst string streets were recognised as specialist furniture, household, motor, clothing and general merchandise complexes occurring along major traffic arteries. The neighbourhood facility and nonconcentrated groups were associated with food, motor, lumber and building material functional groups. The typology may be seen to reflect not only the overall size of centres, but also their functional disposition, urban location and morphology.

Rolph's generalisation was followed by what is perhaps one of the most frequently cited studies, that of Proudfoot (1937a, 1937b, 1938). Proudfoot considered the retail provisions of the cities of Chicago, Philadelphia, Cleveland, Atlanta and Des Moines in detail and completed reconnaissance studies in New York, Washington, Baltimore and Knoxville. Thereby, it was posited that the principal American cities possess five major types of retail configuration, referred to as (1) *the central business district*, (2) *the outlying business center*, (3) *the principal business thoroughfare*, (4) *the neighbourhood business street* and (5) *the isolated store cluster*. It was stated that three criteria, the range of goods sold, the concentration or dispersal of shops, and the character of customer tributary areas were used to distinguish these types, although no definite statistical criteria were advanced for each criterion. Naturally, the C.B.D. was recognised as the heart of the retail system, whilst outlying business centres were considered as miniature C.B.D.s where clothing, furniture, department and convenience stores are found mixed together at focal points of intra-city transport. The principal business thoroughfare was regarded as an amalgam of widely-spaced shopping and convenience stores serving lower-order, local needs, plus a range of traffic artery related demands. The neighbourhood business street was envisaged as drawing customers from mainly within walking distance and to consist of grocery, meat, fruit, vegetable, chemist and other convenience stores. These may occur in a variety of urban locations. Finally, the isolated store cluster consists of two or three complementary convenience stores. The Proudfoot typology, although clearly based on a hierarchical-size principle has connotations concerning the location and morphology of retail centres, and this is a possible area of confusion. Further, the basis of classification in any particular urban context is likely to be entirely subjective.

A further important study was by Ratcliff (1935), who again noted the supremacy of the C.B.D., but argued that two principal conformations, namely *string street developments* and *business nucleations* dominate the retail system outside it. Business nucleations are nodal clusters of retail establishments at major road intersections. These vary in size, essentially forming a hierarchy from isolated stores, though neighbourhood centres, major subcentres to the C.B.D. String streets or business thoroughfares were noted to occur in linear fashion along the main traffic arteries, but rarely extend down intersecting streets. Both local and arterially oriented retail functions are apparent, with the local residential related functions occurring in 'beads'. This recognition of two distinct sub-components of the retail system was really the direct precursor to Berry's three fold typology of urban commercial structure, and served to stress the importance of retail area morphological and land value variations in association with their functional differentiation. As such, the Ratcliff typology was an early indication of the importance of non-size related retail area traits.

In 1946, Canoyer reviewed many of the earlier studies undertaken of urban retailing and on the basis of these re-emphasised the importance of a two-fold division. Firstly, *string street types* were recognised which are characterised by high vehicular but relatively low pedestrian traffic flows and which thus derive a high proportion of their trade from through traffic. On the other hand, a variety of *cluster types* or true nucleated shopping centres were identified, ranging in size from the C.B.D. to the major subcentre at the community level, to the minor subcentre serving a neighbourhood, and then a variety of isolated store types. By this juncture, therefore, in the American city at least, a clear empirical division of the urban retailing system into a set of compact nucleations following a basically hierarchical-size patterning and a set of less compact arterially oriented string street, or ribbon shopping developments had been made. This represented a major advance on the earlier typologies of Proudfoot and Rolph which attempted to integrate these ill-assorted morphological, functional and size variations in a unified framework.

This is not to argue that such marriages of form, function and size were not still suggested. In 1948, for example, Hoover presented commercial land use maps of six major U.S. cities, Louisville, Springfield, San Antonio, Sacramento, Jefferson and Chicago, and argued that four elements were evident: (1) *the downtown area*, (2) *ribbons of commercial development* along principal thoroughfares, (3) *subordinate centres of concentration* and (4) *a 'shotgun' scatter of neighbourhood stores* throughout the built up area. Again, the effort to integrate morphology into a basically size-dominated classification of retail facilities is apparent.

The studies undertaken up to this point, however, had largely been dependent upon the visual examination of plots of retail land use, although some effort was made subsequently to look at functional composition in each case. A change in emphasis was witnessed by the work of Garrison (1950), when he examined the functional structure of some twelve community centres, thirteen major neighbourhood centres and 21 business thoroughfares in Chicago. It was found that community centres had an average of 144 shops performing 53 different functions, notable amongst these being food, cleaning, eating, medical, clothing and car oriented facilities. The major neighbourhood centres consisted of around 31 establishments and 19 functions with little replication of outlets of the same functional type. Particular concentrations of food, fuel, eating, cleaning and laundry, household, furniture, radio sales, auto services, beauty and barber facilities were prominent in such centres. On the business thoroughfares, automobile services, fuel, eating places, building materials, recreational services, car dealers and beverage sales, all functions generally requiring large sites were particularly dominant. Also denoting this move towards more detailed studies, Merry (1955) looked at a single string street development, that of East Colfax Avenue in Denver. In terms of establishment totals, the most commonly occurring activities were restaurant, cleaner/laundry, car sales, gas, beauty, drug, barber and grocery, whilst by ground area occupied, auto sales, gas, grocery, restaurant, drug store, cleaners, car repairs and furniture were most important.

This division into two principal urban retailing conformations, nucleations and ribbons has of course a strong deductive-theoretical foundation in terms of accessibility and land value variations in towns and the rent paying abilities of retail firms, as described in Chapter 2. The recognition of this important distinction has already been described as the precursor to Berry's threefold typology. In fact, this model was based on the further empirical evidence offered by a series of detailed studies by Berry, published from 1959 to 1963 and which represented the logical development of the works cited above. However, Berry's contribution is of such methodological importance that it will be considered separately in the next section of this chapter. Before looking at this, we turn now to review other early studies of urban retailing that were conducted outside the U.S.A., mainly in England and elsewhere in Europe, although many of them postdate Berry's seminal work.

In one such early endeavour, Weekley (1956) identified an array of 43 service centres in Nottingham, England. The axial orientation of the main retailing concentrations was noted by Weekley and a broad distinction was drawn between those intra-urban centres which owed their origin to the engulfment of pre-existing centres during urban growth and those that had developed in a more haphazard manner, where no such nucleus had previously existed, often 'at intervals along the main radial routes' (Weekley, 1956, p. 45). Although this distinction was not taken further or applied in any detail to the centres in Nottingham, its recognition was important. However, sensitivity to such diverse origins and forms was not endemic, and in a volume devoted to British shopping centres, Burns (1959) argued that a four-tier hierarchical structure typified British cities, consisting of (1) *the town centre*, (2) *district centres*, (3) *neighbourhood centres* and (4) *subcentres*, superimposed on a foundation of corner stores. In a frequently redrawn and cited diagram, Burns depicted a clear nested hierarchical arrangement, and perhaps reflecting the planning orientation of the work, no recognition was given to ribbon or linear string street developments. Another early survey of retail and service provision in an English town, this time of the northern part of Leeds was performed by Leeming (1959). Here a clear distinction was drawn between the distribution of shopping facilities in the inner and outer suburbs of the city. In the outer zone it was estimated that over 80 per cent of the functional outlets were to be found in tight clusters, these generally being about 0.5 mile apart and located on main roads. In the inner urban area, a higher overall density of recording was noticeable, but with a lower degree (c.70-90 per cent) of nucleation into groups. As a result, groupings in the inner area were found to be much closer together, often only 100 yards apart and the location of the largest clusters on the most important traffic routes was also observed. Further, Leeming provided an interesting view of the distribution of selected functions in the city, and in a series of maps demonstrated the concentration of shoe shops, soft furnishing and floor covering, pram, bicycle, sports goods, handicrafts and textile suppliers, pawnbrokers and bookmakers and motor-vehicle repairing establishments in the inner urban zone, particularly on the main traffic arteries. In a similar vein, Jones (1960) in his pioneering study of the social structure of Belfast, Northern Ireland started his account of retailing in the city with the comment that 'Along most roads leading from the centre of the city to the suburbs of Belfast the most obvious feature of the landscape is the seemingly endless ribbons of retail shops' (Jones, 1960, p. 85). This is clear from the land use maps presented by Jones, and it was further noted that the size of centres tends to increase gradually inwards.

Other studies pointing to this basic distinction abound. For example, in a comprehensive survey of shopping centres in Greater London, Smailes and Hartley (1961, p. 208) noted that 'the tendency for shops to extend continuously for long stretches of main roads presents special problems of independent ranking'. This predominant radial/ribbon pattern was affirmed in another study of London conducted by Carruthers (1962). On the other hand, Carol (1960) in examining the retail provision of Zurich, Switzerland made a specific effort to apply central place notions to the intra-urban retailing system. Thus, although Carol was clearly aware of Berry's work, arterial business locations were specifically omitted from the analysis. In reverse fashion, this shows the importance of a linear sub-component of the urban retail system which is not fully amenable to a direct central place interpretation. In a similar vein, a study by Parker (1962) looked at the provision of shopping facilities in Liverpool to determine whether they were provided on a hierarchical basis. The conclusion reached was that this was not the case and that facilities occurred in linear fashion, following the main roads, and that such suburban shopping facilities were relatively concentrated in a broad inner urban arc adjacent to the C.B.D. Similarly, as an adjunct to a study of shopping activity patterns, Pocock (1968) classified the elements of the retail system of Dundee into the C.B.D., two major sub-centres and three conspicuous linear concentrations along streets leading from the central area, and a number of neighbourhood clusters and corner stores.

The above review is by no means exhaustive, but nevertheless serves to show that the distinction between compact nucleations and arterial retail developments in the urban business pattern is very important and has a long empirical history. Further studies in towns as different as Melbourne, Australia and Cape Town, South Africa by Johnston (1966) and Beavon (1972) respectively have also noted such features. In fact, even in a study of retailing in Lagos, Nigeria, Mabogunje (1964) applied the Proudfoot typology in unmodified form and linear business streets and thoroughfares stood out as predominant elements. Following on from Chapters 2 and 3, these empirical studies affirm that central place theory is primarily a normative guide, for it applies only broadly to urban retailing spatial patterns due to its strong accent on size-related attributes. In the studies reviewed thus far, the distinction between ribbons and nucleations has been drawn visually on the basis of morphology, and functional, qualitative, locational, accessibility and age differences then brought in subsequently. There is a need for a clear consideration of these variables in retail studies, for the development of techniques to measure them and for detailed examination of their precise interrelationships.

THE EMPIRICAL CONTRIBUTION OF B. J. L. BERRY

Berry's threefold typology of urban commercial structure has already been presented and discussed in Chapter 2 (see, for example, Figures 2.8 and 2.9), and also received a partial empirical verification in Chapter 3. It is probably fair to argue that Berry's work in the context of the American city forms a milestone in urban retailing studies. Berry used the early American research reviewed above as the foundation for a series of more rigorous statistical analyses based on retail functional data.

The principal study emanated from his doctoral dissertation (Berry, 1958), which looked at the spatial groupings and associations of business land uses in Spokane, Washington (185,000 population at the time of the study). This study is also described in Berry (1959) and in Garrison *et al.* (1959, Chapter 3). The frequencies of occurrence of some 60 separate business functions was recorded for the 296 retail centres, although subsequently the functional classification was reduced to 49 items and this entailed a reduction to 285 business centres. The functions were then intercorrelated to show the composite pattern of correspondence of their 49 geographical distributions. Thus, 1,225 correlation coefficients were derived showing the association between each function and all others and the statistical procedure of linkage analysis applied to these to identify groups of spatially associated business types. By this means, nine major sets of functions were derived and these are labelled from 1 to 9 in Table 4.1. Linkage analysis was again used to see if these groups of spatially associated business types themselves displayed any distinctive patterns of association. In this respect it was suggested that two principal conformations existed. Functional groups 1, 2, 3 and 4 were collectively regarded as a 'nucleated' set, whilst groups 5 to 8 were termed an 'arterial' conformation. Group 4 stood as an auto-related system within the nucleations. Group 9 was seen as a separate 'clinic' group, the correlation between doctors and dentists standing at r=0.77. Turning to the actual retail areas of Spokane, 116 of the total of 285 were classified as possessing nucleated business types only and 57 entirely arterial ones. As many as 112 possessed elements of both functional forms, but each of these showed a noticeable concentration of one type or the other. The nucleated centres were found to be widely dispersed throughout the city, whilst arterial centres were more highly concentrated, being oriented to a few major streets and traffic axes. Further comparative and corroborative work was presented for Cedar Rapids, Phoenix and Cincinnati.

There seems little doubt that Berry's work represented a notable advance in urban retailing research for it was the first truly multivariate study of such phenomena. It also brought a new approach with its primary emphasis on functional data and its use of ostensibly objective statistical methods of classification. It was these studies

Table 4.1
Berry's grouping of spatially associated business types

Group 1:	Grocery, barber, cleaner and laundry, drug, real estate and insurance, hardware, beauty, theater.
Group 2:	Clothing, variety, dairy, jewelry, lawyer, post office.
Group 3:	Department, sporting goods and bicycles, other professions, shoe, bank.
Group 4:	Bakery, auto dealer, used auto, florist and nursery, food locker, music and hobby, hotel.
Group 5:	Gas, restaurant, auto repair.
Group 6:	Building supplies, bar, radio-TV sales and service, shoe repair, furniture, auto accessories, appliance, other retail, miscellaneous repair including plumbing, lumber yard, gift and novelty, motel, mission.
Group 7:	Meat, fruit-vegetable and produce.
Group 8:	Printing, office equipment, funeral home.
Group 9:	Doctor, dentist.

(Source: adapted from Garrison *et al.*, 1959, p. 74)

along with the earlier ones that led to the formulation of Berry's classification of the commercial system into nucleations, urban arterials, automobile rows and highway-oriented facilities (Berry, 1959, 1960; Garrison *et al.*, 1959). Thus, Berry (1959) was moved to argue that central place theory alone is not sufficient to explain urban retailing, thereby mirroring the argument presented at the inter-urban scale. Subsequently, Berry advanced the threefold typology of centres, ribbons and specialised areas (Berry, 1962, 1963; Berry and Mayer, 1962). This scheme was shown to apply in the case of Chicago by Berry (1963) where 500 miles of ribbons were identified, as well as in several other urban regions (Garner, 1966; Simmons, 1964). Other American studies have examined the physical and functional characteristics of particular ribbons (Boal and Johnson, 1965, 1968; Pred, 1963) and 'skid row' developments (Ward, 1975; Rowley, 1978).

It is clear that ribbons and nucleations are two vitally important ingredients of the urban retailing system. It is surprising, however, that relatively few systematic studies of such conformations have been carried out in Britain in the post-war period, so that as noted by Davies (1976, p. 124) 'there has been relatively little attempt to apply Berry's type of classification to the business portion of British cities'. In conclusion, it must be stressed that Berry's work was based on functional data and other retail area properties were then brought in as implicit correlates of this functional structure, although the nature of these relationships was not specifically tested (Potter, 1981a). However, Berry's studies and the resultant typology represented a notable advance in the recognition of non-size related intra-urban retail variations. This point appears to have been confused by workers such as Beavon (1977, p. 12-13), who imply that the typology is a part of the Christallerian based theory of tertiary activity, rather than a distinct modification of it as presumably envisaged by Berry.

METHODS OF CLASSIFYING URBAN RETAILING CENTRES

The aim of the previous sections was to review early empirical studies of urban retailing, but a natural outcome has been a growing preoccupation with methods of classifying shopping centres. It would seem worthwhile, therefore, to pull these ideas together at this stage. The procedure of classification is of course basic to all forms of enquiry, for it represents an effort to place the items under scrutiny into natural sets, or groups. As noted in the previous chapter, the basic criterion is that all members of a group should be more like one another than they are members of other groups. The first difficulty encountered, therefore, is to establish the basis on which similarity is to be assessed. It follows from the above account that overall size or functional status has probably been used most frequently in classifying shopping centres. But any salient characteristic such as their morphology, location, functions, quality, age or socio-economic standing may be used. A second consideration is the level of measurement, whether nominal, ordinal, interval or ratio, that is to be employed. Further, the number of separate retail area characteristics to be taken into consideration is another important question. Although there are a number of formidable and recurrent problems involved in classification, given the demands of academic and applied retailing research, it is often necessary to divide the elements of the urban retailing system into discrete sub-sets. It is suggested here that six major types of classificatory procedure may be employed and these are briefly summarised below, although it must be stressed that this division is largely one of convenience only.

1. *The subjective method* - where retail centres are allocated to discrete categories which are labelled in some descriptive manner. Thus, a nominal level of measurement is being employed. In terms of size, for example, centres could be classified into large, medium and small; or nucleated, intermediate and linear with respect to their morphology. This is really the simplest form of classification and centres are generally assigned to particular groups on the basis of a subjective or visual impression rather than by means of precise measurement. Proudfoot's (1937a) classification of retail areas in Philadelphia using his five categories is a prime example.

2. *The univariate method* - if the centres can be given a score on a given variable at the interval or ratio scales, it is possible to use these to classify centres into sets. This is frequently attempted in relation to the size of centres, using measures such as their total turnover, total floorspace, front footage, employees or their total number of constituent establishments or functions. It may be recalled that this method was used in Chapter 3, where the retail centres of Stockport were grouped according to the similarity of their establishment totals (see Figure 3.8). This method has been used widely in other studies (for example, Guy, 1976). Variables other than those representing size could be used in like manner, such as the period of development of centres, their morphology or qualitative tone.

3. *The bivariate method* - two variables may be employed and centres plotted on a graph according to the scores they record on them. In this context, any of the variables listed above could be used and the nearest neighbour criterion applied to identify groups of like centres.

This method was also illustrated in the case study of Stockport, employing the total number of functions performed by centres against their establishment totals. The method has been applied in many intra-urban studies (for example, see Johnston, 1966).

4. *The functional index method* - this was also introduced in Chapter 3, having originally been developed by W.K.D. Davies (1967) and can be used to assess the centrality or functional importance of centres. Each retail function is allocated an arbitrary centrality value of 100 and this is divided by the total number of occurrences of that function within the entire retail system, to give its 'location coefficient'. The functional index value for each centre is the summation of the coefficients recorded by its constituent shops. Thus, the method takes into account the overall frequency of occurrence of functions as well as their presence in a centre. A good illustration of the intra-urban employment of the method is that of McEvoy (1968) for major centres in the Manchester conurbation, using both a 7- and 22-fold functional classification of shop types. Other types of centrality indices have been suggested in the urban context by Dutt (1969) and Johnson (1964).

5. *The functional trait complex method* - this is a shortcut methodology for the classification of retail areas by functional importance, for it obviates the need to conduct a full inventory of shops present and functions performed in centres. The method has been employed frequently and involves the identification of key functional traits which are held to be diagnostic of different levels of functional importance. The method was introduced for service centres at the national scale in England and Wales by Smailes (1944, 1947). An early urban application was in the study of Nottingham by Weekley (1956). A first order centre was regarded as having three banks, one or more cinemas, a Woolworth's store, post office and Boot's chemist. A second order centre was defined as for a first order one, but without a branch of Woolworths or Boots, but with a chain grocery store. The same basic definition was taken for third and fourth order centres, but with only two banks and one bank respectively. The occurrence of a post office in association with a chain grocery store was taken as the threshold for a fifth order centre, whilst a sixth order centre was defined by the presence of just one of these two types. Many variants of this basic methodology are possible and this flexibility is its principal merit. For example, Jones (1960) adopted five indices for Belfast: banks, cinemas, post office, other offices and furniture stores. Centres were then graded according to whether they had one of these services only, two of them, three or four, five or six, or more than six. More complex variations of this type of method have been used by Smailes and Hartley (1961) and Carruthers (1962) in their studies of London. In the Carruthers study, data were compiled from telephone directories and a Grade A centre, for example, had to possess at least eight banks and four chain department stores, 38 clothing, 17 furnishing and 13 radio stores, along with five or more cinemas. Subsequently, a grading according to the rateable values of shops in each centre was also used. The basic problem with the method is of course the arbitrary selection of key criteria and associated thresholds. Thorpe and Rhodes (1966) tried to obviate the dependence on the presence of a few leading stores, taking as their index the number of non-food stores weighted by the number of multiple traders and banks.

6. *The multivariate statistical method* - as previously noted, Berry's

analysis of the occurrence of 49 functions in 285 centres in Spokane is a good example of a multivariate study of urban retailing patterns. The hallmark of the method is that all of the variables deemed to reflect differences between centres may be considered simultaneously. These may relate exclusively to functional traits as in the Berry case study, or to a more diverse set of indices. The two most commonly employed techniques are principal components and factor analysis. Both of these seek to determine whether the variations in an original data set can be accounted for by a smaller number of composite dimensions, referred to as factors or principal components. The statistical methods involved are quite complex and interested readers are referred to a number of standard works describing them (Harman, 1967; Hope, 1968; Comrey, 1973; Johnston, 1978). In all cases, a matrix of correlations is computed. In the usual instance, an *R-mode* analysis is undertaken when correlation coefficients are computed between pairs of measured characteristics. The factors or principal components are then extracted. The relation of the original variables and study items to these derived components is subsequently examined by means of the variable loadings and component scores. In a *Q-mode* analysis, correlations are made directly between the study objects over the range of variables. Direct classification of the study objects may also be performed by cluster or linkage analysis, where the correlation coefficients are used as a measure of similarity between centres. Surprisingly, such multivariate methods were little used in retail and service area research after Berry's pioneering efforts, with perhaps the notable exception of Abiodun (1967). As will be shown later, only relatively recently have they been used in the intra-urban context, and here generally with respect to functional data alone (Beavon, 1970, 1972; Davies, 1971, 1974; Potter, 1976a, 1981a, 1981b). There has been little use made of wider sets of variables in relation to retail centres, although in an interesting study, Davies and Bennison (1978) used cluster analysis to classify individual retail streets in Newcastle upon Tyne C.B.D.

It is undoubtedly true that classification should always be a means to an end rather than an end in itself, so that it is not to be regarded as a sterile or purely academic exercise. This brief summary of methods of classifying retail centres has emphasised that there has been a noticeable trend toward the consideration of a wider range of diagnostic variables in association with evermore rigorous statistical techniques. This is yet another reflection of the move away from a size oriented approach to a more broadly based one in urban retail studies. However, whilst retail centre size and functional status are relatively easy properties to define and quantify, the same is not true of others such as their morphology and qualitative tone, and this has constituted a longstanding problem for researchers in the field.

THE MORPHOLOGY OF URBAN RETAIL CENTRES

In a review paper, Cohen and Lewis (1967) stress the importance of considering both form and function in retailing studies, including an examination of 'shape' under the former heading. Given the early and repeated recognition of morphological variations in the urban retail system, it is surprising that few methods have been developed for quantitatively assessing retail area form. It may be argued that such an oversight has severely curtailed the build up of detailed knowledge concerning the development and structure of the urban retailing system. An examination of the morphology of central places in the Rhondda Valley, South Wales, was made by W.K.D. Davies (1968b) using a points scoring system, but here attention was focused on four aspects of building type and architectural history, rather than morphology or street pattern *per se*. Other research has involved the subjective recognition of centre layout types. Mayer (1942), for example, identified six principal shapes, these being *intersections*, *cruciform*, *attenuated cruciform*, *bimodal*, *cruciform modified by a diagonal* and *quadrilateral*. Similarly, Hartley (1962) in his study of London recognised three main types of centre; *linear*, *carfax* and *complex*.

The retailing system of Stockport may be taken as an example. It is possible to classify the town's 71 centres using the type of subjective assessment advanced by Mayer and Hartley. The basic distinction between *linear* and *nucleated* retail areas is obviously a good starting point. The linear category can be subdivided into *unilateral* and *bilateral* elements, plus *parades*. On the other hand, nucleations can be divided into *minor clusters*, *precincts* and *complex assemblages* (Figure 4.1). However, there are a number of problems involved in the application of such a typology. First and foremost, it is extremely subjective. Many centres show admixtures of both nucleated and linear elements. The shape of centres also appears to be related to their size, with the largest ones showing either distinct linearity or nucleation, whilst smaller centres exhibit a range of intermediate forms.

It can be argued that there are in fact two principal aspects of retail area morphology. First, the spatial distribution of the individual outlets comprising a centre is reflected in its overall shape or street pattern. Secondly, the extent to which these outlets are located in close proximity, without disruption, will influence its fabric contiguity. These two aspects are normally closely interrelated and we would expect a nucleated centre to be less disrupted by non-retail units and other gaps than a linear one. It is tempting to suggest, therefore, that the total number of gaps occurring in a centre's fabric should act as a sound surrogate measure of its morphology. This gives rise to the *fabric-gap index method* as developed by Potter (1976a, 1979c). Firstly, the total number of gaps (G) occurring within a retail area is enumerated:-

$$G = Gr + Gj + Gw$$

where Gr is the number of residential units embedded within the fabric, Gj the number of road intersections and Gw an estimate in terms of approximate residential units of more substantial gaps in retail area fabric. The fabric-gap index (F) may then be calculated for a given retail area employing the formula:-

$$F = \frac{G}{E}$$

where G represents the total number of gaps and E the total establishments comprising the fabric. If distance measures are available they can be used in the formula. Low fabric-gap index values are indicative of highly contiguous fabric arrangements whilst high values imply low levels of contiguity. The method is illustrated in Figure 4.2. A loose-knit assemblage of 25 shops is shown in case A, disrupted by as many as 38 gaps, yielding an index value of 1.52. Examples B, C, D and E show increasingly contiguous fabric arrangements associated with progressively lower index values. The precinct form in case E records

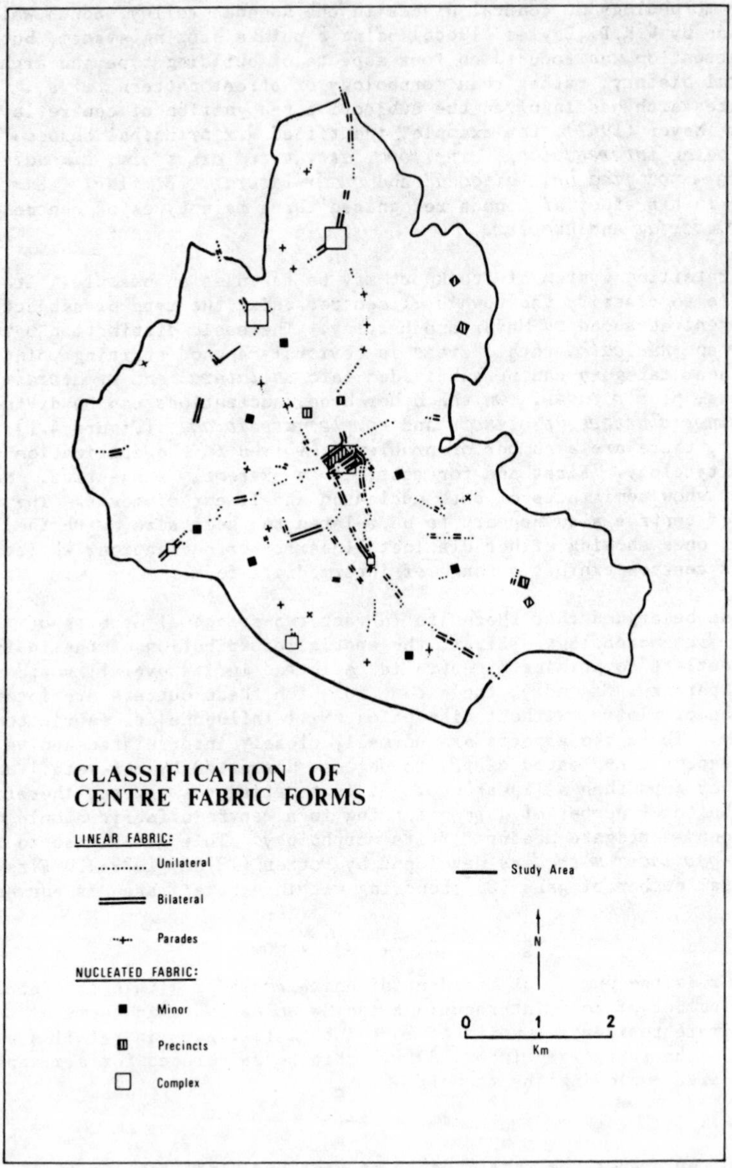

Figure 4.1 A classification of retail area forms in Stockport

a value of 0.08. It must be emphasised that the degree of retail area fabric contiguity may not always reflect shape in a simple fashion. A continuous bilateral retail area as shown in Figure 4.2F would, for example, be considered extremely compact according to this measure. However, this is seldom a difficulty as the more extensive the fabric,

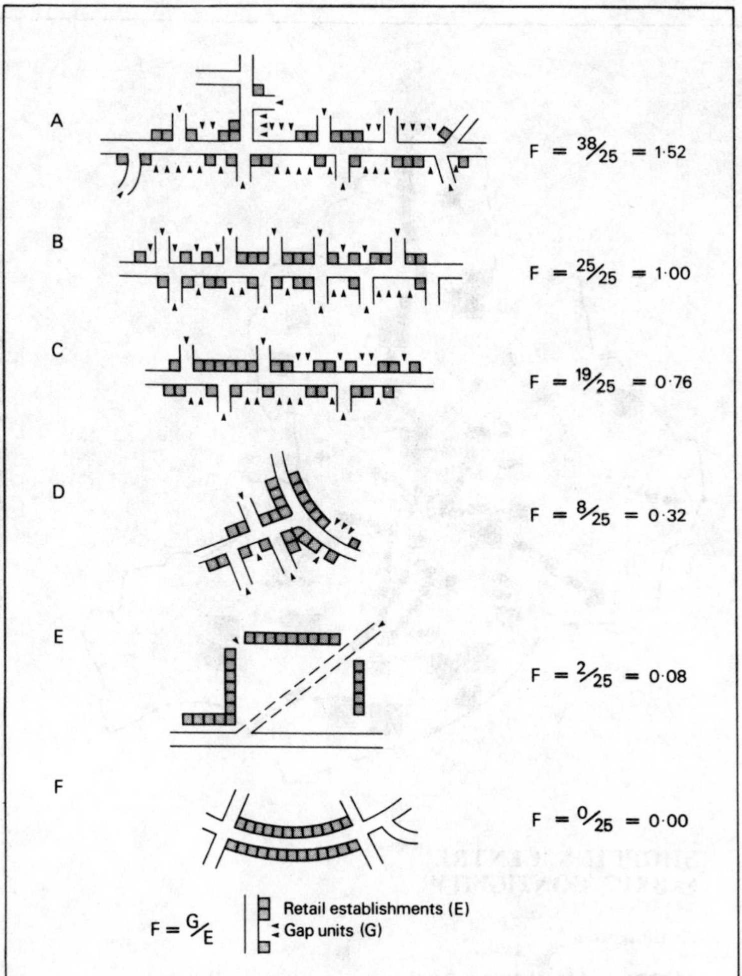

Figure 4.2 Examples of the calculation of fabric-gap index values as a measure of retail area form

generally the greater the number of side roads serving to disrupt it.

The method was used in relation to Stockport, and the index values recorded by the array of centres are shown in Figure 4.3. The overall mean fabric-gap index value for the entire system was 0.54. The range of centre values was from zero to 1.94 (Potter, 1976a). The method clearly makes a quantitative distinction between the major nucleated and ribbon-arterial components of the urban retail system. In the case study, the fabric-gap index values recorded by centres were averaged for centres grouped according to their other salient structural traits (Potter, 1979c). Thereby, it was shown that fabric contiguity tends

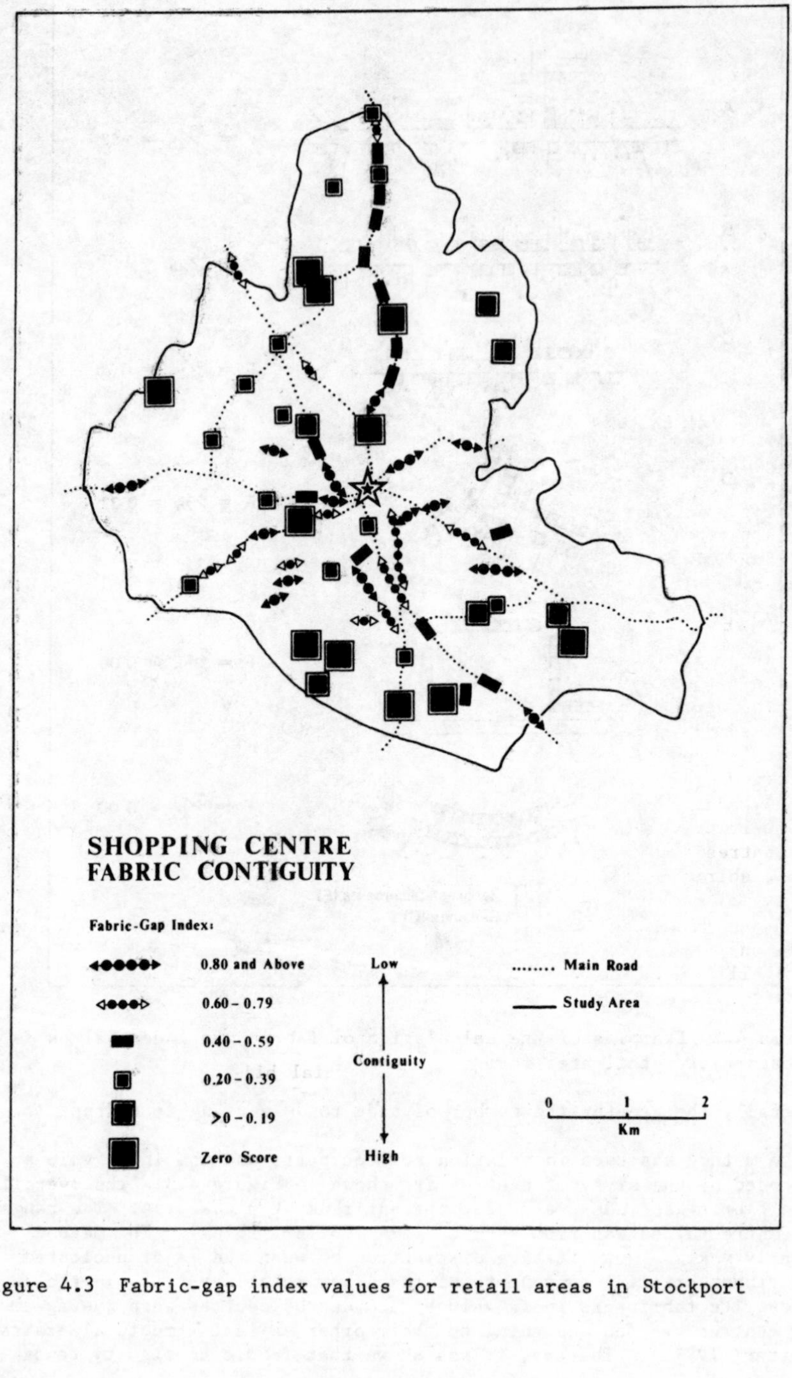

Figure 4.3 Fabric-gap index values for retail areas in Stockport

to increase for centres located with increasing remove from the C.B.D. Contiguity was also demonstrated to decline for retail areas as one descends the retail hierarchy, with the notable exception of the neighbourhood centres. Further, it was shown that the fabric contiguity of retail areas located on the network of main roads was noticeably lower than that of centres situated in the arterial interstices.

Urban retail area morphology is unquestionably an important variable and the fabric-gap index offers a simple method by means of which this attribute can be quantitatively summarised and analysed. The method is not without its problems, however, not the least of which is the meaningful delimitation of retail areas. However, the index should be of some interest and practical relevance to both academics and those involved in commercial planning.

THE QUALITATIVE ATTRIBUTES OF URBAN RETAIL AREAS

Another variable that is frequently cited as being important in the differentiation of urban retailing centres is quality or overall tone, and it is customary for the authors of empirical investigations to make at least some mention of it. Carruthers (1962, p. 9), for instance, states that 'The intangible aspect of quality must be mentioned ... for it inevitably arises in any discussion of shopping centres. Many shoppers would claim that quality of shops is far more important than mere quantity'.

However, retail quality is a nebulous concept which is extremely difficult to define and measure. It seems highly probable that different consumers will employ different sets of criteria in assessing retail areas, so that 'retail quality, like beauty, lies in the eyes of the proverbial beholder' (Potter, 1980a, p. 207). It is tempting, therefore, to suggest that various surrogate measures of quality must be established. For example, Carol (1960) employed the range of brands offered and their prices as variables measuring the importance of urban retailing centres in Zurich. Similarly, the price levels of four standard items, shirts, shoes, wallets and dining sets, were used to denote the quality of retail shops in the central area of Amsterdam by Chatten, Green and Mainwaring (1968). There exists, in fact, an extensive literature on intra-urban and regional variations in retail grocery prices (Campbell and Chisholm, 1970; O'Farrell and Poole, 1972; Rowley, 1972; Parker, 1974a, 1974b, 1979, 1980; Hay and Johnston, 1980).

Another important contribution was made by Berry (1963) in his Chicago case study, where the importance of commercial blight was stressed. Four major types of blight, *economic*, *physical*, *functional* and *frictional* were recognised and associated with intra-urban vacancy rates. McEvoy (1972) also studied vacancy levels in the Manchester conurbation as did Potter (1976a) in relation to Stockport, for they reveal much about physical deterioration and functional obsolescence. Beavon (1970) followed Berry's lead and argued that for classificatory purposes, shops of a particular function that are in poor condition and/or dated should be distinguished from those that are not. This contrast was further developed in an empirical study of shopping centres in Cape Town, by Beavon (1972, 1977) and four grades of shop were recognised. Shops with out-of-date fittings, poor paintwork, cracked glass were designated a B grading. Grade A was thereby defined as being superior in physical appearance to B, whilst Grade C shops showed additional signs of deterioration to B, with respect to plaster and/or woodwork, ceilings and floors. Finally, Grade D was used for cases of complete deterioration. Such gradings were then effectively regarded as separate functional categories. Thus, four types of general dealer and four grades of cafe were identified. This fine division was not apparent for all functional types, so only two groups were noted for chain clothing stores and only one for restaurants. These data were employed as the input for a multivariate study of the retail system, and this will be considered in the next section.

The Berry-type approach is certainly useful but one drawback is its strong emphasis on the physical structure and appearance of shops. Elsewhere, it has been argued that three major components of retail quality can be identified (Potter, 1980a). First there is a strong *commodity* basis with qualitative tone depending on the range, price and reliability of the merchandise offered by retail outlets performing the same basic function. Secondly, it may be suggested that a *service* element contributes to retail quality, including such factors as entrepreneurial skill, spirit and courtesy. Thirdly, there is the *structural* dimension, reflecting the overall design, upkeep and appearance of both individual shops and centres taken as a whole.

An interesting scheme of retail quality grading was, in fact, suggested by Davies (1968) in his study of Leeds, although it has been little used by subsequent workers. In this, six criteria were held to be diagnostic of retail quality levels: shop *appearance*, *window display*, *range of goods*, *type of goods*, *price level* and overall *degree of specialisation*. A high- and a low-income district lying at approximately the same distance from the centre of Leeds were selected as the study areas. For each of the six designated criteria, a rating scale ranging from 1 representing highest to 5 signifying lowest quality was used. Mean quality gradings were derived for each of ten shop types in both areas, employing a points scoring system; 5 points were allocated for each grade 1 shop and 1 point for each grade 5 establishment. Eventually, the grand average quality score of shops serving the predominantly low-income area was found to be 2.06, whilst a markedly higher mean quality value of 3.49 applied to the high-income area shops. Davies (1974) used a similar methodology to grade the 2,542 retail establishments comprising the retail system of Coventry. This time five criteria, *price*, *range*, *window display*, *outside appearance* and *store cleanliness* were used. In the ensuing analysis, total quality scores were aggregated for centres and graphed against shop totals. Those centres visually identified as ribbons seemed to be characterised by relatively low total quality scores.

In an examination of the qualitative standing of the 1,562 outlets comprising the extra-C.B.D. retailing infrastructure of Stockport, it was decided that attention should be focused on the commodity and structural components of retail quality. Further details of the research are given in Potter (1976a, 1980a). It was believed that a modified version of Davies' method would be useful. Further information was therefore obtained regarding the qualitative criteria (Davies, 1972; personal communication), and is shown in Table 4.2. In the Stockport study, the criteria were limited to four and the method involved the subjective appraisal of retail outlet *appearance* (number of advertisements), *window display*, *range of goods* and general *price*

Table 4.2
Possible criteria for the determination of the quality grades of retail outlets

1. *Appearance of retail outlets*	
e.g. *Number of advertisements*	e.g. *Door appearance*
Grade 1 No advertisements	Grade 1 Stylized
2 Few brands names on goods	2 All glass/wood
3 Extensive brand names on goods	3 Glass/thin frames
4 Stickers on window/painted prices	4 Glass/thick frames
5 More advertisement than goods	5 Dirtied/thick frames
2. *Window display*	3. *Range of goods and services*
Grade 1 Spacious and simple	Grade 1 Unusual items offered
2 Intricate/divergent	2 Variety offered
3 Plain but controlled	3 Common brands offered
4 Crammed but controlled	4 Limited range
5 Little apparent control	5 Very limited range
4. *Other criteria*	
e.g. *Price of goods and services*	e.g. *Level of cleanliness*
Grade 1 No prices shown	Grade 1 Excellent upkeep
2 High price level	2 Upkeep good
3 Medium price level	3 Average upkeep
4 Low price level	4 Below average upkeep
5 Very low price level	5 Poor upkeep, dirty

(Based on Davies, 1968; 1972 personal communication. Source: Potter, 1980a)

level in relation to the given anchors of the rating scales (Table 4.3). Each outlet was assessed on the basis of the four criteria using the points scoring system described above (*viz*. grade 1=5 points, grade 5=1 point) and the scores averaged and assigned to the nearest whole number.

Table 4.3
Key criteria employed in determining the quality grades of retail outlets in the Stockport study

1.	Appearance	1	No advertisements
		5	More adverts than goods
2.	Window display	1	Space and simplicity
		5	Little control
3.	Range of goods	1	Unusual
		5	Limited
4.	Price level	1	High
		5	Low

(Source: Potter, 1976a, 1980a)

In the field survey, it proved difficult to assess some 22.15 per cent of the total outlets, a problem previously encountered by Davies (1974) in his study of Coventry. In particular, professional services, travel agents, banks, betting shops, garages, pubs, fried food shops and launderettes were difficult to grade qualitatively.

The quality scores of retail outlets in Stockport were treated in two ways. First, *total quality scores* were summated for the 71 suburban retailing centres and a regression analysis of establishment totals against total quality scores carried out. This suggested the second approach, that of calculating the *mean quality scores* of individual retail areas. As certain retail functional types were excluded from the quality grading, mean quality scores can be calculated in two different ways:-

$$MQE = \frac{TQS}{TE} \qquad (1)$$

$$MQC = \frac{TQS}{TC} \qquad (2)$$

In formula (1) the mean quality score per establishment (MQE) is calculated by dividing the total quality score of a retail area (TQS) by its establishment total (TE). In formula (2), the mean quality score per classified outlet (MQC) is found if the total quality score recorded is divided by the number of outlets that were qualitatively classified (TC). For the majority of retail areas in Stockport there was little difference between quality scores calculated by these two formulas. However, if a retail area contains a large number of non-assessed functions, mainly services, then its mean quality score per classified outlet will tend to be notably higher than its score measured per establishment. This situation is of itself interesting, and it is suggested that both sets of scores should be analysed in parallel, as was done in the Stockport study.

In order to illustrate the method, mean quality scores measured per establishment are shown in Figure 4.4. In Stockport, analysis revealed that retail area mean quality scores increase for retail areas located with increasing distance from the town centre. Furthermore, quality levels were shown to be relatively low for retail areas located on the main arterial roads. Quality levels also displayed a noticeable reduction for successively lower ranks of the retail hierarchy. It was further demonstrated that retail quality levels are closely related to the socio-economic fabric of the town. The spatial configuration of quality levels per establishment depicted in Figure 4.4 is resolved into high, medium and low categories in Figure 4.5A. For comparison, in Figure 4.5B, neighbouring retail areas that record mean quality scores in the same class have been linked, thereby rendering a series of *contiguous retail quality zones*. A decipherable patterning emerges, which may be compared with the socio-economic structure of the town (Figure 4.5C) and the incidence of areas of poor housing (Figure 4.5D). The cross-classification of retail areas by quality levels and socio-economic area type gave a X^2 value of 32.82, significant at p=0.001. As another stage in the analysis, the qualitative properties of the retail areas were related to their morphological attributes. Mean quality scores per establishment were shown to be correlated with retail area fabric-gap index values (r=-0.27, p=0.05). Thus, retail areas with low levels of fabric contiguity generally also exhibit low qualitative attributes. This is an important relationship and the retail areas of Stockport were therefore classified on the basis of their composite quality-fabric

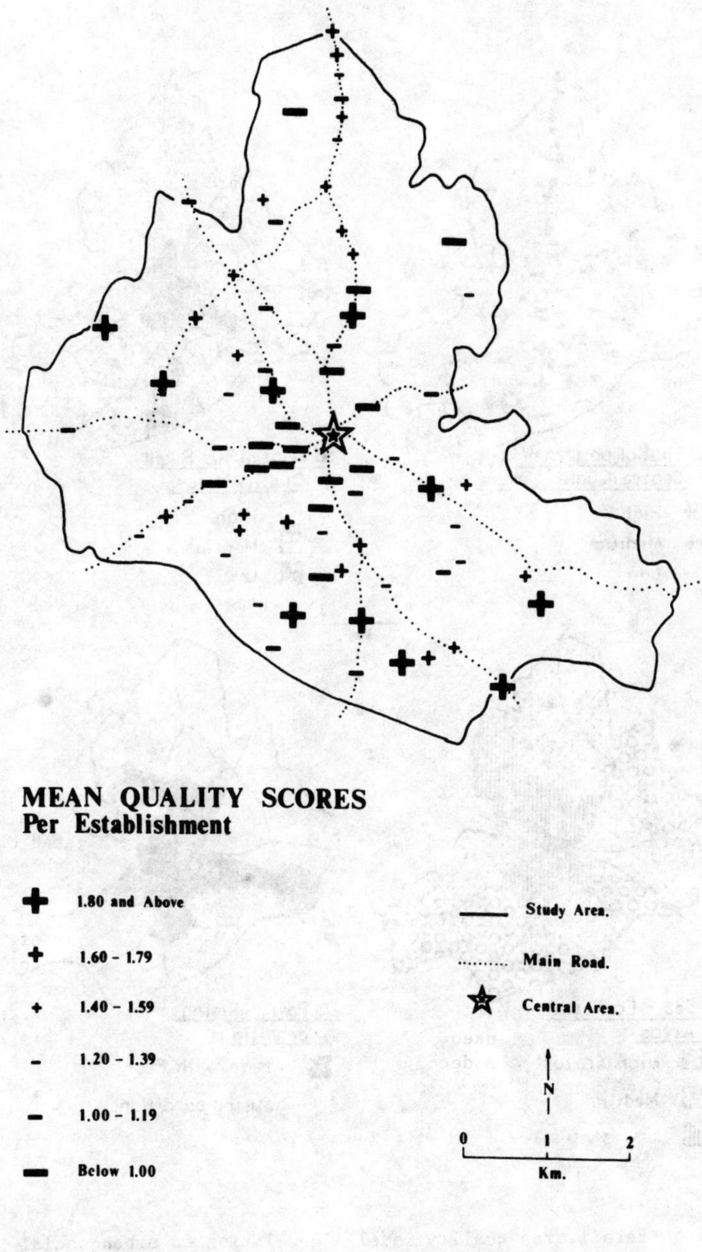

Figure 4.4 Spatial pattern of retail area mean quality scores per establishment (Reproduced by permission from Potter, 1980a)

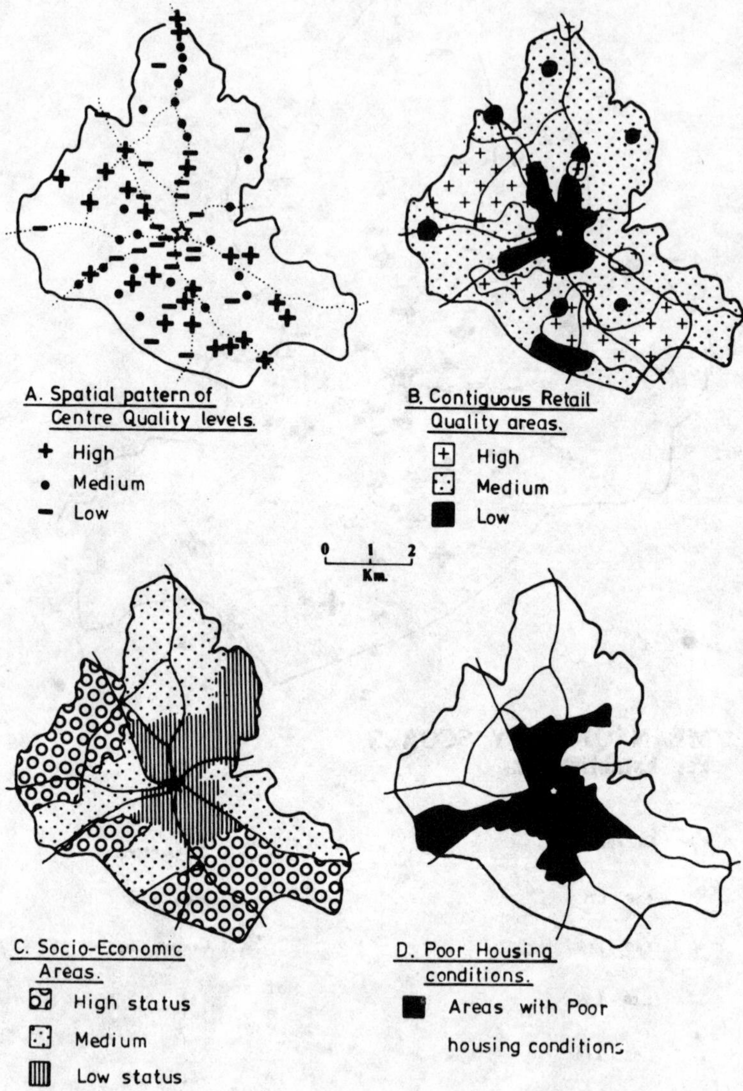

Figure 4.5 Retail area quality levels in relation to urban social patterns (Reproduced by permission from Potter, 1980a)

contiguity attributes (Figure 4.6). The concentration of retail areas with low quality/low fabric contiguity characteristics in the inner urban zone and along the main roads is noticeable. Such qualitative variations allied to configurational differences seem to point to the contrast between nucleated and ribbon components of the urban retail system. This assertion is further evidenced in the next two major sections of this chapter.

Despite its dependence on subjective modes of assessment, the scheme of retail area qualitative grading outlined above is of potential utility to studies of the retailing structure of urban areas. It might well prove to be necessary to develop alternative criteria and methods to measure this important variable in different areas. An interesting case in point here is the effort of Claus, Rothwell and Bottomley (1972) to develop a site rating inventory to determine the quality of low-order retail sites for gasoline service stations. The rating instrument consisted of eleven variables (such as size, neighbourhood) measured on a five point scale from excellent to poor, and was applied to some 110 gasoline service stations. It was argued in conclusion that similar rating instruments could be evolved for other kinds of urban retail outlets.

Retail quality is obviously an important variable in relation to both retail structure and patterns of consumer behaviour. It is likely that establishments of the same functional type but of differing quality will be characterised by different thresholds and ranges (Davies, 1968; Potter, 1980a). Thus, many consumers may be tempted to bypass a nearby offering of a good because of the low qualitative standing of the establishment. Such behaviour has been empirically verified by Schiller (1972) when he showed that centres that have a large number of high-quality restaurants and hotels and those of a pleasant appearance tend to attract a disproportionate number of high income consumers. Such conclusions exemplify why the nearest centre hypothesis is a simplified abstraction at the intra-urban scale.

THE FUNCTIONAL DIMENSION

The functional structure of intra-urban retailing centres is naturally of great significance, as exemplified earlier in this and the previous chapter. A simple means of examining functional disposition in any urban area is to calculate the proportion of total outlets falling into different functional categories for its array of retail centres, as was done in the Stockport case study (see Figure 3.14). However, the starting point for a more detailed analysis of retail functions in the town was the matrix of frequencies of occurrence of some 69 functional types in the 71 centres (Figure 3.6). By means of a simple analysis, incremental sets of functions and non-incremental functional types were identified (see Figures 3.12 and 3.13). These it was argued pointed to nucleated-hierarchical and ribbon-arterial retail area types respectively within the system.

A more detailed way of looking at the functional realm is to apply multivariate statistical methods to functional data sets, as described earlier as a technique of retail area classification. A good example of this kind of analysis is Davies' (1971, 1974) work in Coventry. The analysis was based on a matrix of the frequency of occurrence of 64 functions in some 64 centres. As the principal components initially

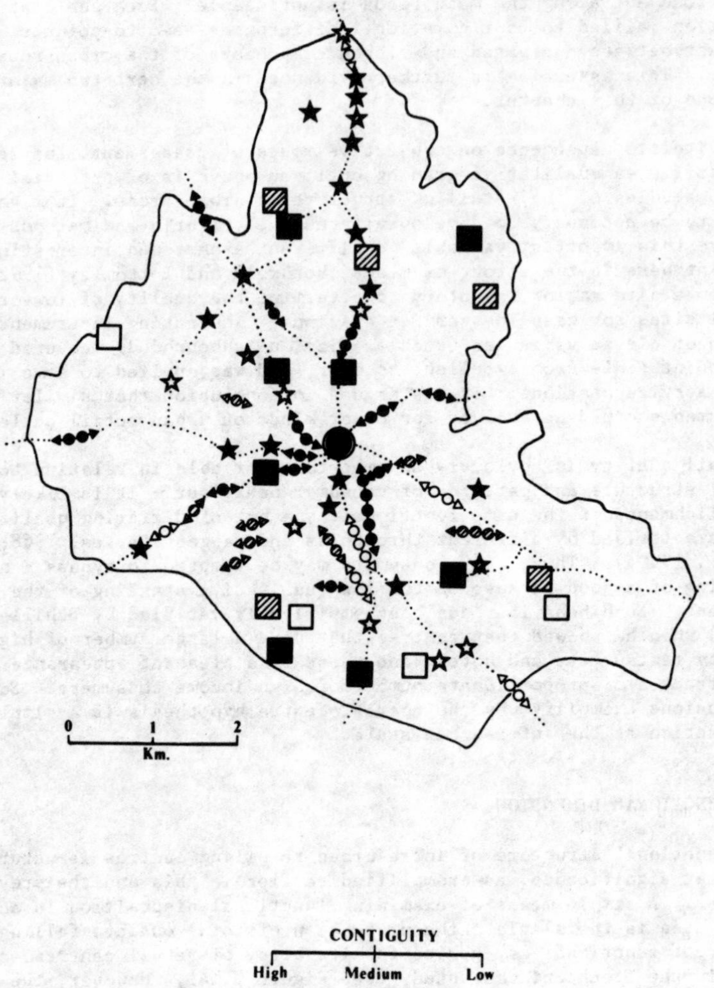

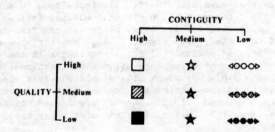

Figure 4.6 Classification of retail areas in Stockport according to their composite quality/fabric contiguity characteristics (Reproduced by permission from Potter, 1980a)

extracted proved difficult to interpret, they were rotated. Rotated Factor I was described as a *convenience group* and Factor II as a set of *uncommonly occurring functions*. Factor III was interpreted as a *more specialised* dimension, Factor IV as a *basic durable goods* set and Factor V a *ribbon-type* functional component. The scores of the centres on these components were not mapped, but were employed with the findings of other analyses to suggest the existence of nucleations and ribbons. Although it was argued that these functional differences were not as clear cut as those occurring in American cities, there was clearly the implication that the Berry threefold typology is of some applicability.

Another interesting example is provided by the work of Beavon (1972) in Cape Town, referred to in the previous section on retail quality. For this analysis, a total of 143 centres with six or more shops were identified and some 142 business categories recognised. The latter consisted of 53 basic retail functions subdivided by gradings of physical blight. Associations within the 142x143 data matrix were measured by a modulated relative homogeneity function (see Beavon, 1970, 1972, 1977 for details of the method). Beavon argued that the basic analysis showed little evidence of a hierarchical structure. To test whether this was the outcome of the occurrence of differential blight, the analysis returned to the original 53x143 functional matrix. It was then concluded that 'a greater amount of structure is discernible' (Beavon, 1972, p. 65) and that 'From the structure of the dendrogram it would appear that at least some basis for hierarchical grouping has been provided through a reduction in the number of property rows of the data matrix' (Beavon, 1972, p. 66). These findings are of significance for they suggest that Beavon's staunch argument that strict intra-urban hierarchies do not occur is based on the recognition of qualitative differences between centres rather than their size. Naturally, these variations would render a less stepped retail pattern, as has been shown in Chapters 2 and 3 of the present work. It seems inappropriate, therefore, that Beavon should have used this empirical evidence to argue the case for an explicitly Löschian intra-urban theory of tertiary location. Further, such a framework appears to accord very poorly indeed with the actual map of the distribution of retail centres in Cape Town presented by Beavon (1972, Figure 5, p. 62), which shows a preponderance of linear and string street developments. It is a pity that Beavon nowhere provides details of the absolute size of the centres with which he is dealing. However, the actual methodology employed by Beavon, constituting a multivariate analysis of functional and qualitative data is of considerable interest and potential utility to workers in the field.

A multivariate analysis of retail functional structure was also carried out as a part of the Stockport case study (see Potter, 1976a, 1981b). The 69x71 functional matrix was first intercorrelated between the functions in an R-mode analysis. This yielded a matrix of 2,346 correlation coefficients summarising the similarity of functions within the system, which was then subjected to principal components analysis (Potter, 1981b). The first ten components explained 93 per cent of the total functional variance, whilst the first two alone were sufficient to account for nearly 51 per cent. The sets of functions loading most significantly upon each component were considered and it was possible to interpret their nature and label them, as shown in Table 4.4. The first component appeared to be a general dimension relating to a *convenience-frequent needs* functional set. Component II brought together a group of *furniture and motor functions* in conjunction with other

Table 4.4
Structure of the eight leading principal components of functional variability

Principal component	Label	Percentage of total variance
I	Convenience-frequent needs	42.22
II	Furniture and motor	8.58
III	Motor-specialised	7.45
IV	Professional services, medical, furnishing	6.46
V	Leisure and motor	4.39
VI	Recreational	3.33
VII	Household amenity	2.81
VIII	Building supplies	2.44

specialist establishments and high vacancy rates. These functional subcomponents seemed to affirm the existence of a Berry-type functional separation, especially when the scores of the centres on the components were mapped. Component I emphasised a size or hierarchical pattern of scores which accorded with its functional nature. Component II, on the other hand, revealed high scores in the inner urban areas and on the main arterial routes. The third component, relating to *motor/specialised* functions also prescribed an inner/outer town pattern, whilst Component IV pinpointed five main concentrations of *professional and medical service* establishments.

As a further stage in the research, cluster analysis was applied to the raw functional data. At the two group level, a clear distinction was revealed between inner town and arterial centres on the one hand, and suburban centres on the other. In fact, the results of the cluster analysis can be broadly replicated by the alternative multivariate research design known as a Q-mode analysis, where correlations are computed between centres themselves as a direct measure of their functional similarity (see Potter, 1976a, 1978). Principal components analysis can then be applied, and in the case of Stockport, the eight leading principal components accounted for 66 per cent of the original variability between centres. The first two Q-components accounted for a little over 44 per cent of this total.

The loadings of the 71 retail areas on these two Q-components are shown in Figure 4.7. Five main groups of retail centres were recognised on the basis of these. The spatial distribution of centres classified in this manner is depicted in Figure 4.8. Group 1 centres are typical of the suburban areas and the upper ranks of the hierarchy are well represented. The centres comprising Group 2 are generally smaller suburban ones. These two groups include those centres shown to have strong convenience-frequent needs functional profiles by the R-mode analysis. The fourth and fifth groups in contrast are predominantly composed of arterial and/or inner town located centres, and taken together are those which have distinctive specialised functional profiles. Finally, Group 3 centres represented an intermediate set, although the majority showed a strong arterial orientation. It appeared, therefore,

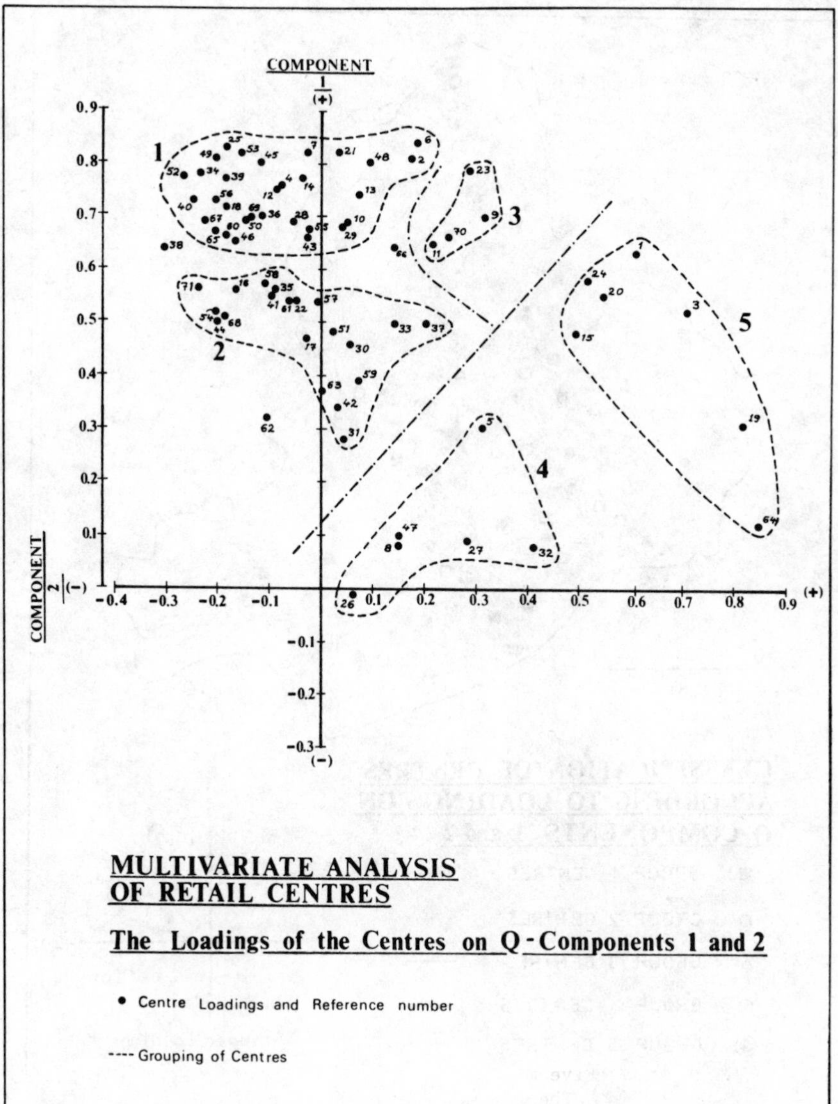

Figure 4.7 The loadings of the retail centres of Stockport on Q-components 1 and 2

that the functional differences that existed between centres in Stockport corresponded to some considerable degree with the type of structuring envisaged in the Berry typology.

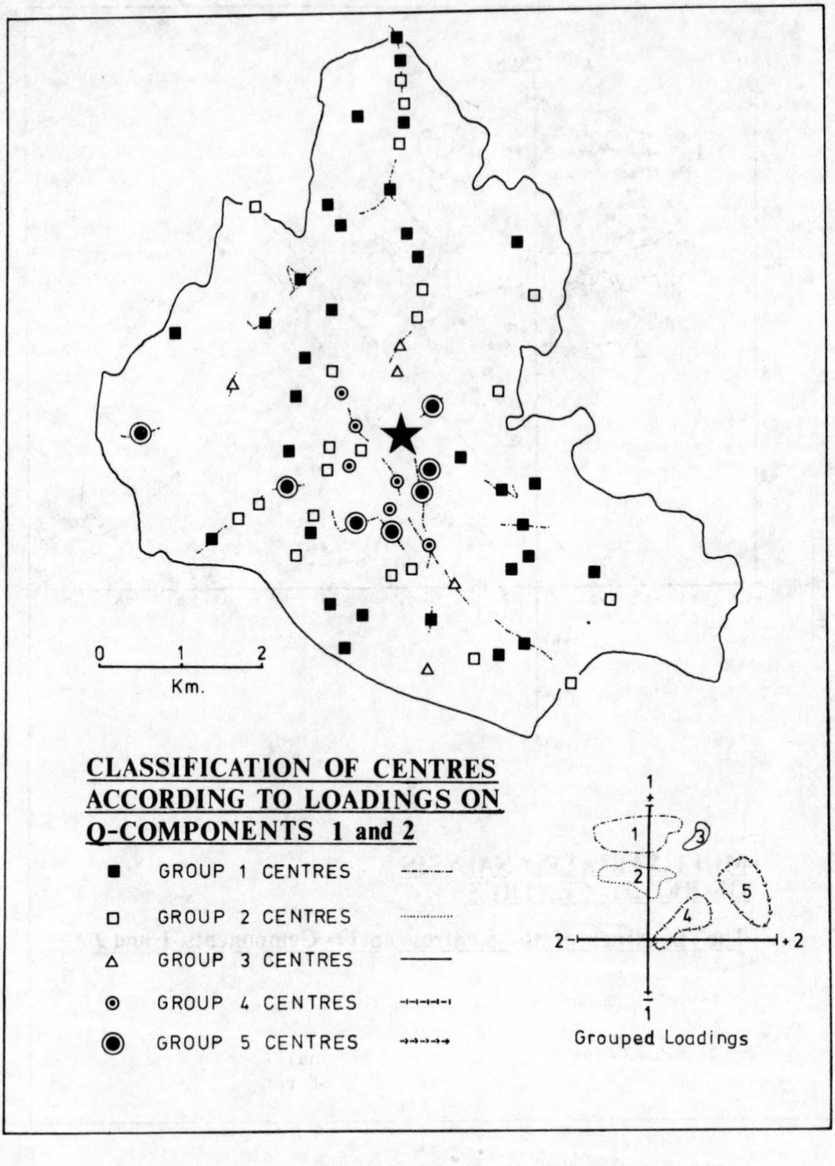

Figure 4.8 The spatial pattern of retail area loadings on Q-components 1 and 2

CORRELATES OF URBAN RETAIL STRUCTURE

Preceding sections of this chapter have examined various retail area properties and through literature reviews and the evidence of case studies, it has been intimated that many of these are closely interrelated. Thus, for instance, it was suggested that the morphology of retail areas in Stockport was related to their quality levels, and perhaps to their functions too. It is surprising, however, that the precise nature of these correlates of urban retailing structure has seldom been investigated in any systematic manner.

This shortcoming has partially been redressed by the work of Potter (1976a, 1981a), who endeavoured to synthesise the relationships existing between such key retail area characteristics for the Stockport system. The two Q-components introduced and mapped in the last section of this chapter were used as a basis for summarising retail area functional structure. Centres with a basically hierarchical functional structure tended to record high loadings on Q-component 1 and low loadings on the second one, whilst specialised functional centres exhibited a reverse pattern of loadings. A statistical analysis was first carried out. The loadings of the retail areas on the first two Q-components were correlated and shown to be negatively associated (r=-0.40, p< 0.01). Other quantifiable retail area attributes were then correlated with their loadings on Q-component 1. Thereby, it was indicated that the hierarchic centres typically have high quality levels but low levels of fabric discontiguity. In contrast, those centres conforming with the second specialised dimension were generally of low qualitative standing and showed high levels of fabric disruption.

These findings were followed up by a graphical analysis, using the technique of *multivariate ordination*. On the functional ordination diagram (see Figure 4.7), as explained previously, hierarchical functional retail areas are located toward the top left, whilst specialised ones appear toward its lower right. Other known differeneces between the array of retail areas were then superimposed on the ordination graph. First, retail area fabric form was considered (Figure 4.9A) and the clustering of nucleated centres toward the hierarchic functional end of the ordination graph is notable, as is the placement of linear shaped centres at the specialised end of the graph. Further, retail areas with high degrees of fabric contiguity were all found to be hierarchic, whilst centres tended to show increasing fabric discontiguity toward the specialised end of the functional spectrum (Figure 4.9B). The relatively high qualitative standing of hierarchic retail areas is also clearly apparent (Figures 4.9C and D). The relationship between the functional disposition and spatial location of centres is depicted in Figure 4.10A, and the virtual total concentration of the main suburban retail areas (2-3 km. from the town centre) at the hierarchic end of the ordination diagram is clearly revealed. The inner urban placement of centres at the specialised end of the functional space is also well demonstrated. When the size differentiation of retail areas is juxtaposed with their multivariate ordination (Figure 4.10B), then within both the hierarchic and specialised retail groups, centre size appears to be positively related to loadings on both functional axes. Further analysis indicated that specialised retail areas tend to have developed prior to 1919 and are situated in the lower socio-economic areas (Figures 4.10C and D). In contrast, hierarchic centres tend to be those developed after 1919 and generally serve the high to medium status districts of the town.

The research thereby showed that classification of the elements of the urban retailing system on multivariate functional grounds is also

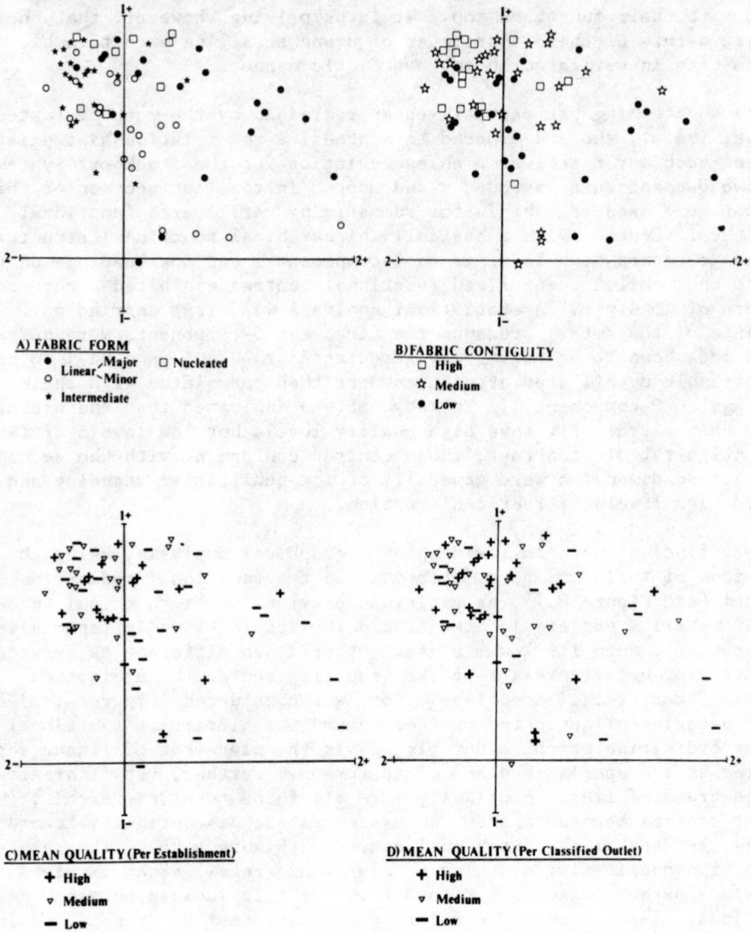

Figure 4.9 The morphological and qualitative attributes of retail areas in relation to their functional ordination (Reproduced by permission from Potter, 1981a)

meaningful when viewed in terms of the location, morphology, contiguity, quality, size, chronological and socio-economic traits of retail areas. In Figure 4.11, the joint quality-fabric contiguity classification of retail centres in Stockport (see also Figure 4.6) is superimposed on the functional ordination graph. The composite low qualitative and fabric contiguity features of the specialised retail centres are highlighted in this manner. These findings tend to suggest the broad efficacy of the Berry threefold typology (Potter, 1981a).

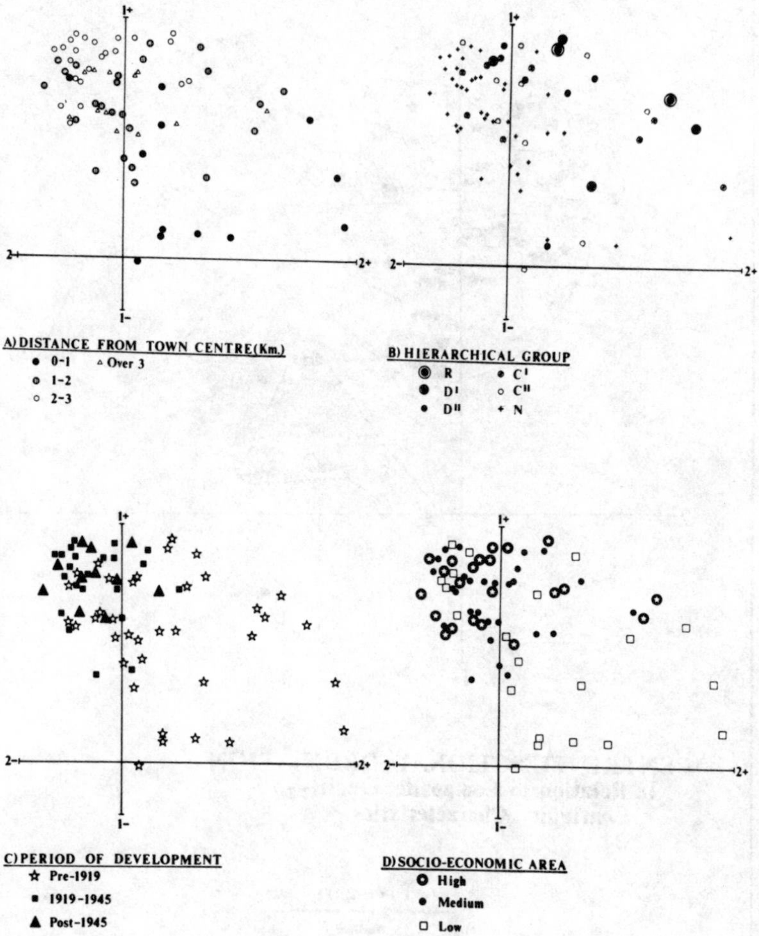

Figure 4.10 The general attributes of retail areas in relation to their functional ordination (Reproduced by permission from Potter, 1981a)

It seemed worthwhile to employ these truly multivariate results to classify retail centres in Stockport (Potter, 1976a). First, mean quality scores and fabric-gap index values were calculated for the five identified retail ordination groups (as shown in Figures 4.7 and 4.8). The findings are shown in Table 4.5. Collectively, the specialised centre groups (numbers 3, 4 and 5) record a mean quality score per establishment of 1.12, as opposed to 1.40 for the hierarchic sets (1 and 2). Levels of fabric disruption tend to rise through the ordination sequence. The mean fabric-gap index value for specialised centres was 0.74 and 0.48 for hierarchic retail areas.

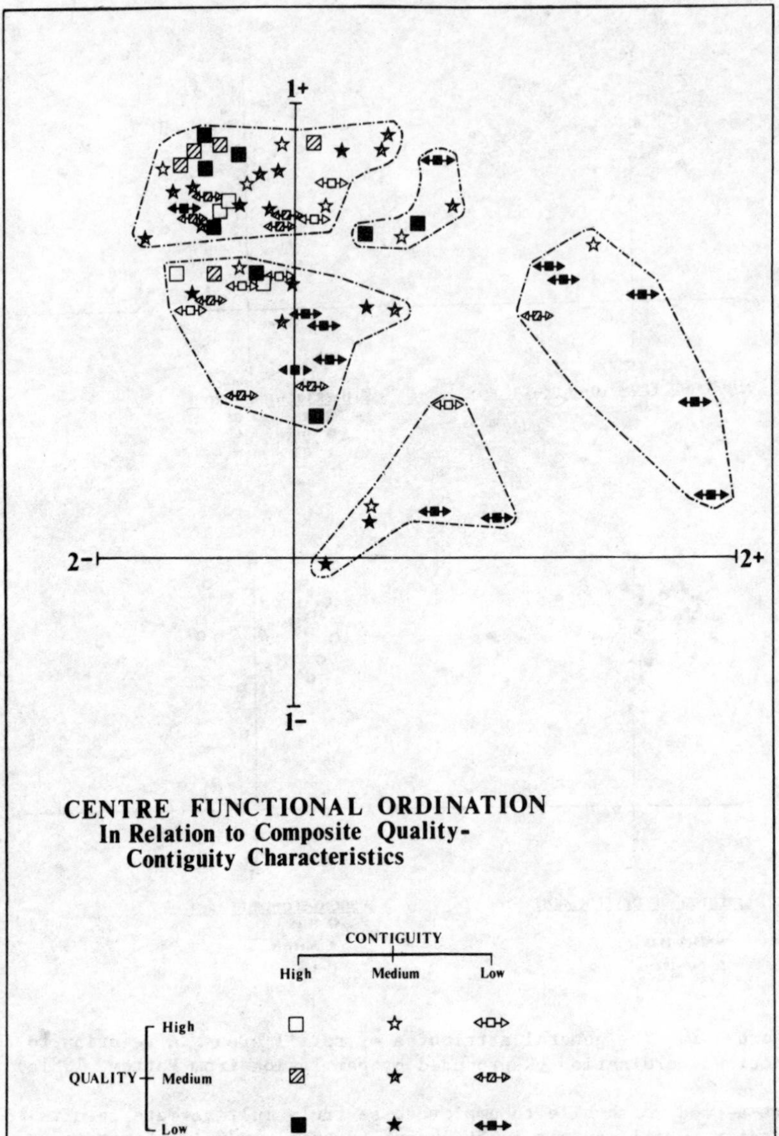

Figure 4.11 The composite quality-fabric contiguity attributes of retail areas in relation to their functional ordination

The specialised centres, showing linear alignments, discontiguity of fabric and low qualitative tone can thus be regarded as *urban arterial ribbons*. In all, 18 such areas were identified and their scores on the original 69 retail functional variables reconsidered. Each of them conformed with the milieu of motor, professional, furniture and building functions, in conjunction with high vacancy rates, as highlighted by the principal components analysis. Whilst some showed a particular specialism, others exhibited a dual specialism amongst these functions. They were therefore sub-divided into specialised and non-specialised urban arterial ribbons. Further, the entire set was disaggregated into three size orders, corresponding with the district (I), community (II) and neighbourhood (III) size levels. This left a residue of six centres which although having been identified as conforming with the specialised principal components, revealed uncharacteristically high contiguity and/or quality levels. Significantly, five of these six centres were in the intermediate ordination group 3. These retail areas were finally assigned to the hierarchic body of centres, but their peripheral fabric areas were classified as *specialised linear extensions*.

Table 4.5

Mean quality and fabric-gap index values for centres in Stockport classified by functional ordination group

Ordination group	Mean quality per establishment	Mean quality per classified outlet	Mean fabric-gap index value
1	1.46	1.72	0.41
2	1.30	1.56	0.58
3	1.20	1.68	0.44
4	1.12	1.77	0.75
5	1.05	1.38	0.94

The remaining centres were referred to as *hierarchic nucleations* and constituted a size-ordered sequence of two regional, six district, two community and 39 neighbourhood centres. The hierarchy of nucleations including the central area and isolated stores gave a 1, 3, 9, 21, 60, 307 numerical sequence of market areas at each level, comparing with the 1, 3, 9, 27, 81, 243, k=3 marketing sequence.

The unravelling of the complex interrelations underlying this classification is probably of greater significance than the classification itself, and the technique of multivariate ordination is recommended for future studies of retailing structure. The mean quality and fabric-gap index values for the final retail area groups in Stockport are shown in Table 4.6. These statistics indicate the magnitude of the disparity existing between the quality and fabric contiguity levels of the two principal divisions of the urban retailing system. The overall mean quality score per establishment of all hierarchic centres was 1.39, and 1.03 for the arterial ribbons. Equivalent statistics measured per classified outlet were 1.66 and 1.53 respectively. The mean fabric-gap index value for all arterial ribbons was as high as 0.90. As noted, certain hierarchic centres showed linear fabric extensions, and their mean fabric-gap index value was 0.85. The main hierarchic centres recorded an index value as low as 0.23.

Table 4.6
Mean quality and fabric-gap index values for the final classification of retail areas in Stockport

Centre group	Mean quality per establishment	Mean quality per classified outlet	Mean fabric-gap index
HIERARCHIC			
Regional	1.58	1.86	0.42
District	1.62	2.02	0.36
Community	1.47	1.80	0.58
Neighbourhood	1.31	1.56	0.46
ARTERIAL			
I	1.21	1.92	0.56
II	0.95	1.38	1.10
III	1.02	1.45	0.82

The spatial representation of this final classification is shown in Figure 4.12, and the classificatory scheme is diagrammatically depicted at the foot of the map. To a considerable degree, this final classification corresponds to the type of structuring suggested to exist in American urban areas by Berry. Certainly, the fundamental distinction appears to be between a set of ribbons which string-out along the main arterial routes in response to enhanced levels of accessibility and a group of nucleated centres. It has to be stressed, however, that it is not suggested that the types of functional conformations envisaged in the Berry typology are directly replicated in British cities. Clearly, where they do exist they are smaller, less clearly developed and have less distinctive functional characteristics.

One further study of such relationships was conducted by Davies (1974) when he recognised distinctive nucleated and ribbon components of the retailing system of Coventry. This work has already been referred to several times in this chapter. A map plot of retail land uses showed the linear nature of many retail conformations. Then, total quality points scores were graphed against centre size, and as discussed earlier, ribbons were found to have lower overall quality scores. Finally, functional differences amongst the centres were investigated by principal components and cluster analyses. Despite arguing that 'It is to be expected perhaps that a classification based on purely functional variations will not be easily equated with one based much more on differences in form' (Davies, 1974, p. 108), a subjective classification on the basis of quality, form and function was attempted. The outcome, shown in Figure 4.13 reveals a set of nucleated shopping centres made up of three levels outside the C.B.D. and conforming broadly with the outer city regions. Further, a set of four size levels of arterial ribbons was identified, occurring mainly in the older, inner urban districts. Finally, a large number of retail areas were shown to have mixed nucleated/ribbon characteristics, especially those located to the north and east of the town centre (Figure 4.13).

THE RETAIL STRUCTURE OF THE C.B.D.

Before attempting to summarise the extensive body of empirical research

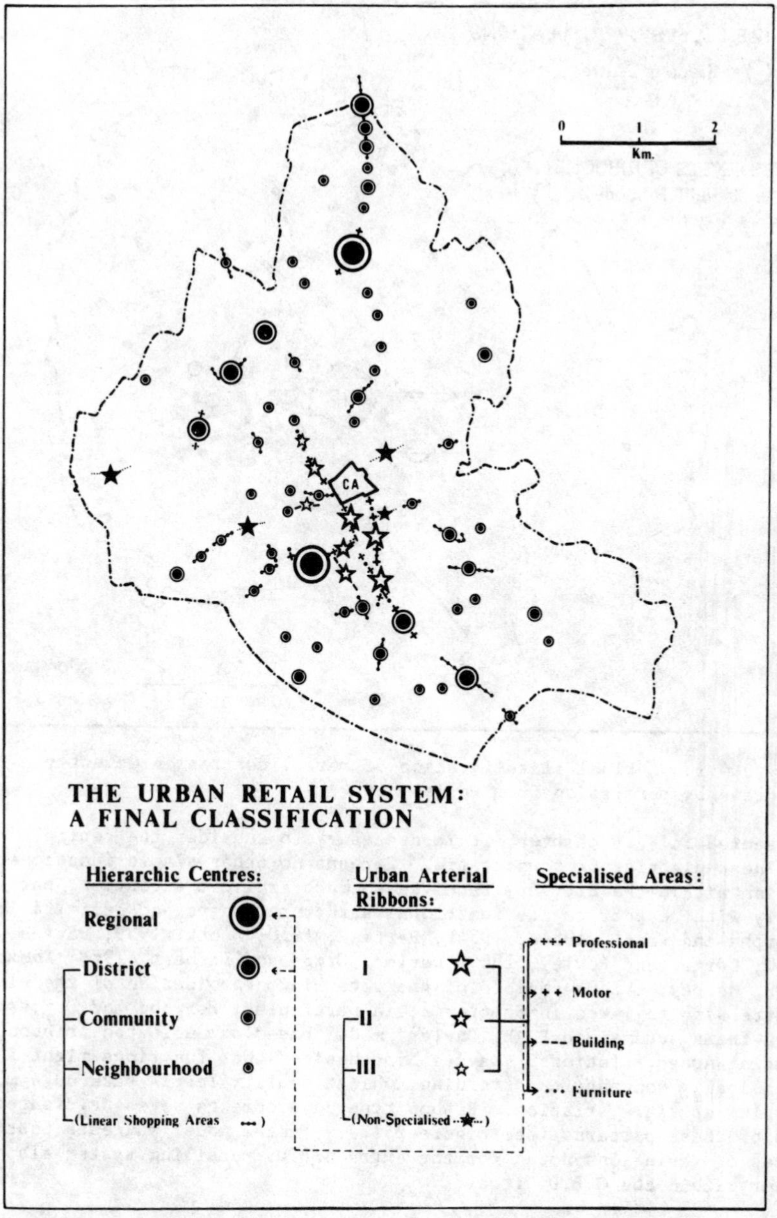

Figure 4.12 A final classification of the urban retailing system of Stockport (Reproduced by permission from Potter, 1978)

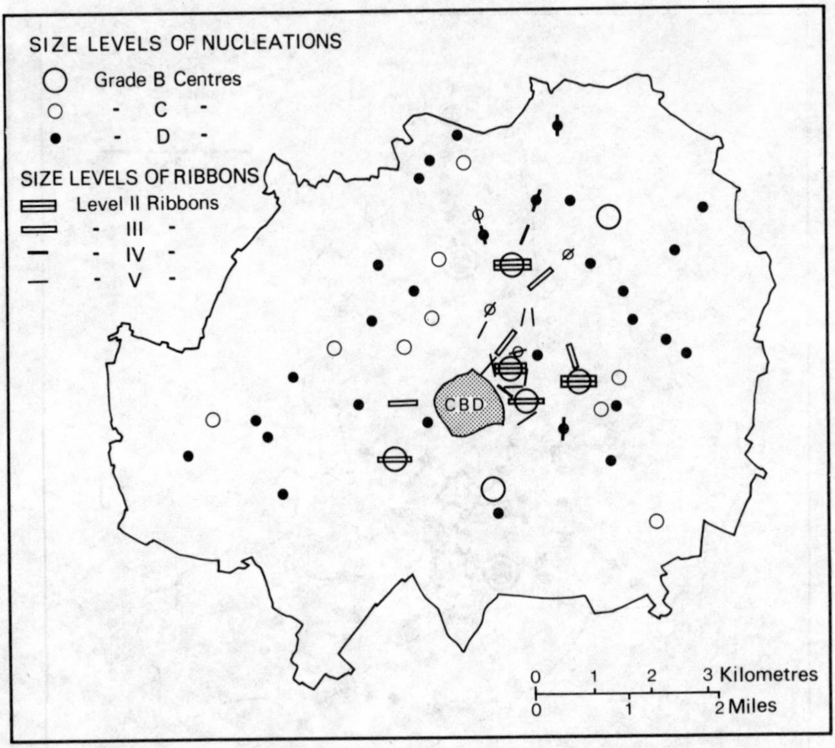

Figure 4.13 A final classification of retail centres in Coventry (Redrawn by permission from Davies, 1974)

presented in this chapter, it is necessary to consider the central business district or town centre. Perhaps no other single functional region within the city has received so much explicit attention, particularly with respect to its functional structure, shape and delimitation (Murphy and Vance, 1954a, 1954b; Hartman, 1950; Scott, 1959; Davies, 1960; Carter and Rowley, 1966; Davies, Giggs and Herbert, 1968; Thomas, 1972; Murphy, 1972). Models of the retailing organisation of the city centre were reviewed in Chapter 2, in particular, Horwood and Boyce's core-frame scheme and R. L. Davies' model based on nucleated, ribbon and special area variations. Davies hypothesised that functions might show a basically concentric patterning, whilst quality levels take on a more complex spatial variation. Ribbon type developments were anticipated on top of these patterns (see Figure 2.12). Such a model suggests that the types of variations noted for the extra C.B.D. retailing system also occur within the C.B.D. itself.

Research has, in fact, shown that this generalisation holds up well to empirical testing. The existence of functional clusters and specialised areas has been noted by Horwood and Boyce (1959), Diamond (1962) and Carter and Rowley (1966) amongst others. Similarly, Chatten, Green and Mainwaring (1968) identified distinct quality variations in the central area of Amsterdam. With regard to morphology, we would expect the core area to be compact and for ribbons to emanate from the periphery, reflecting major growth phases along principal arterials (Davies and Bennison, 1978).

More detailed evidence is supplied by Davies' comprehensive empirical studies of C.B.D. retail structure in Coventry and Newcastle. In the study of Coventry, using centres of gravity and standard distances, Davies (1972b), observed that functions such as apparel and shoes, leisure services, ladies wear and furniture were highly concentrated. Shops of low quality were found to be conspicuously absent from the retailing core, and map evidence suggests that they occur mainly on principal routes in the outer part of the C.B.D. Medium quality shops were typical of the central precinct area catering for a mass market clientele. It was concluded that the high quality shops showed the greatest degree of clustering being highly focused on the precinct, but also showing embryonic clusters on the perimeter of the centre. There is the overall suggestion, therefore, that functions, quality, morphology, location and accessibility are closely interrelated. This relationship was investigated further in a methodologically interesting study of Newcastle undertaken by Davies and Bennison (1978). The individual shopping street was taken as the basic unit of analysis. Twelve variables were selected, reflecting the functional structure, size, ownership patterns, quality and degree of non-retail interruption (retail frontage as a percentage of total street frontage) of the 34 streets identified. Significantly, these variables selected at the C.B.D. street level correspond quite closely with those stressed earlier in this chapter as being of prime importance to studies of the suburban retail system. Cluster analysis was then used and five main groups of streets identified. The five principal C.B.D. shopping streets were grouped together in one set. Eleven centres with either medieval origins or having developed as 19th century ribbons came together as another. Eight adjunct shopping streets were collected together, their outer sections all being given over to non-retail land uses. Two streets stood out as being highly specialised, whilst eight constituted a group of back streets or alleys.

A final illustrative example is drawn from the author's work in Stockport, wherein the street was also taken as the basis of analysis (Potter, 1976a). In all, 484 retail outlets were surveyed, and the entire classificatory array of 68 functions were represented within some 531 functional outlets. The shops are located in seven reasonably distinct assemblages as a result of an historical legacy of fragmentation of the central area (Figure 4.14). The planned Merseyway shopping precinct, opened in 1968, forms the functional heart if not the geometric centre of the district. It is flanked by the Prince's Street shopping area to the north, and the Chestergate/Great Underbank shopping street to its south. St. Petersgate constitutes a fourth major assemblage running to the south of and parallel with Chestergate. The remaining streets, those of Little Underbank, Churchgate/Market Place and Lower Hillgate take the form of linear or ribbon assemblages running southward from the core area.

The use of grid squares or concentric zones as the units of analysis in Stockport would have been inappropriate due to the degree of fabric separation. Although the seven streets do not constitute entirely separate entities, they are sufficiently distinct to allow their employment as units of analysis. In Tables 4.7 and 4.8, the seven sub-areas

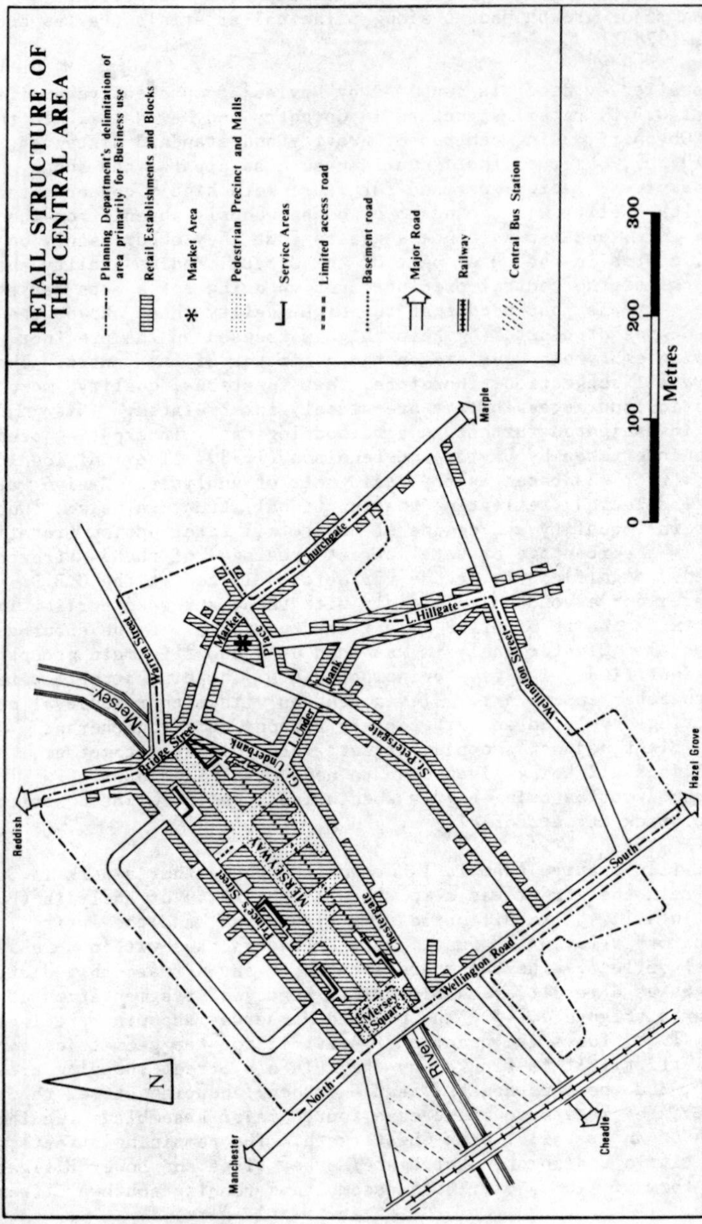

Figure 4.14 The retail structure of the central area of Stockport

Table 4.7
Functional characteristics of the principal shopping streets of the central area of Stockport

Street	Number of establishments	Percentage of total functional outlets		
		Clothing	Household	Professional Service
Merseyway	124	29.78	19.85	2.29
Prince's Street	101	28.07	21.93	1.75
Chestergate/ Great Underbank	67	15.28	18.06	15.28
Little Underbank	32	36.86	13.18	2.63
Market Place/ Churchgate	38	17.79	20.00	2.22
St. Petersgate	64	16.53	13.70	26.02
Lower Hillgate	58	9.69	35.27	2.74
Total	484	22.54	20.87	7.14

Table 4.8
Mean quality and fabric-gap index values for the principal shopping streets of the C.B.D. of Stockport

Street	Mean quality per establishment	Mean quality per classified outlet	Mean fabric-gap index value
Merseyway	3.08	3.44	0.05
Prince's Street	2.26	2.53	0.11
Chestergate/ Great Underbank	1.67	2.55	0.12
Little Underbank	2.47	2.82	0.06
Market Place/ Churchgate	1.08	1.46	0.24
St. Petersgate	1.44	2.42	0.28
Lower Hillgate	1.59	1.84	0.40

are listed in the same order, that is according to their increasing distance of location from Merseyway. Within the central area, it was clear that clothing functions are relatively more profuse in those streets regarded as constituting the core, such as Merseyway, Prince's Street and Little Underbank (Table 4.7). In contrast, within the peripheral shopping streets, clothing outlets formed a much lower proportion of total functional outlets. Household and furnishing group functions were well represented in the peripheral ribbon assemblage of Lower Hillgate. Professional service activities tend to be concentrated in the Chestergate/Great Underbank area and St. Petersgate. These functional variations suggest the existence of a broad core-frame or concentric variation (Table 4.7).

The qualitative standing of the outlets in the central area was also assessed, and affirmed the core-periphery distinction (Table 4.8). Merseyway stands as the qualitative pinnacle, whilst the quality of the immediately adjacent streets is higher than that of the outer ones. Finally, the fabric-gap index value was derived for the entire central area, rendering a value of 0.16, showing that it is the most contiguous component of the entire retail hierarchy. The variation in contiguity levels amongst the constituent divisions of the central area shows the Merseyway precinct to be the most contiguous, followed by the three main shopping streets which flank it. The remaining peripheral assemblages show increasingly greater degrees of fabric disruption (Table 4.8).

The empirical evidence has shown the essential correspondence existing between location, morphology, quality and functional status within the C.B.D. Such complex associations mirror those occurring within the urban retailing system at large, and show the apposite nature of the types of variations first envisaged by Berry and later embodied in the Davies model. There is much temporal and spatial work that remains to be completed on central area retail structure and Rowley and Shepherd (1976) have shown how the fire insurance and shopping centre plans published by C.E. Goad Ltd. since 1885 and 1967 respectively, can be used in such analyses.

HISTORICAL ASPECTS OF DYNAMIC CHANGE AND RETAIL STRUCTURE

Although it has been demonstrated that the structural organisation of urban retailing has been a topic of longstanding concern both in relation to empirical studies and theory formulation, aspects of long-term dynamic change have been scantily treated. This is surprising, for the Victorian city, for example, was the forum for profound changes in the structure of retailing (Shaw and Wild, 1979; Jones, 1979; Mitchell, 1981). Much more attention has been given to short-term and recent changes and their ramifications, via impact studies. This neglect is further manifest in theories and models, few of which incorporate facets of temporal change and adjustment, although some efforts have latterly been made in this direction (White, 1974, 1977; Parr, 1980a, 1980b, 1981), whilst Schiller (1981) has outlined a model showing how retail branches might diffuse through a retail system over time. Often it is suggested that the Löschian system is most appropriate for dealing with population growth and retail change as it initially envisages the spread of low order market areas, whilst the Christaller system starts with the establishment of the largest centres. However, this distinction is largely spurious and the development of suburban centres can be envisaged within a Christallerian-type pattern (Thomas, 1976). Johnston (1980) has also presented a developmental approach to urban retail patterns. It is noted that retailing initially operated from temporary premises at periodic intervals, but that later, permanent shops developed around the market focus. With population growth and urban expansion there is both the duplication of existing shop types and the introduction of a new range of commodities. New shopkeepers can follow one of two locational strategies, either trying for a spatial monopoly or seeking as large a share of the total market as possible by siting near to competitors. The latter strategy can be combined with the former if the aim is to compete only for a portion of the total market, which can be accomplished by locating in district shopping centres.

In broadening the discussion, Simmons' (1964) simple graphical model of the forces leading to retail change is worthy of note. The direct forces of change were identified as population and income, influencing the assortment of business types and their pattern of grouping into business conformations. The indirect forces of income levels, technology and the growth of the urban system were regarded as affecting the direct forces via changes in mobility, consumer preferences, cost structures and economies of scale. This formulation stresses the key relation that exists between developments in transport and mobility on the one hand, and consumer behaviour and retail structure on the other. This important link is illustrated historically in terms of changing transport modes and patterns of urban form (Mayer, 1969; Herbert, 1976; Daniels and Warnes, 1980). Herbert (1976), for example, recognises three main phases in transport technology and urban growth. The first is the stage of *compact growth* during which the city was based on walking, horse and buggies and the trolley, and tended to be small, circular and very dense. The second phase identified was that of *lateral growth*, based on rail and bus developments, during which linear growth spread the urban area in axial fashion. The third stage, that of *dispersed growth*, based on the car and new route developments, allowed great growth in the interstitial areas. With respect to retailing, presumably a single central shopping core would have been sufficient at the first stage, with a tendency towards the development of suburban centres at the second. It is during the third stage that decentralisation of retailing has fully developed in association with polycentric urban forms (Kivell, 1972; Dawson, 1974).

Although empirical evidence is limited in scope, it shows that this progression has indeed occurred. Vance (1962) notes how in the early American city the commercial pattern was core dominated. After the 1890s, the growth of public transport allowed outlying centres to develop at major intersections. The major influences in the post 1930s period were the dramatic increase in private car ownership and the rise of mass selling techniques. More detailed empirical insights have been provided for the British urban scene by Wild and Shaw, using trade directory data for Kingston upon Hull for the period 1823-81 (Wild and Shaw, 1974, 1979; Shaw, 1978). They indicate how less specialised types of shopping were pulled into suburban districts by the rapidly expanding working class population. Whilst in 1823, 58.5 per cent of the city's shops were to be found in the old town, this had fallen to 28.9 per cent by 1851. From 1851 to 1881, there was considerable further suburbanisation of shopping facilities. However, more specialised shop types remained in the town centre, drawing in the more mobile middle-class consumers. Plots of the rateable values of shops in Hull in 1860 show little or no retail site differentiation outside the tight circle of the central area. But by 1880, a major change had occurred, with prongs of high commercial rateable values extending west, north-west and eastwards out from the central area. These linear extensions to the central area were accompanied by a sharp increase in retail site differentiation within the core area.

Wild and Shaw (1975) have also examined the correspondence between retail shops and population growth in the Halifax-Calder Valley area of West Yorkshire during the period 1851-1901, but perhaps their most important paper deals with retailing trends in a number of British urban areas from 1798 to 1881 (Wild and Shaw, 1979). Based on Hull, York, Leeds, Beverley, Wakefield, Huddersfield and Halifax, the work demonstrates that incipient decentralisation of retailing occurred quite early on. At the beginning of the 19th century, the towns showed strong groupings of shops around their respective market places and along the main arterial routes extending out from the historic core. Subsequent growth occurred in an outward fashion and embryonic suburban centres eventually emerged. Huddersfield was used as a detailed illustrative example and shop recordings for 1823, 1851 and 1881 are reproduced in Figure 4.15. The authors recognise three types of retail extension:

> '... firstly, physical expansion of the central concentration into the inner residential districts; secondly, from here, the development of linear axes along the main arterial roads and leading to the outer suburbs; thirdly, as represented at Mold Green, Lockwood, Paddock and Hillhouse, the emergence of nuclear concentrations associated with villages enveloped by the urban growth process' (Wild and Shaw, 1979, p. 41).

The authors further maintain that an historical growth succession is discernible, with physical expansion of the central area initially predominating, but suburban encroachment and linear extension becoming more important during the later period of sustained growth. This identification of nucleated and ribbon growth patterns within the urban retailing system is significant when viewed in relation to the empirical evidence of overall structural ordering presented in this chapter. Corroborative evidence is found for Nottingham in Weekley's (1956) study, whilst Johnston (1968) has shown how the development of the intra-urban commercial hierarchy of south-east Melbourne, Australia was inextricably associated with the location of railway lines and the distances between stations.

A CONCLUDING MODEL

This chapter has provided an overview of empirical studies of urban retailing structure and some effort has been made to relate these to the models and theories reviewed in Chapter 2. It would be foolhardly to endeavour to summarise this vast body of research in its entirety; instead, a simple graphical model of the development and structure of an urban retailing system is presented which hopefully subsumes many of the points raised in the previous discussions. The model is depicted in Figures 4.16 and 4.17 in evolutionary and static structural terms respectively. Details of the general properties of the system shown in Figure 4.17 are summarised in Table 4.9. The model is presented here as a basis for discussion and for future empirical testing.

In developmental terms, in *Stage 1* of the sequence, a compact urban area is dominated by the town centre, and there is little extra-C.B.D. retail development. Embryonic ribbons are to be found along the inner portions of the main roads and are the outcome of recent urban growth. The urban area is surrounded by a series of distinct villages, each with its own local shopping facilities. This stage would conform with the early 19th century in many British cities (see Figure 4.5). With the growth of population and income, directly proportionate development of the town centre becomes impracticable as its average distance from consumers is increasing. Therefore, convenience and other specialist functions start to develop in the suburbs. This may be associated with either entirely new centres built in conjunction with new residential

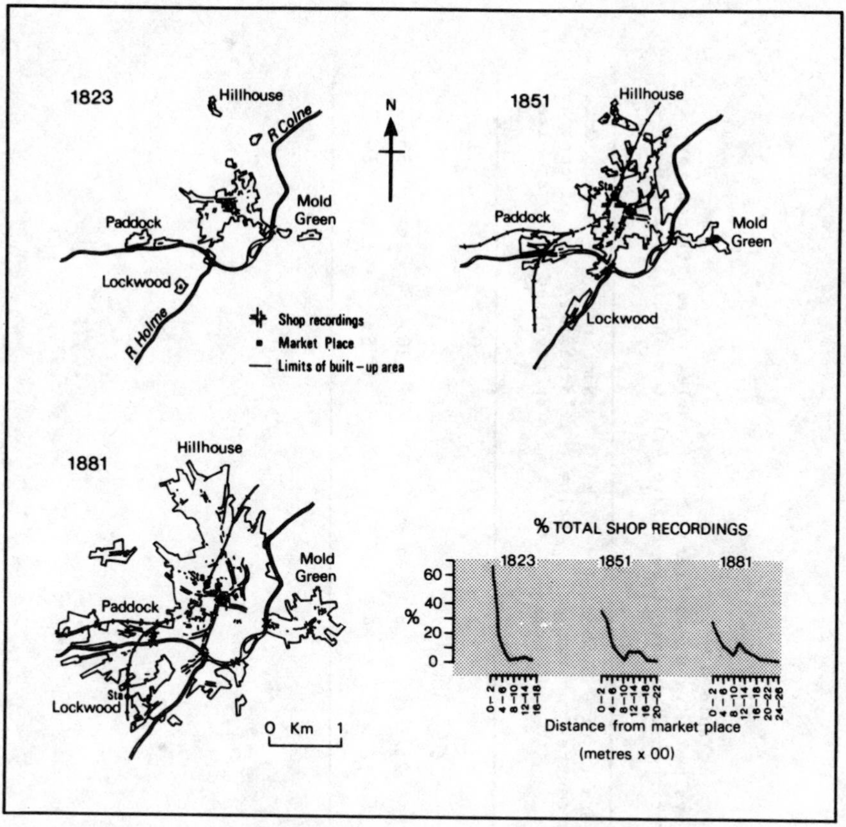

Figure 4.15 Dynamic aspects of the distribution of shops in Huddersfield, 1823-1881 (Adapted by permission from Wild and Shaw, 1979)

districts or the engulfment of former village centres, transforming them into major suburban facilities (see *Stage 2*). The ribbons located along the inner portions of the main arterials continue to grow, but tend to become more specialised, drawing a non-continuous clientele from the entire urban area and/or tracts outside it. This stage conforms approximately with the late 19th century in Britain and the development of a set of nucleated centres and a system of arterial ribbons can be said to have begun. By *Stage 3*, a mature urban retailing system has evolved and a clear hierarchy has emerged, with well-developed ribbons related to car transport superimposed upon it. Centres may well be differentiated in terms of their degree of planning, age, morphology, quality and functional specialisation as well as their overall size. Thus, consumer behaviour will also be highly complex by this stage. The peripheral and in-town location of hypermarkets, superstores and regional centres can be broadly accommodated within this framework, perhaps as a *fourth stage*.

Table 4.9
Hypothetical example of a variable k value intra-urban hierarchy of nucleated retail centres together with a specialised and/or ribbon component (see Figure 4.17 for spatial pattern)

Overall size level	Approx. population served	Approx. no of. shops per centre	Number of centres	Number of market areas	k value	Number of arterial/ specialised areas	Grand total of centres by size
Central area	150,000	500	1	1	-	0	1
District	21,428	100	6	7	7	2	9
Community	5,357	35	21	28	4	10	38
Neighbourhood	1,785	10	56	84	3	5	89

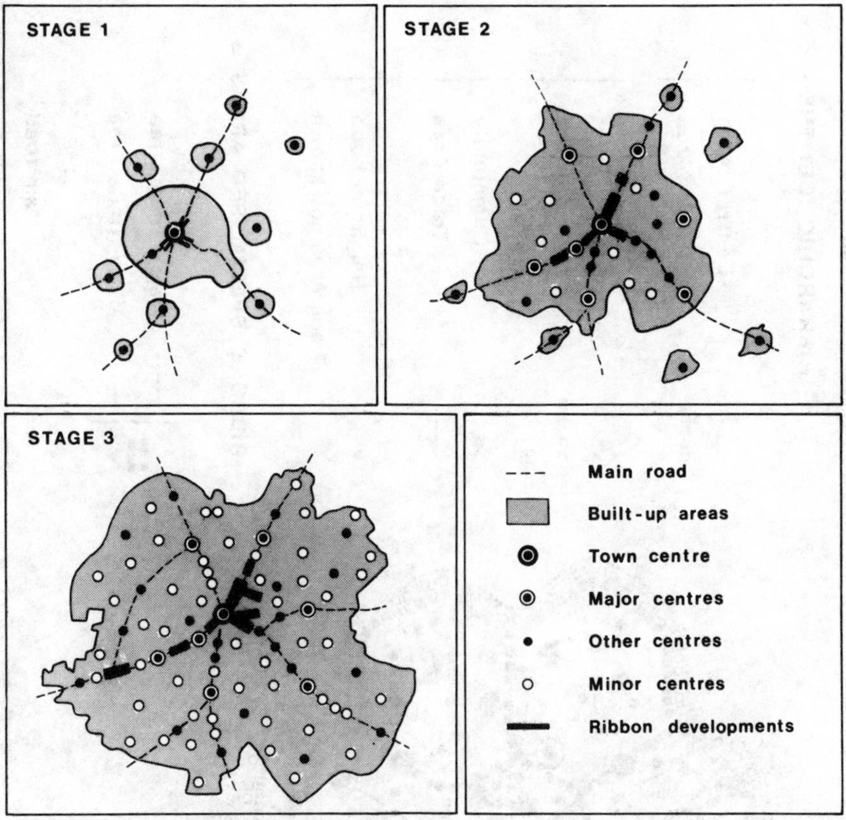

Figure 4.16 A stage model of the evolution of an urban retailing system

Such an evolutionary sequence would give rise to the type of static commercial structure shown in Figure 4.17. This is based on the hypothetical example of a medium-sized urban area of 150,000 population. The central shopping area is surrounded by a ring of six principal district shopping centres, and these are located nearer to the town centre than central place theory would predict. This eccentric location of centres with respect to their market areas not only accords with the findings of empirical structural research but also with the observed spatial behaviour of consumers, as will be illustrated in the next chapter. Thus, a $k_{12}=7$ pattern has been established for the upper echelons of the system. The same principle of distorted market regions is operative for the community and neighbourhood level centres. There are 21 and 56 of these respectively, giving the equivalent of a $k_{23}=4$ and $k_{34}=3$ pattern of urban retail areas. The sub-system of hierarchic nucleations thereby forms a general hierarchical or variable k system (Table 4.9). A separate set of 2, 10 and 5 arterials at the equivalent of the district, community and neighbourhood size levels respectively is then envisaged in this hypothetical example. Two types of trade area are recognised in relation to these developments. Some arterial ribbons

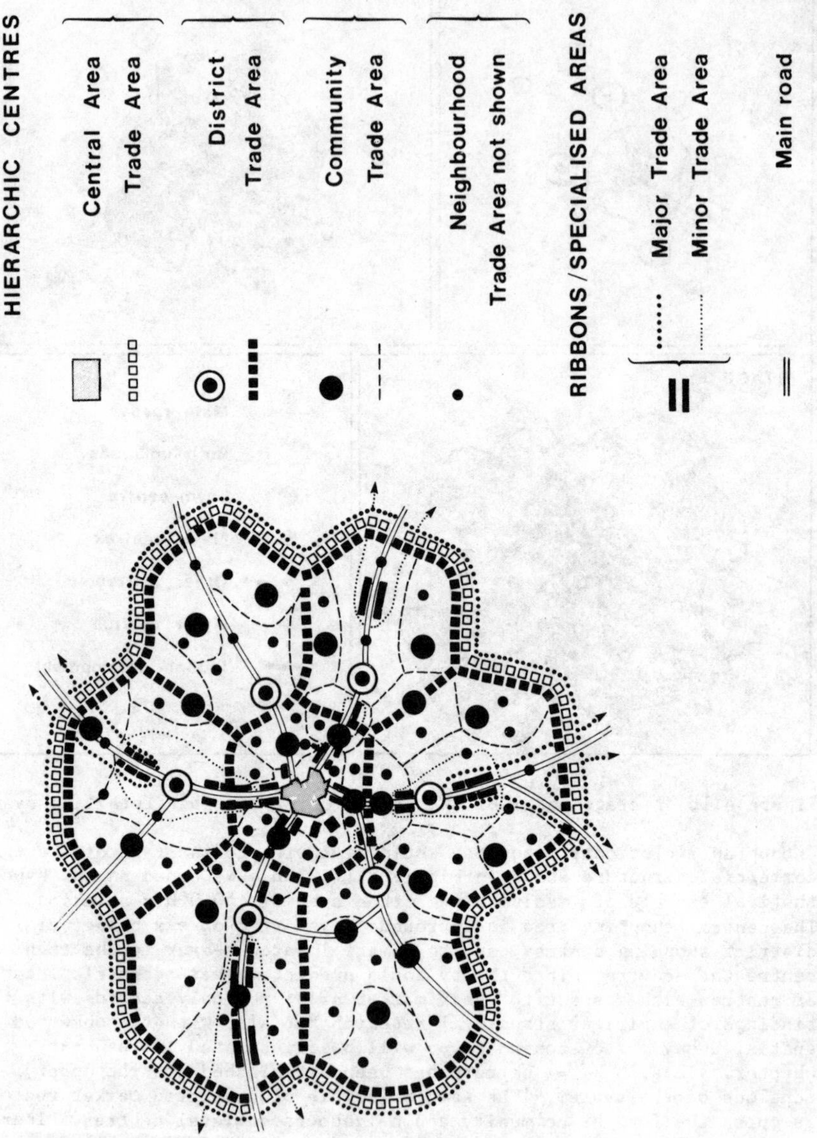

Figure 4.17 A suggested graphical model of urban retail structural organisation

and specialised areas, particularly those placed in the inner town may have major trade zones which relate to a discontinuous population over the whole town (Figure 4.17). Others may be associated with minor trade regions taking the form of corridors along the principal roads, and perhaps incorporating considerable areas outside the contiguous urban district (Figure 4.17). When the hierarchic and ribbon components are aggregated, an ostensibly more haphazard numerical sequence of retail centres is revealed, which perhaps even forms a continuum by size (Table 4.9). Added to this, the system will be further differentiated in qualitative terms according to prevailing socio-economic and income circumstances within the town.

Such a model is very broad, but it is argued here that it is both locationally and behaviourally sensitive. In several respects it represents a graphical and developmental extension of Berry's threefold typology of urban commercial structure. This chapter has stressed that there are many aspects of shopping centre structure that may influence consumers in their decision-making and subsequent overt shopping behaviour, and further, that these variables are interrelated in an extremely complex manner. The behavioural connotations of urban retailing constitute the subject matter of the remainder of this volume. It is tempting to end this section by reiterating the argument first presented in Chapter 1, that despite, or perhaps because of, the common or garden nature of urban retailing and the important role it plays in our daily lives, a great deal of further research remains to be done concerning its precise structural characteristics.

5 Spatial Patterns of Urban Consumer Behaviour

The multi-faceted fabric of the urban retailing system forms the backdrop for the daily shopping activities of urban residents whilst, as stressed in Chapter 1, the structural configuration of the urban retail system is itself the direct outcome of consumer demand and overt behaviour in space. The study of consumer behaviour has been an increasingly popular theme in social and planning studies over the past twenty years, and several general reviews of the resultant body of work have recently appeared (Garner, 1970; Thomas, 1976; Dawson and Kirby, 1980; Shepherd and Thomas, 1980).

In the present chapter, the intention is to examine the research that has been conducted into the spatial nature of urban consumer behaviour, the factors that influence consumer choice of shopping centres, and their motivations. An empirical study of what may be termed 'consumer usage fields' is also presented. The emphasis in this overall account is placed firmly upon the overt behavioural traits exhibited by urban consumers, and at this stage, less stress is placed on their perceptions and cognitions. These vital aspects are dealt with in detail in Chapter 6. In Chapter 7, a study of spatial consumer behaviour and perception conducted by the author in the Swansea urban area is presented.

In the present review, two principal questions are examined: first, how consumer behaviour is related to the attributes of the shopper, and secondly, how such behaviour is related to the physical circumstances of the retailing environment. Thereby, the overall aim of the chapter is to establish the types of generalisable regularities and/or contrasts that occur in urban consumer behaviour, and also to point toward research themes, techniques and possible topics for future investigation. Before looking at these substantive issues in detail, however, it is necessary to provide an overview by examining the relations existing between consumer behaviour and perception/cognition, and at the same time, to define terms basic to this and the next two chapters. These preliminary matters are addressed in the following two sections.

CONSUMER BEHAVIOUR: BASIC CONCEPTS

Spatial consumer behaviour may simply be defined as the aggregate manner in which individual consumers act in the process of acquiring the goods and services that they need and want. Basic aspects of consumer behaviour, such as the frequency of shopping trips, their generally short distance nature and the fact that they represent a major generator of total intra-urban movements were briefly reviewed in Chapter 1. In this account, it was also noted that one stereotype of consumer behaviour envisages a completely rational *economic man* who is constantly seeking an optimal behavioural response, given that such consumers are held to possess perfect levels of information concerning the structure of the retailing environment. In Chapter 2, it was noted that this type of behavioural response is a prime assumption of classical central place structural models, so that consumers are hypothesised to visit the nearest available centre offering the particular good that they require.

However, all of these normative assumptions would only be valid if each and every consumer was characterised by exactly the same motives, values and desires, along with equal incomes, time budgets, levels of mobility and propensities to travel, together with perfect information about the constituent elements of the urban retail system. Clearly, this is a grossly simplified abstraction of reality. In fact, the ideas of Simon (1957, 1959) and Pred (1967), suggesting that spatial behaviour is most accurately viewed as a process of *satisficing* under conditions of bounded rationality have already been discussed in Chapter 1. The salient point here is that consumers are likely to have different subjective impressions of the realities of the urban retailing system. These subjective constructs are frequently referred to as *cognitive images* of the environment, and the informational component is termed the *mental map*. Such concepts will be discussed at length in Chapter 6, and it will suffice here to suggest that these simplified representations of a complex reality are the direct outcome of consumers' *learning process* about the environment, and thereby embody their perceptions and cognitions. Although detailed examination of these terms must also await the next chapter, *perception* may tentatively be defined as the process by means of which we become aware of and interpret or identify the sensations that we receive from our surroundings (Skurnik and George, 1964; Goodey, 1973). By extension, *environmental perception* may be defined as the process and product of individuals' interpretation and structuring of physical and social environments, in which the seemingly objective world is replaced by a simpler, subjectively perceived environment (Pocock, 1971). Although it is difficult to distinguish between the processes of *perception* and *cognition*, the former is properly defined as the process of awareness which occurs due the immediate presence of objects, whilst cognition refers to the sum total of past, present and future anticipated stimuli. Cognition therefore represents a general state of knowing and frequently, it is this more rounded form of general awareness that is being implied when the strictly more limited term 'perception' is used. The interrelations existing between aspects of urban retailing structure, consumer spatial behaviour and perception/cognition were first pointed to in connection with Figure 1.1 of this volume.

Defined in the above manner, the importance of cognition and behaviour to the study of urban retailing starts to become apparent. Retail centres and shops are distributed through space in a complex manner, whilst viewed realistically, the individual has limited mobility, stimulus sensing capabilities, information processing abilities and available time. Thus, the individual consumer interprets the urban retailing environment in a subjective manner and this simplified schema is the individual's cognitive image. The salient point here is that shopping behaviour is likely to be closely related to the consumer's perceptions and cognitions of reality, rather than the real world structure itself. This type of behavioural process has already been illustrated in Chapter 1, via recourse to Pred's conceptualisation of the behavioural matrix (see Figure 1.3). For instance, the consumer may not have perfect knowledge concerning the system, so that information on certain viable shopping alternatives may be missing, or if in existence, may be biased and inaccurate. Thus, a centre might incorrectly be branded as too small, too crowded, too far distant, too noisy, too dispersed or low in qualitative tone. Further, even if the consumer does have the requisite information to hand, he may not wish to employ this to either identify or implement a so called 'optimal' response.

If at this point the behavioural connotations of the structural findings of Chapter 4 are brought into focus, then the likely complexity of urban consumer behaviour can start to be fully envisaged. If retail area structural differences occur over and above those of size and distance to the consumer, such as those of quality, morphology, fabric contiguity, and degree of functional specialisation, then it seems highly probable that different consumers will attach different weightings to each of these characteristics. Thus, for example, one person might feel that retail quality is more important than size or distance, whilst another may regard morphology as the prime criterion in the assessment of centres. This leads on to a further intriguing issue, that is the nature of the choice rules that are employed by consumers, a topic that has been usefully investigated recently by Timmermans (1980a, 1980b, forthcoming). On the one hand, many studies (for example, Schuler, 1979) assume that consumer decision-making follows an *additive* or compensatory rule. In this, a low assessment by a consumer on one structural attribute can be made up for by a high assessment on another. In contrast, the *multiplicative* or non-compensatory decision-making process envisages a situation where if a consumer evaluates a centre to be close to zero with respect to one attribute, then his overall judgment of that centre will tend to be very low as a result. It seems likely that different consumers will employ variant choice rules and this will add to behavioural diversity. The relative importance of multiplicative as against additive modes of choice obviously has important features of urban retailing centres.

This short account gives rise to a number of deductive hypotheses concerning the nature of spatial consumer behaviour in urban areas. First, it seems reasonable to suggest that such overt behaviour is likely to be relatively complex, so that secondly, there will be less dependence on nearest centres than might be expected on the basis of theory alone. Thirdly, a relatively large number of moves may be expected. Fourthly, it may be posited that short distance moves will tend to become increasingly predominant as population densities increase and shopping opportunities become more numerous (Huff, 1961). If this is so, then it also seems appropriate to argue that the larger and more dense the population, the greater the variability in the distance of shopping movements undertaken by different groups (for example, consumers of contrasting social status or age). These and other notions concerning consumer behaviour will be examined in this chapter.

MODELS OF CONSUMER BEHAVIOUR AND COGNITION

Many of the basic ideas introduced in the previous section are integrated in the attempts which have been made to derive simple deductive models of consumer spatial behaviour and cognition. A landmark in this connection is the graph theoretical or topological model of consumer space preferences developed by Huff (1960). The starting point for this formulation was Isard's (1956) concept of *space preference levels*, defined as an individual's propensity to interact with phenomena over distance. Thus, it was argued that 'when placed in the same spatial situation with others, providing all possess identical levels of information, they (consumers) will behave differently' (Huff, 1960, p. 160). Huff then cited Marble (1959), who concluded from empirical research that distances travelled and trip frequencies were not significantly affected by the location of the consumer's residence relative to the retail structure of the city. This implies that variations in behaviour are the direct outcome of the interplay of variant consumer characteristics and inherent differences between retail centres.

Huff then developed his graphical-deductive model using a stage-by-stage approach and the basic model derived is shown in Figure 5.1. The starting point for the model is the desideratum (P_3), that is the consumer's overall readiness to secure an object he desires, and this is conceptualised as being the joint outcome of a stimulus situation (P_1) and/or a physiological drive (P_2). The former represents the physical, social and cultural factors affecting the consumer at a particular time and the latter, the specific condition which produces a need, for example, to eat or to drink. The remainder of the model then consists of the interaction of three major sets of factors. The first of these is the consumer's *value system* (P_4), which is a composite of his geographical location (P_5) and a broad range of personal characteristics (P_6-P_{14}). These include ethical, ethnic, social status, personality, sex and other factors, together with the consumer's mental synthesising abilities. It is argued that these attributes condition the perceptions and resultant actions of consumers in relation to the various locational sources. Here, therefore, the role of perception/cognition is clearly emphasised. The second major set of factors relate to the structural attributes of the available facilities. These are collectively referred to as *behavior-space perception* (P_{15}), although this term is perhaps a little confusing. The point is that shopping centres are 'perceived on the basis of memory and inference' (Huff, 1960, p. 163) according to their structural attributes. It is stressed that consumers assess these characteristics in a subjective manner, and they include reputation (P_{16}), amenities (P_{17}), breadth of merchandise (P_{18}),services offered (P_{19}) and price level (P_{20}). These reflect to a great extent the structural features stressed as being of importance to consumers in Chapters 2-4. At this juncture, Huff has essentially identified the importance of the traits of the consumer and his spatial location on the one hand, and the traits of the retailing environment on the other. But it is obvious that overt behaviour will also depend on the realities of the transport network, and this gives rise to the third major component of the model, that of *movement imagery* (P_{21}). This also has a strong perceived element and relates to travel factors such as transport mode (P_{22}), travel time (P_{23}), travel cost (P_{24}) and parking cost (P_{25}). This cannot be regarded as the complete model, however, as witnessed by Figure 5.1. Although the interaction of these groups of factors will lead to an overt behavioural response, this itself will give rise to a learning or restructuring process. Thus, present behaviour will influence present perceptions and future cognitions of the urban retailing system and will thereby influence future shopping behaviour. This is an important point and a number of researchers have looked at consumer

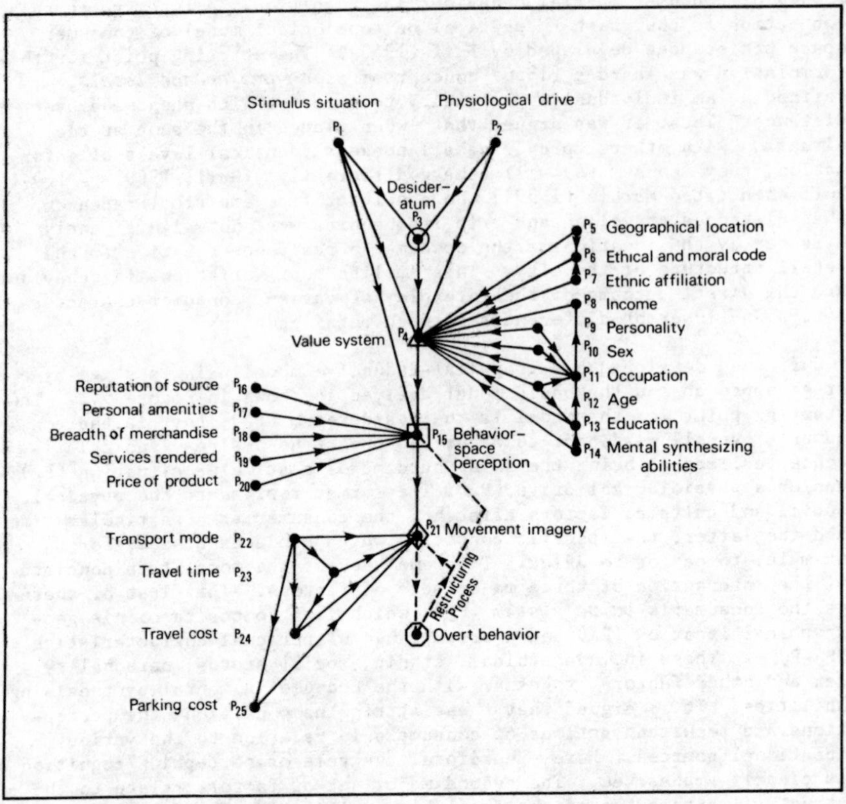

Figure 5.1 Huff's basic model of consumer behaviour and perception (Redrawn by permission from Huff, 1960)

search patterns and learning processes (Golledge and Brown, 1967; Hudson, 1975; Lloyd, 1977).

The basic interactions occurring between these causal factors identified by Huff are those shown in Figure 5.1. But as Huff points out, these will be supplemented by additional or multiple interactions between the elements. Huff takes income as an example of this, for it will not only affect the consumer's value system but will also have a direct influence on the price he is willing and able to pay for specific goods and services. The drawing out of these complex interrelations means that the graphical model thereby becomes extremely complex (see Huff, 1960, Figure 7, p. 166), and Huff tabulated these connections in matrix form. This matrix was then raised to the seventh power in order to establish the proportion of total connectivity accounted for by each of the 25 elements. The most dominant factor was age (26 per cent), followed by personality (14 per cent), sex (13 per cent), education (10 per cent), mental synthesising abilities (10 per cent), occupation (9 per cent) and income (5 per cent).

It is tempting to argue that the main contribution of the model is the stress that it places on the fact that a large number of highly varied factors influence consumer behaviour and cognition. In this sense, this early theoretical formulation acted as a basis for subsequent empirical testing. The results of the connectivity analysis, for instance, suggest that retail centre structural attributes are generally subservient to consumer differences in explaining patterns of consumer space preferences. However, it is probably fair to argue that the model's overall usefulness greatly diminishes at the basic interaction stage depicted in Figure 5.1, for the simple reason that the connectivity analysis depends greatly on the researcher's *a priori* identification of interrelations. The salient point is that the precise nature of linkages is likely to differ from one consumer to the next, and additional, unspecified factors and linkages may play a significant role as well.

Other theoretical models of consumer spatial behaviour have been suggested, for example, by Spence (1971) and Parker (1976), although both would appear to owe much to Huff's original formulation. Spence's general model of shopping behaviour suggests that individual consumer differences together with shopping centre characteristics sum to give the individual's perception, which then serves to channel shopping behaviour. In a similar fashion, Parker starts with social, residential and demographic differences between consumers which relate to their home locations, motivating factors, perceptions and images of the retailing environment. This complex of influences leads to revealed consumer behaviour, and a feedback loop implies the operation of a learning process.

Finally, the present author endeavoured to produce a simple conceptual model of consumer behaviour and cognition in order to afford an operational framework for his empirical studies (Potter, 1979a) and this is reproduced in Figure 5.2. As already discussed above, it is clear that the individual characteristics of consumers will be of considerable importance in influencing their patterns of spatial behaviour and cognition. For example, the status variables of social class, family size, age, personality and car ownership will be reflected in the incomes, propensities to consume, tastes, space preference and mobility levels of different consumer groups. It seems likely, therefore, that such groups will be characterised by contrasting values, needs and wants and shopping goals, as indicated in Figure 5.2.

The main circuit of the model involves the following processes and actions. First, regardless of their personal characteristics and the precise structural arrangement of the urban retailing system, all consumers will be faced with a finite array of locations at which they can satisfy their needs and wants. As a result, it will be necessary for consumers to engage in some form of spatial search process in order to identify the opportunities which are open to them. By this process, consumers will build up knowledge of the retail environment and this latent preference configuration may be termed the *spatial information field*. Such spatial knowledge will be allied with the consumer's emotional reactions to the various centres, a point developed in the next chapter.

It can then be hypothesised that consumers will identify the alternative courses of action that are available to them in fulfilling their

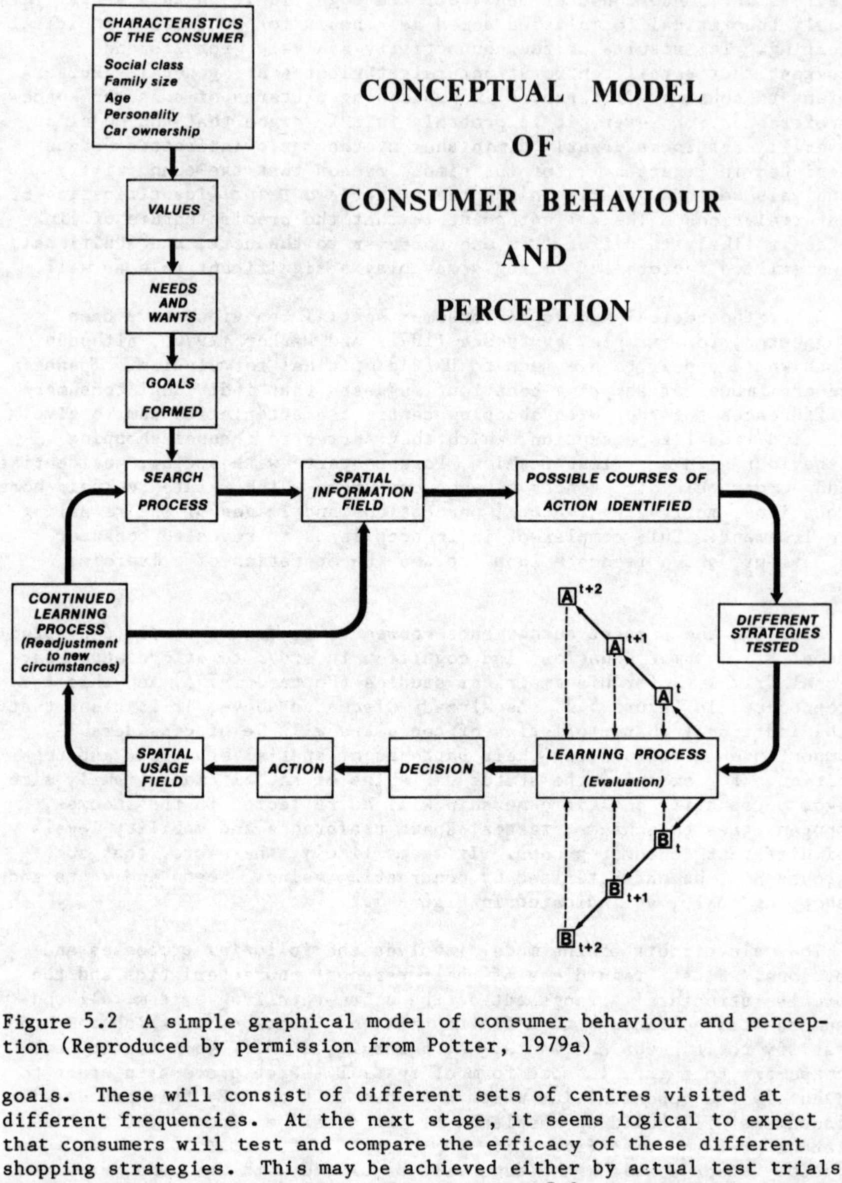

Figure 5.2 A simple graphical model of consumer behaviour and perception (Reproduced by permission from Potter, 1979a)

goals. These will consist of different sets of centres visited at different frequencies. At the next stage, it seems logical to expect that consumers will test and compare the efficacy of these different shopping strategies. This may be achieved either by actual test trials or by a process of mental thought. In Figure 5.2, by way of an example, it is assumed that the consumer has identified two possible strategies, A and B, which he believes will satisfy his needs. Strategy A may involve twice weekly visits to a small neighbouring shopping centre plus a weekly trip to a reasonably close district shopping centre. In contrast, strategy B might be to purchase the same goods by means of a once weekly visit by car to a farther distant hypermarket or superstore. The utility of these two strategies will be evaluated at the present time (A_t, B_t) and perhaps also at various time intervals in the future (A_{t+1}, B_{t+1}). In this fashion, a learning process will occur in which variant courses of behaviour will be evaluated in the light of the consumer's personal characteristics, values, needs, wants and self-imposed goals. Eventually, based on these criteria, the most satisfactory form of behaviour will tend to be implemented when the consumer reaches a decision as to the best way in which to conduct his shopping activities. It is necessary to emphasise at this point that different consumers may employ different criteria and so one person's decision may be entirely different from that of another, even given the same circumstances. Further, the emphasis is placed on the consumer reaching a *satisfactory* rather than an optimal form of spatial behaviour. This decision will be implemented in the form of the consumer's subsequent actions and the entire process will thereby lead to the development of a *spatial usage field* or zone of overt shopping behaviour, which will probably be nested within the spatial information field.

It can be argued that this area of actual shopping activity will be a quasi-stable zone, that is it will be relatively stable only in the short-run period. In the long-term, however, both the personal circumstances of the consumer and the urban retailing environment may undergo change. Thus, new conditions may obtain which require a re-evaluation and perhaps even a readjustment in consumer behaviour. In this respect, the important role played by a continued learning process is revealed (see Figure 5.2). As an example, an entirely new retailing development, such as an out-of-town regional shopping centre, may be established and this may be fed into the spatial information field of a consumer by means of a promotion campaign or by mass media coverage. As a direct result, the decision process will tend to be reiterated. Alternatively, a particular consumer may become dissatisfied with his existing shopping activities and may therefore embark upon a new spatial search phase in order to identify a different and possibly more satisfying form of shopping behaviour. The continued learning process thereby represents a feedback loop within the consumer decision-making process.

Although the model presented above is of necessity highly simplified, it serves to emphasise a number of facts concerning consumer behaviour. First, it demonstrates the close links that exist between consumer cognition, behaviour and retail structure. Further, it also implies that studies of the spatial nature of consumer usage and information fields, both through space and time, are likely to be of great interest and potential utility. Additionally, it is implicit that the consumer usage and information fields pertaining to different sub-groups of the population will exhibit marked contrasts.

STUDIES OF URBAN CONSUMER BEHAVIOUR

It is now perhaps a suitable juncture at which to examine the principal findings of studies of urban spatial consumer behaviour. The customary method used to collect data on such activities is by respondent interview or postal questionnaire, using the technique of shopper self report. Apart from the general problems associated with such methods of acquiring information, including those of respondent recall ability, when examining consumer behaviour, a further difficulty involves the precise wording of the questions seeking information about shopping activities. Frequently, consumers are asked to give details of their 'usual' or 'normal' shopping trips, or alternatively, their most 'recent' journeys. As Brooker-Gross (1981) has commented, this can have the undesirable effect of excluding short term variations in individual shopper behaviour and tends to assume that typical behavioural patterns can be identified. It is also possible that long term shopping patterns will be filtered out by such questions. Another method of collecting data is that of the diary study in which the consumer is asked to record full details of all trips made during a prescribed period, normally a week. Good examples of the use of such diaries are provided by Hanson and Hanson (1972), Davies (1973a) and Daws and McCulloch (1974). The survey by Hanson and Hanson, for example, covered a five week period. A potential problem is that such surveys are quite complex and time consuming for respondents to complete and further, there is the chance that individuals will modify their behaviour as a result of being under such detailed scrutiny. However, as we shall see in Chapter 6, the problems involved in collecting what is basically factual behavioural information are far fewer than those of investigating the subtleties of consumer images and perceptions.

The basic characteristics of urban shopping trips have by now been established in this chapter, and surveys indicating the frequency and short distance of such moves are legion. For example, in an early study, Ambrose (1968) questioned 225 shoppers in Sussex and discovered that there was a sharp distance decay in shopping trips away from the home. Thus, out of a total of 1,395 food shopping trips, 912 covered distances of less than 0.5 mile. Similarly, 1,215 out of a total of 1,928 shopping trips recorded for five different commodity groups occurred within this distance. As a corollary, it was found that whilst 67 per cent of the trips were made on foot, only 14.4 per cent were by car. In a study of retail grocery shopping in Dublin, Ireland it was shown by Parker (1976) that almost 25 per cent of consumers travelled less than 0.3 mile to do their shopping.

Such statistics, however, belie the fact that a substantial body of research has indicated that the hypothesis of nearest centre patronage and travel minimisation are of little direct validity in the intra-urban context. In the study by Ambrose, consumers were asked to make a self-assessment of whether or not they used the nearest centre supplying the goods they purchased. Although the proportion varied quite markedly by functional category, over a third of all trips involved 'excess' travel. The highest degree of additional travel was recorded for clothing trips, with only 51 per cent of movements being to the nearest available place. Such a finding is paralleled in the study of shopping in the city of Christchurch, New Zealand by Clark (1968). Here, it was found that only 50-60 per cent of convenience shopping trips were explained by the nearest centre hypothesis. In fact, the proportion was as low as 46.8 per cent for meat purchases. Corroborative evidence comes from a study of 228 residents of the planned new town of Crawley, Sussex (Day, 1973). For food shopping, 81.8 per cent of the householders indicated that they used their local neighbourhood shops, but such trips only accounted for 37 per cent of total consumer expenditure on food. This indicates that major food oriented shopping trips tend to bypass the nearest available opportunity. The nearest point of supply for non-food items was the planned town centre, but only 82.1 per cent of the respondents stated that they purchased furniture there, and this fell to 36.9 per cent for clothing. Finally, Fingleton (1975) concluded that the nearest centre hypothesis was an apposite behavioural postulate for only 106 of the 401 consumers he studied in the Manchester Conurbation.

The demise of the nearest centre hypothesis as a singular tool for describing urban consumer behaviour is hardly surprising given that it was originally intended as a normative assumption of central place structural models. But the theory has been fruitful in that it has led to many other attempts to explain and model patterns of consumer behaviour. An alternative formulation, that embodied in *spatial interaction theory* seeks to rectify this situation. The idea originated with Reilly's (1931) law of retail gravitation which was introduced in Chapter 1. It was Huff (1963), however, who extended the gravity model to the more realistic situation where more than one centre is used by the residents of an area. It was argued that the probability of a centre being used by residents is directly proportional to its relative attraction and inversely proportional to some function of distance between the centre and the residential area, and in inverse proportion to the competition offered by all other centres in the system. Thus, the probability (p) that a consumer located at i will use shopping centre j is given by the expression:

$$P_{ij} = \frac{A_j}{d_{ij}^b} \Big/ \sum_j \frac{A_j}{d_{ij}^b}$$

where A_j is the attractiveness of shopping centre j, d_{ij} the distance between residential area i and centre j, and b is a distance exponent. The model has frequently been used by planning authorities, despite the fact that only two shopping centre policy variables, relative location and attractiveness are considered, and the need for multi-attribute shopping models has recently been stressed (Timmermans, 1981b). Major considerations involve the precise measure of shopping centre attractiveness to be used (for example, number of businesses, total floorspace or turnover) and the calibration of the distance exponent. A principal criticism of the gravity model is that it is a theory of aggregate consumer behaviour in one region, which is then applied by extrapolation to estimate behaviour in another area (Jensen-Butler, 1972). For this reason, perhaps, the method has generally been employed at the regional scale and application in the intra-urban context has been limited (Pacione, 1974; Lieber, 1977).

Another important approach is that of the *revealed space preference* method, which stems from the original work of Rushton, Golledge and Clark (1967), as elaborated by Rushton (1969, 1971b). The approach maintains that rules of spatial choice can be determined from the examination of overt consumer behaviour. Rushton (1969) stresses that retailing structure and behaviour are both adjusted to one another and are closely interdependent, so that a distinction must be drawn between 'spatial behaviour' and 'behaviour in space'. The former relates to the rules by which alternative locations are evaluated and choices consequently made. In contrast, the term 'behaviour in space' is reserved for the description of actual spatial choices, which are closely related to the existing retail structure, and are not therefore admissable as behavioural postulates in a theory. Thus, the revealed preference approach may be seen as a reaction against the gravity model which deals with behaviour in space (Timmermans and Rushton, 1979). The method initially involves the identification of arbitrarily defined locational types of shopping centre on a graph depicting centre size against distance bands from consumer households. Employing data from an actual survey of shopper behaviour, a centre attractiveness index or *revealed space preference* (I) is calculated for each locational type:

$$I_{ij} = \frac{A_{ij}}{P_{ij}}$$

Thus, the attractiveness of centres of size i at a distance j is equal to the number of households who actually patronise such centres (A_{ij}), divided by the potential number of households who could do so given their residential location (P_{ij}). The derived values of I_{ij} for each cell are then used to draw isopleths on the original graph, and these represent indifference curves of size against distance for the shopping goods under study.

Thomas (1976) has argued that the revealed preference approach is little more successful than the nearest centre hypothesis, for in an empirical study in Christchurch, Clark and Rushton(1970) found that its predictive ability was consistently below 50 per cent for a range of lower order goods. Another major criticism is that the method tends to stress preference and choice on the part of consumers and neglects the formidable constraints that are placed on them (Eyles, 1971; Pirie, 1976; Shepherd and Thomas, 1980). Thus, the approach does not take into account the information levels of consumers (Maclennan and Williams, 1979; Timmermans, 1979b). Another major issue surrounds the degree of transferability of the model between different areas and consumer groups (Timmermans, 1981a). Finally, the method again tends to look at the average responses of a sample of consumers, so that little account is taken of differential behaviour on the part of various sets of consumers.

VARIATIONS IN URBAN CONSUMER BEHAVIOUR

The foregoing account implies that study of the variations that occur in urban consumer behaviour is perhaps as intriguing as the examination of aggregate regularities. Certainly, a great deal of empirical effort has been devoted to this topic over the last twenty years or so. Initially at least, a useful way of examining this work is to address the question as to why it might be that urban consumers do not all behave in exactly the same way by visiting the nearest centres offering particular commodities.

One of the most frequently suggested reasons is that consumers do not choose centres on the basis of a single good, but naturally wish to purchase a range of items on one trip. In the first part of this book it was stressed that multi-purpose shopping trips have important implications for central place and other structural models of retail distribution. A *multi-purpose shopping trip* may be defined as involving the purchase of several orders or types of good on one complete journey. A distinction should be drawn between this and a *combined purpose trip*, where shopping is associated with a work, recreational, entertainment or socialising component. These terms are frequently muddled in the literature. Garrison *et al.* (1959), observed that a higher proportion of single purpose trips tend to be short distance than do multi-purpose ones. Thus, it was posited that consumers are not attempting to minimise travel costs, distance or time for one good, but rather, are endeavouring to get the maximum returns by fulfilling all or many of their purposes on one trip. A similar explanation for a marked lack of distance minimising behaviour on the part of consumers in Uppsala, Sweden was put forward by Hanson and Hanson (1972). It was even suggested that consumers might choose the closest large store offering a good rather than the nearest centre. The importance of multi-purpose travel in relation to choice theory has been fully elaborated by Hanson (1980). Further, Brooker-Gross (1981) has recently examined the phenomenon of 'out-shopping' where exceptionally long trips beyond the nearest place, often leaving the city altogether,are made. It was found that such trips are frequently closely linked with socialising or entertainment activities.

Another potential reason for behavioural complexity is obviously centre structural differences other than size. It has already been ventured in this volume that shopping places of the same functional level may vary with respect to their quality or morphology etc., so that the nearest centre offering a good may not be the consumer's preferred source. There is certainly empirical evidence to support this argument and Schiller (1972) has shown, for example, that middle class consumers exhibit a marked predilection to patronise centres with a large number of high quality hotels and restaurants. This type of explanation is embodied in Warnes and Daniels' (1978) argument that urban shoppers tend to visit the nearest centre that offers the desired type, quality and combination of goods and services. The overall spatial configuration of shopping opportunities may be effective too. For example, Lentnek, Lieber and Sheskin (1975) have suggested the operation of a 'dual assignment rule', whereby a consumer living close to a limited range of shopping places will tend to visit the nearest centre, whilst those living some distance from an opportunity prefer to shop at large places at greater remove. It appears that once a consumer is forced to travel a long distance, then he may well be tempted to continue his journey past available opportunities, to a more preferred centre. Clearly, therefore, we are drawn once again to the point that economic factors alone cannot explain urban shopping patterns.

Research has indicated quite clearly that the assertion that individual shopper characteristics are closely associated with variations in overt behaviour is a valid and important one. An array of studies have, for example, pursued the point that income, occupation and social class are effective in this connection. Davies (1969) investigated the popular consensus view that more movements to a greater variety of retail establishments are made by high income groups than their low income counterparts. Two areas in Leeds situated at approximately the same distance from the city centre were selected for study, one a high income district, the other a low income one. It was found that the high income consumers made a larger number of moves to a more varied set of centres, a higher proportion of which were located outside the immediate neighbourhood. Research using a similar overall design was completed by Thomas (1974) in Swansea. Six residential areas were chosen, each being made up of a low income and a high income district, so that shopping opportunities were similar for the two groups. For grocery shopping trips, at least, the high status consumers tended to travel farther to generally higher order centres. It was further shown that these variations were closely associated with enhanced levels of car ownership and usage. Clearly, variations in both social class and levels of personal mobility are important agents, and corroborative evidence comes from studies by Nader (1969), Grimshaw, Shepherd and Willmott (1970), Parker (1976), Lloyd and Jennings (1978) in a variety of urban settings. The present author has also looked at the influence of these variables in relation to the nature of consumer usage fields (Potter, 1976c, 1977a, 1977c, 1980b) and this work will be summarised in the next section. A recent study of the behaviour of some 681 consumers in Vancouver, Canada can also be cited (Gayler, 1980). In this study, it was established that the higher social class consumers followed the normal rule of travelling further to shop for groceries and women's clothing. However, with respect to furniture, appliance and footwear shopping, it was found that there was little overall distance differentiation. Rather, it appeared that social class variations were expressed in terms of differences in the stores used within particular centres. Such a finding suggests the behavioural importance of quality and other micro-spatial structural variations at the intra-retail centre level (see Chapter 2).

It seems entirely appropriate, therefore, to argue that consumer differences are closely connected to distance minimising behaviour. Fingleton (1975), for example, on the basis of a preliminary data analysis indicated that younger consumers and those owning cars were less likely to purchase bread at their nearest centre. Income however appeared to be of little explanatory value. This analysis was later qualified (Upton and Fingleton, 1979), to suggest that only car ownership had a direct influence, whilst age was related to behaviour via the mobility variable. Interestingly, there appears to be little consensus concerning the influence of age on shopping centre patronage. Davies (1969) in his Leeds study argued that little significant variation in consumer behaviour occurred by age. Potter (1977b) on the other hand identified strong apparent constraints on the shopping behaviour of consumers aged over 60 years. In the same study, size of family was also shown to be effective, with spatially restricted moves being made by consumers with large families. Finally, research also indicates that ethnic, cultural and religious differences between consumers will lead to behavioural diversity. Murdie (1965) showed that Old Order Mennonites were much more dependent on nearest shopping centres than were 'modern' Canadians. Analogous findings have been presented in papers by Ray (1967) and Boal (1969).

THE SPATIAL NATURE OF CONSUMER USAGE FIELDS

It has been shown that there are both clearly recognisable norms and variations in overt consumer spatial behaviour within urban tracts. The present author has suggested that the overall spatial characteristics of urban consumer behaviour may effectively be studied in terms of their *spatial usage fields*. This concept was first introduced in the present chapter with reference to the model of consumer behaviour and perception shown in Figure 5.2. The usage field of a consumer may be defined as the spatial zone which incorporates all of the centres that he patronises in the course of his shopping activities. Further, it has previously been argued that this zone will form part of the consumer's wider information field, that is the area which includes all of the centres about which he possesses knowledge, irrespective of whether or not they are used in the conduct of his shopping.

A simple illustration of these concepts is given in Figure 5.3 (Potter, 1979a). A given consumer will be aware of a finite number of retail centres which exist within his locality. This set of centres comprises the information field of the consumer. Amongst this range of opportunities, a certain number of centres will be visited in order to do shopping. For both usage and information fields thus defined, it is possible to summarise their spatial extent and overall magnitude by means of three simple measures (Potter, 1979a). First, the total number of constituent retail areas may be enumerated. Secondly, the average distance of these centres from the consumer's place of residence may be calculated. Thirdly, two lines radiating from the town centre which encompass all of the centres in the field may be drawn, and the angular extent of the resultant arc measured. These measurements can be clearly understood from Figure 5.3 and should afford good summary measures of the degree of conformity and variation occurring in spatial consumer behaviour.

A pilot questionnaire which sought to investigate consumer usage and information fields was constructed in 1972, and twelve copies were sent out to residents in Stockport. Subsequently, eight responses were received and it was possible to depict their usage and information fields in map form. The examples are shown in Figure 5.4. The variety exhibited by such fields is quite marked, although the majority are relatively simple. There is a noticeable tendency for usage fields to be restricted to the sector of the town in which the consumer is resident. Where an information response is recorded, it is wider than, and envelops the usage field. These preliminary findings indicated the potential utility of a more detailed study of consumer usage fields.

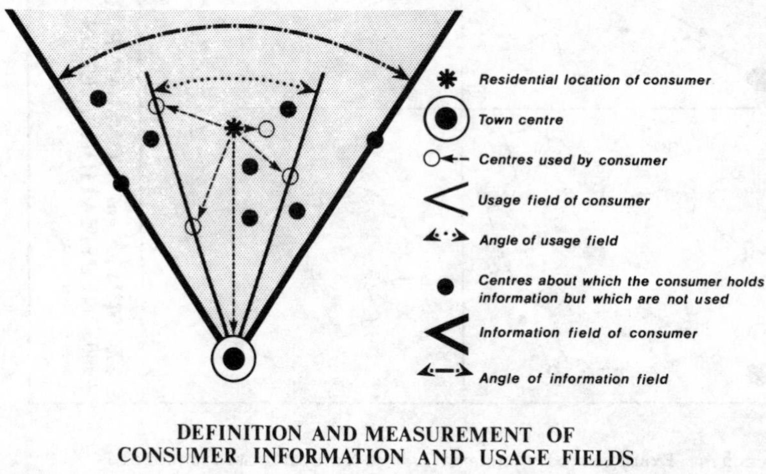

Figure 5.3 The measurement of consumer information and usage fields (Reproduced by permission from Potter, 1979a)

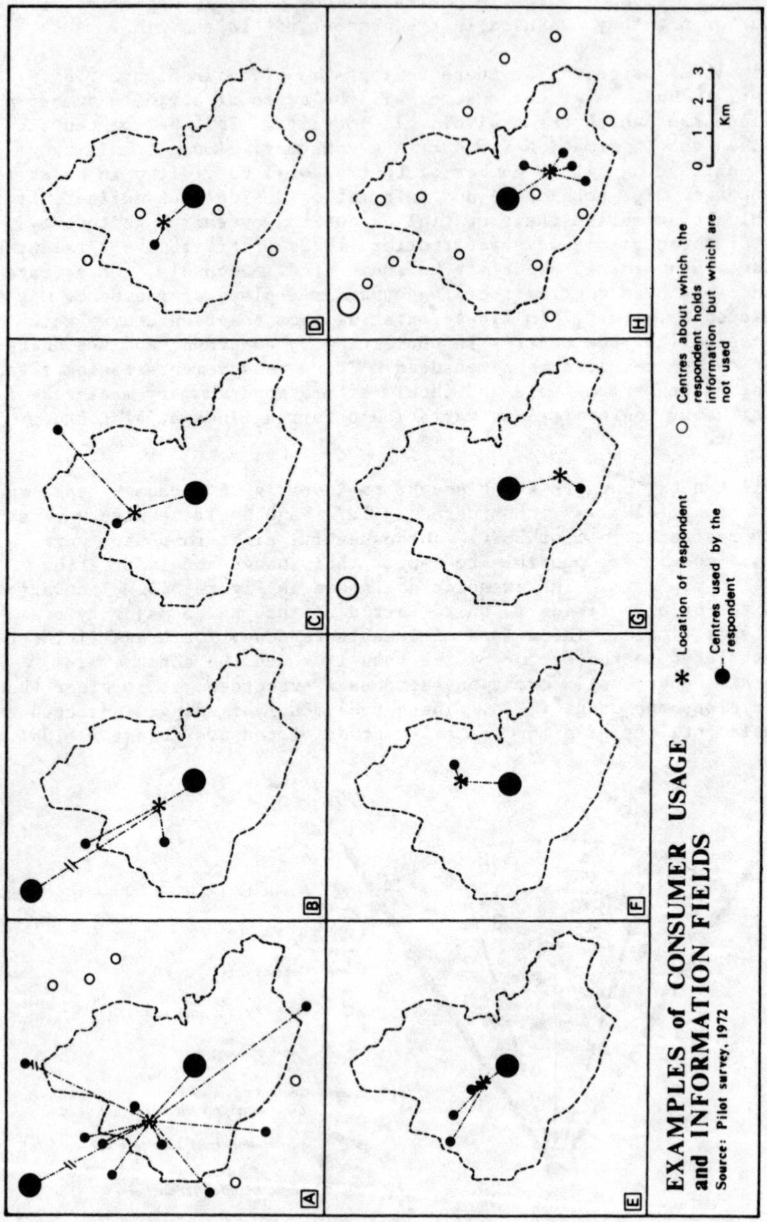

Figure 5.4 Examples of consumer usage and information fields

On the basis of the pilot study, a final version of the questionnaire was prepared, a copy of which is to be found in Appendix 1. Questions in Part 1 focussed on the overt behaviour of the respondents in relation to six broad commodity types. An areally stratified random sample of 800 households was drawn using the Register of Electors. The questionnaires were dispatched at the beginning of February 1973. In all, 192 usable schedules were completed and returned. The distribution of the respondent consumers is shown in relation to the sampling frame in Figure 5.5, and responses were gained from people in all parts of the town. Further, a broadly representative cross-section of the views of people of all ages, social classes and family conditions were gained (see Potter, 1977c, pp. 170-1, for full details). As the association between social status and shopping behaviour was of prime interest, the relative residential location of the various social sets of consumers was established. The high status group members were located at an average of 2.06 km. from the town centre. The same statistics for the other groups were as follows: middle status 2.19 km.; low status 2.02 km.; economically inactive 2.28 km.. Hopefully, this meant that any revealed contrasts in spatial behaviour between the social groups would not merely be the outcome of their differential location with respect to the town centre. However, the more subtle influence of differential location in relation to local shopping opportunities could not be entirely ruled out using this particular study design.

On inspection, wide variations were found to characterise the usage fields pertaining to the 192 sample consumers. Representative examples attesting to this overall variability are depicted in Figure 5.6. Such fields ranged from those which could be described as relatively simple and restricted (examples A, B and C), to those which exhibited greater complexity and spatial extent (examples G and H). As the number of constituent centres increases so the spatial dispersion of centres and the angular extent of such fields tend to increase concomitantly. However, despite these differences, all of the fields displayed a tendency toward residential sector bias. Thus, consumer usage fields typically took the form of wedge-shaped sectoral zones which extended outward from the town centre and focussed on the residential environs of the consumer (Figure 5.6).

A detailed analysis of the usage fields of the sample of 192 consumers was carried out in terms of the three measures of the number of centres, their distance and the angular extent of the entire field. With regard to the former, the total number of centres used ranged from 1 to 7. An overall mean usage total of 3.05 centres was recorded, although the modal class of two centres accounted for 34.9 per cent of the respondents (Table 5.1). The overall mean distance of the centres comprising the respondents' usage fields was 2.04 km.. The average angular extent of the fields was found to be 28 degrees, which is very close to the 30 degree zone that would be expected in a perfect k=3 central place system (see, for example, Figure 1.2A). It should be noted that due to the possible distorting effects of large centres in the Manchester conurbation, only centres located within Stockport were included in the analysis of usage field angles.

However, as already noted, wide variations ocçurred about these average dimensions. In order to examine the bases of these, the respondents were firstly, classified according to their social class

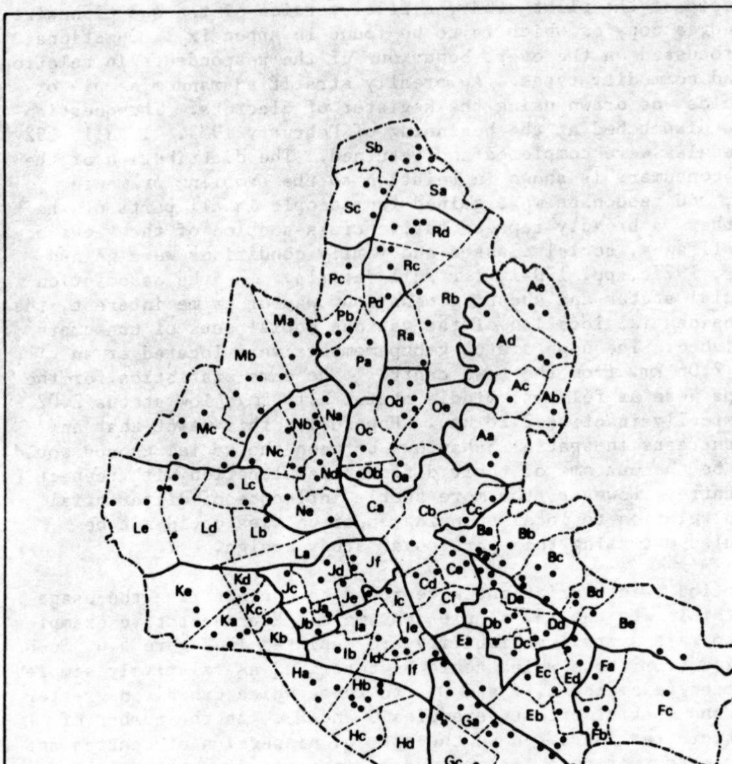

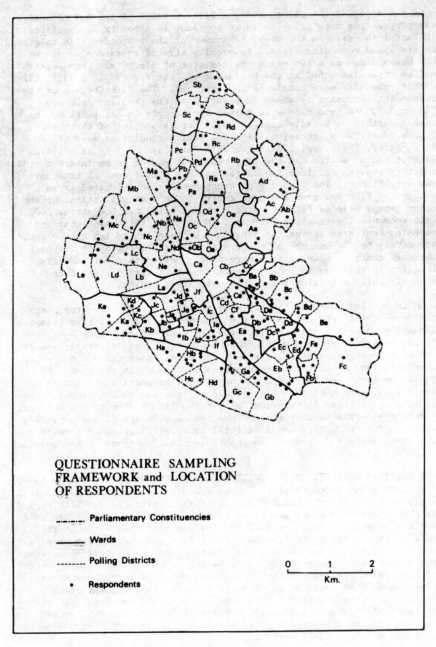

Figure 5.5 The distribution of the questionnaire respondents

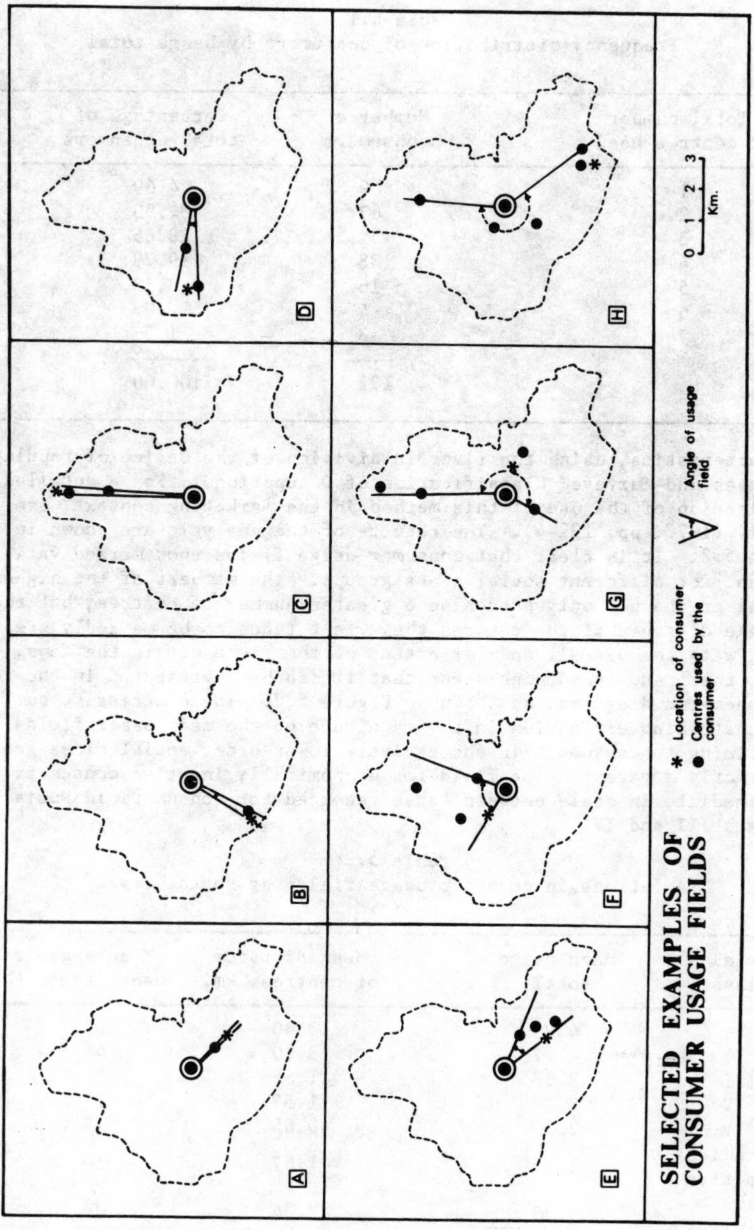

Figure 5.6 Selected examples of consumer usage fields in Stockport

Table 5.1
Frequency distribution of consumers by usage total

Total number of centres used	Number of consumers	Percentage of total consumers
1	9	4.69
2	67	34.90
3	55	28.65
4	38	19.79
5	16	8.33
6	4	2.08
7	3	1.56
	192	100.00

characteristics, using the fivefold division of the Office of Population Censuses and Surveys' Classification of Occupations. For a detailed examination of the use of this method in the marketing context, see Foxall (1977, pp. 192-4). The results of the analysis are shown in Table 5.2. It is clear that consumer usage fields show marked variations for different social class groups. The members of the higher social groups not only patronise a greater number of centres, but the average distance of the centres they visit tends to be markedly greater, along with the overall angular extent of the field within the town. In fact, the trend is so consistent that it can be represented in the form of schematic diagrams, as shown in Figure 5.7. The progressive but quite striking diminution in the magnitude of the mean usage fields pertaining to consumers in successively lower order social class groups is clearly apparent. The field for economically inactive consumers is intermediate in scale between those recorded for consumers in social classes III and IV.

Table 5.2
Variations in consumer usage fields by social class

Social class	Mean usage total	Mean distance of centres, km.	Mean angle of usage field (°)
I	4.45	3.30	83
II	4.27	3.00	45
III	2.87	1.85	23
IV	2.27	1.57	19
V	2.00	0.65	15
Economically inactive	2.45	1.67	14
Entire sample	3.05	2.04	28

The research also looked at variations in consumer usage fields according to age, family size and the use made of cars for shopping (Potter, 1976a, 1977c). As car ownership and more particularly frequency of employment for shopping purposes were closely related to

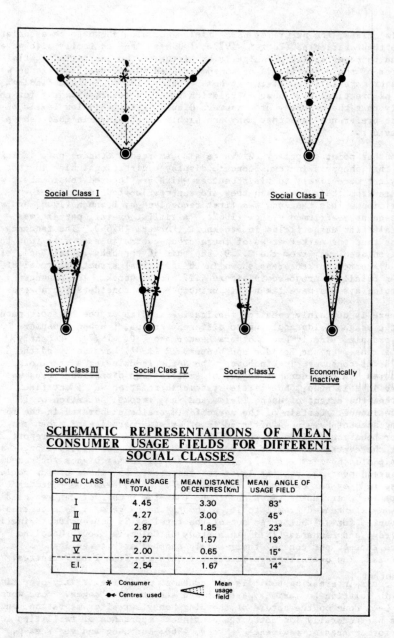

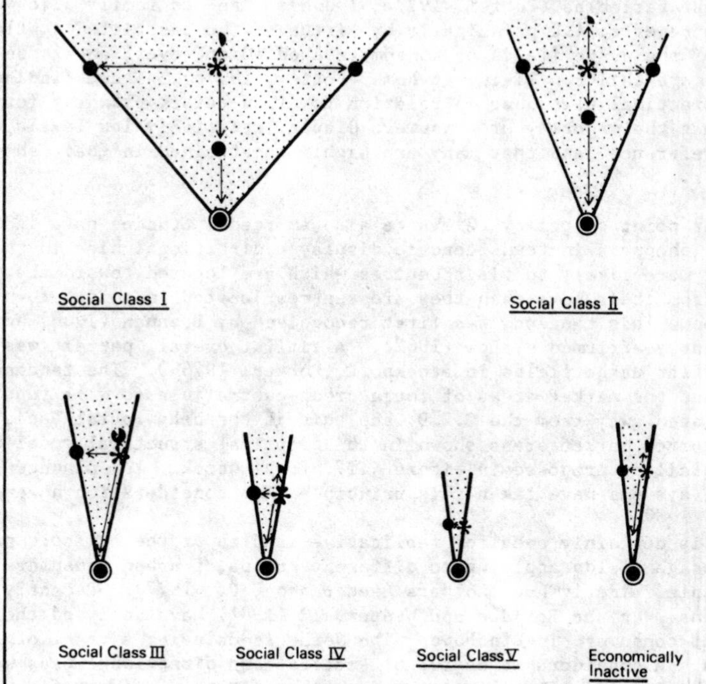

SCHEMATIC REPRESENTATIONS OF MEAN CONSUMER USAGE FIELDS FOR DIFFERENT SOCIAL CLASSES

SOCIAL CLASS	MEAN USAGE TOTAL	MEAN DISTANCE OF CENTRES [Km]	MEAN ANGLE OF USAGE FIELD
I	4.45	3.30	83°
II	4.27	3.00	45°
III	2.87	1.85	23°
IV	2.27	1.57	19°
V	2.00	0.65	15°
E.I.	2.54	1.67	14°

* Consumer
●← Centres used
Mean usage field

Figure 5.7 Social class variations in consumer usage fields in Stockport (Reproduced by permission from Potter, 1977c) social class, the nature of usage fields was also shown to be associated with these variables (Potter, 1977c, 1980b). Age and family size were found to be effective principally by virtue of the restricted spatial extent of the usage fields of consumers aged 60 and over, and those with five or more children living at home (Potter, 1977c). These findings are of practical relevance in relation to urban retail planning for they imply that the majority of consumers display relatively low levels of space preference, and that many are highly constrained in their shopping behaviour.

Another point of policy relevance also emerged. Studies have indicated that shoppers in towns tend to display a directional bias in that they are more likely to visit centres which are located toward the town centre from their home than they are centres located in an out-town direction. This tendency was first recognised by Brennan (1948) and was subsequently affirmed by Lee (1962). A similar overall pattern was revealed for usage fields in Stockport (Potter, 1976b). The tendency means that the market areas of intra-urban central places will tend to be elongated away from the C.B.D. and this is the behavioural basis of the distorted market areas shown in the graphical structural model of urban retailing proposed in Figure 4.17 of this book. Few planned shopping systems have taken this principle into consideration however.

There is certainly need for replicative studies of the holistic nature of the usage fields applying to different groups of urban consumers, say for example, elderly householders (see Hanson, P., 1977). Recently, Timmermans, van der Heijden and Westerveld (1981) have analysed the fields of consumers in Eindhoven, The Netherlands,using a range of measures. A considerable degree of sectoral and directional bias was found in this study, but little systematic relation was identified between the extent of usage fields and age, income, education or length of residence. Certain of the usage field traits elaborated in the foregoing account have been affirmed in other wider studies of urban consumer behaviour. Thus, Daws and Bruce (1971) and Daws (1974) report that the average number of places visited for all foodstuffs amongst a sample of consumers was 2.1. This was significantly higher for consumers aged under 35, but far lower for those over 55, those of low social class and non-car owners. Garrison *et al.* (1959) examined customer trips in Cedar Rapids, Iowa and found that the number of centres used by consumers extended from 1 to 16, although the range of 1 to 8 centres accounted for all but three out of the total of 99 households. Finally, Golledge and Zannaras (1973) in a study of Columbia, South Carolina found that 66 per cent of their sample shopped at between 1 and 3 centres. The overall range in usage totals was from 1 to 7 centres.

Another interesting topic is how consumer usage fields vary over time and in relation to various personal and structural changes. Some work has been done on the nature of shopping behaviour after migration, and this has generally indicated the continued importance of facilities in the former area of residence (Nader, 1968; Korteweg and van Weesep, 1980). Lloyd (1977) studied the behaviour of 75 migrants in Columbia, South Carolina, and found that the use of low order centres near to the old home terminated first and that of higher order centres last. Further studies of temporal changes in consumer usage fields would be of great interest and utility to both planners and academics alike.

CONSUMER DECISION-MAKING AND SHOPPER TYPES

This chapter has exemplified the point that diversity is a hallmark of aggregate consumer behaviour, and that the spatial outcome of such variability is of much interest and significance. It is quite obvious that consumers do not invariably visit the nearest centres available, so that their behaviour is far from optimal if adjudicated on purely economic grounds. It is tempting to suggest, therefore, that consumers have different motives and aspirations, and operate under widely divergent levels of constraint. This line of argument has led to the suggestion that distinct consumer groups or 'shopper types' can be recognised.

Stone (1954), for example, in an early and frequently discussed study of the social psychology of shopping based on suburban Chicago, identified four principal types of consumer. These groups were based on the criteria that shoppers employed to evaluate stores and shopping centres:

1. *Economic consumers* who assess stores with respect to their prices, quality and the variety of goods that they offer. This category accounted for 33 per cent of Stone's sample and formed the largest single consumer group.

2. *Personalising consumers* who tend to evaluate stores according to the relationship existing between the customer and the store personnel. Such consumers wanted to be treated in a personal and friendly manner and constituted 28 per cent of the sample members.

3. *Ethical consumers* were those who felt a moral obligation to shop in certain types of store (for example, the small family run shop). Eighteen per cent of the consumers were categorised in this group.

4. *Apathetic consumers* comprised individuals who were not really interested in shopping and as a consequence, tended to minimise the effort involved. This group accounted for only 17 per cent of the consumers.

The apathetic consumer would obviously be the type who tends to shop at the nearest available centre, whilst those in the economic group would be looking for a 'rational' behavioural response. Members of the other two categories, the personalising and the ethical, would tend to be less constrained by distance and cost. Interestingly, Stone further examined the wider characteristics of the group members. It was significant that economic and personalising consumers were found to be more common amongst recent migrants into the area. On the other hand, established residents were more likely to be either apathetic or ethical consumers. It was also noted that ethical consumers tended to be of a higher social status and this might explain why such consumers are prepared to travel relatively long distances in order to shop. Hoggart (1978) has recently employed Stone's typology in a study of the shopping behaviour of 31 households in North Yorkshire. All four of Stone's original categories were recognised, but three other shopping strategies were added. The *contented* consumer was defined as one who did little shopping around. Such individuals tended to visit the shops that they had grown to like, and might travel some distance in order to do so. This characteristic made these shoppers distinct from those in Stone's apathetic group. The identification of a *constrained* group of consumers recognised that some shoppers face almost insurmountable transport or time induced constraints, which effectively debar them from visiting their preferred locations. Finally, *recreational* shoppers were identified who enjoy visiting different places and who are therefore prepared to travel farther and visit a wider range of centres than is strictly necessary.

The categories provided by such research are useful in that they summarise the types of behavioural diversity that have been explained and examined in this chapter. The chief operational problem of such typologies is that they involve placing consumers into groups on a largely subjective basis. Further, it is highly unlikely that these groupings will be mutually exclusive. In particular, a consumer might well be ethical when shopping for convenience goods, but economic or recreational when purchasing higher order commodities. Similar criticisms may be levelled at other efforts which have been made to define shopper types, such as the largely aspatial fourfold typology presented by Kotler (1965) (see also Golledge, 1970):

1. *Marshallian* - consumers of this type behave as entirely economically rational individuals, thereby reacting instantaneously to market forces.

2. *Pavlovian* - where consumers are regarded as being stimulus prone, reacting, for example, to advertising stimuli.

3. *Freudian* - where consumers are regarded as being fantasy prone, reacting to factors such as packaging and advertising methods. The basic idea is that consumers have repressed feelings which are expressed in socially approved forms.

4. *Veblenian* - consumers are social group prone; as man is basically a social animal, societal norms and customs tend to affect his overt behaviour.

Work along these general lines continues in the urban setting, and Williams (1979) has argued that such an approach enables researchers to adopt a much needed holistic view of shopping behavioural patterns. In Williams' work, some 500 consumers were interviewed in south-west Birmingham concerning their grocery shopping. The trips made by the sample members were classified according to three variables, namely, the mode of travel employed, the trip frequency and the size of centre used. The combination of these three factors that occurred more frequently than expected were regarded as defining shopper types. A total of seven distinct types were thus identified, and together, these accounted for as high a proportion as 73 per cent of the entire sample of consumers. The most commonly occurring shopper type involved the walk/frequent/small centre combination which accounted for 102 consumers, and represents classical low order shopping behaviour. The car/seldom/large centre shopper type was the second most important, with an observed total of 89 respondents. This type conforms with the basic 'one-stop shopping' behavioural pattern. In the ensuing analysis, it was shown that the defined shopper types were closely associated with the consumers' attitudes to shopping as an activity and to the socio-economic variable. In a further analysis of the data, Williams (1981) has identified four basic shopping attitude types:

1. *Economic*: where grocery shopping was carried out as cheaply and as efficiently as possible. Such consumers showed a preference for self-

service stores and supermarkets and a willingness to travel to reach satisfactory outlets.

2. *Convenience*: where shopping was regarded as an onerous task which is to be performed as quickly as possible and with the minimum of effort.

3. *Localised/personal*: where shopping is seen as a local activity involving the use of the nearest offerings and a close personal relationship with the retailer.

4. *Social*: where grocery shopping is seen as an enjoyable social event which affords relief from loneliness, boredom or housework.

A more detailed study of shopper types naturally involves examination of the precise factors that consumers employ in their spatial decision-making. At this juncture, it is perhaps sufficient to observe that the numerous studies that have been conducted on this topic have tended to show that consumers' criteria involve factors other than purely economic ones such as quick journey time, low transport cost, short journey and good access. These factors are of undoubted importance, but shopping centre physical-structural attributes such as variety of stores, shop quality, helpful personnel, good reputation, well-maintained buildings, cleanliness, centre compactness, atmosphere, parking availability and degree of weather protection have been shown to be very influential as well (Davies, 1973a; Pacione, 1975; Patricios, 1978; Potter, 1979b). These findings exemplify the behavioural significance of the broad range of shopping centre structural variables stressed in Chapter 4 of this volume. A more detailed examination of the factors affecting consumer choice and their relative importance will be provided in the next chapter in relation to the nature of appraisive consumer perceptions.

CONSUMER BEHAVIOUR AND AGGREGATE RETAIL STRUCTURE

The final point raised in the section above suggests that studies of aggregate urban consumer behaviour in relation to observed retail area structural differences would be of great potential interest. In fact, it is surprising that there have been comparatively few empirical studies of this sort at the intra-urban scale. However, an interesting prospective approach is suggested by the work of Timmermans (forthcoming). In this research, a laboratory experiment was used involving 16 subjects. Three structural variables, number of shops, travel time and time needed to find a parking space were focused upon. Three conditional states were recognised for each variable (10, 40, 70 shops; 15, 20, 45 minutes travel time; 3, 6, 9 minutes to find a parking space). Combining these gave 27 hypothetical shopping stimulus combinations for respondents to evaluate. This type of approach unquestionably deserves much greater attention, especially as other retail area traits such as morphology, quality and functional specialisation could conceivably be incorporated in such an analysis.

As the present author's research in the Stockport urban area covered both retail structural variations and consumer behaviour, it was possible to examine the links existing between the two, albeit in an exploratory fashion (Potter, 1976a, 1978). It was a simple matter to sum the total number of consumers amongst the sample members who patronised each retail area at some stage in the course of their shopping. This statistic may be referred to as the *aggregate usage total of a retail area*. As the respondent consumers had been drawn from all parts of the town (see Figure 5.5), it was first posited that aggregate usage levels should reflect the overall importance or centrality of the elements of the retailing system. Aggregate usage totals were therefore calculated for retail areas grouped according to their broad hierarchic size categories, and a close positive relationship between overall size and the frequency with which a centre appeared in the behavioural fields of the consumers was clearly evident (Table 5.3). The aggregate usage totals of the 72 centres were then directly correlated with their establishment totals. A correlation coefficient of $r=+0.95$ was recorded, suggesting that some 90 per cent of retail area usage variability was explained by differences in centre size, the two variables being related by the linear expression:

$$U = 0.33E - 3.12$$

where U is the aggregate retail area usage total and E its establishment total.

Table 5.3

Mean aggregate usage totals of retail areas grouped by size

Size category		Number of retail establishments	Mean aggregate usage total
1	Central area	484	182.00
2	Regional	131-140	28.00
3	District	47-109	9.22
4	Community	15- 37	5.15
5	Neighbourhood	2- 11	1.20

A second hypothesis suggested itself in that it was possible that the overall relation between centre size and usage was imperfect due to the occurrence of non-size related contrasts between the retail areas. To investigate this, aggregate retail area usage totals were plotted against establishment totals, as shown in Figure 5.8. The town centre is excluded from this graph, but the remaining 71 elements of the urban retailing system are shown according to the final structural classification derived (see Figure 4.12). The graph shows quite clearly that although there is a high degree of conformity between usage and establishment totals for the hierarchic component of the system, this relationship is weaker and of a different order for the arterial ribbons. These retail area types tend to record low usage totals relative to their absolute size. These visually derived conclusions are affirmed if aggregate usage totals are recalculated for retail areas classified into their final structural groups, as shown in Table 5.4. Comparison of Tables 5.3 and 5.4 indicates that the aggregate usage totals for the retail areas in the third (district), fourth (community) and fifth (neighbourhood) size categories are markedly higher if arterial ribbons of a comparable size are excluded from them. The aggregate usage totals of the three size gradings of urban arterials are shown to be extremely low indeed.

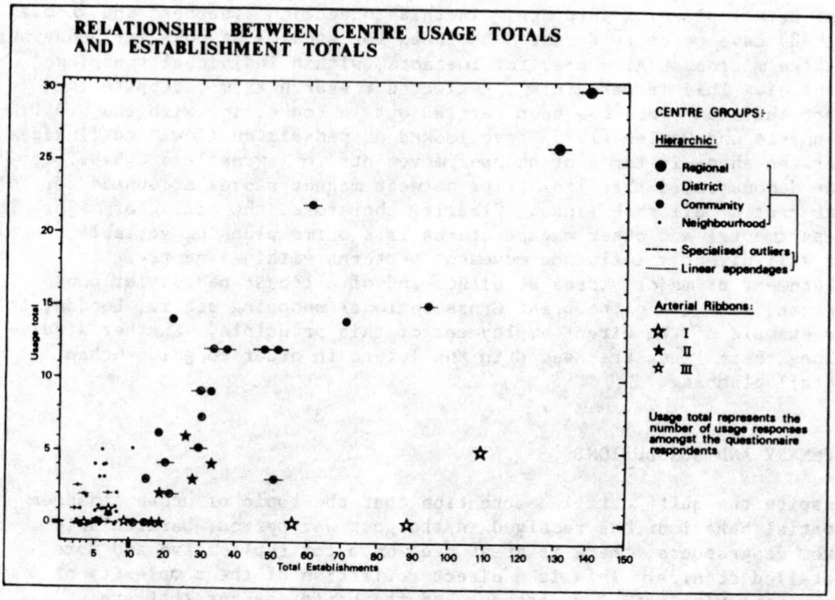

Figure 5.8 Aggregate centre usage totals in relation to urban retailing structure (Reproduced by permission from Potter, 1978)

Table 5.4
Mean aggregate usage totals of retail areas according to the final classification of the system

Hierarchic centres	Mean aggregate usage total	Arterial ribbons	Mean aggregate usage total
Central area (1)	182.00	-	-
Regional (2)	28.00	-	-
District (3)	12.83	I	1.67
Community (4)	5.92	II	2.50
Neighbourhood (5)	1.26	III	0.33

If nothing else, such results provide a behavioural verification of the structural classification of the urban retailing system of Stockport that was presented in the previous chapter. Thus, in terms of their overt behaviour at least, the consumers appeared to be aware of the broad structural characteristics of the urban retailing system. It is tempting to argue that the low usage totals recorded for the arterial ribbons reflect their specialised functional nature and the fact that they draw through traffic and custom from a wide area. These low usage responses may also reflect the aggregate low tonal, qualitative and fabric contiguity characteristics of such areas.

It is clearly the case that more studies of the behaviour of consumers in relation to retailing structural organisation are needed, especially for retail planning purposes. In this connection, Shepherd and Thomas (1980) have recently stressed the need for studies of consumer behaviour at the microspatial scale, for instance, within individual shopping centres. This is certainly a neglected research theme, despite the fact that some work has been carried out in connection with the C.B.D.. Bennison and Davies (1977) have looked at pedestrian flows and linkages between shops in terms of shopper movements in Newcastle's C.B.D.. It was demonstrated that link trips between magnet stores accounted for 74 per cent of all such links. Clearly, therefore, the siting of major departmental and other magnet stores is a prime planning variable, for it will directly influence movement patterns within a centre. The placement of major stores at either end of a linear pedestrian concourse, such as in the Brent Cross regional shopping centre, London, is an example of the direct employment of this principle. Further studies along these lines are needed in the future in order to guide urban retail planning.

SUMMARY AND CONCLUSIONS

Despite the quite detailed attention that the topic of urban consumer spatial behaviour has received in the post war period, particularly from geographers, there is great need both for replicative and more detailed studies. This is a direct reflection of the complexity of urban shopping activity patterns and the rapid changes that are occurring both in retail structural organisation and in general socio-economic consumer traits. The research reviewed in the present chapter has exemplified the wide variations that occur in consumer behaviour according to the status and demographic variables of social class, age and family size. In this connection, many topics remain to be explored in greater detail, for example, the shopping habits of disadvantaged groups, such as the poor, the low status, the old and the infirm. In particular, the identification of the precise nature of the constraints faced by such consumer segments is an important question. Much of the research conducted up to the present, both at the aggregate and group levels has implicitly stressed the importance of preferences over and above that of constraints.

The present survey, especially as supported by the author's and other researchers' work on the spatial configuration of consumer usage fields in urban areas, has stressed that the overt behavioural fields of certain groups are highly restricted indeed. This line of argument is encapsulated in figure 5.9. It may be posited that both family status and socio-economic status variables will influence the spatial extent of such fields, in a manner that is likely to be additive and superimposed. Thus, old/low status households are by and large likely to exhibit the most constrained shopping behavioural patterns and, therefore, the most restricted fields. Similarly, young/large families of a low socio-economic standing are also likely to face a large number of temporal and spatial constraints. The planning implications of such conclusions are of some importance, for they suggest that shopping developments that involve an increased dependency on cars may suit only a limited number of consumer groups and may increase constraints for others. These policy oriented questions are more fully debated in Chapter 8. Another area of interest for further study is that pointed to in the last section, namely, the precise relationships existing

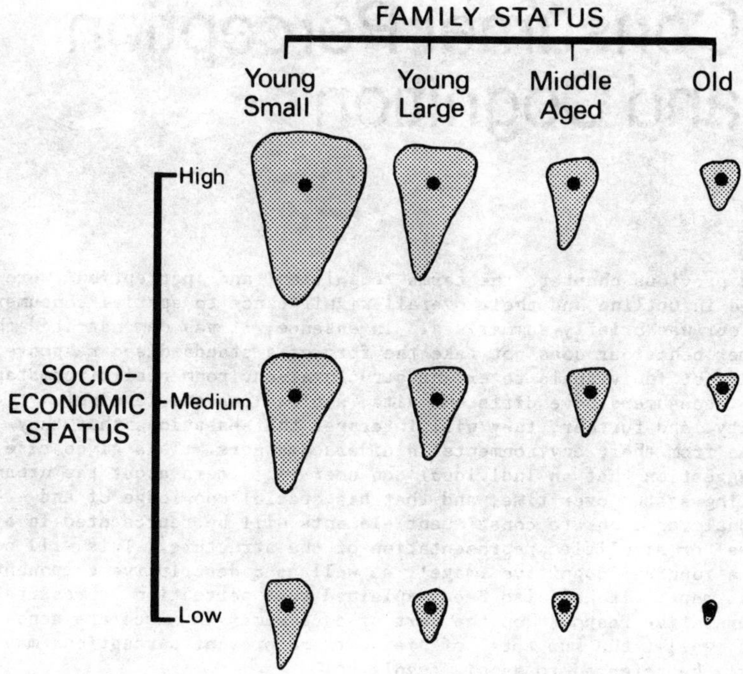

Figure 5.9 The spatial complexity of mean consumer usage fields by family status and socio-economic status

between consumer behaviour and retail structure at both the macro- and micro-spatial scales.

Clearly, the spatial nature of urban consumer behaviour is an extremely interesting and relevant topic of investigation that deserves continued attention. In the next chapter, attention is turned to the equally important subject of the spatial nature of consumer perceptions and cognitions of the urban retail system. This opens up the intriguing but complex question of the precise relations existing between retail structure, consumer attributes and their spatial cognitions, and their manifestation in the form of overt behavioural responses.

6 Aspects of Spatial Consumer Perception and Cognition

In the previous chapter, the terms 'cognition' and 'perception' were defined in outline and their overall significance to spatial consumer behaviour was briefly summarised. In essence, it was demonstrated that consumer behaviour does not take the form of a standardised response on the part of individuals to extant structural-environmental circumstances. Rather, consumers have different aims, aspirations and levels of mobility, and further, they will interpret the sensations that they receive from their environments in diverse manners. This gives rise to the suggestion that an individual consumer will learn about the urban retailing system over time, and that his spatial knowledge of and emotional reactions to constituent elements will be represented in a 'schema' or simplified representation of the structure. This will comprise a rounded 'cognitive image', as well as a descriptive component or 'mental map'. It has also been explained that perception represents the interpretative response on the part of a consumer to immediate sensations, whilst the sum total of his past and present perceptions may properly be referred to as his cognition.

As is implied above, there are really two separate although closely interlinked components of consumer cognition-perception. First, there is a basically *designative aspect*, which involves pure environmental-spatial knowledge of the location, size, disposition, shape and texture of phenomena (Pocock, 1973; Pocock and Hudson, 1978). In simple terms, this component involves the 'whatness' and 'whereness' of environmental objects. By and large, if represented in graphical-spatial form, this aspect is akin to the mental map of the consumer. In the present volume, this has already been referred to as the consumer information field (see Chapter 5, especially Figures 5.2 and 5.3, and the accompanying text). There is, however, another important ingredient of cognition-perception and that is the *appraisive response*, which involves 'the meaning attached to, or evoked by, the physical form' (Pocock and Hudson, 1978, p. 68). This essentially comprises consumers' emotional reactions, including the meaning that they attach to structural attributes and whether they like, dislike or are indifferent to particular retail centres. Taken together, the appraisive and designative components of consumer cognition comprise the mental image of a consumer and this obviously connotes aspatial as well as spatial aspects of retail structure.

The present chapter aims to provide a basic outline of research carried out on these important topics. In the first section, aspects of designative consumer information fields are considered through the author's research and that of others. The problems involved in eliciting, measuring and analysing such phenomena are stressed, a point which is returned to in the conclusion to the chapter. A more detailed examination of research dealing with the factors affecting consumer decision-making is then provided, which follows on from the material presented on this topic in Chapter 5. This is followed by a consideration of studies of appraisive aspects of consumer cognition. In this account, the methods used to examine such responses, for example, repertory grids and personal construct theory and multidimensional scaling are examined. Once again, problems of measurement and interpretation are shown to be formidable. The question of consumer cognition at the intra-centre level of the C.B.D. is then examined. Another area of significance involves the precise relations existing between cognition and aggregate urban retailing structure. This is obviously an important topic, although it is one that has received relatively little direct attention. Finally, in this chapter, the study of urban retail cognition is evaluated in the context of the current debate surrounding the overall efficacy of the behavioural-perceptual paradigm in environmental research. In Chapter 7, this is followed by a replicative study of consumer behaviour and spatial cognition carried out by the author in the Swansea urban area.

DESIGNATIVE COGNITION AND CONSUMER INFORMATION FIELDS

A fundamental point concerning the spatial nature of consumers' designative cognition of urban retailing facilities emanates from the generalisations reached about overt urban consumer behaviour in Chapter 5. If consumer behaviour shows features such as sectoral and directional bias, and marked variation by consumer status variables, it is tempting to ask whether similar spatial properties characterise their information fields. This forms the major substantive topic investigated in this section.

In asking such a question, however, a basic problem must be faced, namely, how is the researcher to go about the task of collecting accurate and meaningful data on designative consumer cognitions? The difficulties involved in obtaining information on the spatial perceptions of individuals have been usefully reviewed by Reiser (1972), and it is fair to comment that regardless of the precise method used to elicit environmental cognitions, problems of response bias and unreliability are likely to occur. Reiser notes that three major symbolic methods can be employed to elicit the designative component of spatial cognitions:

1. *Iconic method*, which depends upon the visual representation of phenomena, often at a reduced scale. For example, subjects might be asked to identify environmental features depicted in photographs or accurate line drawings.

2. *Graphic method*, where respondents indicate their knowledge of places by drawing a sketch map or by identifying features on a topographic map.

3. *Verbal method*, where a verbal description or listing of salient environmental features is provided by the survey respondents.

Undoubtedly, the most frequently employed method of acquiring data has been to ask respondents to draw a sketch map of the environment under study. All three methods can of course be used to look at the individual's cognition of urban retailing facilities. It is important to note, before examining this topic in detail, that certain groups of respondents might find it difficult to use the symbolic languages involved in different methods, so that the task may not be testing their designative perception as much as their ability to use the method selected (Reiser, 1972; Spencer, 1973). For example, it has been posited that studies such as those conducted by Orleans (1973) and Francescato and Mebane (1973), investigating ethnic and social contrasts in cognition using sketch maps, tend to run into this difficulty. Spencer (1973) has argued that lower working class respondents may find it difficult to represent their environments in this way. Another potential problem involves the precise instructional set given to the respondents, as this may also influence the form of the graphical response gained (Murray and Spencer, 1979). Further, issues such as whether a blank piece of paper should be given to interviewees, or whether they should be provided with an outline base map of the area, including details of road and district names can also be raised. The other methods of eliciting cognitive responses are not without their problems too. If the iconic approach is employed then the importance of light conditions, photograph angle and orientation loom large, and it is equally true that some individuals will be more adept at photographic recognition than others. The verbal method seems very tempting, therefore, but there are also potential difficulties with this method. For example, if environmental objects are listed by name on a questionnaire, and the respondents asked whether they know of each one, they may know the place and not the name, or *vice versa*. Similarly, different names may be used by different people for the same place. If the interviewee is asked to provide a verbal self-report of known places, then it is not possible to consider the perceived spatial relations existing between the places in his cognitions. These problems of measurement and elicitation must be constantly borne in mind in studies of designative environmental cognition and will be exemplified in the review of research in the field of retailing which follows.

The early impetus to work on designative cognition in urban areas stemmed from the seminal research of Lynch (1960), which will be discussed fully in a later section. In particular, Lynch inspired a series of papers dealing with the behavioural bases of human migration at various spatial scales (see, for example, Wolpert, 1966; Brown and Moore, 1970). Adams (1969), in a frequently quoted paper, took these ideas further in the urban setting. He argued that a resident will develop a mental map of his home town that is based on his 'kinetic' or movement field, reflecting the repeated journeys that he makes to work and to shop. Thus, the central hypothesis advanced was that the typical urban based mental map would conform to a wedge-shaped view of the city. This notion of cognitive sectoral bias is interesting when juxtaposed with the behavioural findings presented in Chapter 5. Adams argued that if this is a valid assertion, intra-urban residential migration will also occur in a predominantly sectoral fashion. This was shown to be true in Adams' limited empirical study with 75.63 per cent of all recorded moves occurring within a 90^{0} sector. Sectoral bias in the mental maps, search spaces and migrations of urban residents has been confirmed in several further studies (Simmons, 1968; Johnston, 1971, 1972; Donaldson and Johnston, 1973; Donaldson, 1973; Poulson, 1977).

Further insights were provided by Horton and Reynolds (1969, 1971), who were concerned with the relative familiarity that residents had with different parts of the city. They defined an *action space* as that part of the urban area that is most familiar to an individual, whilst the *activity space* is the zone which encompasses the area within which he undertakes the majority of his daily movements. These two components are akin to the information and usage fields defined by the present author in the urban retailing context. Horton and Reynolds maintained that a strong distance decay would occur in the action spaces of individuals away from their places of residence. Two contrasting socio-economic areas were chosen in Cedar Rapids, Iowa and respondents selected in both were asked to indicate their degree of overall familiarity on a five point scale with 27 areas making up the city. The low income group, located near to the C.B.D. showed a strong familiarity with their home area and adjacent tracts. The peripherally situated middle class group showed a marked sectoral bias in their familiarity, but overall they were familiar with a wider set of urban areas.

This type of work suggests that social differences will occur in designative cognitions, and that spatial regularities such as sectoral bias will also be evident. The present author, therefore, set out to examine whether such features characterised the retail cognitions of the respondents included in the Stockport shopping survey (Potter, 1976a, 1976c, 1977a, 1979a). To examine information fields, Part 5 of the questionnaire reproduced in Appendix 1 was devised. A base-map of Stockport and its immediately adjacent environs was included and on it, features such as the town boundary, main roads, town centre and surrounding districts were clearly denoted. The sample respondents were then invited to draw on to the map all of the shopping centres they 'use, have seen or have personally heard about'. They were then requested to indicate those centres that they actually visited in the course of their shopping.

Although as explained in Chapter 5, some 192 completed schedules were returned, usable completed base-maps were received in only 179 of these. As was found in relation to consumer usage fields, wide variations characterised the information fields pertaining to the respondents. Selected examples of these fields are included in Figure 6.1. Cases A to H are examples of relatively restricted fields which display a high degree of sectoral bias. Examples I to L are spatially more extensive and demonstrate that as the number of centres incorporated in the information fields increases, so the angular magnitude of the field and the spatial dispersion of centres tend to increase concomitantly. Complex and quite extensive retail information fields are witnessed by cases M to P. However, the tendency toward residential sector bias in available information remains evident in each of these.

The frequency distribution of the 179 respondent consumers by total number of separate retail centres comprising their information field is shown in Table. 6.1. The overall range was from one to 14 centres, although as many as 75.98 per cent of the sample had an information total of between two and five centres. The mean was 4.12 and the modal category three centres. Only including those centres located within the town, the average distance between the centres comprising the information fields of the respondents and their homes was 1.55 km., whilst the mean angular extent of such fields was 76 degrees.

These three aggregate measures of information field spatial complexity were calculated separately for consumers disaggregated by social class,

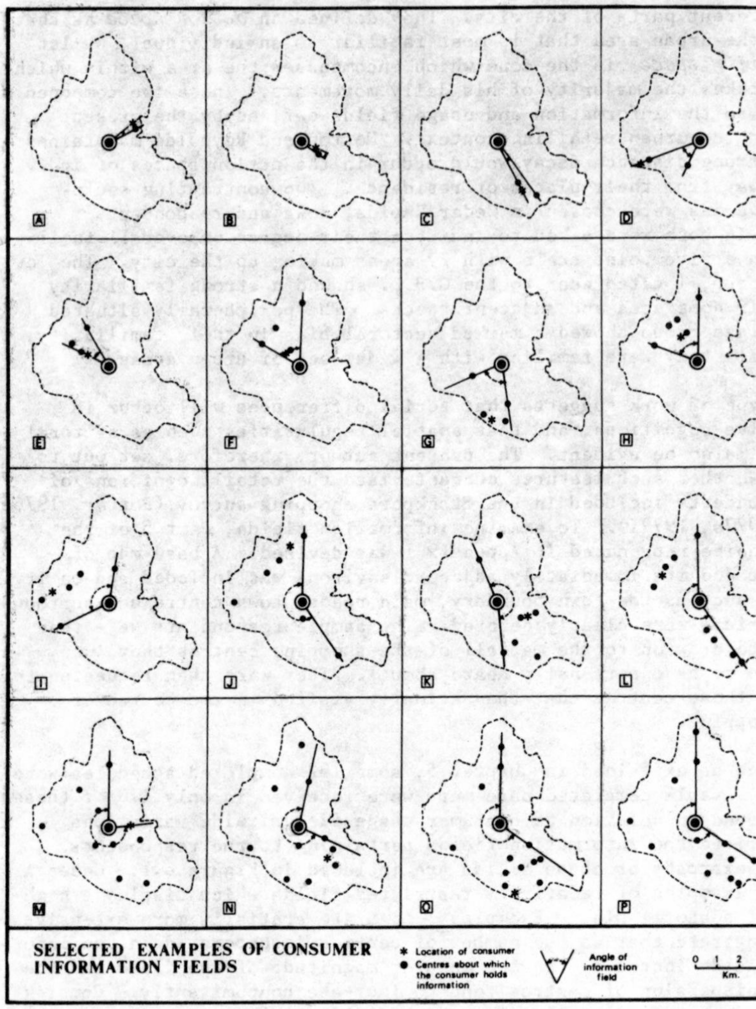

Figure 6.1 Selected examples of consumer information fields in Stockport (Reproduced by permission from Potter, 1979a)

and the results are shown collated in Table 6.2. Just as was found in connection with spatial consumer usage fields, mean information totals exhibit a striking and progressive decline for consumers in the successively lower social class groupings. Thus, mean information totals are above the average recorded for all consumers in the case of those in the upper three social classes, but are below this level for the members of social classes IV and V. Further, the average distance of constituent centres and the angular extent of the information zone both increase with movement up the social hierarchy. Thus, it is the high status consumers who show the most detailed and most spatially extensive designative cognition of the urban retailing system. Schematic

Table 6.1
Frequency distribution of consumers by information total

Total number of centres known	Number of consumers	Percentage of total consumers
1	5	2.79
2	37	20.67
3	46	25.70
4	30	16.76
5	23	12.85
6	15	8.37
7	11	6.15
8	5	2.79
9	1	0.56
10	2	1.12
11	2	1.12
12	0	0.00
13	1	0.56
14	1	0.56
	179	100.00

Table 6.2
Variations in consumer information fields by social class

Social class	Mean information total	Mean distance of centres, km.	Mean angle of information field (°)
I	5.78	1.74	143
II	5.18	1.79	110
III	4.19	1.59	75
IV	3.38	1.31	55
V	1.67	1.82	15
Economically inactive	3.20	1.43	49
Entire sample	4.12	1.55	76

representations of the overall mean dimensions of the information fields pertaining to different social class groups of urban consumers are reproduced in Figure 6.2. It is interesting to compare these revealed variations in urban consumer information fields by social class with the generally similar spatial variations found for consumer usage fields (see Figure 5.7).

Information totals, mean distances and angular magnitudes were also calculated for the consumers classified according to the age and family size variables, and again it was found that the variations paralleled those established for usage fields (Potter, 1977b, 1979a). Although there was noticeably little difference in the magnitude of the information fields pertaining to consumers up to the age of 59 years, those

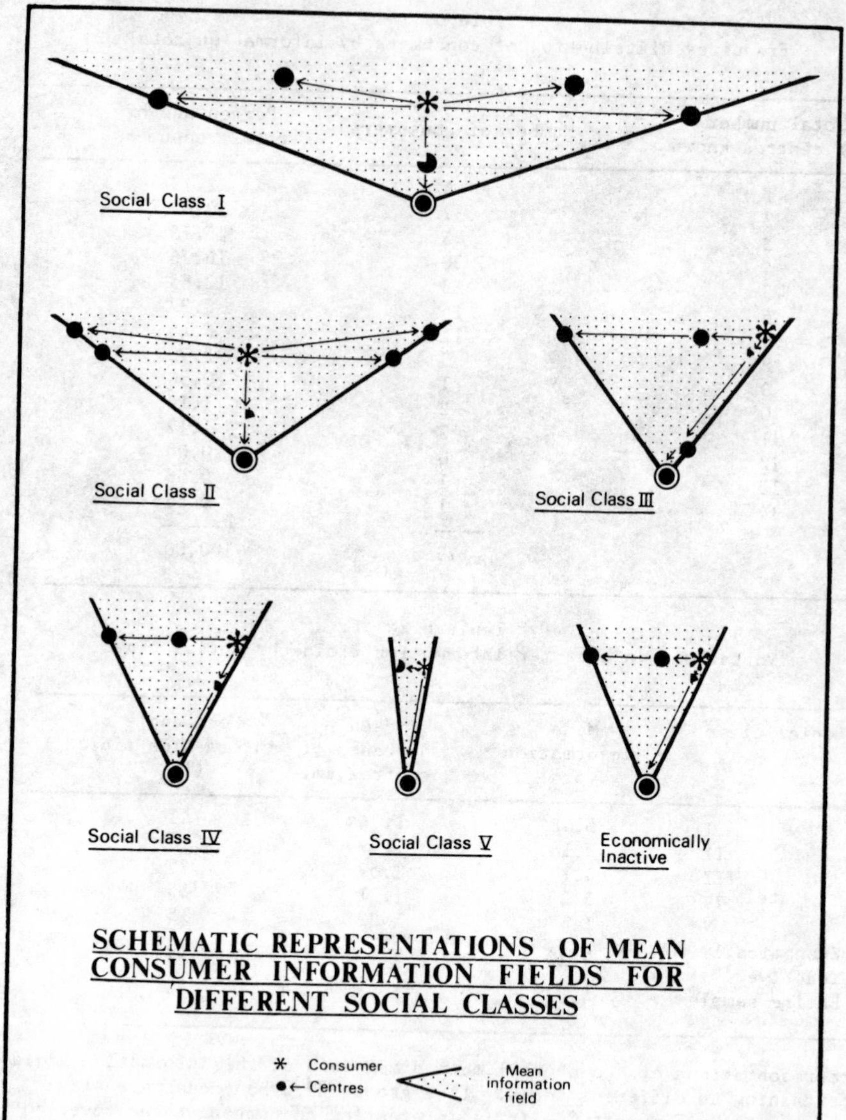

Figure 6.2 Social class variations in consumer information fields in Stockport (Reproduced by permission from Potter, 1979a)

of consumers aged 60 or over were notably restricted. Such spatial zones were also limited in the case of households with four or more children, in all probability reflecting the time, income and mobility constraints faced by such groups. Finally, a marked tendency towards a 'downtown' directional bias in designative consumer cognition was also revealed, with respondents tending to know more about those centres located toward the town centre from their places of residence than those in an uptown direction (Potter, 1976b). This finding again stresses the behavioural-cognitive relevance of the structural model of urban retailing developed and presented in Chapter 4.

In summary, the study indicated that many consumers are characterised by information fields that display a high degree of spatial propinquity. It seems significant that information fields show the same types of regularities and variations as those displayed by usage zones, so that they appear to be closely related. In terms of policy imperatives, it is tempting to suggest that the results imply that out-of-town and peripheral large-scale shopping developments that are largely dependent on car borne trips will be suited to the requirements of only a limited number of consumers (Potter, 1979a, 1980b). This argument is exemplified if graphical representations of the average dimensions of the information and usage fields pertaining to the Stockport consumers according to their stated frequency of use made of cars for shopping are examined. Figure 6.3 shows that there is a clear relationship between these two variables, and the planning implications of this association will receive attention in Chapter 8. Figure 6.3 also demonstrates that restricted behaviour appears to be associated with restricted cognition. Certainly, more studies of an holistic nature that look at both shopper cognition and behaviour together are needed.

It might be argued that as a graphical method of response acquisition was used in the Stockport study of information fields, the variations found in them by social class are simply a reflection of the ability of consumers of different educational backgrounds to complete a graphical exercise (see Mackay, 1976). It is difficult to entirely refute this argument, although it can be said that as the study was looking at perceptions of spatial phenomena, it appears reasonable that a graphical method should have been used. Further, the close correspondence shown between usage and information fields tends to give credence to the findings concerning consumer cognitions.

Other holistic studies of urban consumer information fields are unfortunately relatively few and far between. Studies along these lines, completed mainly in the mid-1970s, have generally looked at consumers' cognitions of restricted retail phenomena such as supermarkets (Mackay, Olshavsky and Sentell, 1975) and grocery stores (Hanson, 1976, 1977; Smith, 1976; Parker, 1976). Further, few studies have examined simultaneously, aspects of consumer behaviour and cognition. An exception is offered by the recent work of Timmermans, van der Heijden and Westerveld (1981) in the context of Eindhoven, The Netherlands. Here, some 194 respondents were asked to assess their familiarity with 24 shopping centres using a five-point rating scale. Numbers of centres, mean distances and several measures of directional and sectoral bias were enumerated for each sample consumer. Information totals were found to range from one to 17 centres, although 92.8 per cent of consumers knew of between one and ten centres. The mean information total was 6.41 centres, and considerable evidence of distance, directional and sectoral bias in shopping centre cognition was revealed. However, only limited relationships were found to exist between information field complexity and personal characteristics in the Dutch setting.

Parker (1976) has provided an interesting examination of consumers' knowledge of shopping facilities in Dublin, Ireland. Sample consumers

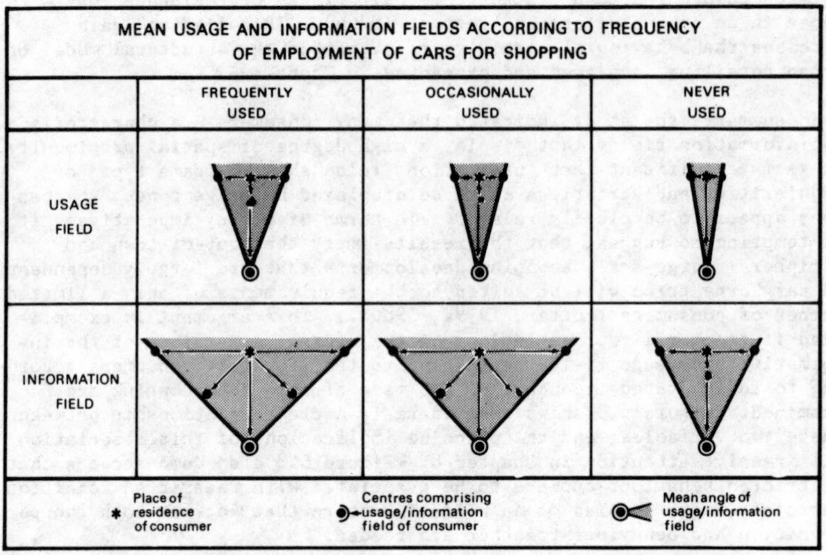

Figure 6.3 Mean usage and information fields in Stockport according to use made of cars for shopping

in 12 different areas of the city were asked to indicate their level of awareness of retail areas. Dublin was divided into its 31 constituent wards and respondents were invited to rate their familiarity with the facilities existing in each. A score of one indicated extreme familiarity and a score of four complete unfamiliarity. The method is of note for it does not depend upon a graphical or iconic mode of response, although some fineness of detail is clearly lost as a consequence. Average familiarity scores were then calculated for each sub-area. Examples of the results obtained are to be found in Figures 6.4 and 6.5. The awareness spaces of consumers in two of the outer suburban districts of Dublin are shown in Figure 6.4. In both cases, a marked sectoral bias in degree of familiarity is witnessed, for residents are aware of facilities in their home area, in the city centre, and in the tracts between these two locations. In Figure 6.5, similar awareness maps are shown for two inner urban area samples of consumers. The residents of the 'Rotunda B' district show fairly low levels of awareness and a strong home bias, whilst those living in the 'Merchants Quay C' district have a more extensive information field, but nevertheless one with a very high degree of home sector bias.

Another study which is of some methodological interest was carried out by Poulsen (1977) in Hamilton, New Zealand, a city with a population of 80,000. Respondents were presented with photographs of 20 shopping centres in the town which they had to identify and locate. In the case of two of the centres, photographs were taken at both ends of the main street so as to take into account the direction of approach customarily employed by consumers. It was found that levels of correct identification were closely related to the size of centres. However, some evidence of spatially restricted knowledge occurred at the neighbourhood centre level. Poulsen's work raises the interesting issue of the possible influence of city size on the incidence of sectoral bias. It seems reasonable to posit that the smaller the city, the less the likelihood of restricted cognition. This is certainly an hypothesis that warrants further study.

In another survey, Hanson (1976, 1977) investigated individuals' 'information' or 'cognitive' levels about food retailing stores, this time in Uppsala, Sweden. A total of 90 grocery stores, all located within a 8 km. radius of the C.B.D. were selected and presented to the consumers as stimuli. Each store was named and its location described. A seven point rating-scale of familiarity was employed. It was found that information levels declined rapidly with distance away from the home, with 2-2.5 km. emerging as a critical distance. Higher overall levels of familiarity were found for facilities situated in the C.B.D.-oriented sector, confirming the existence of strong sectoral bias. Finally, Smith (1976) completed a study of mental information about grocery stores in a section of Hamilton, Ontario. The information fields of residents were measured by the number of individual stores reported and their mean distance. It was found that information field complexity increased with increasing social class and length of residence in the urban area.

In conclusion, it would appear that distance, directional and sectoral biases in consumer behaviour and spatial cognition are important and recurrent features, and as such, they must be taken into account both in models of urban retail organisation and urban retail structural plans. The manifest variations that characterise the usage and information fields of different social groups of consumers, and the limited nature of the fields recorded for certain disadvantaged consumer groups must also be regarded as being of great practical relevance. Despite the problems of measurement and interpretation encountered, further studies of these features are therefore required as a basis for sound planning and academic observation.

CONSUMER CHOICE AND APPRAISIVE COGNITION

Although it is an obvious truism to observe that shopping centres cannot form a part of the behavioural fields of urban consumers unless they are known to them, it is just as clear that designative perceptions cannot alone explain overt shopping behaviour. Rather, designative cognitions must be regarded as setting the spatial limits within which consumer behaviour will occur at a given time. Further, it hardly seems necessary to debate whether cognition influences behaviour or *vice versa*, for there is patently a reciprocal and cumulative link between the two. The actual choice of shopping centres for particular purchases will be influenced by a consumer's appraisive or emotional response to the constituent elements of his designative cognitions. In fact, changes in the appraisive perceptions of a consumer may lead to changes in his information field. For example, a fall in income might lead an individual to place more stress on the proximity and price levels of shopping centres than was formerly the case. In these circumstances, the consumer might embark on a new search phase in order to find a cheaper centre located closer to his home. These sorts of changes in designative and appraisive cognitions are implicit in the present author's model of spatial consumer behaviour, presented in

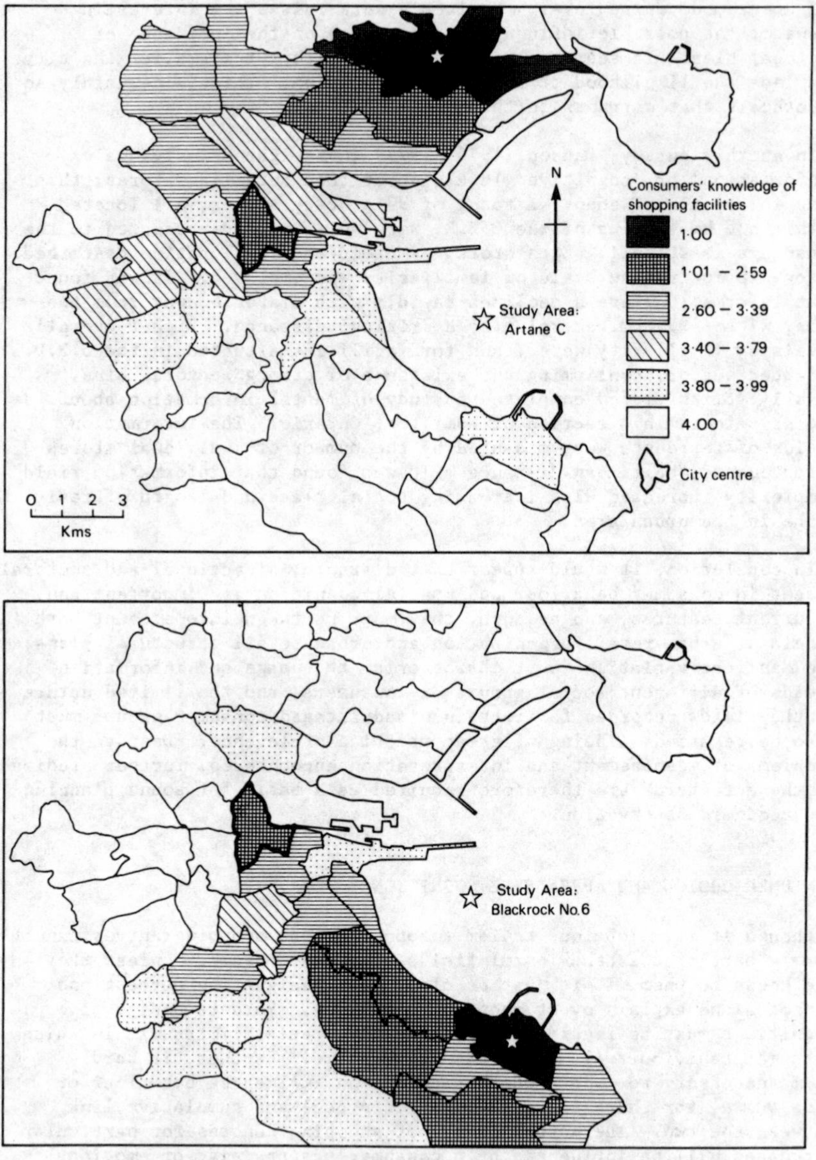

Figure 6.4 Consumer awareness spaces in the outer suburbs of Dublin (Redrawn by permission from Parker, 1976)

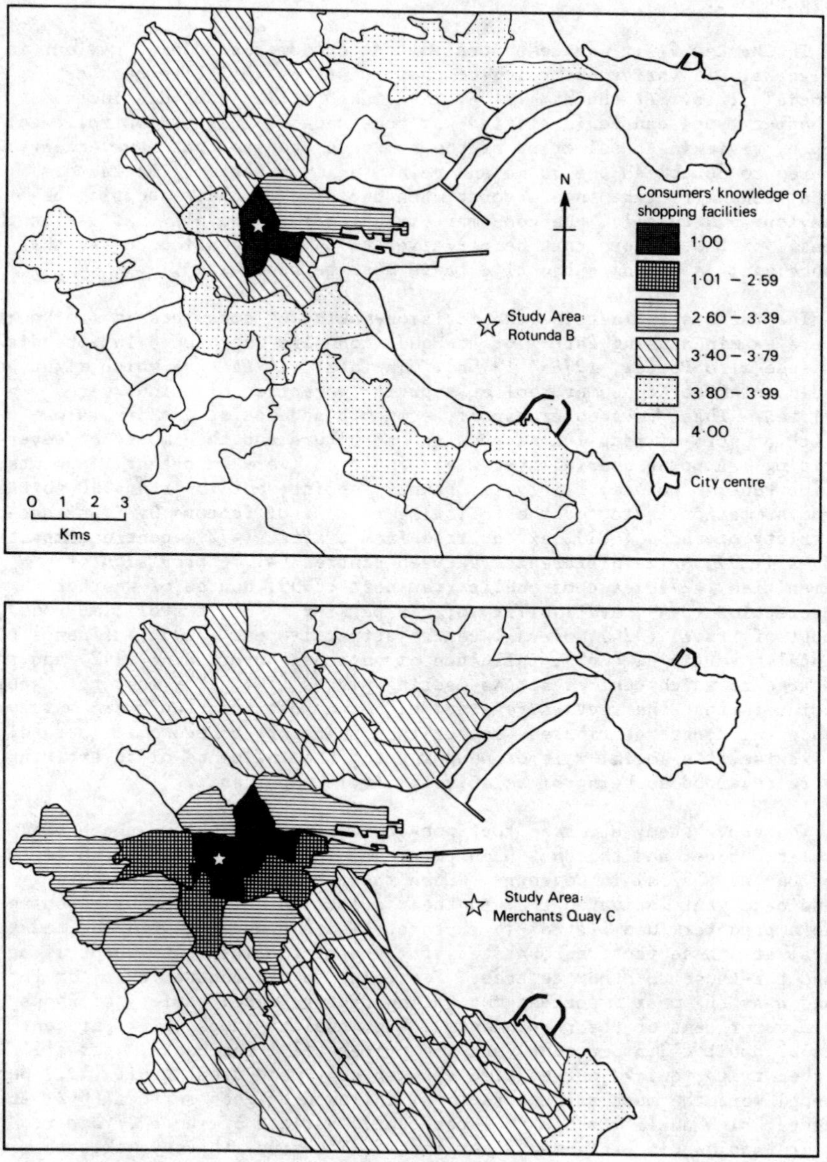

Figure 6.5 Consumer awareness spaces in the inner suburbs of Dublin (Redrawn by permission from Parker, 1976)

Figure 5.2.

In Chapter 5, it was demonstrated that consumer spatial behaviour is diverse, and varies according to shopper status variables such as social class. At the same time, the linked notion that distinct shopper types can be identified was considered. This can be followed up by reviewing a selection of the numerous studies that have endeavoured to establish the range and relative importance of the factors that consumers take into account when deciding on their shopping behaviour. Naturally, the consumer evaluates shopping alternatives on the basis of the factors that he perceives to be of significance, so that once again a strong subjective basis must be recognised.

The factors influencing the decision-making of consumers in Stockport were examined using Part 4 of the questionnaire reproduced in Appendix 1 (see also Potter, 1976a, 1979b). In total, 14 factors which might be held to affect consumer choice, especially centre selection, were listed. These covered transport, economic and social factors, along with aspects of retail area physical structure and the impact of advertising. A point scoring system was employed (very important: 3 points; important: 2 points; fairly important: 1 point; not important: 0 points), and summation indicated the following ranking of factors by importance: variety of shops (491), extent free from traffic (472), centre compactness (428), price differences between centres (427), provision of amenities (427), ease of public transport (395), degree of weather protection (394), availability of car parking (371), travel time (344), cost of travel (324), overall centre attractiveness (322), influence of local advertising (163), influence of national advertising (142) and the degree to which centres act as meeting places (74). The most noticeable point is that the factors regarded as being most important were mainly shopping centre attributes, rather than transport or economic factors. Likewise, the social role of shopping and the influence of advertising were regarded as being of relatively little importance.

The above study stresses that non-economic variables influence consumer choice, and this has been borne out in other surveys, such as that of Davies (1973a) in Coventry. Here the respondents were asked to indicate what motivated them in their selection of centres by recourse to a predetermined list of 15 factors. The respondents were invited to evaluate these factors separately for shopping trips to the central area and for those to other centres. For trips to the central area, by far and away the most important motivating factors were: variety of shops (12.6 per cent of the respondents), high quality shops (12.4 per cent), usual habit (12.3 per cent) and low prices (12.1 per cent). For all other trips, quick journey time (22 per cent) and usual habit (19.7 per cent) were the most salient factors, followed by good service (8.2 per cent), high quality shops (8.1 per cent), variety of shops (7.1 per cent) and meeting friends (7 per cent). The study thereby makes the obvious but very important point that the factors affecting consumer choice vary according to the purpose of the trip. Once again, non-economic factors such as good service, high quality goods and variety of shops are shown to be influential. Similarly, the significance of retail area structural variables over pure accessibility considerations was also demonstrated by Pacione (1975) in a study based on the Tayside region of Scotland. Seven pre-selected criteria were evaluated by the respondents on a seven point scale, and the revealed order of importance was shop quality, price levels, shop reliability, variety, accessibility, combined trips and centre atmosphere/appearance. The factors influencing the selection of convenience good stores by 443 consumers in the northern area of Johannesburg were examined by Patricios (1978, 1979, 1980) using 33 variables categorised on an *a priori* basis. Of the 14 most influential variables, eight were related to the character of shops (helpful personnel, clean shop, high quality, wide selection, good reputation, convenient opening times, adequate number of personnel and easy to move through the shop). The remaining six variables reflected movement considerations (short journey, near, easy car access, short walking distance from car to shop, low travel cost, easy to find parking). Shopping centre related factors on the other hand were evaluated far less highly. Patricios concludes that many planners will be surprised that aggregate shopping centre attributes are of secondary importance, although the author stresses that a well designed centre as the container of good individual shops remains a highly desirable goal. One important methodological point should be considered when interpreting Patricios' results, however, and that is that the questions related directly to the reasons why consumers chose particular establishments, so it hardly seems surprising that shopping centre attributes were not revealed as being of prime motivating influence.

The final study considered here is that of Parker (1976) where 12 preselected motivating factors were identified, and respondents in Dublin asked to rank them in order of importance in connection with their grocery shopping. For the sample taken as a whole, the most important factors were accessibility, cleanliness, range of goods and prices. Middling importance was attached to reputation, service and opening hours. The other factors included, such as easy parking, the offering of credit, trading stamps and deliveries, and the opportunity to meet people were found to be relatively unimportant. An interesting further insight is provided in this work, for it was shown that the relative importance attached to different factors varied by social status, and car ownership. For example, consumers in professional occupations placed greater emphasis on the range of goods offered than they did on accessibility, cleanliness and price levels.

Such studies indicated that non-economic factors, especially shopping centre and retail establishment physical, service and visual characteristics are important determinants of shopper choice. Such a finding affirms the importance of the structural variables and associated indices of measurement reviewed in Chapter 4. Further, it is apparent that the factors influencing consumer decision-making not only vary according to the purpose of the trip, but the emphasis placed on these factors will differ between individuals. Once again, we return to the argument that although general trends can be deduced, shoppers cannot be regarded as a uniform and undifferentiated mass. In fact, consumer choice is highly subjective, and may well be based on inaccurate or even entirely erroneous information. This assertion is well illustrated by research carried out to examine individuals' perception of distance in urban areas. Canter and Tagg (1975) stressed the importance of such work within cities and suggested that a confusing city structure may lead to the general overestimation of distances, whilst a more coherent urban form may result in underestimation. Interestingly, Lee (1970) in a study based on Dundee found that distances between points tended to be consistently overestimated. However, it was revealed that distances in an outward direction from the city centre were constantly overestimated by a greater margin than inward ones. Lee maintained that this was the result of urban residents' focal orientation towards the city centre, so that the phenomenon of downtown directional bias occurs. In another study, Pacione (1975) compared consumers' perception of distance to shopping centres with actual distances and found that perceptual accuracy was inversely related to objective distance. Further, a far greater degree of perceived accuracy was found in connection with those centres which were actually visited by consumers. Similarly, the centres most preferred by consumers were also more accurately perceived in terms of distances, a finding that tends to imply that overt behaviour is closely related to spatial cognition. Similar perceptual distortions may occur in relation to other variables, such as price levels, and some researchers have argued that behaviour can be quite unrelated to price (Trinkaus, 1980). However, price is likely to be a very important factor for certain consumer groups, such as old age pensioners (see Parker, 1978, for example).

A more rigorous technique for the examination of appraisive consumer cognitions is that of the *semantic differential*, which is often associated with principal components or factor analytic methods. The technique was first developed by Osgood (see Osgood, Suci and Tannenbaum, 1957, and Oppenheim, 1966) and involves the use of a number of bipolar seven point rating scales, the extremes of which are defined by an adjective. The respondent is presented with a set of relevant scales and is asked to rate the objects or concepts under study on them. Subsequently, it is possible to factor analyse sets of scales in an effort to look for basic dimensions of meaning amongst the respondents. A good example of the use of this method in the study of consumers' cognitions is offered by Downs (1970), who examined the views of 202 housewives of the Broadmead shopping centre in Bristol. It was initially hypothesised that the image of such a city centre shopping district would be based on the nine cognitive categories of price, structure, ease of internal movement, visual appearance, reputation, range, service, opening hours, atmosphere. Four scales were then derived for each cognitive category, giving a total of 36 seven point scales. Examples of these are well designed/badly designed, clean/dirty, busy/not busy. Each of the respondents rated the centre on each of the 36 scales and the emergent matrix was factor analysed. It was concluded that consumers' cognition of the centre consisted of eight principal dimensions: firstly, service quality, which accounted for 21.9 per cent of the original variance, followed in order of importance by price, structure-design, shopping hours, internal pedestrian movement, range, visual appearance, and traffic conditions. It is notable that retail establishment factors were of especial importance as opposed to aggregate shopping centre traits.

A particularly thorny problem with the above method involves the interpretation and naming of the derived components. However, there is a more fundamental criticism in that the semantic differential method, in common with the other studies reviewed earlier in this section, involves the prespecification of factors by the researcher (Burnett, 1973; Timmermans, 1980a). Partly as a reaction to this problem, some workers have suggested that the method of *multidimensional scaling* should be used in studies of consumer cognition. This involves the consumer in specifying the preferences that he holds between pairs of study objects, in the present context, shopping centres. An advantage of the method is that no preselection of attributes or motivating factors is required, for these are derived directly from the computational procedure itself and hence are neither named or brought to the interviewee's attention (Spencer, 1980; Timmermans *et al.*, forthcoming). The method results in the derivation of a configuration of the study objects in a multidimensional space according to their perceived similarity amongst the respondents. The researcher then views this patterning and seeks to identify the meanings of the dimensions. Multidimensional scaling methods have been used by Burnett (1973) in relation to women's shopping for clothing, and also recently by Spencer (1978, 1980) and Blommenstine, Nijkamp and van Veenendaal (1980). A likely problem with this method, however, is that consumers may not know of all the centres included in the survey by the researcher, and may thus be unable to make pairwise comparisons of them all. This appears to have been the case in Spencer's (1978, 1980) study, and only 200 out of 381 consumers interviewed felt able to complete the task. Significantly, Spencer included seven shopping centres in his study and this is considerably greater than the information totals shown to apply to the majority of urban consumers earlier in this chapter (see Table 6.1, for example). Another point to bear in mind is that subjectivity occurs when the researcher interprets and seeks to name the attributes underlying the dimensions (Timmermans, *et al*, forthcoming; Spencer, 1980). Added to these problems of elicitation and interpretation is the fact that the method has little or no theoretical foundation.

The requirement is for a flexible yet robust method that affords the consumer the opportunity of expressing his own cognitive structure. Increasingly, researchers in the field have turned to Kelly's (1955) *Personal Construct Theory* and the associated *Repertory Grid* technique (see Fransella and Bannister, 1977). The approach essentially focuses on the individual and the way in which he structures phenomena by means of his own personal constructs. A *construct* is the way in which two objects are alike and thereby different from a third. Operationally, the technique involves the interviewee being presented with the study objects in sets of three or 'triads'. He is asked to stipulate in what way two of these are similar and thus different from the third. For example, in connection with shopping centres, a consumer might say that two are big whilst the third is small, or that two are dispersed and the other compact. Thus, the constructs elicited would be big/small and compact/dispersed respectively. The process is continued until successive triads reveal no further new constructs. The method is extremely flexible and both the study objects and/or constructs may be either freely elicited from respondents or given by the researcher. The responses of an individual may be tabulated in a *repertory grid*, with the study objects appearing in the columns and the constructs in the rows. Respondents can then be asked to scale the study objects on each of the constructs.

The flexibility of the method also applies to analysis, and as Hudson (1980) has noted, there are two approaches that can be followed. First, a soft/subjective analysis may be pursued, involving examination of the number, nature and types of elements and constructs derived. In particular, the labels of the constructs can be viewed so as to establish the dimensions consumers employ in evaluating the study objects. Secondly, a hard/objective approach can be followed if principal components, factor analysis or multidimensional scaling are applied to either individual or group grids. In the latter case, individual grids may be combined to form a 'supergrid' if the elements and/or constructs are standardised. At this juncture, however, the method is largely analogous to the multivariate analysis of semantic differential scales.

These methods have been employed since the early 1970s in order to study consumer cognitions of shops (Hudson, 1974), and retailers' images of the retail environment (Harrison and Sarre, 1975). An excellent illustration of the utility of the method is given by the recent work of Timmermans *et al.* (forthcoming). Twelve shopping centres were selected in the Woensel district of Eindhoven by the researchers. For the 20 consumers interviewed, the number of separate constructs elicited varied from 8 to 16, with an average of 11.8. The number of shops present in a centre was the most frequently elicited construct, applying to 19 of the consumers. This was followed by parking, location relative to home, atmosphere, range, presence of non-retail functions, upkeep, possibility of shopping around, degree of specialism; all of these constructs being mentioned by ten or more of the consumers. Finally, a factor analysis was performed on each grid to check for redundancy, and the two most important dimensions were found to be centre size in relation to atmosphere, and overall accessibility. Such findings serve to exemplify the potential utility of the method. However, Hudson (1980) has stressed one important cautionary point in noting that whilst the method explains cognitive structure, it cannot directly explain overt behaviour as this is influenced by constraints as well as by preferences.

Clearly, the study of consumer choice and appraisive cognitions is a complex but potentially extremely rewarding task, for it is only by knowing how consumers evaluate the urban retailing environment that planners can design and build better ones. Accordingly, there is little doubt that methodological and substantive research will continue in this important field of enquiry in the future.

COGNITION AT THE C.B.D. LEVEL

Despite the fact that as observed in Chapter 5, relatively little research has been carried out into consumer spatial behaviour at the intra-retail centre and C.B.D. scales, a number of studies have investigated consumer cognition of the structure of C.B.D.s. In great part, this attention probably reflects the fact that Kevin Lynch's (1960) seminal study, *The Image of the City*, was conducted at this level. As a planner and architect, Lynch was primarily concerned with the visual quality of the city and the degree to which its structure was legible or 'imageable' to its residents. Denizens of three American cities, Boston, Jersey and Los Angeles were interviewed and requested to provide a sketch map of the central city together with descriptions of a number of trips through it and a listing of its most distinctive elements. This was the first major designative-sketch map drawing exercise to be carried out in an urban setting. Lynch posited that the elements of derived images of urban structure could be classified into five broad categories, namely:

1. *Paths*: which are channels of movement such as roads and railways.

2. *Edges*: linear elements which cannot be travelled along, which mainly comprise boundaries between zones.

3. *Districts*: areas which display a common character.

4. *Nodes*: strategic points which can be entered.

5. *Landmarks*: important points which cannot be entered.

These categories are not without ambiguity, however, and in practice, for instance, it can be difficult to distinguish between nodes and landmarks, whilst many paths may also act as very strong edges. It is notable, however, that shop related phenomena are likely to play a prominent part in such urban images. For example, major stores tend to coincide with major nodes, and may themselves constitute important landmarks if defined in the widest sense. Similarly, shops are linked along paths and spatial clusters of shops may form distinct districts (for example, a high quality retail area, a professional and banking district). Shop elements certainly featured quite prominently in residents' views of all three cities. The images of the three cities studied by Lynch, as derived from the consensus of both sketch maps and verbal interviews were mapped. The features mentioned or drawn by respondents were categorised into the five above listed elements, and were shown according to the overall frequency of citation made by them. Notably, for each of the three cities, the image based on verbal responses was much more complex than that based on sketch maps.

The Lynchian methodology has been employed in a large number of further studies, mainly as the result of its simplicity and ease of operation. Thus, Goodey *et al.* (1971) summated residents' sketch maps of Birmingham city centre and showed that features associated with shopping, especially magnet stores, predominated. Interestingly, Goldman (1975) asked residents of Jerusalem to name as many of the city's stores selling ladies' shoes and furniture as they could, and found that a large proportion of recalls were made in terms of nearby landmarks rather than by the name of the store. Similarly, Davies and Bennison (1978) asked a sample of students to draw sketch maps of the central shopping area of Newcastle and noted that a heavy accent was placed on major landmarks and non-retailing activities. Presumably such features are of considerable assistance to consumers in planning their shopping trips within the C.B.D.. Other studies have revealed that the spatial extent and complexity of central city images are positively related to factors such as social class, age and length of residence (Orleans, 1973; Francescato and Mabane, 1973; Goodchild, 1974; Matthews, 1980), in much the same way as was found in connection with consumer information totals. In fact, the parallels existing between city-wide retail cognitions, and those of the C.B.D. are clearly exemplified in a study of children's perception of the Broadmead planned shopping district of central Bristol, completed by Smith, Shaw and Huckle (1979). Children in three broad age groups were asked to name verbally as many shops in the area as they could in a five minute period. Then, amongst these they were asked to indicate those stores that they had visited in the preceding year. These counts were referred to as the 'awareness' and 'activity' spaces of the children and represent the equivalents of intra-centre information and usage totals respectively. It was shown that both cognition and actual usage of different shops increased progressively with age. At the same time, the children's attitudinal response to the centre was also shown to become more positive over time. This is an interesting study of the relations existing between behaviour, designative and appraisive cognitions at the C.B.D. level and further work along these lines, looking at social class variations for instance, would be productive. Research has also affirmed the operation of the principle of sectoral bias at the C.B.D. level. Klein (1967) examined residents' definition of the town centre of Karlsruhe, Germany and found that there was a tendency for respondents to exaggerate the extent of the C.B.D. towards their home and to contract it in other directions. Biases in distance perception within the C.B.D. were also demonstrated in Meyer's (1977) study of Erlangen, Germany. Here, it was found that the length of shopping streets tended to be consistently over-estimated. Significantly, however, the distances of preferred shopping streets and those leading towards the respondent's home tended to be relatively underestimated. It is interesting to observe that Meyer originally wanted respondents to draw sketch maps of the C.B.D., but had to abandon this approach, when 19 out of 31 respondents interviewed were unable to do so. Clearly, problems of image elicitation and measurement are recurrent ones, regardless of the spatial scale at which behavioural-perceptual studies are conducted.

COGNITION AND AGGREGATE RETAIL STRUCTURE

In this final major section of the chapter, we briefly return to the author's Stockport-based case study, for the survey design made it possible to calculate the number of times each shopping centre in the system was known amongst the 192 survey respondents. Thus, just as the aggregate usage totals of retail areas were analysed in Chapter 5, so it is possible to consider their *aggregate information totals* (see also Potter, 1976a, 1978).

Mean aggregate information totals were first calculated for the 71 retail areas grouped by their broad size divisions, and a positive association between the two variables was revealed (Table 6.3). The correlation between establishment totals and mean aggregate information totals was +0.95, suggesting that 90 per cent of overall cognitive variability was accounted for by centre size. The two variables were associated by the linear equation:

$$I = 0.38E - 0.36$$

where I denotes the information total recorded by a retail area and E its establishment total. This association between knowledge and shopping centre size was also revealed in Poulsen's (1977) photograph based study of shopping centre identification in Hamilton, New Zealand.

Just as with aggregate usage statistics, however, it seemed worthwhile to look at centre information totals in relation to the final multivariate based classification of retail area groups. Figure 6.6 affirms the general correspondence existing between retail area size and information levels, but also shows that arterial ribbons of a given size order record noticeably lower information totals than their hierarchic counterparts. This is quantitatively demonstrated by the statistics listed in Table 6.4. The salient point is that the mean information totals recorded for hierarchic centres in the third, fourth and fifth size categories are considerably higher than those recorded for all centres in these size categories. Thus, when disaggregated from the other retail areas, the arterial ribbons are characterised by very low mean information responses relative to hierarchic centres of an equivalent size (Table 6.4).

Although only of an exploratory nature, this research implies that

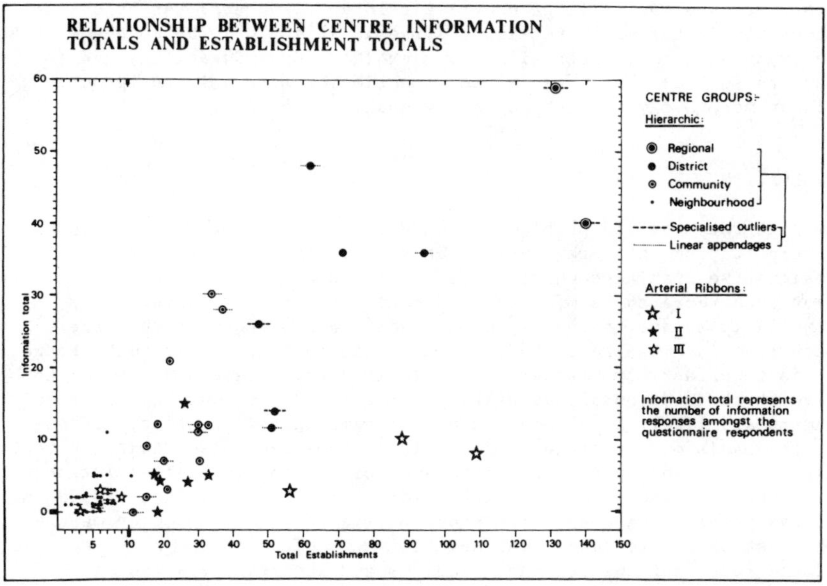

Figure 6.6 Aggregate centre information totals in relation to urban retailing structure (Reproduced by permission from Potter, 1978)

Table 6.3
Mean aggregate information totals of retail areas grouped by size

Size category	Number of retail establishments	Mean aggregate information total
1 Central area	484	192.00
2 Regional	131 - 140	49.50
3 District	47 - 109	21.44
4 Community	15 - 37	9.84
5 Neighbourhood	2 - 11	2.20

Table 6.4
Mean aggregate information totals of retail areas according to final classification of the system

Hierarchic centres	Mean aggregate information total	Arterial ribbons	Mean aggregate information total
Central area (1)	192.00	-	-
Regional (2)	49.50	-	-
District (3)	29.67	I	7.00
Community (4)	11.85	II	5.50
Neighbourhood (5)	2.24	III	1.67

consumers are aware of the non-size related structural variations that occur within the urban retailing system. It can only be concluded that in Lynchian terms, arterial ribbons exhibit low imageability due to factors such as their specialised functional nature, discontiguous, linear morphology and generally low qualitative tone.

EVALUATION

Despite the manifold problems of data elicitation, measurement and interpretation that are involved in studies of the appraisive and designative spatial cognitions of urban consumers, it is concluded here that such research is of vital and continuing significance. This is especially so due to the rapid pace and scale of changes that are occurring in urban retail structural organisation. Given such change, it is important for planners, retailers, developers and academics to have at their disposal, detailed information as to how precisely consumers are likely to respond to new circumstances. Further, although on the basis of the present review it must be recognised that the mental maps, images and spatial cognitions of consumers are manifestly subjective, personal and sometimes highly idiosyncratic, this fact should in no way deter researchers from endeavouring to study such phenomena by the most objective means available to them. This is the case regardless of the fact that the methods, findings and theoretical standing of perceptual-cognitive environmental studies have received much criticism of late, and heated debate concerning the overall efficacy of research in the field has ensued (Bunting and Guelke, 1979; Rushton, 1979; Saarinen, 1979; Downs, 1979). One criticism that needs emphasising, however, is that mental maps should not be regarded as objects which exist in cartographic form in people's heads (Bunting and Guelke, 1979; Graham, 1976). In fact, in many circumstances an individual's spatial behaviour may be guided by little more than a series of habitual stimulus-response links (Downs and Stea, 1973). Thus, Tuan (1975) has commented that 'Mental maps, then, are not representable images that people carry in their heads as they go about their business' (p. 209-10) and that as a result the terms 'schema' or 'cognitive structure' are more useful 'in that they do not suggest "picture", whether material or mental' (p. 206). Another major line of criticism is that work in the field has achieved relatively little in the way of explaining the precise nature of overt spatial behaviour (Bunting and Guelke, 1979). Here, however, we come back to an argument presented earlier, in that it must be clearly recognised that constraints are likely to influence behaviour just as much as perceptions and preferences. It thus seems rather harsh to condemn cognitive studies on these grounds. Finally, it must also be accepted that cognitive-behavioural studies will always face methodological problems of some complexity. The recent work of Murray and Spencer (1979) is illustrative in this respect for, although they found that basic drawing ability was an important intervening variable affecting the ability of respondents to produce environmental sketch maps, they concluded that whilst 'mental mapping techniques may be flawed, ... they do reflect differences in the skill of cognizing the environment which could only otherwise be brought out by laborious interviews or questionnaire techniques' (p. 391). Thereby, the stage seems set for further research in this difficult but patently intriguing and very rewarding aspect of retail and marketing research.

7 Consumer Behaviour and Cognition: A Swansea Case Study

In the foregoing chapters, it has been stressed that studies of consumer cognition and perception, together with their relationship to overt consumer behaviour entail considerable problems of both measurement and interpretation. At the same time, however, the pure and applied relevance of such studies has also hopefully been demonstrated and it has been suggested in several places that replicative studies are required. The term 'replication', however, does not merely mean the repeating of exactly the same type of work in precisely the same area, but rather, the repeated examination of a particular phenomenon of consumer behaviour and cognition in different environmental and socio-economic settings and/or using different research designs and techniques. The use of different techniques is particularly important with respect to further studies of both appraisive and designative aspects of consumer perception/cognition, for it has already been shown that formidable difficulties exist in eliciting images and mental maps in a clear and unbiased manner. Thus, although strong evidence has been furnished in the previous two chapters to indicate that there are clearly generalisable patterns of consumer behaviour and perception within urban tracts, a replicative study conducted in Swansea, Wales is presented here as corroborative evidence. The rationale behind this work, published in this volume for the first time is set out in detail in the next two sections.

AIMS OF THE RESEARCH

The principal aim of the study was to replicate the type of research into consumer usage and information fields previously carried out by the present author in Stockport, but this time using different methods in order to make up for the various shortcomings of the earlier research. The detailed aims of the project are set out below.

1. A principal aim was to counteract the possible effects of differences in retail structural provision on the consumer behaviour and perceptions of different social groups. A major problem with the type of study carried out in Stockport is that different social groups may be located in different parts of the town. If, for example, low income residents are largely situated in the inner city zone with its surfeit of small retail assemblages, whilst high income groups are mainly confined to the outer city, then this alone might account for the fact that the latter group travel farther in order to shop. Although in the Stockport research it was shown that the average distance of residential location of the five different social groups from the town centre

was not markedly different, the effects of retail structural differences cannot be entirely isolated from that of the social variable. The solution is to select a micro-spatial study area that houses residents of different circumstances in close juxtaposition.

2. A further intention was to control for non-social class differences between consumers. In the earlier study it was shown that differences in consumer behaviour and perception occurred not only by social class, but according to age, family size and car ownership/usage as well. However, the small size of the sample made it virtually impossible when looking at the influence of any one of these variables to control for the influence of the others. In order to examine class based differences in consumer behaviour/perception it is necessary to have different social groups that are matched in all other respects, for example, in terms of age, length of residence etc.

3. It was also thought desirable to use a non-graphical method of eliciting details of consumer information fields. It might be argued in the case of the Stockport study that the differences revealed in information field complexity were a reflection of the contrasting abilities of different social groups to translate their knowledge into the form of a map. It is difficult to entirely counter such an argument on the basis of the Stockport data, and so it was decided to use a written means of data elicitation.

4. A further desire was to initially restrict the definition of usage and information fields to the intra-urban realm. Taken to the extreme, a consumer might cite New York or Tokyo as forming part of his information field merely because he knows that all large cities act as major shopping nodes. This does not mean that such information should be disregarded. Rather, it can be analysed separately as the extra-urban component of the information field.

THE SURVEY DESIGN

The area in which the case study was conducted was the Swansea urban region, located at the western edge of the South Wales coalfield. Swansea had a total population of 189,853 persons in 1971. The city forms the economic, social and cultural focus of the West Glamorgan County Council administrative area which contained 373,000 persons in 1971. In fact, Swansea acts as the major urban centre for the entire south west Wales region. Thus, for example, 34 per cent of the total retail turnover of West Glamorgan occurs in Swansea.

A survey area was needed within Swansea that would satisfy the first aim listed above. The selection of such an area was facilitated by the fact that Thomas (1974) had examined the influence of socio-economic status on consumer behaviour in Swansea, as noted in Chapter 5, and in so doing, he identified six areas where high and low income groups were located in very close proximity. One of these residential neighbourhoods, that of West Cross was adopted as the case study area. West Cross is located on the coast of the south western section of the city, just to the north of Oystermouth, as shown in Figure 7.1.

The northern half of the West Cross neighbourhood consists of local authority rented housing of various ages, whilst the southern part is

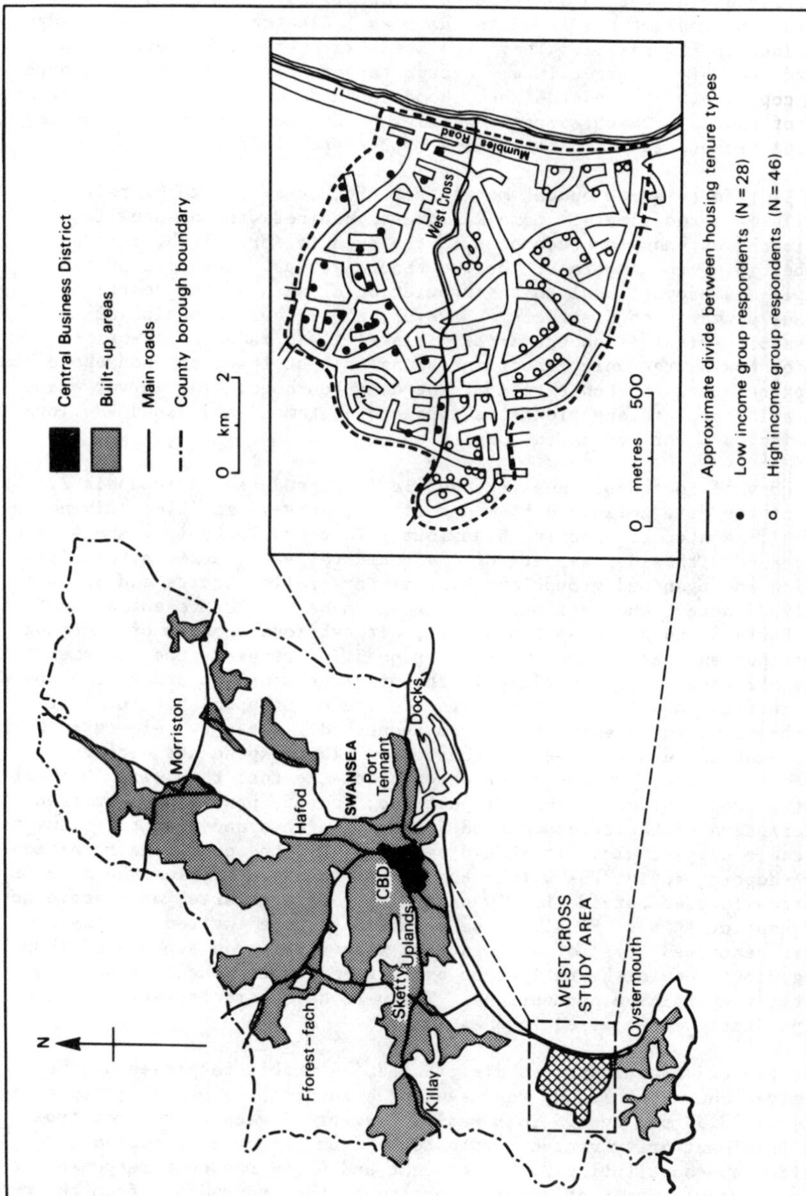

Figure 7.1 The West Cross study area and location of survey respondents

entirely given over to owner-occupied dwellings. The divide between these two tenure types is quite sharp as indicated by the inset diagram included in Figure 7.1. These two areas were therefore regarded as surrogates of different income groups rather than social class groups per se. The West Cross neighbourhood taken as a whole forms a distinct entity and is a favoured residential zone for members of both housing tenure groups, as shown in studies by Herbert (1973).

A limited research budget meant that the survey had to be relatively small-scale and simple. Some 222 questionnaires were eventually delivered by hand to households in the area in April 1978, an equal number going to members of the two tenure groups. The size of the sample was proportional to the population of each of the constituent census enumeration districts. However, the actual selection of the households within each enumeration district was made on an entirely random basis, the only constraint being that at least one household had to be selected in each street of the neighbourhood. The survey was of the self-complete questionnaire type and a stamped addressed envelope was included for return on completion.

A copy of the questionnaire schedule is reproduced in Appendix 2. Not all of the data collected by means of this survey, entitled 'Living in towns', related to shopping behaviour. In fact, Parts 1, 2 and 4 were concerned with wider aspects of environmental satisfactions, participation in organised groups and general personality traits and are not analysed here. The sections that are germane to the present account are Parts 3 and 5. Question 3 deals with various aspects of shopping behaviour and perception. The first question requests the consumer to list all those places visited in the previous month in order to shop. Any centres normally visited in the course of shopping but not listed in the previous category were then requested. These two elements should represent the usage fields of consumers. The respondents were then asked to list all of the other shopping places that they were aware of in the area, but which they did not use, thereby providing a written description of their information fields when combined with the elements of their usage field. It should be noted that the questions referred to 'shopping activities within the town', so where mention was made of centres located outside the Swansea County Borough area, a separate note was kept of these. Finally, the respondents were invited to assess their perceived level of satisfaction with five broad aspects of shopping provision in the region, so as to gain a more rounded impression of their appraisive perceptions. The personal characteristics of the respondents were covered in question 5.

Of the 222 questionnaires distributed, 74 usable responses had been received one month later, representing a respectable overall completion rate of 33.33 per cent. This varied however between 28 returns from the local authority rented sample to 46 from the owner occupied residents, constituting 25.53 per cent and 41.44 per cent response rates respectively. The spatial distribution of the respondents from the two areas is shown in Figure 7.1.

From this point onward, the local authority residents are referred to as the *low income sample* and the owner occupiers as the *high income sample*. The characteristics of the two sets of respondents are listed in Table 7.1. Although matched samples were required in all respects apart from social status, given the survey design it was not possible

Table 7.1
Characteristics of the sample consumers in the West Cross area of Swansea

(a) Sample size			
	High income group	Low income group	Entire sample
	46	28	74

(b) Age distribution			
	Percentage of total sample:		
	High income group	Low income group	Entire sample
Under 30	13.04	10.72	12.16
30-39	43.48	32.14	39.19
50 and over	43.48	57.14	48.65
Total	100.00	100.00	100.00

(c) Car ownership			
	High income group	Low income group	Entire sample
Percentage owning a car	100.00	71.43	89.20

(d) Length of residence			
	High income group	Low income group	Entire sample
Length of residence in the West Cross area (years)	13.14	16.19	14.29
Length of residence in Swansea (years)	25.70	42.30	32.15

to sample on a quota basis. Table 7.1 shows, however, that the high and low income samples are broadly matched in terms of their age, although the low income group respondents tended to be a little older. On the other hand, the sub-samples were noticeably different in terms of car ownership levels. All of the high income sample members possessed a car, as opposed to 71.43 per cent of those in the low income group. A further variable of importance is that of length of residence. Table 7.1(d) shows that whilst there was little difference in the average length of residence in the West Cross area between the two groups, there was a marked contrast in the time that they had lived in the Swansea region as a whole. Thus, whilst the low income respondents had lived in the city for an average of 42.3 years, the equivalent statistic for the more mobile high income group was much lower at

25.7 years.

THE URBAN RETAIL SYSTEM OF SWANSEA

The importance of Swansea as a regional shopping centre has already been mentioned. In fact, in 1971, the City recorded a retail turnover of £60.3 millions, representing some 59 per cent of the West Glamorgan County total. As much as £35.1 million, or as previously noted, 34 per cent was accounted for by the C.B.D. alone. The central area of Swansea has undergone considerable redevelopment since the Second World War, when it was badly damaged by bombing. In particular, the retail core has expanded westward, whilst the northern areas have tended to decline in importance.

The County Planning Department in their 1977 Structure Plan Report of Survey identified an intra-urban hierarchy consisting of the C.B.D., six district and 24 neighbourhood level centres. However, the district centres identified by the Department seemed highly disparate in terms of their size levels, and it was concluded that this classification was inadequate as a framework for the present work. A field survey of urban retailing facilities in Swansea, undertaken in 1979 by two undergraduate students supervised by the author, was therefore employed.

The distribution of commercial land in the city is shown in Figure 7.2. The high density of retail establishments in the inner city zone, especially along the main roads leading from the C.B.D. is noticeable. Almost continuous string street developments extend westward out of the city centre. Ribbon developments are also noticeable to the north of the C.B.D. The major suburban shopping centres generally occur at the intersections of the principal roads, whilst smaller centres are scattered in the interstitial areas.

In total, 55 separate retail centres were recognised within the urban area, and their size differentiation as measured by establishment totals is depicted in Figure 7.3. The elements of the system were divided into five size orders, and the spatial patterning of this classification is shown in Figure 7.4. The numerical notation used in this diagram represents the rank ordering of centres by establishment totals. The *city centre* houses as many as 627 separate retail establishments and dominates the retailing system. The second largest centre is Morriston, which is located in the north of the city and consists of 153 establishments. This is far larger than any other suburban centre and was therefore designated as a *sub-regional centre*. There are four centres with a total of between 65 and 86 shops. These were classified as *district level centres* and comprise Oystermouth (number 3) to the south of the West Cross study area, Bryn-y-Mor Road (4) to the south west of the C.B.D., and Uplands (5) and Sketty (6) both to the west of the city centre. Below this level, a continuum of centres by size is apparent, but there are eight centres with between 20 and 35 shops and these were classified as *community level centres* (Figure 7.3). The remaining 41 centres, with between five and 16 shops were labelled as *neighbourhood level facilities*. Overall, therefore, there was a 1, 2, 6, 14, 54 numerical sequence of retail centres performing functions at the five identified levels of the system.

One point about which concern has recently been expressed by the

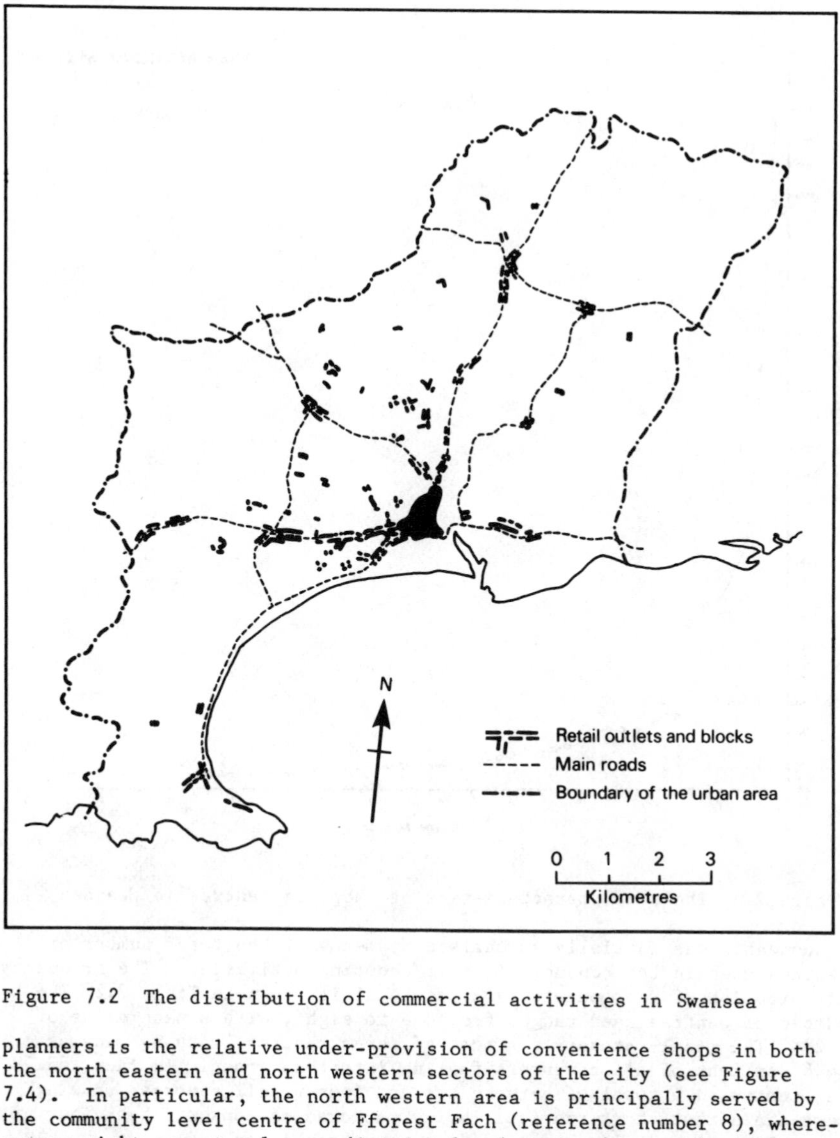

Figure 7.2 The distribution of commercial activities in Swansea

planners is the relative under-provision of convenience shops in both the north eastern and north western sectors of the city (see Figure 7.4). In particular, the north western area is principally served by the community level centre of Fforest Fach (reference number 8), whereas one might expect a larger district level centre here. The other major retail policy issue has involved several proposals to build hypermarkets and superstores. These schemes have generally been rejected in favour of the development of more adequate district level facilities.

CONSUMER BEHAVIOUR AND USAGE FIELDS

The overall shopping behavioural patterns of the entire group of 74

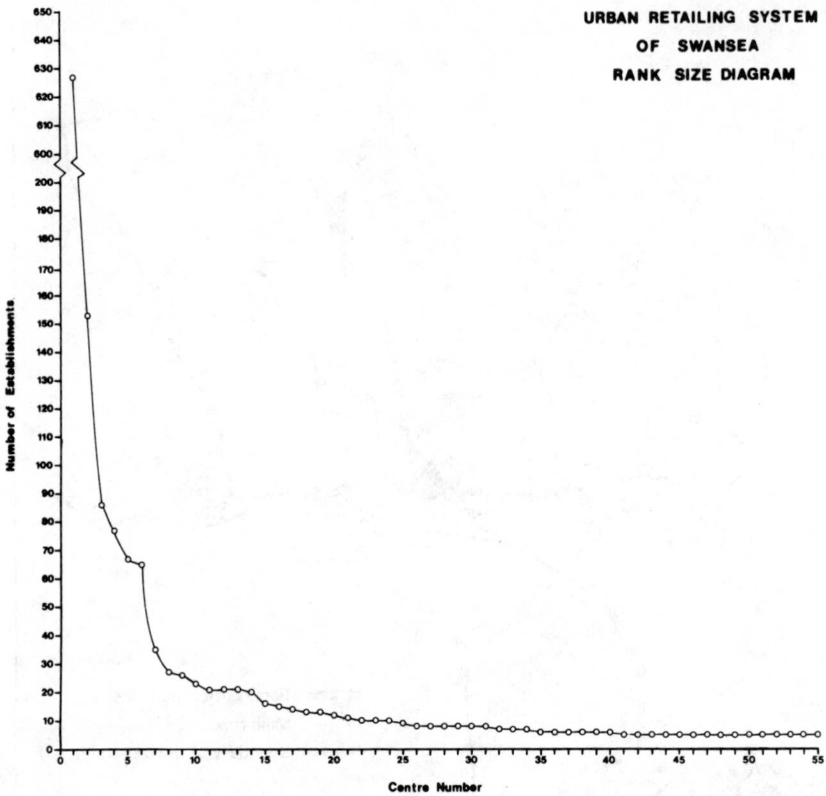

Figure 7.3 The size characteristics of shopping centres in Swansea

respondents was initially summarised by means of the total number of centres used in the conduct of their shopping activities. The frequency distribution of respondents by usage total is shown in Table 7.2 The number of centres used ranged from one to eight, with a mean value of 3.28. The modal category was that of three centres, with as many as 44.6 per cent of all consumers falling into this group. In fact, 83.79 per cent used a total of between two and four retail centres, showing once again that short-run equilibrium patterns of consumer behaviour are relatively simple when viewed in aggregate terms.

In this analysis, the overall distribution of the centres comprising the usage fields of consumers was also examined by distance from their places of residence (Table 7.3). For the sample taken as a whole, as high a proportion as 46.5 per cent of the centres visited were within 2 km. of the consumers' homes, showing the predominance of short distance shopping trips. The retail hierarchy of the area is such that it can be assumed that the majority of these moves were to quite small centres, or to the district centre of Oystermouth, in order to purchase

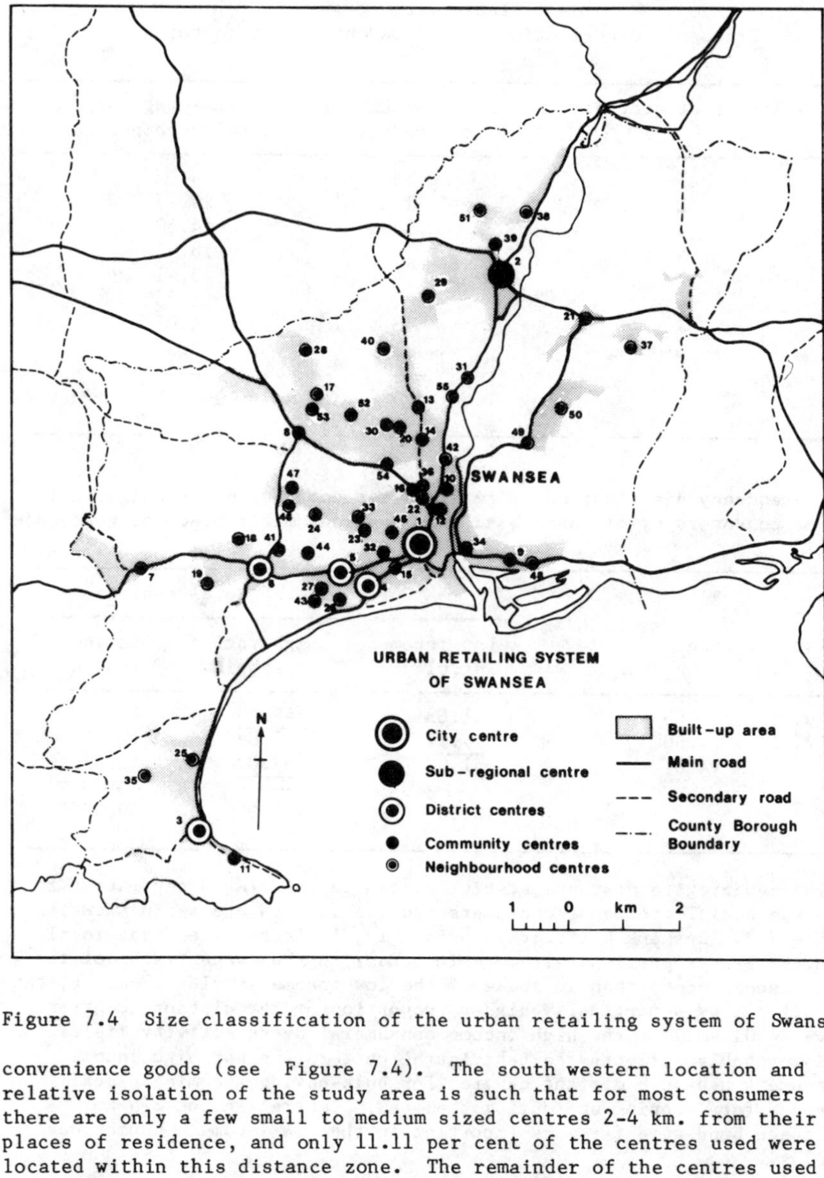

Figure 7.4 Size classification of the urban retailing system of Swansea

convenience goods (see Figure 7.4). The south western location and relative isolation of the study area is such that for most consumers there are only a few small to medium sized centres 2-4 km. from their places of residence, and only 11.11 per cent of the centres used were located within this distance zone. The remainder of the centres used by the sample members, some 42.39 per cent, were located farther than 4 km. from the consumer. This reflects the location of the city centre and specialist retail assemblages at around 5-6 km. from the residents of West Cross. Such statistics imply the operation of a trade off between small centres located close to the consumer's home which are used frequently, and large centres farther away that are visited less frequently.

Table 7.2
Frequency distribution of respondents by usage total

Number of centres	Total number of respondents	Percentage of total respondents
1	3	4.05
2	15	20.27
3	33	44.60
4	14	18.92
5	4	5.41
6	1	1.35
7	3	4.05
8	1	1.35
	Total 74	100.00

Table 7.3
Frequency distribution of retail areas comprising the usage fields of consumers by distance band from the consumer's place of residence

	Percentage of total centres		
Distance zone (km.)	Low income sample	High income sample	Entire sample
0.00 - 2.00	41.03	49.09	46.50
2.01 - 4.00	17.95	7.88	11.11
⩾ 4.01	41.02	43.03	42.39
	100.00	100.00	100.00

These aggregate distance statistics can be calculated separately for the two social groups of consumers and the results are again shown in Table 7.3. Perhaps a little surprisingly, it is revealed that local centres are proportionately more important in the usage fields of the high income group than in those of the low income sample. However, this is off-set by a marginally higher proportion of far distant centres (over 4.01 km.) in the high income consumers' overt activity fields. This probably reflects the behavioural pattern whereby high income consumers use more distant centres for bulk-buying and minor local centres for 'topping-up' during the week. Centres in the 2-4 km. distance band were far more important in the low income consumer usage fields.

Other salient features of consumer behaviour amongst the respondents are revealed if aggregate usage fields are constructed for the two groups of shoppers. These are reproduced in Figures 7.5A and 7.5B for the low and high income groups respectively. The retailing centres are shown classified by size, and minor centres (less than five shops) are also depicted within the West Cross case study area. The centres are shaded according to the percentage of total consumers stating that they

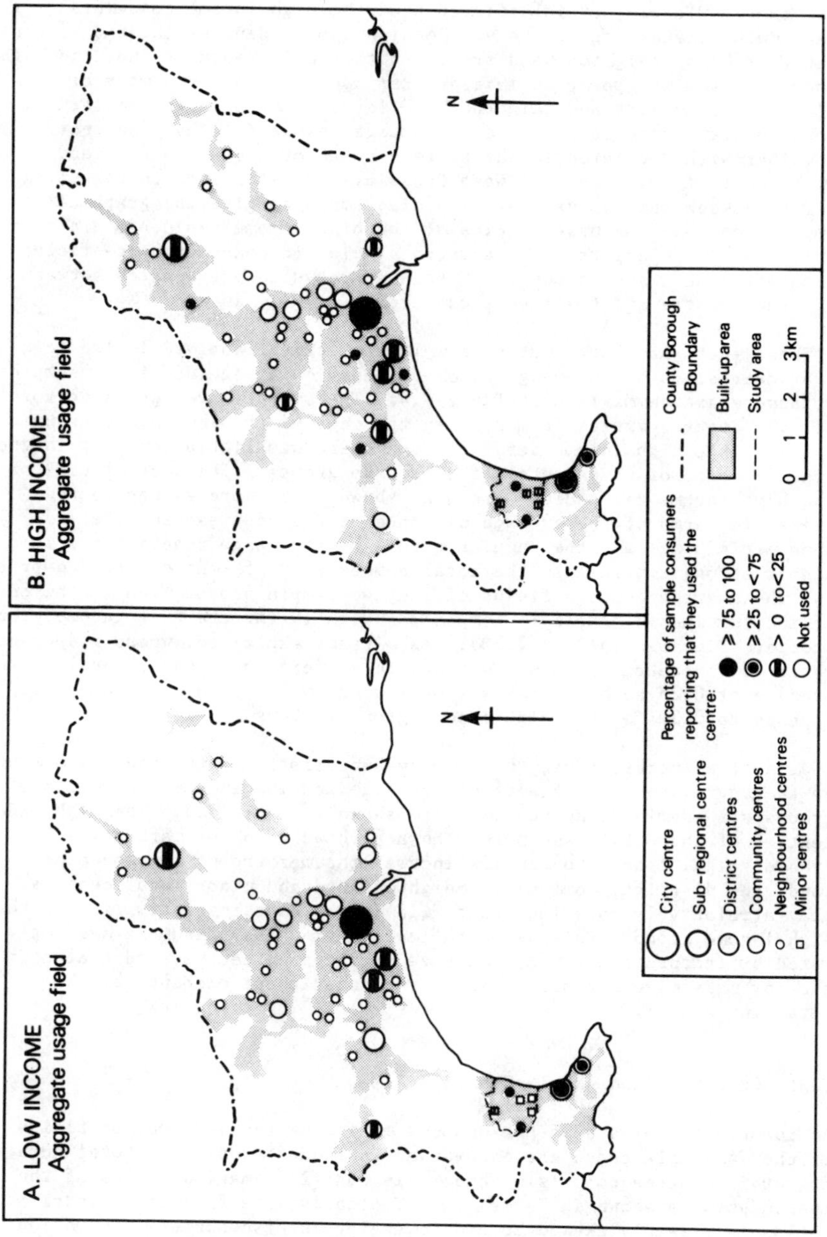

Figure 7.5 The aggregate usage fields of the low and high income consumer groups in Swansea

use them. Clearly, it is affirmed that the high income consumers do make much greater use of the six local shopping centres located within the West Cross neighbourhood area. Another difference is that the high income consumers appear to make greater use of a larger number of district, community and neighbourhood level centres in the western and north western suburbs of the city. Usage levels for the town centre together with Morriston in the extreme north of the urban area and Oystermouth to the south of West Cross are much the same in percentage terms between the two groups. The diagrams also give the graphical impression that the usage fields of the high income residents are more extensive. The existence of a sectoral bias in consumer usage fields is also witnessed, for in the main, the centres used are located between the town centre and the case study area.

These facts are borne out by simple statistical analyses. The mean characteristics of the usage or overt behavioural fields of the sample consumers are summarised in Table 7.4. The overall average usage total of 3.28 centres varies from 2.79 in the case of the low income group to 3.59 for the high income set, although there was little contrast in the overall range of usage totals for the two groups. The usage fields of the high income respondents are also shown to be more extensive when viewed in terms of the average distance of the centres from the consumer's home and the angular extent of the usage zone. There is also a strong contrast in the total number of different centres comprising the aggregate usage fields of the two sample groups, ten in the case of the low income sample in comparison with 19 for the high income group (compare Figures 7.5A and 7.5B). As already explained, where responses referred to centres outside Swansea, these were counted separately. An average of 0.25 such centres was mentioned by low income consumers as opposed to 0.30 for the high income group members.

As a final perspective, the size characteristics of the centres making up the aggregate usage fields of the high and low income consumer sub-groups was examined and the data are shown in Table 7.5. The high order centres of the C.B.D. and Morriston are shown to be of marginally greater significance to the low income consumer group. On the other hand, the district, community, neighbourhood and minor local centres play a relatively more important role in the shopping activities of the high income group. This seems to imply that these consumers are motivated by factors other than the size of shopping centres and that they thereby make more extensive use of the constituent elements of the retailing system.

CONSUMER PERCEPTION AND INFORMATION FIELDS

An identical analysis of the centres making up the information fields of the 74 sample consumers in Swansea was undertaken. The total number of retail centres comprising the individual information fields of the respondents is shown in Table 7.6. Typically, the frequency distribution is markedly skewed toward lower levels of consumer information, implying that consumers generally make decisions about their spatial shopping behaviour on the basis of quite limited designative knowledge of city wide retailing facilities. However, the range of centres in the information fields was quite great, extending from 1 through to 11. The overall mean information total was 4.78 centres, but the modal category was again that of three centres, with 27.03 per cent of the respondents

Table 7.4
Characteristics of the usage (Behavioural) fields of consumers in the West Cross area, Swansea

	Low income group	High income group	Entire sample
Mean usage total (centres)	2.79	3.59	3.28
Range (centres)	1-7	2-8	1-8
Mean distance (km.)	3.11	3.26	3.21
Mean angle of field (degrees)	24.82	42.85	36.07
Total number of different centres used by sample members	10	19	20
Mean number of centres used outside Swansea	0.25	0.30	0.28

Table 7.5
Size characteristics of the centres comprising the usage fields of the consumers

Hierarchical group	Low income sample		High income sample	
	N	%	N	%
City centre	26	33.33	44	26.67
Sub-regional centre	2	2.56	4	2.42
District centres	15	19.24	33	20.00
Community centres	13	16.67	32	19.39
Neighbourhood centres	20	25.64	44	26.67
Minor centres	2	2.56	8	4.85
Total	78	100.00	165	100.00

being grouped in this single category. More significantly, 74.33 per cent of the sample respondents knew of between two and six centres within the town. Only two consumers stated that they knew of only one retailing centre.

The frequency distribution of the retail areas comprising the aggregate information fields of the consumers according to distance shows a very similar pattern to that displayed by the elements of the usage field (Table 7.7). Thus, for the sample treated as a whole, whilst 36.44 per cent of the centres were located within 2 kms. of the homes of consumers, 46.61 per cent were farther than 4.01 km. away and only 16.95 per cent were located in the 2-4 km. zone. A similar patterning of relative importance of centres in different distance bands by social class was revealed in the aggregate information fields as in the aggregate usage fields (compare Table 7.7 with Table 7.3). Far distant and local centres are of relatively enhanced significance in the information fields of the high income consumers. But overall, it is noticeable that

Table 7.6
Frequency distribution of respondents by information total

Number of centres	Total number of respondents	Percentage of total respondents
1	2	2.70
2	10	13.51
3	20	27.03
4	11	14.87
5	6	8.11
6	8	10.81
7	5	6.76
8	2	2.70
9	4	5.41
10	3	4.05
11	3	4.05
Total	74	100.00

Table 7.7
Frequency distribution of retail areas comprising the information fields of consumers by distance band from the consumer's place of residence

Distance zone (km.)	Percentage of total centres:		
	Low income sample	High income sample	Entire sample
0.00 - 2.00	33.04	38.08	36.44
2.01 - 4.00	26.09	12.56	16.95
≥ 4.01	40.87	49.37	46.61
	100.00	100.00	100.00

far distant centres are more prevalent in the information fields of both social groups than in their usage fields, suggesting that the usage field is normally a relatively parochial sub-set of the information field.

The spatial form of the aggregate low and high income group information fields is shown in Figures 7.6A and 7.6B respectively. These diagrams are effectively the urban retailing equivalent of Lynchian type maps of residents' public images of the city. Once again, it is apparent that local, including minor centres, form a more important component of the high income group's information field. The major district centres of Sketty and Uplands, which lie in a line running directly westward from the city centre are known by a greater proportion of the high income respondents than of the low income ones. The former group also appear to be marginally more aware of the sub-regional centre of Morriston along with several other community and neighbourhood level

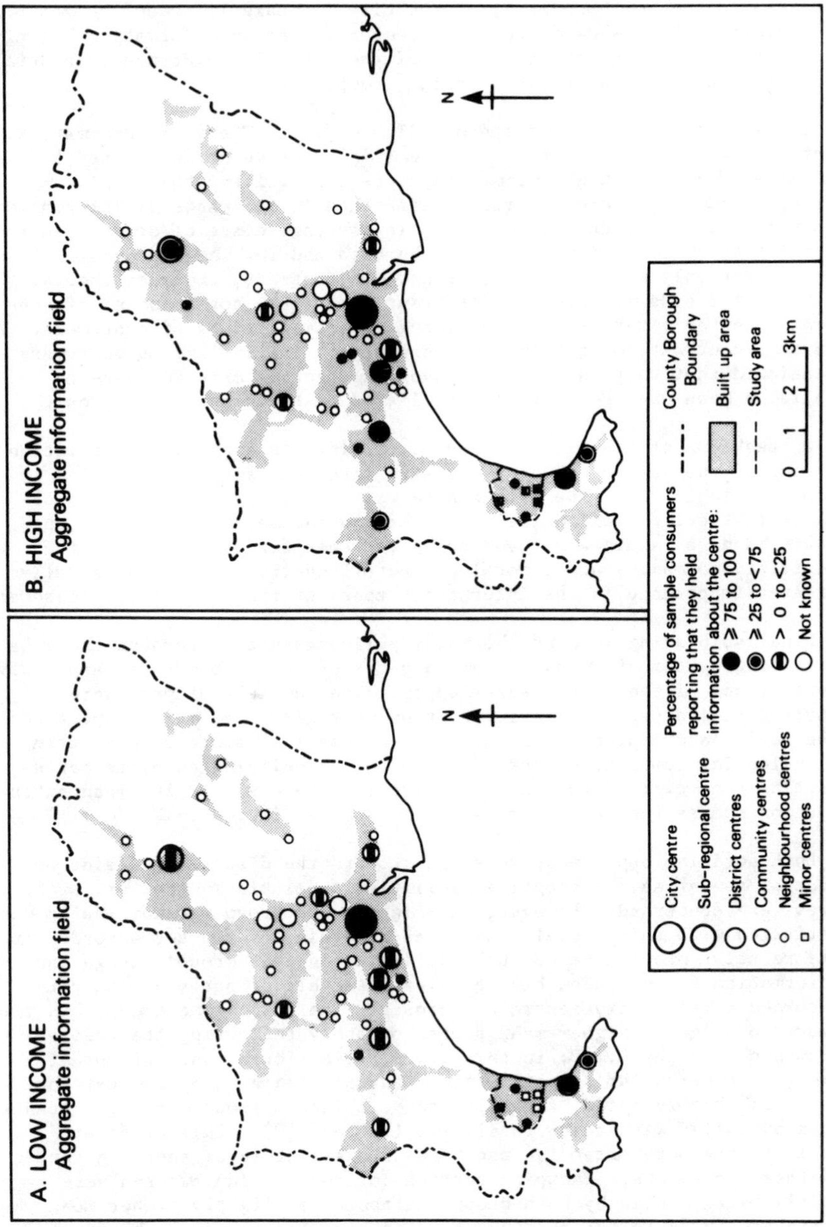

Figure 7.6 The aggregate information fields of the low and high income consumer groups in Swansea

centres in the northern parts of the city (compare Figures 7.6A and B). The diagrams also show evidence of sectoral bias in informational fields and give a good general indication of the overall difference in spatial scale of the zones of the two social groups.

These contrasts are summarised in Table 7.8. The mean information total of 4.78 centres for the entire sample may be disaggregated to give a value of 5.2 for high income consumers and 4.11 for the low income group. However, there is little difference in the range of information values recorded by the two groups. The average distance of the centres forming the information fields of the high and low income consumer groups are only marginally different. In contrast, the mean angular extent of fields is markedly different, as is the total number of separate centres cited by the two aggregate social groups of consumers. A further contrast emerged in that on average, the low income consumers mentioned that they knew of 0.75 shopping centres outside Swansea, whilst a mean of 1.04 centres were listed by the high income group.

A breakdown of the retail areas comprising the aggregate information fields of the sample consumers by size level was again informative as shown by Table 7.9. The city centre was of greater relative significance in the information fields of the low income consumers. On the other hand, as again was found to be the case for usage fields, the district, community and minor local retail centres were of marginally greater importance in the information zones of the high income consumers.

Finally, bearing in mind the major policy issues concerning the urban retailing system of Swansea, some aspects of the respondents' appraisive perceptions of the system were tapped. The sample consumers were invited to indicate how satisfied they felt with five major aspects of the region's shopping environment, on a numerical scale ranging from 1 indicating complete dissatisfaction to 7 signifying complete satisfaction (see p. 2 of the questionnaire in Appendix 2). The mean satisfaction scores for the two consumer groups are listed in Table 7.10.

Both social groups recorded scores toward the dissatisfied side of neutral as far as the shopping facilities available in the West Cross area were concerned. However, the high income group was marginally more satisfied with these local facilities and this, of course, accords with the relative prominence of such facilities in this group's usage and information fields. The highest overall levels of satisfaction were recorded for the city centre of Swansea. The low income group this time showed a slightly higher mean score, probably reflecting the greater prominence of the C.B.D. in this group's behavioural and perceptual fields. Other shopping centres in Swansea taken as a single category were less highly rated, although the high income group was significantly more satisfied with these facilities (Table 7.10). This no doubt reflects the more extensive use made of district level shopping centres by these consumers. Shopping centres located outside Swansea were fairly highly rated by both groups, although a slightly higher mean satisfaction score was recorded for the high income set. The final question involved a prospective appraisal on the part of the consumers of their likely satisfactions if a hypermarket or superstore were to be built in the suburbs of Swansea. For both sets of consumers, the overall reported degree of satisfaction with such a development was quite high. Almost paradoxically perhaps, the low income sample of consumers recorded a mean satisfaction score that was significantly higher than

Table 7.8
Characteristics of the information (perceptual) fields of consumers in the West Cross area, Swansea

	Low income group	High income group	Entire sample
Mean information total (centres)	4.11	5.20	4.78
Range (centres)	1-11	2-11	1-11
Mean distance (km.)	3.49	3.75	3.66
Mean angle of field(°)	57.32	82.26	72.82
Total number of different centres known by sample consumers	16	22	23
Mean number of centres known outside Swansea	0.75	1.04	0.84

Table 7.9
Size characteristics of the centres comprising the information fields of the consumers

Hierarchical group	Low income group		High income sample	
	N	%	N	%
City centre	28	24.34	45	18.83
Sub-regional centre	6	5.22	17	7.11
District centres	27	23.48	65	27.19
Community centres	22	19.13	47	19.67
Neighbourhood centres	30	26.09	56	23.43
Minor centres	2	1.74	9	3.77
	115	100.00	239	100.00

that of the high income group. In this respect, it seems reasonable to assume that the anticipated price reductions associated with such a store would be a strong attraction for the low income consumers. The high income group on the other hand are already more able to shop around and would perhaps be inclined to feel that such a development would be of less direct benefit to them and further, might even have grave environmental repercussions. A point worth bearing in mind here is that the question as posed did not mention where exactly in the suburbs it was envisaged that such a large store would be sited. If the respondents interpreted this to mean in the south western suburbs of the city, then this would be seen as more of an advantage by the somewhat less mobile low income consumer group.

SUMMARY AND CONCLUSIONS

The analysis presented in this chapter has indicated that the general

Table 7.10
Perceived satisfaction with major aspects of the Swansea urban retailing system

Aspect	Mean satisfaction score		
	Low income group	High income group	Significance
Shopping centres in West Cross	3.32	3.85	-
Swansea city centre	5.57	5.27	-
Other shopping centres in Swansea	3.92	4.66	0.10
Shopping centres outside Swansea	4.30	4.41	-
If a 'hypermarket' or 'superstore' were to be built in the surburs	5.30	4.50	0.20

traits of consumer spatial behaviour and cognition identified and enumerated in the earlier chapters were replicated in the case of the Swansea urban area. This implies that the marked variations that characterise the usage and information fields of consumers are not merely a reflection of the method of response elicitation employed by these earlier studies. Such a conclusion is especially significant in relation to consumer information fields which are difficult to identify and measure in an entirely unbiased manner. Further, the Swansea study has shown that the strong social contrasts identified in the overall scale and complexity of such fields appear to be genuine in the sense that the effects of the differential residential placement of consumers in relation to urban retailing structure were negated in this research, as were the effects of consumer status variables such as age and length of residence in the area.

As a final summary analysis, the aggregate spatial usage and information fields of the entire sample of 74 respondents are shown mapped in Figures 7.7A and 7.7B respectively. In both of these, the relationship between the proportion of the sample consumers reporting that they used or held information about centres, and the size and distance of such centres is extremely interesting. The aggregate usage field of the consumers shown in Figure 7.7A highlights the fact that centres located close to the consumers are generally quite regularly used regardless of their size. Quite naturally, with distance away from the study area, only the larger district and sub-regional centres are used by a significant number of consumers. The same overall patterning is true of the aggregate information fields of the consumers (Figure 7.7B). In both cases, a 'corridor' or broadly sectoral pattern of high usage or knowledge occurs in the area between the C.B.D. and the West Cross study area.

If the broad results of research conducted in different contexts are compared, then some interesting similarities are revealed (Tables 7.11 and 7.12). For example, the overall number of centres used by sets of sample consumers appears to be broadly similar. Comparative statistics

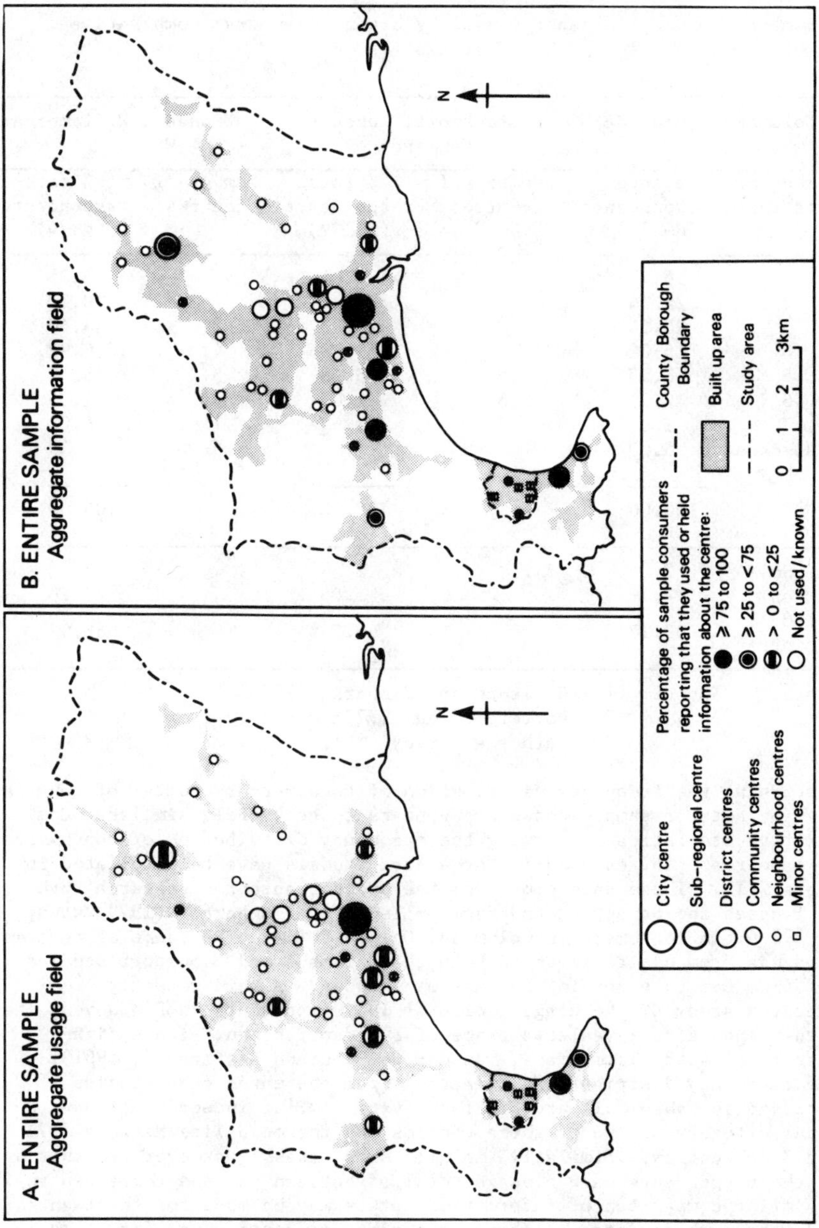

Figure 7.7 The aggregate usage and information fields of the entire sample of consumers in Swansea

Table 7.11
Number of shopping centres used by urban consumers: comparative statistics

Columbus, Ohio, USA[1]		Stockport, Cheshire England[2]		Swansea, W. Glamorgan Wales[3]	
Number of centres	% total respondents (N=293)	Number of centres	% total respondents (N=192)	Number of centres	% total respondents (N=74)
1	18.77	1	4.69	1	4.05
2	25.94	2	34.90	2	20.27
3	25.24	3	28.65	3	44.60
4	15.02	4	19.79	4	18.92
5	8.53	5	8.33	5	5.41
6	2.39	6	2.08	6	1.35
7	1.02	7	1.67	7	4.05
No data	3.07			8	1.35
	100.00		100.00		100.00
Mode	2		2		3
Mean	2.71		3.05		3.28
1-3 centres	69.97%		68.24%		68.92%

(Notes:- Source: 1 Golledge and Zannaras (1973)
2 Potter, 1976a, 1977c
3 Author's survey)

concerning the frequency distribution of consumers by number of centres used by sets of sample consumers appears to be broadly similar. Comparative statistics concerning the frequency distribution of consumers by number of centres used in three case studies have been collated in Table 7.11. These data come from the present author's research work in Swansea and Stockport and from Golledge and Zannaras' (1973) study of 293 urban consumers in Columbus, Ohio, U.S.A. The range of centres used was from one to seven in both the Columbus and Stockport studies and from one to eight in the case of Swansea. A more recently executed study of the usage fields of 194 respondents in Eindhoven, The Netherlands also revealed a range of 1-7 centres, but with a higher average of 4.58 (Timmermans, van der Heijden and Westerveld, 1981). The frequency distributions emanating from the three case studies included in Table 7.11 are, in fact, very similar indeed. All have a modal category of two or three centres and the mean lies between 2.71 and 3.28 centres. Similarly, in all three cases, just over two-thirds of the respondents have a usage total of between one and three centres. A similar comparison of information totals may be made for the Swansea and Stockport studies. Although the range of centres was from 1 to 14 in the case of Stockport, and 1-11 in Swansea, the mode was 3 in both cases and the average around 4. In both, a little less than half the consumers knew of between one and three centres in all. Timmermans *et al.* (1981) have also examined information totals, but here, both the range and average values were markedly higher at 1-17 and 6.41 respect-

Table 7.12
Number of shopping centres comprising the information fields of consumers: comparative statistics

Stockport, England[1]		Swansea, Wales[2]	
Number of centres	% total respondents (N=192)	Number of centres	% total respondents (N=74)
1	2.79	1	2.70
2	20.67	2	13.51
3	25.70	3	27.03
4	16.76	4	14.87
5	12.85	5	8.11
6	8.37	6	10.81
7	6.15	7	6.76
8	2.79	8	2.70
9	0.56	9	5.41
10	1.12	10	4.05
11	1.12	11	4.05
12	-		
13	0.56		100.00
14	0.56		
	100.00		
Mode	3		3
Mean	4.12		4.78
1-3 centres	49.16%		43.24%

(Notes:- Source: 1 Potter 1976a, 1979a
2 Author's survey)

Table 7.13
Comparison between the characteristics of consumer usage and information fields in Swansea and Stockport

Social group	Stockport (N=192)		Swansea (N=74)	
	Mean usage total	Mean information total	Mean usage total	Mean information total
High	4.32	5.30	3.59	5.20
Middle	2.87	4.19	-	-
Low	2.24	3.18	2.79	4.11
Entire sample	3.05	4.12	3.28	4.78

ively, in all probability reflecting the planned basis of neighbourhood facilities in Eindhoven.

The average characteristics of the usage and information fields of the different sub-groups of consumers in the Swansea case study have

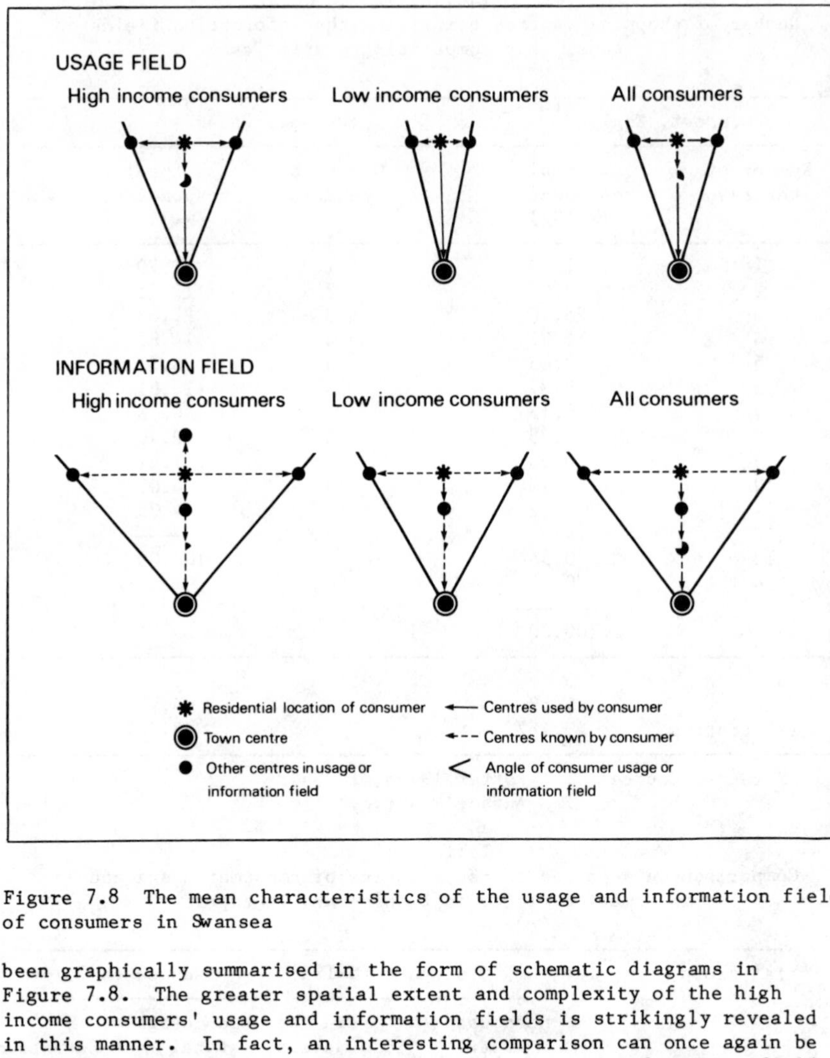

Figure 7.8 The mean characteristics of the usage and information fields of consumers in Swansea

been graphically summarised in the form of schematic diagrams in Figure 7.8. The greater spatial extent and complexity of the high income consumers' usage and information fields is strikingly revealed in this manner. In fact, an interesting comparison can once again be made with the social class differences in usage and information fields revealed in Stockport (Table 7.13). The data show that these disparities are of approximately the same order of magnitude.

In conclusion, it is hoped that the present study represents a truly replicative piece of research in the sense that it has reaffirmed the appropriateness of the conclusions reached and inferences drawn in earlier studies, using different methods and case study areas. Further, the work has provided some additional insights into the nature of spatial consumer behaviour and perception in urban areas, for example, with respect to the size characteristics of the centres comprising the usage and information fields of different social groups of consumers. The study also demonstrates how a few simple questions concerning the appraisive perceptions of consumers can shed light on both the behaviour of consumers and major retail policy issues such as the development of hypermarkets. Finally, the work has hopefully indicated that despite the plethora of studies conducted into aspects of consumer behaviour and perception in the post war period, much research still remains to be done, both in terms of the search for generalisations and the examination of particular local circumstances.

8 Location, Cognition, Behaviour and Retail Planning

This volume has focused attention on the two important topics of the overall spatial-structural organisation of urban retailing systems, and the form of consumer cognition and behaviour within them. At the same time, efforts have also been made to identify the manifold links existing between these facets of retail provision and consumer demand. Overall, the complex and essentially dynamic nature of these phenomena has been exemplified throughout this work, and the need for regulation, guidance and some form of control has been implied in a number of sections. In this concluding chapter, these applied issues are raised and examined in greater depth. It is necessary to stress, however, that the aim here is not to describe in detail the urban retail planning machinery and policies as they exist in any particular country or group of countries, nor to outline a comprehensive blueprint for the development of an ideal planning machinery of this type. In this regard, excellent accounts already exist, particularly those contained in Davies' (1979) monograph on urban retail planning in the European Community and Guy's (1980) catholic overview of the role of retail planning in the British context. Rather, the present intention is to consider some of the major contemporary urban retail planning issues as they exist in the majority of western industrial countries, viewing them specifically in the light of the empirical and theoretical findings that have been presented in the previous seven chapters of this book. Thus, the present brief account is perforce both partial and speculative, rather than comprehensive and purely factual.

URBAN RETAIL PLANNING

Whilst it is perhaps not unduly helpful to state that there are as many definitions of 'planning' as there are planners, such an extreme suggestion does serve to emphasise that the noun 'plan' has a number of different meanings. In an environmental context, however, Hall (1974) has suggested that planning is concerned with the deliberate achievement of objectives by means of assembling actions in an orderly sequence. Essentially, therefore, *physical* or *town and country planning* is concerned with foreseeing and guiding change with respect to the future configuration of land use patterns. Retailing, as a vital ingredient of the land use mosaic and the generator of major traffic and pedestrian flows, qualifies for detailed attention on the part of planners, along with residential, industrial, recreational, agricultural and other functional land use categories. Thought of in this light, we may follow Wade (1979, p. 51) who has ventured that:

'Retail planning can be summarised as being the planned provision of retail outlets in which the following questions assume critical importance: How much or how many? What type? When? Where?'

Wade's definition does not just apply at the level of individual retail outlets, but extends to aggregates of them in the guise of shopping centres, and even complete urban-regional retailing systems.

It is necessary to stress, however, that a large number of different individuals and groups are involved in the retail planning process, and these agents include retailers, consumers, planners, politicians, property developers and conservationists (Schiller, 1979; Wade, 1979; Guy, 1980), each of whom are likely to hold divergent views on various critical issues. The potential conflicts that might arise between interest groups may be seen as the *raison d'être* of retail planning in a free-market or mixed economy. For example, the optimal situation for developers or retailers may be at variance with the demands of consumers and/or conservationists, in either economic or social terms, so that some form of intervention or arbitration is required. However, it is necessary to realise that urban retail planning does not exist as an entirely independent activity, but rather as an integral part of the overall physical development planning process (Wade, 1979). In Britain, for instance, the local planning authorities at the County and District Authority levels are vested with the responsibility of drawing up *structure* and *local* land use development plans respectively, and these will both contain a retailing ingredient. But as Wade (1979) has noted, such authorities 'do not, however, have the power to insist that these plans are positively adhered to' (p. 57). In essence, they afford an overall framework for the future organisation of land use, and all proposed developments, such as a new building, changing the use of an existing one or even the construction of a new shop front, require the granting of planning permission. Thus, the planner tends to exercise a predominantly negative form of control in most contexts (Wade, 1979).

The need for some degree of planned control in the field of retailing has perhaps never been more apparent than today, with the rapid developments that are occurring in the urban market place. Aspects of contemporary urban retailing change have been discussed briefly in several of the earlier chapters of this volume, in particular, with respect to the derivation of a dynamic model of urban retail structural change in Chapter 2, and also in relation to the overall organisation of retailing as an economic activity in Chapter 1. Essentially, major changes have occurred in consumer behaviour, in association with increasing real incomes and car ownership, the suburbanisation of population, increasing female participation in the labour force and improvements in food storage and refrigeration. Concomitantly, changes such as the trend towards self-service, and in the use of floorspace, range of goods offered and diversification have occurred in retail trading methods. As a result, this has led to pressure for large scale shopping developments such as hypermarkets and superstores in edge- and out-of-town locations. Other structural and locational issues, involving local stores, the rise of multiples and the future of small independent retailers, district centres, arterial ribbons and town centres have also become highlighted during this era of unprecedented change.

Clearly, the material presented in this book has indicated that there are strong links between urban retailing structure and location on the one hand, and consumer cognition-behaviour on the other. It almost goes without saying that all those who are interested in the urban retail planning process need to understand the reciprocal links existing between retailing structure and consumer behaviour-cognition. Whilst it is probably fair to comment that planners generally affect structure and thereby influence overt behaviour, it is just as true that plans may reflect the influence of changes in consumer behaviour that have stemmed from broad social and economic developments. Further, planned change in the structure of one part of the urban retailing system may affect behaviour and thereby structure in other parts. The need to consider the nature of these important reciprocal links existing between behaviour and structure forms the background to the discussion of major contemporary urban retail planning issues.

CURRENT RETAIL PLANNING ISSUES

The issues briefly enumerated above are well represented in a simple diagram depicting contemporary elements of urban retail planning policy recently produced by Davies (1977b). The hypothetical distribution of commercial activities shown in Figure 8.1A mirrors the overall spatial pattern customarily found in cities, and this may be fitted into the geographical classification of the C.B.D., encircled by a zone of mixed commerce and industry, with a number of clusters of activity, or nucleations existing in the suburbs (Figure 8.1B). Additionally, a conspicuous number of ribbon or unplanned strip developments are classified along the main arterial roads, together with a mixed commercial-industrial zone on the periphery. In Figure 8.1C, an idealised representation of the main types of planning proposals frequently embodied in local authority development and structure plans is shown. The principal element of control depicted here is the replacement of extant arterial ribbon developments with a series of redeveloped facilities, generally of a compact nucleated-precinct form. Although a planned mixed commercial-industrial area is included on the eastern side of the town, it is noticeable that no explicit recognition has been given to large peripheral stores or shopping centres. The sorts of future planning proposals for urban retailing envisaged by Davies are shown in Figure 8.1D. Notably, this system comprises a number of new service plazas or planned strip/ribbon developments to replace the existing ribbons, plus a number of trading marts. Also, two new commercial estates are recognised on the urban periphery. Similarly, a planned out-of-town development is envisaged on the north-western side of the urban region. The overall perceived disparity existing between the spatial and structural organisation of the urban retailing systems depicted in Figure 8.1A and 8.1B reflects the major urban retail planning issues that are of particular current importance.

There is little doubt that the interconnecting planning issues surrounding the development of large scale retail establishments have had primacy since the early 1970s. The currency and intensity of this issue is amply illustrated by Davies' (1977b, p. 42) comment that an

> 'emotive debate over the desirability of hypermarkets and "out-of-town" shopping centres has tended to divert attention away from more pressing issues in the rest of the city'.

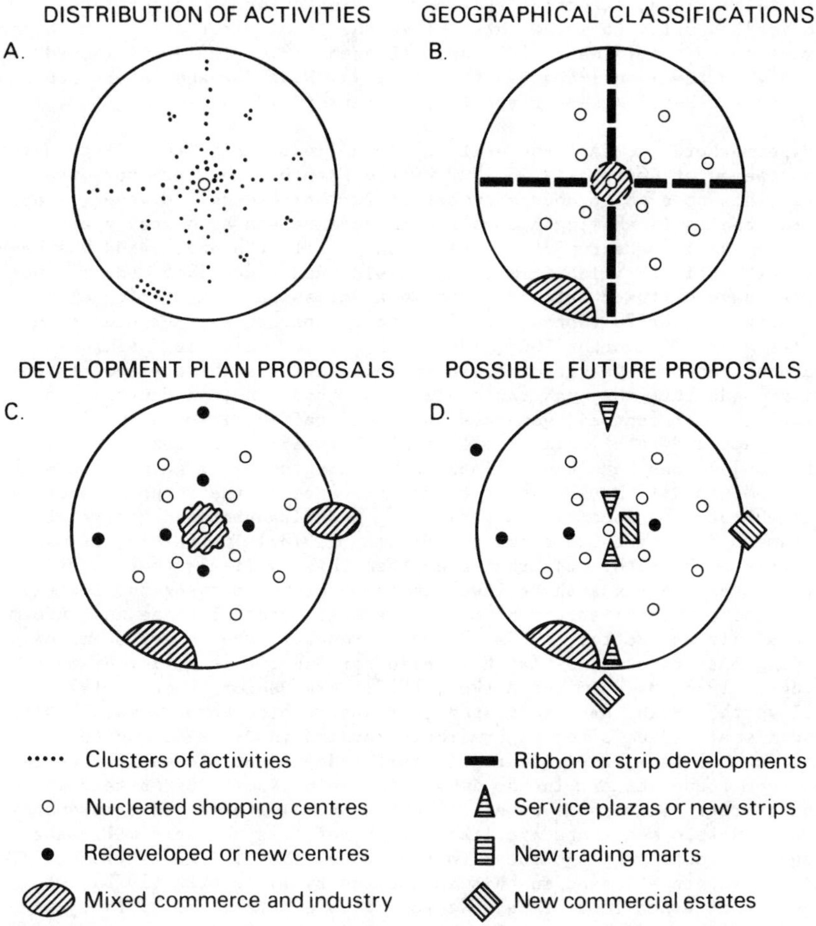

Figure 8.1 Elements of urban retail planning policies (Redrawn by permission from Davies, 1977b)

A *hypermarket* may be defined as a single level self service store selling both food and non-food items and having a sales area in excess of 50,000 square feet (5,000 square metres). Similar developments, but with 25-50,000 square feet (2,500-5,000 m^2) are generally referred to as *superstores*. The latter frequently place greater emphasis on the sale of food and household items. Hypermarkets and superstores are essentially to be seen as the logical development of supermarkets and the rise of multiple grocery retail firms. Such stores reap the benefits of economies of scale by means of mass merchandising techniques, thereby generally offering consumers lower prices. Initially, they were developed on green field out-of-town and edge-of-town sites, where land costs are low. Further, such stores are normally located along major roads and are predominantly based on attracting a car-borne clientele. Thus, extensive free car parking at ground floor level is provided, usually covering three times the sales floor area. The hypermarket concept originated in France (Dawson, 1976, 1981) and spread rapidly in the late 1960s, so that in 1973, West Germany and France had 406 and 212 hypermarkets respectively (Parker, 1975).

Hypermarkets are far less well developed in Britain, the first having been opened at Caerphilly in 1972 by the French firm Carrefour, who have since gone on to open a number of further stores. However, superstore trading is showing a consistent increase and such stores are becoming an important part of the urban retailing scene. Asda has been the most active British firm in the field, and since 1965, their superstores have diffused outwards from West Yorkshire, with the total now standing at over 70 (Jones, 1981). Other superstores have been opened by Tesco and Woolworths (Guy, 1980). The major point is that the planning response has generally been to restrict such developments on the grounds that they may cause a loss of trade in town centres and existing local centres, generate unwanted traffic, involve the loss of open space and entail visual blight (Davies, 1977c; Potter, 1980b). Other objections have been raised on social grounds, arguing that such developments will have a deleterious influence on the shopping provision available to low income, non car-owning and disadvantaged groups of consumers if they cause closures (Hillman, 1973). Certainly, if many closures occur within an urban area then this is likely to be a major worry given the research reviewed in this volume, showing the restricted and quite parochial nature of many consumers' spatial usage and informational fields (Potter, 1979a, 1980b). However, the numerous impact and trading pattern studies that have been carried out (see, for example, Bridges, 1976; Malcolm and Aitken, 1977; York Junior Chamber, 1977; Hallsworth, 1981a) have indicated that such stores compete mainly with traditional medium sized supermarkets located in district and town centres. In fact, the closure of small independent stores has generally not been found, except in the immediate vicinity of hypermarkets and superstores. Thus, some have argued that small stores are complementary to such developments and are likely to benefit as shoppers will make frequent 'topping-up' journeys to them (Guy, 1980). One cautionary point has been stressed in this connection by Hallsworth (1978), who argues that a non-local impact at some future date is more likely than a local and immediate one. For example, if a superstore 'creams off' part of all grocery retailers' profits, already marginal firms may become even more so, and perhaps go into eclipse when their leases fall due for renewal. Given this complex array of pros and cons, the only reasonable answer would seem to be to allow and even encourage such developments in acceptable forms and locations, wherever they are unlikely to lead to the irrevocable deterioration of the shopping facilities serving those who are not able to use the new large store. This point will be returned to in the following discussion.

The trend towards large-scale and multiple retailing has inevitably been paralleled by the increasing plight of the small unit and independent retailer. In fact, there has been a consistent decline in total shop numbers in Britain since the 1950s. In the period 1961-1971, for example, shop numbers fell 10.5 per cent from 542,000 to 485,000. Between 1971 and 1975, the number of independent retail outlets declined by seven per cent (Berry, 1977). Frequently, urban redevelopment schemes, high rents and planning regulations have been cited as contributing to this overall reduction in shop numbers (Berry, 1977). Obviously, such facilities fulfil an essential role for many consumers, given the preponderance of short distance shopping trips on foot revealed in Chapter 5. The question of personal mobility is an important one, and Hillman (1973) has noted that only 20 per cent of women in the U.K. held driving licences in 1972, despite an overall car ownership level of 51 per cent of total households. It seems highly likely that the poor, the elderly and those with large families will make frequent use of small shops along with those who fall into Stone's (1954) *personalising* and *ethical* consumer groups. Further, the role of small shops in facilitating 'topping-up' shopping trips has already been stressed. In this light, Berry (1977) has argued that the small shop performs an important social as well as an economic function, and has argued that Government policy must seek to ensure the future survival of such enterprises.

Neighbourhood shopping centres have generally taken the form of planned precinct forms in post-war redeveloped residential zones, and these have normally been sited at the mean centre of neighbourhood areas (Low, 1975). It is noticeable, however, that planners have rarely if ever taken the occurrence of *downtown directional bias* and Brennan's law into consideration. The location of retail facilities at the town centre end of residential areas, such as in the pattern shown in Figure 4.17, would take this behavioural tendency into account. At the same time, such a planned design would allow housing for the elderly, the poor and less mobile groups to be located closer to the neighbourhood and town centre facilities than that of other groups.

Another major urban retail planning issue involves arterial ribbons, and generally speaking, planners have endeavoured to eradicate these low tonal, discontiguous and specialist assemblages on the grounds that they are associated with congestion and visual blight. However, work in this volume has indicated that they comprise an important integral component of the intra-urban retailing system. Davies (1977c) argues that multiple retailers, especially supermarkets have been the chief beneficiaries of planned inner urban shopping schemes, whilst ribbon functions have generally found them ill-suited to their needs. Redeveloped centres at this level tend to be precincts sited off main roads oriented to local convenience shopping trips, rather than motorised through trips. Thus, Davies has suggested that ribbon type businesses will in the future 'need to be allocated to new strip forms which, within and around the central area, might be thought of in terms of service plazas' (Davies, 1977b, p. 45). This call has been backed up by suggesting designs for a number of new planned ribbon forms, as shown in Figure 8.2. These redeveloped ribbons need not cause vehicular congestion or danger to pedestrians, although catering for a primarily motorised trade that is diverted off the main roads. For example, the *convenience oriented strip* consists of a bilateral row of shops that is approached by car from the main road by means of slip-ways (Figure 8.2A). Similarly, in Figure 8.2B, a possible design for a somewhat larger *auto oriented strip* is shown which allows for off street access and parking, and also provides space for future expansion. Two further developments, *service plazas* and *trading marts*, which involve different functions but similar physical layouts have also been envisaged by Davies (1977b) (see Figure 8.2C). These forms would provide a rational

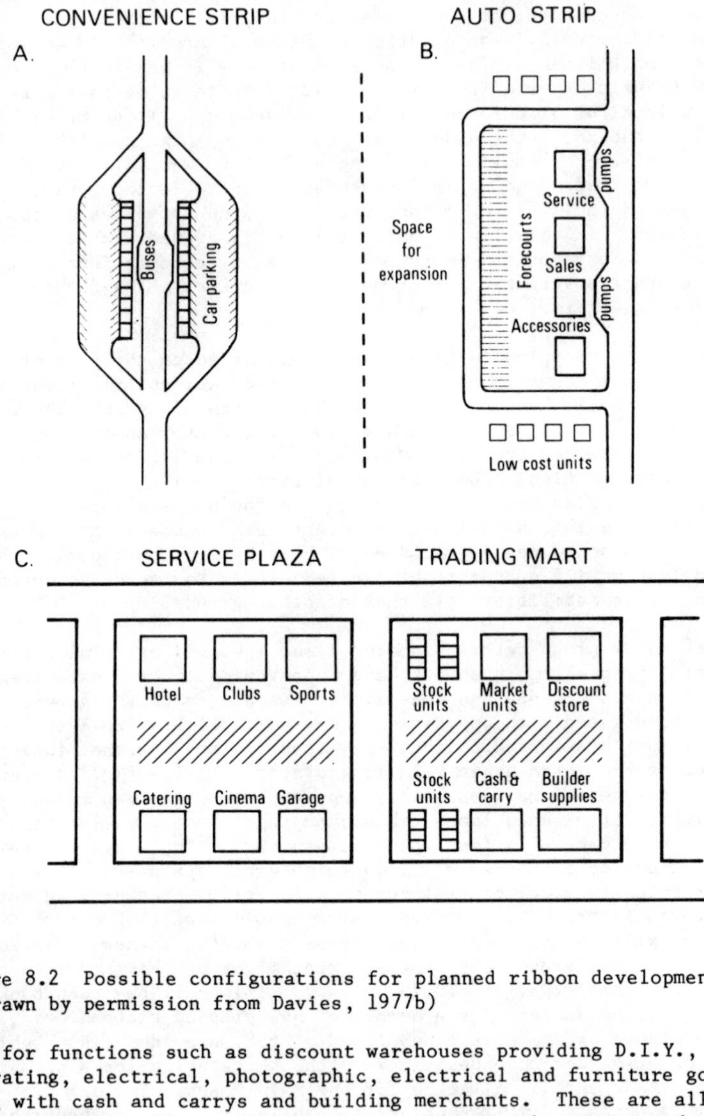

Figure 8.2 Possible configurations for planned ribbon developments (Redrawn by permission from Davies, 1977b)

home for functions such as discount warehouses providing D.I.Y., decorating, electrical, photographic, electrical and furniture goods, along with cash and carrys and building merchants. These are all functions which require vehicular access along with storage and parking space, but which cannot afford very high rents. In the recent past, they have tended to occur along main urban roads. Planned clusters would have the beneficial effect of increasing the likelihood of multi- and combined purpose trips. Similar advantages are inherent in the clustering of recreational and vacational oriented functions in service plazas. It is notable that these planned ribbon/specialised areas all recognise the functional significance of such areas, as shown in this book, but combine them in a form which diminishes their poor layout, accessibility problems, fabric disruption, low imagability, and thereby, greatly enhances their overall acceptability.

Another development of note in western industrial urban areas has been the rise of the planned *regional shopping centre*, particularly in North America, where they originated. Such facilities are generally dominated by department or variety stores, but consist of an entire complex of shops of different sizes and functions. They normally occupy green field sites on the outskirts of cities near to major transport routes, and take the form of enclosed units composed of shopping malls (Davies, 1977c). Another characteristic is the provision of ample car parking spaces. In Britain, planning application for regional centres of this type have been made at Haydock Park (Cole, 1966), Stonebridge and Cribbs Causeway (Davies, 1977c). All of these were refused permission, and the only example of such a centre is that of Brent Cross located in north west London, which was opened in 1979 (Blake, 1976; Newby and Shepherd, 1979). This development, on a 21 hectare site and which provides 3,500 car parking spaces is an out-of-centre rather than out-of-town facility. In fact, London Transport have routed nine bus services to the centre which is also served by a nearby underground station. However, surveys have shown that even so, 75 per cent of the shoppers travel to the centre by car (Newby and Shepherd, 1979).

It is notable that hypermarkets, superstores and regional centres located in peripheral and out-of-town locations are all based on increased car ownership and levels of personal mobility, which have afforded increasing space-time convergence over the past 25 years. However, recently, several commentators have noted that present and possible future problems of petrol supply and increasing costs, may well militate against such car oriented developments, unless that is, rapid developments occur in automobile technology, such as the electric car (Wood and Lee, 1980; Lee and Wood, 1980; Newby and Shepherd, 1979). Wood and Lee cite the interesting example afforded by the collapse of the sole river bridge in Hobart, Tasmania, which left 30 percent of the urban population on the eastern shore cut off from the principal metropolitan shopping areas. The major response on the part of consumers was to place a greater emphasis on multi-purpose journeys. The importance of multi- and combined purpose trips in both structural and behavioural terms has been stressed in this book, and this factor appears to be of some significance in relation to the development of large free-standing retail stores.

Such a consideration is perhaps reflected in the movement toward superstore- rather than hypermarket-sized developments in British urban areas. Further, it is increasingly being suggested that large retail stores should be included as the anchor traders in new *district level centres*, which also house an array of smaller supporting units (see URPI, 1977; Hallsworth, 1981b). This line of argument is also embodied in the Department of Environment's *Development Control Policy Note 13* (1977), which states that large retail stores may be beneficial 'where they form part of a district centre and are not built on greenfield sites or on the fringes of existing towns'. This appears to be a laudable stance, although under these conditions the question of the precise tenant mix becomes a very important one, since the larger the anchor trader, the greater the likely competition for certain supporting units (URPI, 1977). As Jones (1981) has recently noted, however, Asda are increasingly cooperating with local authorities in providing schools, clinics and other social services along with their new superstores. A similar approach seems to be evolving in relation to town centres, with the development of *in-town hypermarkets* (see, for example, Pacione, 1979). The massive investments made by local authorities and developers in the redevelopment of town centre shopping areas in the post-war period has led to concern that peripheral large scale developments will drain expenditure away from them. Again, the in-town development will facilitate greater multi-purpose shopping activity and afford easy access by public transport. On the other hand, such developments may exacerbate traffic congestion in town centres and also involve higher land and site preparation costs. In a similar vein, Dawson (1981) has observed the rise of *hypermarket centres* in France, where 10-30 specialist shops group around a hypermarket. Such developments may well be appropriate in the suburban tracts of many British urban areas. The development and testing of techniques for the evaluation of the locational impacts of superstores and hypermarkets is an important requirement, and both Rogers (1979) and Guy (1980) have recently suggested such formulations. Guy, for instance, has identified a range of 15 criteria which may be used to evaluate superstores located in city centres, existing district centres, inner and outer suburban planned district centres, edge-of-town and other positions. Although the subjectivity involved in any such process of evaluation has been criticised by Davies and Sparks (1981), such techniques are likely to be extremely useful in offering the analyst and policy maker an initial perspective on the problems involved in different urban locales.

It is no doubt fair criticism to venture that planners have been over-zealous in their adherence to the notion of a neat intra-urban retailing hierarchy. It is clear that in the future, a more flexible attitude will be required, although it is equally important to recognise that developments which entail further erosion of the possibility of multi-purpose travel could prove to be shortsighted. But as has been emphasised throughout this volume, the pure size related characteristics of urban retailing facilities have perhaps been overstressed in the past, at the expense of other salient attributes; and more specialised retail forms would appear to be both inevitable, and highly desirable, if they are appropriately planned and implemented.

CONCLUDING COMMENTS

Urban retailing is manifestly an important and complex activity and, therefore, constitutes a relevant, interesting and rewarding topic for investigation. It is hoped that this book, as well as summarising the research effort in this broad field of study, has also served to pinpoint at least some of the significant gaps that exist in our extant factual knowledge and technical expertise. There is certainly great need for further work to be conducted both in relation to features of urban retailing structural organisation and consumers' latent and overt behavioural-cognitive responses. This future research, covering theoretical, empirical, descriptive and predictive approaches is especially required given the nature and scope of the changes that are at present occurring within the urban retail system, and the associated need for careful planning and control. Further, it is apparent that research contributions are likely to be made by the full gamut of social science disciplines, with economics, history, sociology, regional science, geography, marketing, planning, architecture, design and psychology standing prominently amongst them. Notwithstanding the broad interdisciplinary nature of the field, it is hoped that the present book has also served to exemplify the utility of and continued need for an overtly *spatial* approach in the study of urban retailing phenomena.

Appendix 1
Stockport Shopping Survey

Bedford College
(University of London)

Department of Geography

REGENT'S PARK LONDON NW1 4NS

Dear

I am conducting research at the University of London, and as a part of my work I am making a study of shopping habits in the Stockport area. I need the views of a cross-section of people throughout the town.

For this reason I would be very grateful if you could spare the time to answer a few questions about your shopping habits. Much of the space has been reserved for your own comments and opinions which will be of invaluable help to my study. I know that we are all cautious when asked to fill in a survey sent through the post, and quite rightly too, but I am conducting this survey in such a way that all your answers will be treated in strict confidence, and no individual will be referred to in the report. It is hoped that the information you provide will be of great use to all those concerned with improving shopping facilities.

You will find a stamped addressed envelope in which to return the completed questionnaire. I hope that you will be able to take part so that a true cross-section of opinions can be considered. May I take this opportunity to extend my warm thanks to you if you do feel that you can help me with my study.

Yours sincerely,

Robert B.Potter. B.Sc. (Lond.)

STOCKPORT SHOPPING SURVEY

PART 1

We are interested in WHERE you usually purchase the different items listed below. In each case give the name of the District, (eg. Stockport Centre or Reddish), and the name of the Road as well, if it is a small centre or a single shop. If you regularly visit more than one place for any particular type of good you can list these in order of preference on the lines provided, (i..ii..iii..). Please also state how often you visit these centres, (eg. 1 visit per week or 6 months etc,) and the method of transport which you generally use, (eg. walking, cycle, bus, train, motorcycle, motorcar).

ITEM	PLACE WHERE YOU BUY THIS ITEM (DISTRICT & ROAD)	HOW OFTEN	MEANS OF TRANSPORT
1. Small, casual	i..	....	....
purchases (eg.	ii..	....	....
bread, cigarettes.)	iii..	....	....
2. Regular purchase	i..	....	....
of meat and	ii..	....	....
groceries.	iii..	....	....
3. Minor household	i..	....	....
goods, (eg. light-	ii..	....	....
bulbs.)	iii..	....	....
4. Minor clothing,	i..	....	....
(eg. socks, hand-	ii..	....	....
kerchiefs.)	iii..	....	....
5. Major purchases,	i..	....	....
(eg. furniture, cloth-	ii..	....	....
ing).	iii..	....	....
6. Expensive goods,	i..	....	....
(eg. jewellery.)	ii..	....	....
	iii..	....	....

PART 2

In this section we would like you to state briefly what you think of the shopping facilities available to you in your locality and in the area as a whole. You might like to say what you think of your local shops, what you think of the Merseyway Precinct and the Town Centre or any other place that you visit to shop. (eg. Manchester etc.) Your

1.

PLEASE TURN OVER

comments will be of great assistance:–

....

....

....

....

....

....

....

PART 3

In this section you will find a few questions for you to answer:–

a) Have your shopping habits changed at all since the opening of the Merseyway shopping centre? (Write YES or NO.) ....

IF YOU HAVE ANSWERED NO PROCEED TO NEXT QUESTION. IF YOU HAVE ANSWERED YES PROCEED TO QUESTION c).

b) Are there any particular reasons why you have not changed your shopping habits?

....

....

....

c) Do you visit Manchester centre less since the opening of Merseyway? (Write YES or NO and state reasons if you wish.) ....

....

....

d) Do you visit your local shopping centres less since the opening of Merseyway? (Write YES or NO and give reason).

....

....

....

e) Do you find that Merseyway is suited to your shopping needs? (Write YES or NO and give reasons.) ....

....

....

....

f) Do you think that Merseyway is an attractive, pleasant place to shop in? (Write YES or NO and give reasons)

....

....

....

PLEASE TURN OVER

PART 4

Below you will find a list of factors which might influence the way in which you shop, especially in determining the centres you visit. In each case consider the factor and then tick the appropriate box according to how important you feel the factor to be. A space has been left at the bottom for you to note down any factors which you think are important but have not been listed.

	Very Important	Important	Fairly Important	Not Important
Cost of travel to centres.				
Availability of Parking Facilities.				
Whether centres are places where you meet friends and neighbours.				
Variety of Shop types present.				
Price differences between centres.				
Time spent in travelling to centre.				
Frequency and Reliability of Public Transport to centres.				
Provision of Amenities, (eg. seats, toilets, provision for disabled.) at centres.				
Influence of Advertising by stores in national newspapers. (eg. C & A, Mace).				
Influences of Local Advertisements, (eg. local and district papers, local cinemas).				
Whether shops are close together.				
Provision of covered areas.				
Degree to which centres are attractive, (eg. trees, plants and bright architecture).				
Extent to which centres are free from Traffic.				

 PLEASE TURN OVER

PART 5

Below you will find an outline map of Stockport and the surrounding areas. The dashed line, (-·-·-·-·) shows the boundary of Stockport and the surrounding areas are named. Look at this map and the key below it, and then show clearly where you live by means of a cross. (X) Then on the map mark with a circle (O) all the shopping areas that you USE, HAVE SEEN or HAVE PERSONALLY HEARD ABOUT within the entire area of the map, (Stockport and the surrounding districts.) Then draw arrows (⟶) from where you live to all those centres that you ACTUALLY SHOP AT. There is no need to check up or guess as we are only interested in the centres which you know personally.

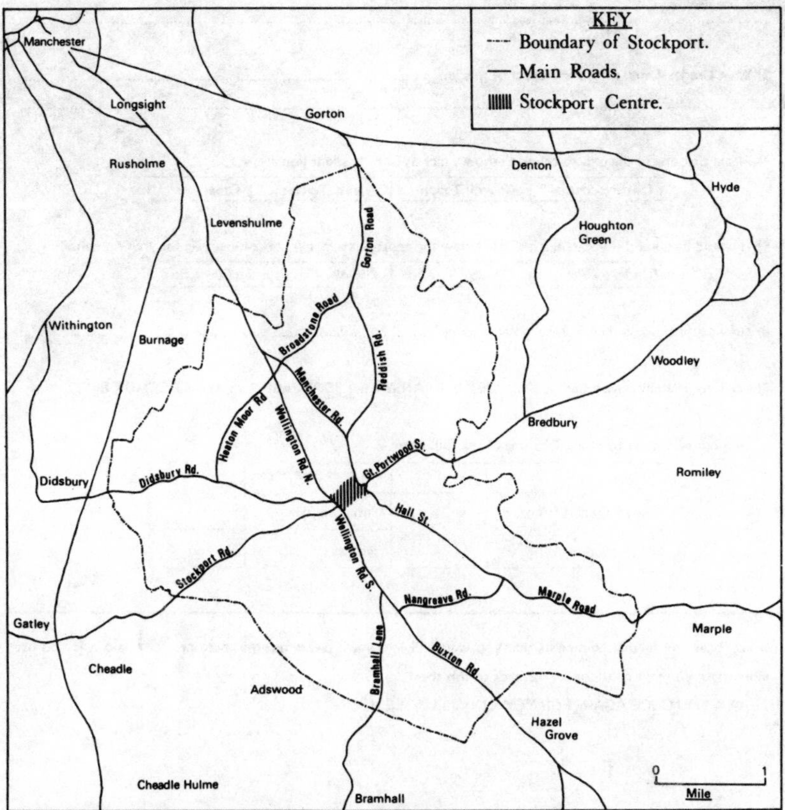

TO BE DRAWN ON THIS MAP BY YOU:

X To show WHERE YOU LIVE.

O To show Shopping Centres YOU USE, HAVE SEEN or HEARD ABOUT.

⟶ Arrows pointing from your home to the places you ACTUALLY SHOP AT.

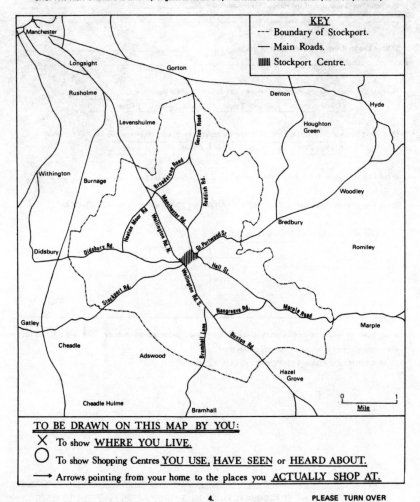

4. **PLEASE TURN OVER**

PART 6

The questions in this part of the survey are of a slightly more personal nature than those in the earlier parts, but are essential if we are to take account of the views of the whole cross-section of people in the area. Your answers will be treated in the strictest confidence throughout.

1) Please indicate your approximate age by ticking one of the age groups below:—

Under 30	30–39	40–49	50–59	Over 60

2) What is the Occupation of the Head of the household? ....

....

3) What Grade, if any, is held in respect of this job? ....

....

4) Please tick one of the groups below to show which type of resident you are:—

Owner-occupier	Council Tenant	Private Tenant	Other

5) It would be helpful if you could indicate below the appropriate weekly take-home pay for your household:—

Under £25	£25-35	£36-49	£50 +

6) How many children do you have living at home?..

7) Does your family have a Car? .... (IF YOU ANSWER YES PLEASE ANSWER QUESTION 8)

8) Do you use the car to shop? Tick one of the following:—

Always.		Only at weekends.	
Always, apart from local shopping.		Infrequently.	
		Never.	

If you have any further comments that you would like to make please use the space provided below. If you need more space you may continue on the back of this sheet.

THANK YOU ONCE AGAIN FOR YOUR INVALUABLE HELP.

YOU HAVE NOW FINISHED THE QUESTIONNAIRE. COULD YOU PLEASE RETURN IT AS SOON AS POSSIBLE USING THE STAMPED ADDRESSED ENVELOPE. THANK YOU FOR YOUR CO-OPERATION.

5.

Appendix 2
Swansea Survey: Living in Towns

Bedford College
(University of London)
Department of Geography
REGENT'S PARK LONDON NW1 4NS
Telephone: 01-486 4400
Telegrams: Edforcoll London NW1

Dear Sir or Madam,

Living in Towns

May I ask for your help? I am conducting research at the University of London, and as part of my work I am making a study of the Swansea area. In particular, I am interested in how people feel about living in towns and cities. As so many of us now live in urban areas, you can appreciate that this is an interesting and potentially rewarding field of enquiry.

I need the views of a cross-section of people living in the West Cross area. I would be grateful, therefore, if you could spare the time to answer a few simple questions. I must stress that I am conducting this survey in such a way that all answers will be treated in the strictest confidence, and no individual will be referred to in the report. It is hoped that the results obtained will help us to understand how people react to urban areas.

I do hope that you will be able to take part so that a true cross-section of views can be considered. You will find a stamped addressed envelope in which to return the survey. May I take this opportunity to extend my sincere thanks to you if you feel able to participate.

Yours faithfully,

R.B. Potter

Dr. R.B. Potter,
Lecturer in Geography.

S W A N S E A   S U R V E Y

1. We are interested in how satisfied you feel with certain broad aspects of your life within the town. For each aspect listed below, give a score from 1 to 7 according to how satisfied you feel. Use 1 to show complete dissatisfaction and 7 to indicate complete satisfaction. Use scores from 2 to 6 to convey reactions between these end-points. Tick the appropriate box in each case:-

Completely Dissatisfied ◄—— Neutral ——► Completely Satisfied

	1	2	3	4	5	6	7
Your home..................							
Your job....................							
Your neighbourhood...........							
The West Cross area..........							
Swansea as a place to live....							
Being a housewife............							
Your health..................							
Your leisure time............							
Your family's education......							
Your standard of living.......							
The economic state of Britain.							
Democracy in Britain..........							
Religion in Britain...........							

-1-

2. Do you, or does any member of your family belong to any of the following kinds of organization? If so, please tick the appropriate box:-

a) Sports club............		g) Womens' Institute..........	
b) Social club............		h) Housing or Community group..	
c) Recreational club......		i) Political party...........	
d) Environmental group....		j) Professional society.......	
e) Charity organization...		k) Church organization........	
f) Trade union............		l) Adult education group......	

3. We would also like to ask a few simple questions about your shopping activities within the town.

a) Can you recall all the places you visited in the last month in order to do shopping? Please list these places below. For large shopping areas just give the name of the district (e.g. 'Swansea city centre'/'Morriston'). For small centres and single shops give both the name of the road and the district (e.g. 'Alderwood Road, West Cross'):-

....
....
....
....
....

b) Are there any other places which you normally visit to shop but which are not listed above? If so, please list below in the same manner:-

....
....
....

c) Finally, can you think of any other shopping centres that you know about, but which you do not use? Please list below in the same manner:-

....
....
....
....

d) We are also interested in how satisfied you feel with various aspects of your shopping activities. For each aspect, give a score ranging from 1 to 7 according to how satisfied you feel, (as in question 1). Use 1 to indicate complete dissatisfaction and 7 to show complete satisfaction:-

Completely Dissatisfied ◄——Neutral——► Completely Satisfied

	1	2	3	4	5	6	7
a) Shopping centres in West Cross.......							
b) Swansea city centre..................							
c) Other shopping centres in Swansea....							
d) Shopping centres outside Swansea.....							
e) If a 'hypermarket' or 'superstore' were to be built in the suburbs of Swansea							

-2-

4. As a part of this study, we wish to consider how urban residents react to a number of everyday roles and situations. Consider each of the following questions and answer yes or no:-

a) Do you sometimes feel happy, sometimes depressed, without apparent reason?..YES/NO

b) Do you prefer action to planning for action?......................YES/NO

c) Do you have frequent ups and downs in mood, either with or without apparent cause?..................................YES/NO

d) Are you happiest when you get involved in some project that calls for rapid action?....................................YES/NO

e) Are you inclined to be moody?...YES/NO

f) Does your mind often wander while you are trying to concentrate?..YES/NO

g) Do you usually take the initiative in making new friends?........YES/NO

h) Are you inclined to be swift and sure in your actions?...........YES/NO

i) Are you frequently "lost in thought" even when supposed to be taking part in a conversation?...............................YES/NO

j) Would you rate yourself as a lively individual?..................YES/NO

k) Are you sometimes bubbling over with energy and sometimes very sluggish?..YES/NO

l) Would you be very unhappy if you were prevented from making numerous social contacts?.......................................YES/NO

5. Finally, we need the views of a cross-section of people living in the area. Answering these last few questions will help us to achieve this. Your answers will be treated in the strictest confidence throughout.

a) How long have you lived in the West Cross area?...........................
b) How long have you lived in Swansea?..
c) Do you or does any member of your family have a car?.................YES/NO
d) Please indicate your approximate age by ticking one of the boxes below:-

Under 30	30-49	50 and over

e) What is the occupation of the chief breadwinner of the family? Please give full details including grade if any:- ....
....
....

YOU HAVE NOW FINISHED THE QUESTIONNAIRE. PLEASE RETURN IT AS SOON AS POSSIBLE USING THE STAMPED ADDRESSED ENVELOPE PROVIDED. THANK YOU FOR YOUR ASSISTANCE. If there are any further comments which you would like to make please use the back of this sheet.

-3-

Bibliography

Abiodun, J.O., (1967), 'Urban hierarchy in a developing country', *Economic Geography*, 43, 347-67.

Adams, J.S., (1968), 'Review of Behavior and Location', *London School of Economics, Graduate School of Geography Discussion Paper, 20.*

Adams, J.S., (1969), 'Directional bias in intra-urban migration', *Economic Geography*, 45, 302-23.

Alchian, A.A., (1950), 'Uncertainty, evolution, and economic theory', *Journal of Political Economy*, 58, 211-21.

Alexander, D., (1970), *Retailing in England during the Industrial Revolution*, Athlone Press, London.

Alexander, I. and Dawson, J.A., (1979), 'Employment in retailing: a case study of employment in suburban shopping centres', *Geoforum*, 10, 407-25.

Alonso, W., (1960), 'A theory of the urban land market', *Papers and Proceedings of the Regional Science Association*, 6, 149-57.

Ambrose, P., (1968), 'An analysis of intra-urban shopping patterns', *Town Planning Review*, 39, 327-34.

Applebaum, W., (1954), 'Marketing geography', in James, P.E. and Jones, C.F. (Eds.), *American Geography: Inventory and Prospect*, Syracuse University Press.

Applebaum, W., (1961), 'Teaching marketing geography by the case method', *Economic Geography*, 37, 48-60.

Beaujeu-Garnier, J. and Delobez, A., (1979), *Geography of Marketing*, Longman.

Beavon, K.S.O., (1970), 'An alternative approach to the classification of urban hierarchies', *South African Geographical Journal*, 52, 129-33.

Beavon, K.S.O., (1972), 'The intra-urban continuum of shopping centres in Cape Town', *South African Geographical Journal*, 54, 58-71.

Beavon, K.S.O., (1973), 'A procedure for constructing Lösch's regional system of markets', *South African Journal of Science*, 69, 377-9.

Beavon, K.S.O., (1974a), 'Interpreting Lösch on an intra-urban scale', *South African Geographical Journal*, 56, 36-59.

Beavon, K.S.O., (1974b), 'Generalising the intra-urban model based on Lösch', *South African Geographical Journal*, 56, 137-54.

Beavon, K.S.O., (1975), 'Christaller's central place theory: reviewed, revealed, revised', *Department of Geography and Environmental Studies, University of Witwatersrand, Johannesburg, Occasional Paper No. 15.*

Beavon, K.S.O., (1976), 'The Lösch intra-urban model under conditions of changing cost functions', *The South African Geographic Journal*, 58, 36-9.

Beavon, K.S.O., (1977), *Central Place Theory: A Reinterpretation*, Longman.

Beavon, K.S.O., (1978a), 'City-rich and city-poor sectors: a comment on the construction of the Löschian landscape', *Geographical Analysis*, 10, 77-82.
Beavon, K.S.O., (1978b), 'Löschian regions of homogeneous structure: an expository note', *Tijdschrift voor Economische en Sociale Geografie*, 69, 172-5.
Beavon, K.S.O., (1978c), 'A comment on the procedure for determining the general structure of a Löschian hierarchy', *Journal of Regional Science*, 18, 127-32.
Beavon, K.S.O., (1979), 'The Lösch constraints - again', *Journal of Regional Science*, 19, 505-9.
Beavon, K.S.O. and Hay, A.M., (1978), 'Long run average cost, price and Christaller's concept of range: an explanatory note', *Geography*, 63, 98-100.
Beavon, K.S.O. and Mabin, A.S., (1975), 'The Lösch system of market areas: derivation and extension', *Geographical Analysis*, 7, 131-51.
Beavon, K.S.O. and Mabin, A.S., (1976), 'A pedagogic approach to the Löschian system of market areas', *Tijdschrift voor Economische en Sociale Geografie*, 67, 29-37.
Beckmann, M.J. and McPherson, J ., (1970), 'City size distribution in a central place hierarchy: an alternative approach', *Journal of Regional Science*, 10, 25-33.
Bennison, D.J. and Davies, R.L., (1977), 'The movement of shoppers within the central area of Newcastle upon Tyne', *University of Newcastle upon Tyne, Department of Geography, Seminar Papers*, 34.
Berry, B.J.L., (1958); 'Shopping centers and the geography of urban areas', *Ph.D. thesis, University of Washington*.
Berry, B.J.L., (1959), 'Ribbon developments in the urban business pattern', *Annals of the Association of American Geographers*, 49, 145-55.
Berry, B.J.L., (1960), 'The impact of expanding metropolitan communities upon the central place hierarchy', *Annals of the Association of American Geographers*, 50, 112-16.
Berry, B.J.L., (1962), *The Commercial Structure of American Cities: A Review*, Community Renewal Program, Chicago.
Berry, B.J.L., (1963), 'Commercial Structure and Commercial Blight', *University of Chicago Department of Geography Research Paper*, No. 85.
Berry, B.J.L., (1964), 'The case of the mistreated model', *Professional Geographer*, 16(3), 15-16.
Berry, B.J.L., (1967), *Geography of Market Centers and Retail Distribution*, Prentice-Hall.
Berry, B.J.L. and Garrison, W.L., (1958a), 'Recent developments of central place theory', *Papers and Proceedings of the Regional Science Association*, 4, 107-20.
Berry, B.J.L. and Garrison, W.L., (1958b), 'A note on central place theory and the range of a good', *Economic Geography*, 34, 304-11.
Berry, B.J.L. and Mayer, H.M., (1962), 'Design and preliminary findings of the University of Chicago's studies of the central place hierarchy', in Norborg, K. (Ed.), *Proceedings of the IGU Symposium in Urban Geography Lund 1960*. Lund Studies in Geography, Series B. Human Geography No. 24, Gleerup, Lund, 247-52.
Berry, B.J.L. and Pred, A., (1961), *Central Place Studies: A Bibliography of Theory and Applications*, Regional Science Research Institute, Bibliographic Series, 1.
Berry, R.K., (1977), *Small Unit Retailing in Urban Britain - a Review of Present Trends and the Policies Affecting the Small Shop*, St. David's University College, University of Wales.

Bird, J., (1977), *Centrality and Cities*, Routledge and Kegan Paul.
Blake, J., (1976), 'Brent Cross shopping centre', *Town and Country Planning*, 44, 231-36.
Blommestein, H., Nijkamp, P., van Veenendaal, W., (1980), 'Shopping Perceptions and preferences: a multidimensional attractiveness analysis of consumer and entrepreneurial attitudes', *Economic Geography*, 56, 155-74.
Blumenfeld, H., (1959), 'The tidal wave of metropolitan expansion', *Journal of the American Institute of Planners*, 25, 3-14.
Boal, F.W., (1969), 'Territoriality on the Shankill-Falls divide', *Irish Geography*, 6, 30-50.
Boal, F.W. and Johnson, D.B., (1965), 'The functions of retail and service establishments on commercial ribbons', *Canadian Geographer*, 9, 145-69.
Boal, F.W. and Johnson, D.B., (1968), 'Nondescript streets', *Traffic Quarterly*, 22, 329-44.
Brennan, T., (1948), *Midland City*, Dobson, London.
Bridges, M.J., (1976), *The York Asda: a study of changing shopping patterns around a superstore*, University of Manchester, Centre for Urban and Regional Research.
Bromley, R.J., Symanski, R. and Good, C.M., (1975), 'The rationale of periodic markets', *Annals of the Association of American Geographers*, 65, 530-07.
Brooker-Gross, S.R., (1981), 'Shopping behavior in two sets of shopping destinations: an interactionalist interpretation of outshopping', *Tijdschrift voor Economische en Sociale Geografie*, 72, 28-34.
Brown, L.A. and Moore, E.G., (1970), 'The intra-urban migration process: a perspective', *Geografiska Annaler*, 52B, 1-13.
Bullock, N. *et al.*, (1974), 'Time budgets and models of urban activity patterns', *Social Trends*, 5, 45-63.
Bunge, W., (1962), *Theoretical Geography*, Lund Studies in Geography, Series C, No. 1.
Bunting, T.E. and Guelke, L., (1979), 'Behavioral and perception geography: a critical appraisal', *Annals of the Association of American Geographers*, 69, 448-62.
Burnett, P., (1973), 'The dimensions of alternatives in spatial choice processes', *Geographical Analysis*, 5, 181-204.
Burns, W., (1959), *British Shopping Centres*, Leonard Hill, London.
Burns, W., (1967), *Traffic and Transportation in Newcastle-upon-Tyne*, Newcastle-upon-Tyne Corporation.
Burton, I., (1963), 'The quantitative revolution and theoretical geography', *Canadian Geographer*, 7, 151-62.
Campbell, C.K., (1966), 'Research in recreational geography', *British Columbia Geographical Series*, 7.
Campbell, W.J. and Chisholm, M., (1970), 'Local variation in retail grocery prices', *Urban Studies*, 7, 76-81.
Canoyer, H.G., (1946), *Selecting a Store Location*, Government Printing Office, Washington.
Canter, D. and Tagg, S.K., (1975), 'Distance estimation in cities', *Environment and Behavior*, 7, 59-80.
Carol, H., (1960), 'The hierarchy of central functions within the city', *Annals of the Association of American Geographers*, 50, 419-38.
Carruthers, W.I., (1962), 'Service centres in Greater London', *Town Planning Review*, 33, 5-31.
Carter, H., (1981), *The Study of Urban Geography* (3rd. Edition), Arnold, London.

Carter, H. and Rowley, G., (1966), 'The morphology of the central business district of Cardiff', *Transactions of the Institute of British Geographers*, 38, 119-34.
Chatten, I.M., Green, M.D. and Mainwaring, J., (1968), 'Quality retailing variations in the central area of Amsterdam', *South Hampshire Geographer*, 1, 1-16.
Christaller, W., (1933), *Die zentralen Orte in Suddeutschland*, Verlag. Translated by Baskin, C.W., (1966), *Central Places in Southern Germany*, Prentice-Hall.
Christaller, W., (1950), 'Das grundgerüst der raumlichen ordnung in Europa: die systeme der Europäischen zentralen orte', *Frankfurter Geographische Hefte*, 24, 5-14.
Christaller, W., (1962), 'Die hierarchie der Städte', *Lund Studies in Geography, Series B*, 24, 3-11.
Clark, C., (1940), *Conditions of Economic Progress*, London.
Clark, C., (1951), 'Urban population densities', *Journal of the Royal Statistical Society, Series A*, 114, 490-6.
Clark, P.J. and Evans, F.C., (1954), 'Distance to nearest neighbour as a measure of spatial relationships in populations', *Ecology*, 35, 445-53.
Clark, W.A.V., (1967), 'The spatial structure of retail functions in a New Zealand city', *New Zealand Geographer*, 23, 23-33.
Clark, W.A.V., (1968), 'Consumer travel patterns and the concept of range', *Annals of the Association of American Geographers*, 58, 386-96.
Clark, W.A.V., (1969), 'Applications of spacing models in intra-city studies', *Geographical Analysis*, 1, 391-99.
Clark, W.A.V. and Rushton, G., (1970), 'Models of intra-urban consumer behavior and their implications for central place theory', *Economic Geography*, 46, 486-97.
Claus, R.J., Rothwell, D.C. and Bottomley, J., (1972), 'Measuring the quality of a low order retail site', *Economic Geography*, 48, 168-78.
Cohen, S.B. and Lewis, G.K., (1967), 'Form and function in the geography of retailing', *Economic Geography*, 43, 1-42.
Colby, C.C., (1933), 'Centrifugal and centripetal forces in urban geography', *Annals of the Association of American Geographers*, 23, 1- 20.
Cole, H.R., (1966), 'Shopping assessments at Haydock and elsewhere: a review', *Urban Studies*, 3, 147-56.
Comrey, A.L., (1973), *A First Course in Factor Analysis*, Academic Press.
Dacey, M.F., (1962), 'Analysis of central place and point patterns by a nearest neighbor method', *Lund Studies in Geography, Series B*, 24, 55-75.
Dacey, M.F., (1965), 'The geometry of central place theory', *Geografiskä Annaler*, 47B, 111-24.
Daniels, P.W. and Warnes, A.M., (1980), *Movement in Cities: Spatial Perspectives in Urban Transport and Travel*, Methuen.
Davies, D.H., (1960), 'The hard core of Cape Town's central business district: an attempt at delimitation', *Economic Geography*, 36, 53-69.
Davies, K. and Sparks, L., (1981), 'Policies for the location of large stores', *Area*, 13, 232-5.
Davies, R.L., (1968), 'Effects of consumer income differences on the business provisions of small shopping centres', *Urban Studies*, 5, 144-64.
Davies, R.L., (1969), 'Effects of consumer income differences on shopping movement behavior', *Tijdschrift voor Economische en Sociale Geografie*, 60, 111-21.

Davies, R.L., (1970), 'Variable relationships in central place and retail potential models', *Regional Studies*, 4, 49-61.
Davies, R.L., (1971), 'The urban system of retailing in Coventry', *Coventry Shopping Studies Progress Report*, 8.
Davies, R.L., (1972a), 'Structural models of retail distribution: analogies with settlement and land-use theories', *Transactions of the Institute of British Geographers*, 57, 59-82.
Davies, R.L., (1972b), 'The retail pattern of the central area of Coventry', *Institute of British Geographers, Urban Study Group, Occasional Publication*, 1, 1-32.
Davies, R.L., (1973a), 'Patterns and profiles of consumer behaviour', *University of Newcastle-upon-Tyne, Department of Geography, Research Series, No. 10*.
Davies, R.L., (1973b), 'The location of service activities', in Chisholm, M. and Rodgers, B. (Eds.), *Studies in Human Geography*, Heinemann.
Davies, R.L., (1974), 'Nucleated and ribbon components of the urban retail system in Britain', *Town Planning Review*, 45, 91-111.
Davies, R.L., (1976), *Marketing Geography: With Special Reference to Retailing*, Retailing and Planning Associates (1976) Corbridge, Northumberland and Methuen, London (1977).
Davies, R.L., (1977a), 'Store location and store assessment research: the integration of some new and traditional techniques', *Transactions of the Institute of British Geographers*, 2, 141-57.
Davies, R.L., (1977b), 'A framework for commercial planning policies', *Town Planning Review*, 49, 42-58.
Davies, R.L., (1977c), 'Issues in retailing', Chapter 5 in Davies, R.L. and Hall, P. (Eds.), *Issues in Urban Society*, Penguin, Harmondsworth.
Davies, R.L. (Ed.), (1979), *Retail Planning in the European Community*, Saxon House.
Davies, R.L. and Bennison, D.J., (1978), 'Retailing in the city centre: the characters of shopping streets', *Tijdschrift voor Economische en Sociale Geografie*, 69, 270-85.
Davies, W.K.D., (1965), 'Some considerations of scale in central place analysis', *Tijdschrift voor Economische en Sociale Geografie*, 56, 221-6.
Davies, W.K.D., (1966), 'The ranking of service centres: a critical review', *Transactions of the Institute of British Geographers*, 40, 51-65.
Davies, W.K.D., (1967), 'Centrality and the central place hierarchy', *Urban Studies*, 4, 61-79.
Davies, W.K.D., (1968a), 'The need for replication in human geography: some central place examples', *Tijdschrfit voor Economische en Sociale Geografie*, 59, 145-55.
Davies, W.K.D., (1968b), 'The morphology of central places: a case study', *Annals of the Association of American Geographers*, 58, 91-110.
Davies, W.K.D. and Briggs, R., (1967), 'Automobile establishments in Liverpool: a steady state distribution', *The Professional Geographer*, 19, 323-29.
Davies, W.K.D., Giggs, J.A. and Herbert, D.T., (1968), 'Directories, rate books and the commercial structure of towns', *Geography*, 53, 41-54.
Davis, D., (1966), *A History of Shopping*, London, Routledge and Kegan Paul.
Daws, L.F., (1974), 'On shoppers' requirements for the location of shops in towns', *Building Research Establishment Current Paper*, *CP23/74*

Daws, L.F. and Bruce, A.J., (1971), *Shopping in Watford*, Building Research Station, Department of the Environment.
Daws, L.F. and McCulloch, M., (1974), 'Shopping activity patterns: a travel diary study of Watford', *Building Research Establishment Current Paper*, 31/74.
Dawson, J.A., (1973), 'Marketing geography', in Dawson, J.A. and Doornkamp, J.C. (Eds.), *Evaluating the Human Environment: Essays in Applied Geography*.
Dawson, J., (1974), 'The suburbanisation of retail activity', in Johnson, J.H. (Ed.), *Suburban Growth*, Wiley, London.
Dawson, J.A., (1976), 'Hypermarkets in France', *Geography*, 61, 259-62.
Dawson, J.A., (1979a), *The Marketing Environment*, London, Croom Helm.
Dawson, J., (1979b), 'Retail trends in the E.E.C.', in Davies, R.L. (Ed.), *Retail Planning in the European Community, Saxon House*, 21-49.
Dawson, J. (Ed.) (1980a), *Retail Geography*, London, Croom Helm.
Dawson, J.A.,(1980b), 'Research priorities in retail geography', *Interim report of S.S.R.C. sponsored seminar group on geography of retailing*.
Dawson, J.A., (1981), 'Shopping centres in France', *Geography*, 66, 143-6.
Dawson, J. and Kirby, D.A., (1980), 'Urban retailing and consumer behaviour: some examples from Western Society', in Herbert, D.T. and Johnston, R.J., (1980), (Eds.), *Geography and the Urban Environment: Progress in Research and Applications*, Volume III, John Wiley, London.
Day, R.A., (1973), 'Consumer shopping behaviour in a planned urban environment', *Tijdschrift voor Economische en Sociale Geografie*, 64, 77-85.
Dent, B.D., (1980), 'Metropolitan retail structure', Chapter 16 in Hartshorn, T.A., (1980), *Interpreting the City: An Urban Geography*, Wiley, New York.
Diamond, D.R., (1962), 'The central business district of Glasgow', Proceedings of the IGU Symposium in Urban Geography, *Lund Studies in Human Geography*, 24, 525-34.
Dixon, O.M., (1972), 'Models of nodal regions', in The Retail Structure of Cities, *Institute of British Geographers, Urban Studies Group, Occasional Publication*, No. 1, 33-48.
Donaldson, B., (1973), 'An empirical investigation into the concept of sectoral bias in the mental maps, search spaces and migration patterns of intra-urban migrants', *Geografiska Annaler*, 55B, 13-33.
Donaldson, B. and Johnston, R.J., (1973), 'Intra-urban sectoral mental maps: further evidence from an extended methodology', *Geographical Analysis*, 5, 45-54.
Downs, R.M., (1970), 'The cognitive structure of an urban shopping centre', *Environment and Behavior*, 2, 13-39.
Downs, R.M., (1979), 'Critical appraisal or determined philosophical skepticism', *Annals of the Association of American Geographers*, 69, 468-71.
Downs, R.M. and Stea, D., (1973), *Image and Environment*, Aldine, Chicago.
Dutt, A.K., (1969), 'Intra-city hierarchy of central places: Calcutta as a case study', *Professional Geographer*, 21, 18-22.
Epstein, B., (1969), 'Review of Geography of Market Centers and Retail Distribution by B.J.L. Berry', *Economic Geography*, 45, 88-9.
Eyles, J., (1971), 'Pouring new sentiments into old theories: how else can we look at behavioural patterns?', *Area*, 3, 242-50.

Fernie, J. and Carrick, R.J., (1981), 'Quasi-retail activity in Britain', *Paper presented at the annual conference of the Institute of British Geographers, Leicester.*
Fingleton, B., (1975), 'A factorial approach to the nearest centre hypothesis', *Transactions of the Institute of British Geographers*, 65, 131-39.
Fox, H.S.A., (1970), 'Going to market in 13th century England', *Geographical Magazine*, 42, 658-67.
Foxall, G.R., (1977), *Consumer Behaviour: a practical guide*, Retailing and Planning Associates, Corbridge, Northumberland.
Francescato, D. and Mebane, W., (1973), 'How citizens view two great cities: Milan and Rome', in Downs, R.M. and Stea, D. (Eds.), *Image and Environment*.
Fransella, F. and Bannister, P., (1977), *A Manual for Repertory Grid Technique*, Academic Press, London.
Freeman, T.W., (1959), *The Conurbations of Great Britain*, Manchester University Press.
Funck, R. and Parr, J.B., (Eds.), (1978), *The Analysis of Regional Structure: Essays in Honour of August Lösch*, Pion, London.
Garner, B.J., (1966), *The Internal Structure of Shopping Centres*, Northwestern University, Studies in Geography, 12.
Garner, B.J., (1967), 'Models of urban geography and settlement location', Chapter 9 in Chorley, R.J. and Haggett, P. (Eds.), *Models in Geography*, Methuen, London, 302-60.
Garner, B.J., (1970), 'Towards a better understanding of shopping patterns', in Osborne, R.H., Barnes, F.A. and Doornkamp, J.D. (Eds.), *Geographical Essays in Honour of K.C.Edwards*, Department of Geography, University of Nottingham.
Garrison, W.L., (1950), 'The Business Structure of the Consumer Tributary Area of the Fountain Square Major Outlying Business Center of Evanston, Illinois', *Ph.D. thesis, Northwestern University.*
Garrison, W.L., Berry, B.J.L., Marble, D.F., Nystuen, J.D. and Morrill, R.L., (1959), *Studies of Highway Development and Geographical Change*, Greenwood Press, New York.
Gayler, H.J., (1980), 'Social class and consumer spatial behaviour: some aspects of variation in shopping patterns in metropolitan Vancouver, Canada', *Transactions of the Institute of British Geographers*, N.S., 5, 427-45.
Getis, A., (1964), 'Temporal analysis of land use patterns with the use of nearest neighbor and quadrat methods', *Annals of the Association of American Geographers*, 54, 391-9.
Giggs, J.A., (1977), 'The changing commercial structure of Barry, 1884-1976', *Papers presented to the Urban Geography Study Group of the Institute of British Geographers, Leicester.*
Gold, J.R., (1980), *An Introduction to Behavioural Geography*, Oxford University Press.
Goldman, A., (1975), 'The use of landmarks in recalling retail stores', *Urban Studies*, 12, 319-24.
Golledge, R.G., (1970), 'Some equilibrium models of consumer behavior', *Economic Geography*, 46, 415-24.
Golledge, R.G. and Brown, L.A., (1967), 'Search, learning, and the market decision process', *Geografiska Annaler*, 49B,
Golledge, R.G., Rushton, G. and Clark, W.A.V., (1966), 'Some characteristics of Iowa's dispersed farm population and their implications for the grouping of central place functions', *Economic Geography*, 52, 261-72.

Golledge, R.G. and Zannaras, G., (1973), 'Cognitive approaches to the analysis of human spatial behavior', in Ittelson, W.H. (Ed.), *Environment and Cognition*, Seminar Press, 59-94.
Goodchild, B., (1974), 'Class differences in environmental perception: an exploratory study', *Urban Studies*, 11, 157-69.
Goodey, B., Duffett, A.W., Gold, J.R. and Spencer, D., (1971), 'City-Scene: An Exploration into the image of central Birmingham as seen by Area Residents', *University of Birmingham, Centre for Urban and Regional Studies, Research Memorandum,* 10.
Graham, E., (1976), 'What is a mental map?', *Area*, 8, 259-62.
Grimshaw, P.N., Shepherd, M.J. and Willmott, A.J., (1970), 'An application of cluster analysis by computer to the study of urban morphology', *Transactions of the Institute of British Geographers*, 51, 143-61.
Guy, C.M., (1976), 'The location of shops in the Reading area', *University of Reading, Geographical Papers*, 46.
Guy, C.M., (1980), *Retail Location and Retail Planning in Britain*, Gower Press, Farnborough.
Gwynne, R.N., (1978), 'City size and retail prices in less-developed countries: an insight into primacy', *Area*, 10, 136-40.
Haggett, P., (1965), *Locational Analysis in Human Geography*, Arnold.
Haggett, P., Cliff, A.D. and Frey, A., (1977), *Locational Analysis in Human Geography. Second Edition, Volume 1*, Arnold, London.
Haites, E.F., (1976), 'A note on the general structure of a Löschian hierarchy', *Journal of Regional Science*, 16, 257-60.
Hall, P., (1974), *Urban and Regional Planning*, Penguin, Harmondsworth.
Hallsworth, A.G., (1978), 'A caveat on retail assessment', *Area*, 10, 24-25.
Hallsworth, A., (1981a), Trading Patterns of a Freestanding Hypermarket: Havant Hypermarket, *Department of Geography, Portsmouth Polytechnic.*
Hallsworth, A., (1981b), Trading patterns of a District Centre Superstore: Asda Waterlooville, *Department of Geography, Portsmouth Polytechnic.*
Hanson, P., (1977), 'The activity patterns of elderly households', *Geografiska Annaler*, 59B, 109-24.
Hanson, P. and Hanson, S., (1972), 'Distance minimization in intra-urban household travel', *Proceedings of the New England - St. Lawrence Valley Geographical Society*, 2, 80-2.
Hanson, S., (1976), 'Spatial variations in the cognitive levels of urban residents', Chapter 9 in Golledge, R.G. and Rushton, G. (Eds.), *Spatial Choice and Spatial Behavior: Geographical Essays on the Analysis of Preferences and Perceptions*, 157-77.
Hanson, S., (1977), 'Measuring the cognitive levels of urban residents', *Geografiska Annaler*, 59B, 67-81.
Hanson, S., (1980), 'Spatial diversification and multipurpose travel: implications for choice theory', *Geographical Analysis*, 12, 245-57.
Harman, H.H., (1967), *Modern Factor Analysis*, Chicago.
Harrison, J. and Sarre, P., (1975), 'Personal construct theory in the measurement of environmental images', *Environment and Behavior*, 7, 3-58.
Hartley, G., (1962), *A Study of Central Places and their services within the London Area*, Unpublished Ph.D. thesis, University of London.
Hartman, G.W., (1950), 'The central business district: a study in urban geography', *Economic Geography*, 26, 237-44.

Hartshorn, T.A., (1980), *Interpreting the City: An Urban Geography*, Wiley, New York.
Harvey, D., (1969), *Explanation in Geography*, London.
Harvey, D., (1973), *Social Justice and the City*, Arnold, London.
Hay, A.M., (1971), 'Notes on the economic basis for periodic marketing in developing countries', *Geographical Analysis*, 3, 393-401.
Hay, A.M. and Johnston, R.J., (1980), 'Spatial variations in grocery prices: further attempts at modeling', *Urban Geography*, 1, 189-201.
Hay, A.M. and Smith, R.H.T., (1980), 'Consumer welfare in periodic market systems', *Transactions of the Institute of British Geographers, New Series*, 5, 29-44.
Hayes, C.R., (1957), 'Suburban residential land values along the C.B. & Q. railroad', *Land Economics*, 33, 177-81.
Herbert, B., (1976), 'Urban morphology and transportation', *Traffic Quarterly*, 20, 633-49.
Herbert, D.T., (1973), 'Residential mobility and preference: a study of Swansea', in *Social Patterns in Cities*, Institute of British Geographers Special Publication No 5, 103-121.
Hillman, M., (1973), 'The social costs of hypermarket developments', *Built Environment*, 2, 89-91.
Hodder, B.W., (1968), *Economic Development in the Tropics*, London, Methuen.
Hoggart, K., (1978), 'Consumer shopping strategies and purchasing activity: an exploratory investigation', *Geoforum* , 9, 415-23.
Hoover, E.M., (1948), *The Location of Economic Activity*, McGraw-Hill, New York.
Hope, K., (1968), *Methods of Multivariate Analysis*, London.
Horton, F.E. and Reynolds, D.R., (1969), 'An investigation of individual action spaces', *Proceedings of the Association of American Geographers*, 1, 70-5.
Horton, F.E. and Reynolds, D.R., (1971), 'Effects of urban spatial structure on individual behavior', *Economic Geography*, 47, 36-48.
Horwood, E. and Boyce, R., (1959), *Studies of the Central Business District and Urban Freeway Development*, Settle.
Hoyt, H., (1958), 'Classification and significant characteristics of shopping centres', *Appraisal Journal*, April, 214-22.
Hudson, R., (1974), 'Images of the retailing environment: an example of the use of the repertory grid methodology', *Environment and Behavior*, 6, 470-94.
Hudson, R., (1975), 'Patterns of spatial search', *Transactions of the Institute of British Geographers*, 65, 141-54.
Hudson, R., (1980), 'Personal construct theory, the repertory grid measure and human geography', *Progress in Human Geography*, 4, 346-59.
Huff, D.L., (1960), 'A topographical model of consumer space preferences', *Papers and Proceedings of the Regional Science Association*, 6, 159-73.
Huff, D.L., (1961), 'Ecological characteristics of consumer behavior', *Papers and Proceedings of the Regional Science Association*, 7, 19-28.
Huff, D.L., (1963), 'A probabilistic analysis of shopping centre trade areas', *Land Economics*, 39, 81-90.
Isard, W., (1956), *Location and Space-Economy*, M.I.T. Press.
Jefferys, J.B., (1954), *Retail Trading in Britain, 1850-1950*, Cambridge University Press.
Jefferys, J.B. and Knee, D. (1962), *Retailing in Europe*, Macmillan, London.
Jensen-Butler, C., (1972), 'Gravity models and planning tools: a review of theoretical and operational problems', *Geografiska Annaler*, 54B,

68-78.
Johnson, J.H., (1967), *Urban Geography: An Introductory Analysis*, Pergamon, Oxford.
Johnson, L.J., (1964), 'Centrality within a metropolis', *Economic Geography*, 40, 324-36.
Johnston, R.J., (1966), 'The distribution of an intra-metropolitan central place hierarchy', *Australian Geographical Studies*, 4, 19-33.
Johnston, R.J., (1968), 'Railways, urban growth and central place patterns: an example from south-east Melbourne', *Tijdschrfit voor Economische en Sociale Geografie*, 59, 33-41.
Johnston, R.J., (1971), 'Mental maps of the city: suburban preference patterns', *Environment and Planning*, 3, 63-72.
Johnston, R.J., (1972), 'Activity spaces and residential preferences: some tests of the hypothesis of sectoral mental maps', *Economic Geography*, 48, 199-211.
Johnston, R.J., (1978), *Multivariate Statistical Analysis in Geography*, Longman, London.
Johnston, R.J., (1979), *Geography and Geographers: Anglo-American Human Geography since 1945*, Arnold.
Johnston, R.J., (1980), *City and Society: An Outline for Urban Geography*, Penguin, Harmondsworth.
Jones, E., (1960), *A Social Geography of Belfast*, Oxford University Press.
Jones, P., (1981), 'Retail innovation and diffusion - the spread of Asda stores', *Area*, 13, 197-201.
Jones, R., (1979), 'Consumers' co-operation in Victorian Edinburgh: the evolution of a location pattern', *Transactions of the Institute of British Geographers*, N.S., 4, 292-305.
Kay, G., (1975), 'Stages of technology and economic development', *Geography*, 60, 89-98.
Kelly, G.A., (1955), *The Psychology of Personal Constructs*, Norton, New York.
King, L.J. and Golledge, R.G., (1978), *Cities, Space and Behavior: The Elements of Urban Geography*, Prentice-Hall, New Jersey.
Kivell, P.T., (1972), 'Retailing in non-central locations', *Institute of British Geographers, Urban Study Group, Occasional Publication*, 1, 49-58.
Kivell, P.T. and Shaw, G., (1980), 'The study of retail location', Chapter 2 in Dawson, J. (Ed.), *Retail Geography*, Croom Helm, London.
Klein, H.J., (1967), 'The delimitation of the town centre in the image of its citizens' in Bull, E.J. (Ed.), *Urban Core and Inner City*, University of Leiden, 286-306.
Knos, D., (1962), *Distribution of Land Values in Topeka, Kansas*, Lawrence, Kansas.
Korteweg, P.J. and van Weesep, J., (1980), 'Shopping patterns of suburbanites', *Tijdschrift voor Economische en Sociale Geografie*, 71, 318-26.
Kotler, P., (1965), 'Behavioral models for analyzing buyers', *Journal of Marketing*, 29, 37-45.
Kutter, E., (1973), 'A model for individual travel behaviour', *Urban Studies*, 10, 235-58.
Lee, T.R., (1962), 'Brennan's law of shopping behaviour', *Psychological Reports*, 11, 662.
Lee, T.R., (1970), 'Perceived distance as a function of direction in a city', *Environment and Behavior*, 2, 40-51.
Lee, T.R. and Wood, L.J., (1980), 'The city in an era of restricted car usage: some potential responses and adjustments to future oil

shortages', *Geoforum*, 11, 27-29.
Leeming, F.A., (1959), 'An experimental survey of retail shopping and service facilities in parts of North Leeds', *Transactions of the Institute of British Geographers*, 26, 133-52.
Lentnek, B., Lieber, S.R. and Sheskin, I., (1975), 'Consumer behaviour in different areas', *Annals of the Association of American Geographers* 65, 538-45.
Leven, C.L., (1969), 'Determinants of the size and spatial form of urban areas', *Papers of the Regional Science Association*, 22, 7-28.
Lewis, P.W., (1980), 'Christaller, Lösch and after', (book review essay) *Progress in Human Geography*, 4, 146-52.
Ley, D., (1977), 'Social geography and the taken-for-granted world', *Transactions of the Institute of British Geographers*, N.S., 2, 498-512.
Lieber, S.R., (1977), 'Attitudes and revealed behaviour: a case study', *Professional Geographer*, 29, 53-8.
Lipsey, D., (1971), 'Productivity in distribution: a summary of the literature', *Distributive Trades EDC, NEDO*.
Lloyd, P. and Dicken, P., (1977)(1972), *Location in Space: A Theoretical Approach to Economic Geography* (Second/First Editions), Harper and Row.
Lloyd, R.E., (1977), 'Consumer behavior after migration: a reassessment process', *Economic Geography*, 53, 14-27.
Lloyd, R. and Jennings, D., (1978), 'Shopping behavior and income: comparison in an urban environment', *Economic Geography*, 54, 157-67.
Loewenstein, L.K., (1963), 'The location of urban land uses', *Land Economics*, 39, 406-20.
Logan, A., (1968), 'The pattern of service centres in Warringah Shire, Sydney', *University of Sydney Planning Research Centre* (cited in Scott, 1970).
Lomas, G.M., (1964), 'Retail trading centres in the Midlands', *Journal of the Town Planning Institute*, 50, 104-19.
Lösch, A., (1938), 'The nature of economic regions', *Southern Economic Journal*, 5, 71-8.
Lösch, A., (1940), *Die räumliche Ordnung der Wirtschaft*, Jena. Translated by Woglom, W.H. and Stolper, W.F., (1954), *The Economics of Location*, Yale University Press.
Low, N., (1975), 'Centrism and the provision of services in residential areas', *Urban Studies*, 12, 177-91.
Lynch, K., (1960), *The Image of the City*, Cambridge, Mass., M.I.T.
Mabogunje, A.L., (1964), 'The evolution and analysis of the retail structure of Lagos, Nigeria', *Economic Geography*, 40, 304-23.
Mackay, D.B., (1976), 'The effect of spatial stimuli on the estimation of cognitive maps', *Geographical Analysis*, 8, 439-52.
Mackay, D.B., Olshavsky, R.W. and Sentell, G., (1975), 'Cognitive maps and spatial behavior of consumers', *Geographical Analysis*, 7, 19-34.
MacLennan, D. and Williams, N.J., (1979), 'Revealed space preference theory - a cautionary note', *Tijdschrift voor Economische en Sociale Geografie*, 70,307-9.
Malcolm, J.F. and Aitken, C.P., (1977), *The Impact of a Superstore: Fine Fare, St. Ninians, Stirling*, Department of Town and Regional Planning, University of Glasgow, Discussion Papers in Planning.
Marble, D.F., (1959), 'Transportation inputs at urban residential sites' *Papers of the Regional Science Association*, 5, 253-66.
Marshall, J.U., (1964), 'Model and reality in central place studies', *Professional Geographer*, 16(1), 5-8.

Marshall,J.U., (1969), *The Location of Service Towns: an approach to the analysis of central place systems*, University of Toronto Press.
Marshall, J.U., (1975), 'The Löschian numbers as a problem in number theory', *Geographical Analysis*, 7, 421-26.
Marshall, J.U., (1977a), 'Christallerian networks in the Löschian economic landscape', *Professional Geographer*, 29, 153-9.
Marshall, J.U., (1977b), 'The construction of the Löschian landscape', *Geographical Analysis*, 9, 1-13.
Marshall, J.U., (1978a), 'On the structure of the Löschian landscape', *Journal of Regional Science*, 18, 121-5.
Marshall, J.U., (1978b), 'The truncated Löschian landscape: a reply to Beavon', *Geographical Analysis*, 10, 83-6.
Marshall, J.U., (1979), 'Lösch revisited - again', *Journal of Regional Science*, 19, 501-3.
Matthews, M.H., (1980), 'The mental maps of children: images of Coventry's city centre', *Geography*, 64, 169-79.
Mayer, H.M., (1942), 'Patterns and recent trends of Chicago's outlying business centres', *Journal of Land and Public Utility Economics*, 18, 4-16.
Mayer, H., (1969), 'The Spatial Expansion of Urban Growth, *Association of American Geographers Resource Papers*, No. 7.
McEvoy, D., (1968), 'Alternative methods of ranking shopping centres', *Tijdschrift voor Economische en Sociale Geografie*, 59, 211-17.
McEvoy, D., (1972), 'Vacancy rates and the retail structure of the Manchester conurbation', *Institute of British Geographers, Urban Study Group, Occasional Publication*, 1, 59-67.
Mercer, D.C., (1970), 'Urban recreational hinterlands: a review and example', *Professional Geographer*, 22, 74-8.
Merry, P.R., (1955), 'An inquiry into the nature and function of a String Retail Development: A Case Study of East Colfax Avenue, Denver, Colorado', *Ph.D. thesis, Northwestern University*.
Meyer, G., (1977), 'Distance perception of consumers in shopping streets', *Tijdschrift voor Economische en Sociale Geografie*, 68, 355-61.
Mitchell, I., (1981), 'Pitt's shop tax in the history of retailing', *Local Historian*, 14, 348-51.
Morrill, R.L. and Earickson, R.J., (1968), 'Variations in the character and use of hospital services', *Health Services Research*, 3 (reprinted in Bourne, L.S. (1971), *Internal Structure of the City*, Oxford.
Morrill, R.L. and Earickson, R.J. and Rees, P., (1970), 'Factors influencing distances travelled to hospitals', *Economic Geography*, 46, 161-71.
Murdie, R. A., (1965), 'Cultural differences in consumer travel', *Economic Geography*, 41, 211-33.
Murphy, R. (Ed.) (1961), 'Marketing Geography comes of age', *Economic Geography*, 37 (special issue).
Murphy, R.E., (1972), *The Central Business District: A Study in Urban Geography*, Longman, London.
Murphy, R.E. and Vance, J.E., (1954a), 'A comparative study of nine Central Business Districts', *Economic Geography*, 30, 301-36.
Murphy, R.E. and Vance, J.E., (1954b), 'Delimiting the CBD', *Economic Geography*, 30, 189-222.
Murray, D. and Spencer, C., (1979), 'Individual differences in the drawing of cognitive maps: the effects of geographical mobility, strength of mental imagery and basic graphic ability', *Transactions of the Institute of British Geographers*, N.S. 4, 385-91.

Nader, G.A., (1968), 'Private housing estates: the effects of previous residence on workplace and shopping activities', *Town Planning Review*, 39, 65-74.
Nader, G.A., (1969), 'Socio-economic status and consumer behaviour', *Urban Studies*, 6, 235-45.
NEDO, (1970), *Urban Models in Shopping Studies*, National Economic Development Office, London.
NEDO, (1971), *The Future Pattern of Shopping*, National Economic Development Office, London.
Nelson, H.J., (1955), 'A service classification of American cities', *Economic Geography*, 31, 189-210.
Newby, P.T. and Shepherd, I.D.H., (1979), 'Brent Cross: a milestone in retail development', *Geography*, 64, 133-7.
Newling, B., (1969), 'The spatial variation of urban population densities', *Geographical Review*, 59, 242-52.
O'Farrell, P.N. and Poole, M.A., (1972), 'Retail grocery price variation in Northern Ireland', *Regional Studies*, 6, 83-92.
Oppenheim, A.N., (1966), *Questionnaire Design and Attitude Measurement*, Heinemann, London.
Orleans, P., (1973), 'Differential cognition of urban residents: the effects of social scale on mapping' in Downs and Stea (Eds.), *Image and Environment*, Aldine.
Osgood, C.E., Suci, G.J. and Tannenbaum, P.M., (1957), *The Measurement of Meaning*, University of Illinois Press, Urbana.
Pacione, M., (1974), 'Measures of the attraction factor: a possible alternative,*Area*, 6, 279-82.
Pacione, M., (1975), 'Preference and perception: an analysis of consumer behaviour', *Tijdschrift voor Economische en Sociale Geografie*, 66, 84-92.
Pacione, M., (1979), 'The in-town hypermarket: an innovation in the geography of retailing', *Regional Studies*, 13, 15-24.
Pacione, M., (1980), 'Redevelopment of a medium-sized central shopping area: a case study of Clydebank', *Tijdschrift voor Economische en Sociale Geografie*, 71, 159-68.
Parker, A.J., (1974a), 'An analysis of retail grocery price variations', *Area*, 6, 117-20.
Parker, A.J., (1974b), 'Intra-urban variations in retail grocery prices', *Economic and Social Review*, 5, 393-403.
Parker, A.J., (1975), 'Hypermarkets - the changing pattern of retailing', *Geography*, 60, 120-4.
Parker, A.J., (1976), 'Consumer Behaviour, Motivation and Perception: A study of Dublin', *Research Report, Department of Geography, University College Dublin*.
Parker, A.J., (1978), 'Old age-pensioners: shopping behaviour and attitudes towards price', *National Prices Commission Monthly Report*, 76, 40-57.
Parker, A.J., (1979), 'A review and comparative analysis of retail grocery price variations', *Environment and Planning*, A, 11, 1267-88.
Parker, A.J., (1980), 'Retail grocery price variations: a consideration of the structural and locational characteristics of stores', *Journal of Consumer Studies and Home Economics*, 4, 35-49.
Parker, H.R. (1962), 'Suburban shopping facilities in Liverpool', *Town Planning Review*, 33, 197-223.
Parr, J.B., (1970), 'Models of city size in an urban system', *Papers of the Regional Science Association*, 25, 221-53.
Parr, J.B., (1973), 'Structure and size in the urban system of Lösch', *Economic Geography*, 49, 185-212.

Parr, J.B., (1978a), 'An alternative model of the central-place system', in Batey, P.W.J., *Theory and Method in Urban and Regional Analysis*, London Papers in Regional Science, 8, Pion.
Parr, J.B., (1978b), 'Models of the central place system: a more general approach', *Urban Studies*, 15, 35-49.
Parr, J.B., (1980a), 'Health care facility planning: some developmental considerations', *Socio-Economic Planning Sciences*, 14, 121-7.
Parr, J.B., (1980b), 'Frequency distributions of central places in Southern Germany: a further analysis', *Economic Geography*, 56, 141-54.
Parr, J.B., (1981), 'Temporal change in a central-place system', *Environment and Planning A*, 13, 97-118.
Parr, J.B. and Denike, K.G., (1970), 'Theoretical problems in central place analysis', *Economic Geography*, 46, 568-86.
Parr, J.B., Denike, K.G. and Mulligan, G., (1975), 'City-size models and the economic base: a recent controversy', *Journal of Regional Science*, 15, 1-8.
Patricios, N.N., (1978), 'Consumer images of spatial choice and the planning of shopping centres', *South African Geographical Journal*, 60, 103-20.
Patricios, N.N., (1979), 'Human aspects of planning shopping centers', *Environment and Behavior*, 11, 511-38.
Patricios, N.N., (1980), 'Rating-scale methodology for environmental designs', *Environment and Planning, B*, 7, 273-87.
Pirie, G.H., (1976), 'Thoughts on revealed preference and spatial behaviour', *Environment and Planning, A*, 8, 947-55.
Pocock, D.C.D., (1968), 'Shopping patterns in Dundee: some observations', *Scottish Geographical Magazine*, 84, 108-16.
Pocock, D.C.D., (1971), 'Urban environmental perception and behaviour: a review', *Tijdschrift voor Economische en Sociale Geografie*, 62, 321-6.
Pocock, D.C.D., (1973), 'Environmental perception: process and product', *Tijdschrift voor Economische en Sociale Geografie*, 64, 251-7.
Pocock, D. and Hudson, R., (1978), *Images of the Urban Environment*, Macmillan.
Potter, R.B., (1976a), 'The Structural Characteristics of the Urban Retailing System and the Nature of Consumer Behaviour and Perception: A Case Study Based on Stockport', *Unpublished Ph.D. thesis, University of London*.
Potter, R.B., (1976b), 'Directional bias within the usage and perceptual fields of urban consumers', *Psychological Reports*, 38, 988-90.
Potter, R.B., (1976c), 'Spatial nature of consumer usage and perceptual fields', *Perceptual and Motor Skills*, 43, 1185-86.
Potter, R.B., (1977a), 'Spatial patterns of consumer behaviour and Perception in relation to the social class variable', *Area* , 9, 153-6.
Potter, R.B., (1977b), 'Effects of age and family size on consumer behaviour and perception', *Perceptual and Motor Skills*, 45, 842.
Potter, R.B., (1977c), 'The nature of consumer usage fields in an urban environment: theoretical and empirical perspectives', *Tijdschrift voor Economische en Sociale Geografie*, 68, 168-76.
Potter, R.B., (1978), 'Aggregate consumer behaviour and perception in relation to urban retailing structure: a preliminary investigation', *Tijdschrift voor Economische en Sociale Geografie*, 69, 345-52.
Potter, R.B., (1979a), 'Perception of urban retailing facilities: an analysis of consumer information fields', *Geografiska Annaler*, 61B, 19-29.

Potter, R.B., (1979b), 'Factors influencing consumer decision-making', *Psychological Reports*, 44, 674.
Potter, R.B., (1979c), 'The morphological characteristics of urban retailing areas: a review and suggested methodology', *Bedford College, University of London, Papers in Geography*, 2.
Potter, R.B., (1980a), 'Spatial and structural variations in the quality characteristics of intra-urban retailing centres', *Transactions of the Institute of British Geographers*, New Series, 5, 207-28.
Potter, R.B., (1980b), 'What is convenient shopping?', *Town and Country Planning*, 49, 115-17.
Potter, R.B., (1981a), 'Correlates of urban retail area functional structure: an approach employing multivariate ordination', *Professional Geographer*, 33, 208-15.
Potter, R.B., (1981b), 'The multivariate functional structure of the urban retailing system: a British case study', *Transactions of the Institute of British Geographers*, New Series, 6, 188-213.
Potter, R.B. and Hunte, M.L., (1979), 'Recent developments in planning the settlement hierarchy of Barbados: implications concerning the debate on urban primacy', *Geoforum*, 10, 355-62.
Poulsen, M.F., (1977), 'Sectoral residential mobility and the restricted image', *New Zealand Geographer*, 33, 15-25.
Pred, A., (1963), 'Business thoroughfares as expressions of urban negro culture', *Economic Geography*, 39, 217-33.
Pred, A., (1967), *Behavior and Location: Foundations for a geographic and dynamic location theory, Part I*, Lund Studies in Geography, Series B, Human Geography No. 27.
Price, D.G., (1967), 'A geographical study of retail distribution in Buckinghamshire, Berkshire and Oxfordshire', *Unpublished Ph.D. thesis, University of London.*
Proudfoot, M.J., (1937a), 'City retail structure', *Economic Geography*, 13, 425-8.
Proudfoot, M., (1937b), 'The outlying business centers of Chicago', *Journal of Land and Public Utility Economics*, 13, 57-70.
Proudfoot, M. J., (1938), 'The selection of a business site', *Journal of Land Public Utility Economics*, 14, 370-82.
Rabiega, W.A. and Lamoureux, L.F., (1973), 'Wholesaling hierarchies: a Florida case study', *Tijdschrfit voor Economische en Sociale Geografie*, 64, 226-30.
Ratcliff, R.U., (1935), 'An examination into some Characteristics of Outlying Retail Nucleations in Detroit, Michigan', *Ph.D. thesis, University of Michigan.*
Ray, D.M., (1967), 'Cultural differences in consumer travel behaviour in Eastern Ontario', *Canadian Geographer*, 11, 143-56.
Reilly, W.J., (1931), *The Law of Retail Gravitation*, Knickerbocker Press, New York.
Rieser, R.L., (1972), 'Urban spatial images: an appraisal of the choice of respondents and measurement situation', *London School of Economics, Graduate School of Geography Discussion Paper, No. 42.*
Rogers, A., (1969a), 'Quadrat analysis of urban dispersion: Part 1: theoretical techniques', *Environment and Planning*, 1, 47-80.
Rogers, A., (1969b), 'Quadrat analysis of urban dispersion: Part 2: case studies of urban retail systems', *Regional Studies*, 13, 395-408.
Rolph, I.K., (1929), *The Locational Structure of Retail Trade*, Domestic Commerce Service, U.S. Bureau of Foreign and Domestic Commerce. Vol. 80, Washington, Government Printing Office.
Rowley, G., (1972), 'Spatial variations in the prices of central goods: a preliminary investigation', *Tijdschrift voor Economische*

en Sociale Geografie, 63, 360-8.
Rowley, G., (1978), '"Plus ça change...": a Canadian skid row', *Canadian Geographer*, 22, 211-24.
Rowley, G. and Shepherd, P. McL., (1976), 'A source of elementary spatial data for town centre research in Britain', *Area*, 8, 201-8.
Rushton, G., (1969), 'Analysis of spatial behavior by revealed space preference', *Annals of the Association of American Geographers*, 59, 391-400.
Rushton, G., (1971a), 'Postulates of central-place theory and the properties of central-place systems', *Geographical Analysis*, 3, 140-56.
Rushton, G., (1971b), 'Preference and choice in different environments', *Proceedings of the Association of American Geographers*, 3, 146-50.
Rushton, G., (1972), 'Map transformations of point patterns: central place patterns in areas of variable population density', *Papers of the Regional Science Association*, 28, 111-29.
Rushton, G., (1979), 'Commentary on behavioral and perception geography', *Annals of the Association of American Geography*, 69, 463-4.
Rushton, G., (1980), 'Review of Beavon, Central Place Theory: A Reinterpretation and Angel and Hyman, Urban Fields: A Geometry of Movement for Regional Science', *Geographical Analysis*, 12, 282-3.
Rushton, G., Golledge, R.G. and Clark, W.A.V., (1967), 'Formulation and test of a normative model for the spatial allocation of grocery expenditure by a dispersed population', *Annals of the Association of American Geographers*, 57, 389-400.
Saarinen, T.F., (1979), 'Commentary-Critique of Bunting-Guelke paper', *Annals of the Association of American Geographers*, 69, 464-8.
Saey, P., (1973), 'Three fallacies in the literature on central place theory', *Tijdschrift voor Economische en Sociale Geografie*, 64, 181-94.
Santos, M., (1979), *The Shared Space: The Two Circuits of the Urban Economy in Underdeveloped Countries*, Methuen, London.
Schiller, R.K., (1972), 'The measurement of the attractiveness of shopping centres to middle class luxury consumers', *Regional Studies*, 6, 291-7.
Schiller, R., (1979), 'The responsibilities of retail planning', Chapter 1 in Davies, R.L. (Ed.), *Retail Planning in the European Community*, Saxon House, Farnborough, 7-20.
Schiller, R., (1981), 'A model of retail branch distribution', *Regional Studies*, 15, 15-22.
Schuler, H.J., (1979) 'A disaggregate store-choice model of spatial decision-making', *Professional Geographer*, 31, 146-56.
Schultz, G.P., (1970), 'The logic of health care facility planning', *Socio-Economic Planning Sciences*, 4, 383-93.
Scola, R., (1975), 'Food markets and shops in Manchester 1770-1870', *Journal of Historical Geography*, 1, 153-68.
Scott, P., (1959), 'The Australian CBD', *Economic Geography*, 35, 290-314.
Scott, P., (1970), *Geography and Retailing*, London, Hutchinson.
Shaw, G., (1978), 'Processes and patterns in the geography of retail change, with special reference to Kingston-upon-Hull, 1880-1950', *University of Hull, Occasional Papers in Geography, No. 24*.
Shaw, G. and Wild, M.T., (1979), 'Retail patterns in the Victorian city', *Transactions of the Institute of British Geographers*, N.S., 4, 278-91.

Shepherd, I.D.H. and Thomas, C.J., (1980), 'Urban consumer behaviour', Chapter 1 in Dawson, J.A. (Ed.), *Retail Geography*, Croom Helm.
Sherwood, K.B., (1970), 'Some applications of the nearest neighbor technique to the study of the movement of intra-urban functions', *Tijdschrift voor Economische en Sociale Geografie*, 61, 41-8.
Sibley, D., (1972), 'Strategy and tactics in the selection of shop locations', *Area*, 4, 151-7.
Sibley, D., (1973), 'The density gradients of small shops in cities', *Environment and Planning*, 5, 223-30.
Simmons, J., (1964), *The Changing Pattern of Retail Location*, University of Chicago, Department of Geography, Research Paper No. 92.
Simmons, J.W., (1968), 'An urban information field', *Ontario Geographer*, 2, 35-48.
Simon, H.A., (1957), *Models of Man: Social and Rational*, New York.
Simon, H.A., (1959), 'Theories of decision-making in economics and behavioural science', *American Economic Review*, 49, 253-83.
Skinner, G.W., (1964), 'Marketing and social structure in rural China', *Journal of Asian Studies*, 24, 3-39.
Skurnik, L.S. and George, F., (1964), *Psychology for Everyman*, Penguin, Harmondsworth.
Smailes, A.E., (1944), 'The urban hierarchy in England and Wales', *Geography*, 29, 41-51.
Smailes, A.E., (1947), 'The analysis and delimitation of urban fields', *Geography*, 32, 153-61.
Smailes, A.E. and Hartley, G., (1961), 'Shopping centres in the Greater London area', *Transactions of the Institute of British Geographers*, 29, 201-13.
Smith, G.C., (1976), 'The spatial information fields of urban consumers', *Transactions of the Institute of British Geographers*, New Series, 1, 175-89.
Smith, G.C., Shaw, J.B. and Huckle, P.R., (1979), 'Children's perception of a downtown shopping center', *Professional Geographer*, 31, 157-64.
Smith, H., (1948), *Retail Distribution: A Critical Analysis* (Second Edition), Oxford University Press, London.
Spence, P.S., (1971), 'Orderliness in the journey to shop', *Tijdschrift voor Economische en Sociale Geografie*, 62, 22-34.
Spencer, A.H., (1978), 'Deriving measures of attractiveness for shopping centres', *Regional Studies*, 12, 713-26.
Spencer, A.H., (1980), 'Cognition and shopping choice: a multi-dimensional scaling approach', *Environment and Planning, A*, 12, 1235-51.
Spencer, D., (1973), 'An evaluation of cognitive mapping in neighbourhood perception', *Centre for Urban and Regional Studies, University of Birmingham, Research Memorandum*, No. 23.
Stine, J.H., (1962), 'Temporal aspects of tertiary production elements in Korea', in Pitts, F.R. (Ed.), *Urban Systems and Economic Development*, University of Oregon Press.
Stolper, W.F., (1955), 'Spatial order and economic growth of cities', *Economic Development and Cultural Change*, 3, 137-46.
Stone, G., (1954), 'City shoppers and urban identification: observations on the social psychology of city life', *American Journal of Sociology*, 60, 35-54.
Tarrant, J.R., (1967), 'A classification of shop types', *Professional Geographer*, 19, 179-83.
Tarrant, J.R., (1973), 'Comments on the Lösch central place system', *Geographical Analysis*, 5, 113-21.

Taylor, P.J., (1976), 'An interpretation of the quantification debate in British Geography', *Transactions of the Institute of British Geographers, N.S.*, 1, 129-42.
Teitz, M.B., (1968), 'Towards a theory of urban public facility location', *Papers and Proceedings of the Regional Science Association* 21, 35-51.
Thomas, C.J., (1974), 'The effects of social class and car ownership on intra-urban shopping behaviour in Greater Swansea', *Cambria*, 1, 38-12(
Thomas, C.J., (1976), 'Sociospatial differentiation and the use of services', Chapter 1 in Herbert, D.T. and Johnston, R.J. (Eds.), *Social Areas in Cities, Volume II: Spatial Perspectives on Problems and Policies*, Wiley, London, 17-63.
Thomas, R.W., (1972), 'The retail structure of the central area', *Institute of British Geographers, Urban Study Group, Occasional Publication*, 69-94.
Thomas, R.W., (1978), 'Review of Central Place Theory: A Reinterpretation by K.S.O. Beavon', *Regional Studies*, 12, 484.
Thompson, D.L., (1963), 'New concept: "subjective distance"', *Journal of Retailing*, 39, 1-6.
Thompson, D.L., (1966), 'Future directions in retail area research', *Economic Geography*, 42, 1-18.
Thorpe, D., (1978), 'Progress in the study of the geography of retailing in Britain', *Geoforum*, 9, 83-106.
Thorpe, D. and Rhodes, T.C., (1966), 'The shopping centers of the Tyneside urban region and large scale grocery retailing', *Economic Geography*, 42, 52-73.
Tietz, B., (1971), 'The future development of retail and wholesale distribution in Western Europe: an analysis of trends up to 1980', *British Journal of Marketing*, 5, 42-55.
Timmermans, H., (1979a), 'Centrale Plaatsen Theorieën en Ruimtelijk Koopgedrag', *Ph.D. thesis, Catholic University of Nijmegen*.
Timmermans, H., (1979b), 'A spatial preference model of regional shopping behaviour', *Tijdschrift voor Economische en Sociale Geografie*, 70, 45-8.
Timmermans, H., (1980a), 'Unidimensional conjoint measurement models and consumer decision-making', *Area*, 12, 291-300.
Timmermans, H., (1980b), 'Consumer spatial choice strategies: a comparative study of some alternative behavioural spatial shopping models', *Geoforum*, 11, 123-31.
Timmermans, H., (1981a), 'Spatial choice behaviour in different environmental settings: an application of the revealed preference approach', *Geografiska Annaler*, 63B, 57-67.
Timmermans, H.J.P., (1981b), 'Multiattribute shopping models and ridge regression analysis', *Environment and Planning A*, 13, 43-56.
Timmermans, H., (forthcoming), 'Consumer choice of shopping centre: an information integration approach', *Regional Studies*.
Timmermans, H. and Rushton, G., (1979), 'Revealed space preference theory - a rejoinder', *Tijdschrift voor Economische en Sociale Geografie*, 70, 309-12.
Timmermans, H., van der Heijden, R. and Westerveld, H., (1981), 'Perception of urban retailing environments: an empirical analysis of consumer information and usage fields', *University of Technology, Eindhoven, Department of Architecture, Building and Planning Working Paper*.
Timmermans, H., van der Heijden, R. and Westerveld, H., (forthcoming), 'Cognition of urban retailing structures: a Dutch case study', *Tijdschrift voor Economische en Sociale Geografie*.

Tinkler, K.T., (1973), 'The topology of rural periodic market systems', *Geografiska Annaler*, 55B, 121-33.
Trinkaus, J., (1980), 'Buyers' price perception at a flea market - an informal look', *Psychological Reports*, 46, 266.
Tuan, Y-F., (1975), 'Images and mental maps', *Annals of the Association of American Geographers*, 65, 205-13.
Tucker, K.A. and Yamey, B.S., (1973), *Economics of Retailing*, Penguin, Harmondsworth.
Turner, R. and Cole, H.S.D., (1980), 'An investigation into the estimation and reliability of urban shopping models', *Urban Studies*, 17, 139-57.
Ullman, E.L., (1974), 'Space and/or time: opportunity for substitution and prediction', *Transactions of the Institute of British Geographers*, 63, 125-39.
Upton, G.J.G. and Fingleton, B., (1979), 'Log-linear models in geography', *Transactions of the Institute of British Geographers*, N.S., 4, 103-15.
U.R.P.I., (1977), *District Shopping Centres: Report of an URPI Workshop*, The Unit for Retail Planning Information Limited, Reading.
Valavanis, S., (1955), 'Lösch on location', *American Economic Review*, 45, 637-44.
Vance, J.E., (1962), 'Emerging patterns of commercial structure in American cities', in Norberg, K. (Ed.) *Institute of British Geographers Symposium in Urban Geography*, Lund.
Vance, J.E., (1970), *The Merchant's World: The Geography of Wholesaling*, Prentice-Hall.
Vance, J.E., (1973), 'On freedom of evolution in the geography of wholesaling: comments on a Florida hierarchical case study', *Tijdschrift voor Economische en Sociale Geografie*, 64, 231-6.
Von Böventer, E., (1962), 'Towards a unified theory of spatial economic structure', *Papers of the Regional Science Association*, 10, 163-87.
Wade, B., (1979), 'Retail planning in Britain', Chapter 3 in Davies, R.L. (Ed.), *Retail Planning in the European Community*, Saxon House, 51-63.
Ward, J., (1975), 'Skid row as a geographic entity', *Professional Geographer*, 27, 286-96.
Warnes, A.M. and Daniels, P.W., (1978), 'Intra-urban shopping travel: a review of theory and evidence from British towns', *Paper presented to the annual conference of the Institute of British Geographers*.
Warnes, A.M. and Daniels, P.W., (1979), 'Spatial aspects of an intra-metropolitan central place hierarchy', *Progress in Human Geography*, 3, 384-406.
Warnes, A.M. and Daniels, P.W.,(1980), 'Urban retail distributions: an appraisal of the empirical foundations of retail geography', *Geoforum*, 11, 133-46.
Watts, H.D., (1977), 'Market areas and spatial rationalization: the British brewing industry after 1945', *Tijdschrift voor Economische en Sociale Geografie*, 68, 224-40.
Webber, M.J., (1972), *The Impact of Uncertainty on Location*, M.I.T. Press.
Webber, M.J. and Symanski, R., (1973), 'Periodic markets: an economic location analysis', *Economic Geography*, 49, 213-27.
Weekley, I.G., (1956), 'Service centres in Nottingham: a concept in urban analysis', *East Midland Geographer*, 6, 41-6.
White, J. and Case, K.E., (1974), 'On covering problems and the central facilities location problem', *Geographical Analysis*, 6, 281-93.

White, R.W., (1974), 'Sketches of a dynamic central place theory', *Economic Geography*, 50, 219-27.
White, R.W., (1977), 'Dynamic central place theory: results of a simulation approach', *Geographical Analysis*, 9, 226-43.
Wild, M.T. and Shaw, G., (1974), 'Locational behaviour of urban retailing during the nineteenth century: the example of Kingston upon Hull', *Transactions of the Institute of British Geographers*, 61, 101-18.
Wild, M.T. and Shaw, G., (1975), 'Population distribution and retail provision: the case of the Halifax-Calder Valley area of West Yorkshire during the second half of the nineteenth century', *Journal of Historical Geography*, 1, 193-210.
Wild, M.T. and Shaw, G., (1979), 'Trends in urban retailing: the British experience during the nineteenth century', *Tijdschrift voor Economische en Sociale Geografie*, 70, 35-44.
Williams, N.J., (1979), 'The definition of shopper types as an aid in the analysis of spatial consumer behaviour', *Tijdschrift voor Economische en Sociale Geografie*, 70, 157-63.
Williams, N.J., (1981), 'Attitudes and consumer spatial behaviour', *Tijdschrift voor Economische en Sociale Geografie*, 72, 145-54.
Wilson, A.G., (1972), 'Theoretical geography: some speculations', *Transactions of the Institute of British Geographers*, 57, 31-44.
Woldenberg, M.J., (1968), 'Energy flow and spatial order: mixed hexagonal hierarchies of central places', *Geographical Review*, 58, 552-74.
Wolpert, J., (1964), 'The decision process in a spatial context', *Annals of the Association of American Geographers*, 54, 537-58.
Wolpert, J., (1966), 'Behavioral aspects of the decision to migrate', *Papers and Proceedings of the Regional Science Association*, 15, 159-69.
Wood, L.J. and Lee, T.R., (1980), 'Time-space convergence: reappraisal for an oil short future', *Area*, 12, 217-22.
Yeates, M., (1965), 'Some factors affecting the spatial distribution of Chicago land values, 1910-60', *Economic Geography*, 41, 57-70.
Yeates, M. and Garner, B.J., (1980/1971), *The North American City* (Third/First Editions), Harper and Row, New York.
York Junior Chamber, (1977), *York: a Study of Shopping with Particular Reference to the Impact on Food Shopping of an Out-of-Town Superstore*, York Junior Chamber.

Index